CHOICES & INCEPTIONS:

Traditional Electional Astrology

TRANSLATED & EDITED BY
BENJAMIN N. DYKES, PHD

The Cazimi Press
Minneapolis, Minnesota
2012

Published and printed in the United States of America
by the Cazimi Press
621 5th Avenue SE #25, Minneapolis, MN 55414

ISBN-13: 978-1-934586-23-5
Library of Congress Control Number: **2012911024**

Acknowledgements

I would like to thank the following friends and colleagues, in alphabetical order: Chris Brennan, Charles Burnett, Deb Houlding, and David Juste.

Also available at www.bendykes.com:

The famous medieval horary compilation *The Book of the Nine Judges* is now available in translation for the first time! It is the largest traditional horary work available, and the third in the horary series.

Designed for curious modern astrology students, *Traditional Astrology for Today* explains basic ideas in history, philosophy and counseling, dignities, chart interpretation, and predictive techniques. Non-technical and friendly for modern beginners.

Two classic introductions to astrology, by Abū Ma'shar and al-Qabīsī, are translated with com-mentary in this volume. *Introductions to Traditional Astrology* is an essential reference work for traditional students.

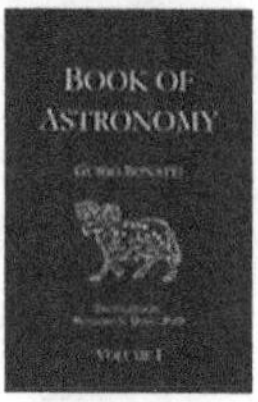

The classic medieval text by Guido Bonatti, the *Book of Astronomy* is now available in paperback reprints. This famous work is a complete guide to basic principles, horary, elections, mundane, and natal astrology.

The Search of the Heart is the first in the horary series, and focuses on the use of victors (special significators or *almutens*) and the practice of thought-interpretation: divining thoughts and predicting outcomes before the client speaks.

The Forty Chapters is a famous and influential horary work by al-Kindī, and is the second volume of the horary series. Beginning with a general introduction to astrology, al-Kindī covers topics such as war, wealth, travel, pregnancy, marriage, and more.

The first volume of the *Persian Nativities* series on natal astrology contains *The Book of Aristotle*, an advanced work on nativities and prediction by Māshā'allāh, and a beginner-level work by his student Abū 'Ali al-Khayyāt, *On the Judgments of Nativities.*

The second volume of *Persian Nativities* features a shorter, beginner-level work on nativities and prediction by 'Umar al-Tabarī, and a much longer book on nativities by his younger follower, Abū Bakr.

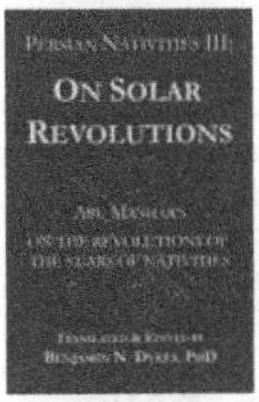

The third volume of *Persian Nativities* is a translation of Abū Ma'shar's work on solar revolutions, devoted solely to the Persian annual predictive system. Learn about profections, distributions, *firdārīyyāt*, transits, and more!

This compilation of sixteen works by Sahl bin Bishr and Māshā'allāh covers all areas of traditional astrology, from basic concepts to horary, elections, natal interpretation, and mundane astrology. It is also available in paperback.

Expand your knowledge of traditional astrology, philosophy, and esoteric thought with the *Logos & Light* audio series: downloadable, college-level lectures on CD at a fraction of the university cost!

TABLE OF CONTENTS

Book Abbreviations ix
Table of Figures x
INTRODUCTION 1
§1: What is an election? 2
§2: Epistemological and moral issues in elections 14
§3: The Māshā'allāh transmission and the relation of questions to elections 22
§4: Al-'Imrānī and al-Rijāl 32
§5: The Moon and Lunar mansions 39
§6: Planetary Hours 47
§7: Times in al-'Imrānī and al-Rijāl 50
§8: Remoteness from angles, and house systems 56
§9: A translation note 58
PART I: THE MOON *&* LUNAR MANSIONS 59
Al-Kindī: The Choices of Days 59
Al-Rijāl: The Book of the Skilled VII.101: On Elections according to the Moon's Motion through the Mansions 61
PART II: PLANETARY HOURS 76
Bethen: On the Hours of the Planets 77
§1: Planetary hours 77
§2: Triplicities, when on the Ascendant 79
§3: Quadruplicities, based on Sahl's *On Elect.* 80
§4: General instructions and planetary significators, from Sahl's *On Elect.* 83
§5: On the hour and sign of Saturn, and his Ascendant 85
Al-Rijāl: The Book of the Skilled VII.100: On the Significations of the Hours 86
PART III: COMPLETE ELECTIONS 91
Sahl bin Bishr: On Elections 91
The Ascendant and whatever is in it concerning elections 94
The second sign from the Ascendant, and whatever is in it, in terms of elections 103
The third sign and whatever is in it concerning elections 106
The fourth sign and whatever is in it, in the manner of elections 106
The fifth sign and whatever is in it in terms of elections 110

The sixth sign and whatever is in it in terms of elections....................111
The seventh sign and whatever is in it in terms of elections 117
The eighth sign and whatever is in it in terms of elections.................121
The ninth sign and whatever is in it in terms of elections...................122
The tenth sign and whatever is in it in terms of elections...................127
The eleventh sign and whatever is in it in terms of elections.............130
The twelfth sign and whatever is in it in terms of elections................131
On that which is not in the twelve signs in terms of elections...........133
Al-'Imrānī: The Book of Choices 134
Chapter I.1.0: Whether elections are useful...135
Chapter I.2.0: On the general works of elections for every man 140
Chapter I.3: On the elections of those whose nativities are known...168
Chapter I.4: On elections after an inquiry has been made, whether the matter is perfected or not 172
Chapter I.5.0: In what hours we may have trust that what was undertaken in them, would be perfected 174
Chapter II.1.0: Electing for powerful people 182
Chapter II.1.1: On the confirmation of dignities.................................183
Chapter II.1.2: On the removal of dignities..184
Chapter II.1.3: On the building of cities and forts 185
Chapter II.1.4: On the building of houses and the rest of what is in a city and fort...186
Chapter II.1.5: On the destruction of the buildings of enemies 186
Chapter II.1.6: On the rerouting of rivers and springs........................187
Chapter II.1.7: On the building of ships for defeating enemies..........188
Chapter II.1.8: On going out to battle or something else 189
Chapter II.1.9: On the reconciliation of enemies 193
Chapter II.1.10: On returning..194
Chapter II.1.11: On searching and hunting..195
Chapter II.1.12: On racing horses 196
Chapter II.1.13: On games...197
Chapter II.2.1: On works whose significations are taken from the Ascendant, and first on breastfeeding..197
Chapter II.2.2: On taking boys away from the breast..........................198
Chapter II.2.3: On the cutting of the nails 198
Chapter II.2.4: On cutting the hair of the head or the body...............198
Chapter II.2.5: On entering a bath 199

Chapter II.2.6: On healing the sick 199
Chapter II.2.7: On remedies pertaining to surgery 200
Chapter II.2.8: On the letting of blood by phlebotomy or cupping...200
Chapter II.2.9: On the circumcision of boys 201
Chapter II.2.10: On giving purgatives 202
Chapter II.2.11: On binding drugs 203
Chapter II.2.12: On sneezing [drugs] and gargles and vomiting, through potions or any other [means] 203
Chapter II.2.13: On putting on new vestments 204
Chapter II.3.1: On the elections of those things which particularly pertain to the second house, and first on the restoring or recovery of assets loaned to someone 204
Chapter II.3.2: On buying 205
Chapter II.3.3: On the selling of seeds and other things which pertain to open fields, and anything for sale 206
Chapter II.3.4: On lending money 206
Chapter II.3.5: On raising the hand [to receive money] 207
Chapter II.3.6: On changing one's lodging-place 208
Chapter II.4.1: On elections pertaining to the third house, and first on the reconciliation of brothers 208
Chapter II.4.2: Instruction in those things which pertain to devotion to God 209
Chapter II.4.3: On the sending of legates 209
Chapter II.5.1: On those things which pertain to the fourth house, and first on the purchase of real estate 210
Chapter II.5.2: On beginning to cultivate real estate 212
Chapter II.5.3: On the building of a mill 213
Chapter II.5.4: On planting trees and sowing seeds, and all things which are fruitful in that year (namely in its own season) 213
Chapter II.5.5: On contracting [to work] the land 214
Chapter II.5.6: On the leasing out of houses and produce 214
Chapter II.6.1: On those things which pertain to the fifth house, and first on the conceiving of a son 216
Chapter II.6.2: On gifts 217
Chapter II.7.1: On the sixth house, and first on the buying of captives 218

Chapter II.7.2: On the manumission of captives and the imprisoned, and domesticating horses....219
Chapter II.7.3: On the buying of animals....219
Chapter II.7.4: On the buying of animals with which we hunt....220
Chapter II.8.1: On the seventh house....220
Chapter II.8.2: On an association....221
Chapter II.8.3: On a purchase and sale....221
Chapter II.8.4: On the betrothal of women....221
Chapter II.9: On the eighth house, and first on the fitness of an inheritance....222
Chapter II.10.1: On the ninth house, and first on moral teaching....223
Chapter II.10.2: On instruction in singing and those things which pertain to gladness....223
Chapter II.11.1: On the tenth house, and first on instruction in swimming....224
Chapter II.11.2: On instruction for fighting....224
Chapter II.11.3: On instruction in other works....225
Chapter II.12.1: On the eleventh house, and first on those things which pertain to acquiring a good name and reputation....225
Chapter II.12.2: On seeking a matter, both one promised and one sought....226
Chapter II.12.3: On seeking love and friendship....227
Chapter II.13.1: On the twelfth house, and first if you wanted to hinder any enemy, or on the king catching his enemy or a less powerful person....228
Chapter II.13.2: On searching for a fugitive....228
Chapter II.13.3: On searching for a fugitive....228
Chapter II.13.4: On making a robber or watchman reveal what we are seeking....229

Al-Rijal: The Book of the Skilled VII: On Elections....231

Prologue to the book:....231
Prologue of the author....231
Chapter VII.1: On the rules and roots which are necessary in this method, and which cannot be avoided....236
Chapter VII.2.0: On the principles of deeds....238
Chapter VII.3.0: On the signs and their significations....250
Chapter VII.4: On the first house and its elections....256

Chapter VII.5: On entering a bath 256
Chapter VII.6: On cutting the hair on the head 257
Chapter VII.7.0: On bloodletting and cupping 257
Chapter VII.8: On cutting the nails 259
Chapter VII.9: On the second house and its elections 260
Chapter VII.10: On managing assets and seeking them, and taking on debts 260
Chapter VII.11.0: On buying and selling 261
Chapter VII.12: On selling produce 266
Chapter VII.13: On giving capital 266
Chapter VII.14: On accepting capital 267
Chapter VII.15: On changing from one house to another 268
Chapter VII.16: On the work of alchemy 269
Chapter VII.17: On the third house and its elections 270
Chapter VII.18: On beginning to demonstrate the sciences of the law 270
Chapter VII.19: On the fourth house and its elections 272
Chapter VII.20.0: On making the foundations of estates and homes 272
Chapter VII.21: On extracting waters by digging and making streams or brooks flow off 279
Chapter VII.22: On buying real estate 280
Chapter VII.23: On settling land 282
Chapter VII.24: On making a mill 282
Chapter VII.25: On sowing, and planting trees 283
Chapter VII.26: On leasing lands 283
Chapter VII.27: On leasing out homes and produce for payment 284
Chapter VII.28: On removing phantasms from the home 285
Chapter VII.29: On the fifth house and its elections 287
Chapter VII.30: On lying with a woman so that one may have a son 287
Chapter VII.31: On giving the native to be nourished 288
Chapter VII.32: On taking the native from the breast 289
Chapter VII.33: On circumcising and baptizing 289
Chapter VII.34: On cutting and putting on new clothes 290
Chapter VII.35: On handing over gifts 290
Chapter VII.36: On sending couriers 291
Chapter VII.37: On writing papers 291
Chapter VII.38: On foods 291

Chapter VII.39: On drinks....293
Chapter VII.40: On getting involved in things with a good smell....293
Chapter VII.41: On sending pigeons so that they would lead others 294
Chapter VII.42: On taking a created [fetus] from the mother's belly 294
Chapter VII.43: On the sixth house and its elections....295
Chapter VII.44: On healing the infirm....295
Chapter VII.45: On healing with a syringe....296
Chapter VII.46: On healing the eyes....297
Chapter VII.47: On taking laxative medicine....297
Chapter VII.48: On giving binding medicine....300
Chapter VII.49: On giving medicine through the nose and for vomiting and gargling....300
Chapter VII.50.0: On buying slaves....301
Chapter VII.51.0: On giving the law to slaves and captives, and domesticating horses....302
Chapter VII.52.0: On buying beasts, large and small....304
Chapter VII.53: On the seventh house and its elections....306
Chapter VII.54: On marriage-unions....306
Chapter VII.55: On elections for a dispute....310
Chapter VII.56: On buying arms for war....315
Chapter VII.57.0: On confronting [others] in wars and making peace....316
Chapter VII.58: On tearing down the forts and estates of enemies...323
Chapter VII.59: On making arms and clever devices for subduing enemies—namely galleys and other vessels of the sea....324
Chapter VII.60: On a partnership, and every matter which comes to be between two people....325
Chapter VII.61: On searching for a fugitive....326
Chapter VII.62: On making a robber reveal [what we are seeking]....326
Chapter VII.63: On hunting by land and by water....327
Chapter VII.64: On playing at board games, chess, dice, and what is like that....330
Chapter VII.65: On lying down with women....332
Chapter VII.66: On the eighth house and its elections....334
Chapter VII.67: On a testament of death....334
Chapter VII.68: On the situation of what is left by the dead....335
Chapter VII.69: On the ninth house and its elections....336

Chapter VII.70.0: On an election for travel....336
Chapter VII.71: On journeys for reasons of touring around....341
Chapter VII.72: For one who wanted to return quickly from his journey....343
Chapter VII.73: On journeys which a man wants to make in secret..343
Chapter VII.74: On journeys by water....344
Chapter VII.75.0: On buying the ship, and boarding it, and moving it....346
Chapter VII.76.0: On putting the ship in the water....348
Chapter VII.77: On learning sciences and teachings....352
Chapter VII.78: On learning singing and other entertaining things...353
Chapter VII.79: For the entrance into a city, by the one who comes from a journey....354
Chapter VII.80: On the tenth house and its elections....356
Chapter VII.81.0: For entering into a dignity....356
Chapter VII.82: On an election for a dignity of the land, or for tax revenues or the law....363
Chapter VII.83: On adapting the dignity of magistrates....363
Chapter VII.84: On adapting the dignity of a chancery-clerk or clerkship, or those who bear books of computations....364
Chapter VII.85.0: On choosing from among equal men, which of them they will make a lord and a greater [person]....365
Chapter VII.86: For one who wanted to go with the king or another lord....368
Chapter VII.87: On putting the king in the house of his rulership....368
Chapter VII.88: For one who wanted to give his argument in the presence of the king....369
Chapter VII.89: On seeking the defense of the king....369
Chapter VII.90: On learning masteries....370
Chapter VII.91: On learning to bear arms....370
Chapter VII.92: On learning to swim in waters....371
Chapter VII.93: On the eleventh house and its elections....372
Chapter VII.94: On matters which happen for the sake of acquiring a good name and reputation....372
Chapter VII.95: On fulfilling promises and demanding petitions....373
Chapter VII.96: On seeking love and friendship....374
Chapter VII.97: On the twelfth house and its elections....375

Chapter VII.98: On the racing of horses 375
Chapter VII.99: On the hour at which a king would catch his enemy or a less powerful person....376
Chapter VII.100: On the significations of the hours 377
Chapter VII.101: On elections according to the Moon's motion through the mansions....377
Chapter VII.102.0: On the times in which hope is had that [one's] petitions would be fulfilled....377
Appendix A: Rulerships....396
Appendix B: Types of Signs....398
Appendix C: General Instructions on Elections, from al-Kindī 400
Appendix D: Three Versions of the *Bust*....404
Appendix E: The *Essential Medieval Astrology* Cycle 406
Glossary 408
Bibliography 427
Index....431

BOOK ABBREVIATIONS

Anth.	Vettius Valens	*The Anthology*
BOA	Bonatti, Guido	*The Book of Astronomy*
Carmen	Dorotheus of Sidon	*Carmen Astrologicum*
Cent.	pseudo-Ptolemy	*Centiloquium*
Forty Chapters	Al-Kindī	*The Forty Chapters*
ITA	Abu Ma'shar et al.	*Introductions to Traditional Astrology: Abū Ma'shar & al-Qabīsī*
Judges	Various	*The Book of the Nine Judges*
On Elect.	Sahl bin Bishr	*On Elections* (in *WSM*)
On Quest.	Sahl bin Bishr	*On Questions* (in *WSM*)
PN 1-3	Various	*Persian Nativities I-III*
Search	Hermann of Carinthia	*The Search of the Heart*
Skilled	Al-Rijāl	*The Book of the Skilled in the Judgments of the Stars*
TBN	'Umar al-Tabarī	*Three Books on Nativities* (in *WSM*)
Tet.	Claudius Ptolemy	*Tetrabiblos*
WSM	Sahl bin Bishr & Māshā'allāh	*Works of Sahl & Māshā'allāh*

TABLE OF FIGURES

Figure 1: General scheme of the logic of action 11
Figure 2: The logic of action as a basic rooted election 13
Figure 3: Select passages in the Māshā'allāh transmission 28
Figure 4: Divergence between Sahl and reports of al-Khayyāt 31
Figure 5: Planetary hours during day (from sunrise) 48
Figure 6: Planetary hours during night (from sunset) 49
Figure 7: Proposed "ways" of measuring time (Dykes) 54
Figure 7: Arabic 28-mansion system, with the likely stars comprising them.. 75
Figure 5: Planetary hours during day (from sunrise) 76
Figure 6: Planetary hours during night (from sunset) 76
Figure 10: Straight and crooked signs, in northern and southern hemispheres 96
Figure 11: Venus rescuing Sagittarius from besiegement by body 146
Figure 12: Jupiter and Saturn sending right aspects to the Moon 147
Figure 13: Angles for buying land for cultivation (al-Kindī, *Forty Chapters* §470) 211
Figure 14: Angles for buying land for cultivation (Māshā'allāh group [*Judges* §4.5, 4.8-9], *Carmen* V.10.1) 212
Figure 15: Approximate chart for the completion of the al-'Imrānī translation 230
Figure 16: The Moon and prices, by declination (from *Carmen* V.43.1-4) 264
Figure 17: The Moon and prices, by lunar phase (from *Carmen* V.43.5-8) ... 264
Figure 18: The Moon and prices, by quadrant (from *Carmen* V.43.5-8) 265
Figure 19: Foundation chart for Baghdad, from al-Bīrūnī 273
Figure 20: Approximate chart for founding of Baghdad (modern calculations) 273
Figure 21: Al-Kindī's cardinal directions for fighting 317
Figure 22: Al-Rijāl's proposed correction to al-Kindī 317
Figure 23: Time-based scorched period, from New Moon on Sunday morning 319
Figure 24: Years given to planets aspecting the Lot of Fortune (*Anth.* III.12) 382
Figure 25: Years given to the signs (derived from the planets' lesser years) when the lord of Fortune is in them (*Anth.* III.12) 383
Figure 26: Table of planetary years 383

Figure 27: Major dignities and counter-dignities 396
Figure 28: Triplicity lords 396
Figure 29: Table of Egyptian bounds 397
Figure 30: Table of "Chaldean" faces or decans 397

INTRODUCTION

I am happy to present *Choices & Inceptions*, the electional volume of my *Essential Medieval Astrology* series.[1] It is the only volume, because for the most part electional texts are repetitive and exhibit little variety in approach. Moreover, there is much overlap in the four most widely known electional texts, three of which are translated here in Part III (see below).[2] Taking some statements by Deborah Houlding as a guide, I have divided the book into three parts:

> Part I includes two texts which describe elections based solely on the Moon's position: her position in the Lunar mansions, and her applications to the other planets. This is the crudest and most general type of consideration, because it describes conditions which apply to everyone, everywhere, at the same time, for periods up to a day or so. This Part includes al-Kindī's short *The Choices of Days* and Ch. VII.101 of al-Rijāl's *The Book of the Skilled in the Judgments of the Stars.*
>
> Part II includes two texts which focus on electing by planetary hours. This is slightly more sophisticated than the previous type, because the lengths of planetary hours are sensitive to season and latitude, and their periods are shorter than those of the Lunar applications (thereby requiring more sensitive planning). Nevertheless they barely employ the full battery of astrological concepts and lore in determining auspicious times. This Part includes *On the Hours of the Planets* by Bethen,[3] and Ch. VII.100 of al-Rijāl.
>
> Part III includes what I am calling "complete" elections: a complete consideration of all features of an electional chart, such as house rulerships and positions, planetary hours, planetary configurations, sect, malefic and benefic distinctions, and even distinctions between more

---

[1] For a list of works in the series (and projected, forthcoming works), see Appendix E.

[2] The fourth is Book V of Dorotheus, which I will discuss later on.

[3] My own view is that "Bethen" is a medieval Latin writer of the 11th or 12th Centuries, since the section of his work which derives from Sahl's *On Elect.* is taken verbatim from the John of Seville translation (at least, it was probably translated by John, and I will refer to it as such). The name "Bethen" may in fact be a rendering of the name of the second Lunar mansion and its primary fixed star, Botein.

general elective approaches and very specific ones based on a client's nativity or question. This Part includes a revised translation of Sahl bin Bishr's *On Elections*, al-'Imrānī's famous *The Book of Choices*, and Tr. VII of al-Rijāl (which is completely devoted to elections and timing procedures).

Before introducing some of the contents of these works, I would like to address some issues of terminology, the relation of elections to questions (horary), event charts, thought-interpretation, and so on.

§1: What is an election?

In one sense elections are simple to understand, and they form a clearly-defined branch in traditional astrology (along with nativities, questions or "horary,"[4] and mundane astrology). The word "election" simply means "choice," from the Latin *eligo* ("to pick out, choose"). Electional astrology chooses advantageous times to perform deliberate actions: from when to go to war, to the forming of a business partnership, to the right times for travel. For the most part, this is all we have to know before jumping into the practice of elections.

On the other hand, there are complications with respect to the relation between elections and questions, and their relation to thought-interpretation and "event charts." Moreover, there were medieval debates about the appropriateness of elections, and whether and how to cast an election chart for someone with an unknown nativity. This latter point brings in the medieval theory of "roots," and has a connection to some uses of ancient logic. So, elections occupy a complicated position within the branches of astrology. Let us first turn to some points of terminology.

Terminology

Above, I mentioned the Latin verb *eligo*, whence we get the Latin *electio* and our English *election*. In Arabic, elections or choices are normally called

---

[4] For the most part I will use "questions" and "interrogations" instead of "horary," which simply means "pertaining to the hour" (i.e., pressing questions of the moment).

ikhtiyārāt, "choices," from the verb *khāra* ("to choose, pick out"): so, these words mean exactly the same thing in Arabic and Latin.

But this notion of choosing is ambiguous, because it mainly refers to the intellectual *commitment to* an action, not the actual undertaking of it. In fact, one might even suppose that this notion of choice really refers to what the *astrologer* does in choosing an auspicious time, rather than what the client or agent of the action does: so that "election" may have begun as an insider term of art among professional astrologers. For the action itself, Arabic writers (such as al-Kindī,[5] Sahl,[6] and al-Qabīsī[7]) used *ibtidā'āt* ("beginnings, undertakings"), from *badā'* ("begin, start, make the first step"). This was translated accurately into Latin as *inceptiones* ("beginnings, undertakings," whence we get the English "inception"), from the verb *incipio*—and the person who actually performs the action and undertaking, is an *inceptor* ("one who undertakes, begins").[8] So again, the Arabic and Latin match perfectly.

Now, it happens that the earlier Greek writers on elections (such as Hephaistio of Thebes and Dorotheus of Sidon) did not refer to this branch as "choices." Rather, they used the Greek equivalent of the second group of words in the previous paragraph: *katarchē* ("beginning"), from *katarchō* ("to make a beginning").[9] And so, while later Arabic and Latin authors seemed to speak on the one hand of how an astrologer "chooses" an auspicious time, they followed the Greek-language writers by referring to the actions themselves as "beginnings" and "undertakings." This branch of astrology is about the choosing of times, but for successful actions, beginnings, undertakings.

Questions, elections, and thought-interpretation: overlap and ambiguity

Now, it would seem that elections are clearly distinguishable from questions or interrogations. According to our normal understanding, interrogational astrology has to do with getting answers to specific questions, whereas elections have to do with choosing a time for a topic that is already

---

[5] Burnett 1993, pp. 82-83.

[6] See references in Crofts, p. 237.

[7] Al-Qabīsī, pp. 136-37.

[8] Remember that the paying client might not be the same person as the one undertaking the action.

[9] See for example Hephaistio vol. 1, p. 403. But as I will show below, there are good reasons to suppose that *katarchai* should be understood as "relative" or "secondary" beginnings.

known (and which we want to be successful). But things are not that simple. It is true that some matters can be considered more or less "pure" questions, such as "where is my lost cow?" Others may be considered more or less "pure" elections, such as "when should I set out on my journey?" Again, questions may be asked about matters in which one is not personally involved or cannot make much of a contribution to, such as "will X win the war?"—while elections suppose that one is personally involved and has the power to make a decision. However, there are a number of reasons why questions and elections are not so clearly distinct.[10] Let's start with some observations about questions and elections.

(1) Some questions imply an action. In some interrogational texts, the answers to questions of the form "will it happen?" take the form of "yes, but only if you do X." An instructional example from Sahl[11] expresses this in the form of a rule, to the effect that if the querent seeks an honor, the lord of the Ascendant in the tenth shows that he will get it, but only through his own effort; but if the lord of the tenth is in the Ascendant, he will get it without effort. Bonatti provides a chart from his own practice,[12] responding to a question as to whether a general would successfully besiege and occupy an enemy castle. Bonatti's answer is basically of the form, "yes you can, but you won't": he points out that the general "ought to have it," but only "provided that first the things that needed to be done to capture it, came to pass"; however, he points out that certain features of the chart indicated "they would not apply themselves to those things by which the castle ought to and could be taken. And this was the reason it was not taken, when it could have been taken." In these cases, an abstract answer of "yes" or "no" may be given, but it is connected with the necessity of some future action. If the answer is "yes," one might well elect a time to perform that action, but sometimes (as in Bonatti's example), the question shows that while the action is possible, it will not take place.

(2) Some elections require a successful question. As we will see below, medieval writers recognized that some actions need to be confirmed by a reliable nativity (with annual predictions, *etc.*), or even a successful question. For instance, suppose the nativity is neutral or ambiguous as to the success of business travel: one might well need to ask a question as to the success of

---

[10] I am also aware that there is a debate on the use of *katarchē* to describe elections, questions, and event charts under one umbrella, but will not address it here.

[11] *On Quest.* §10.1 (*Judges* §10.1).

[12] *BOA* Tr. 6, Part II, 7th House, Ch. 29.

business travel this year, and then elect a good time if one receives a positive answer. In some cases, the chart of the question was used as a proxy for the nativity, and its features used to craft an effective election.

(3) Some questions and electional charts refer to past actions and events which were not of interest or deliberately chosen at the time. For example, one might ask how long a king will reign: Māshā'allāh says[13] one may cast the chart for the time when the king ascended the throne (what is now called an "event" chart), and even cast subsequent solar revolutions based on that time—treating the unplanned event as being like a nativity. This would be like an election, but for a past event which had not been astrologically chosen, implying less than the deliberate choice we normally assign to elections. Likewise, in *Carmen* V.35 Dorotheus assumes that the client has had property stolen and wants to find it: much of the chapter is concerned with where the property is and how to recognize the thief, but V.35.57ff tells the astrologer how to recognize what the stolen property was. But shouldn't the client know that already? In this case, the consultation uses present information (in the form of a question) to say something about what happened in the past, even if it is simply so as to confirm astrologically what the situation of concern is. One might also ask a question about (or get information about) an event which has happened in the past, especially looking at the recent separations of the Moon to identify past events connected with a present concern. So although one might think that questions seek the truth about a present or future situation, and elections seek times for a future action, each may be applied to past events not deliberately chosen or previously of concern.

(4) Questions and undertakings can each be linked to thought-interpretation procedures. In *The Search of the Heart*, I provided texts and arguments to show that both ancient and medieval astrologers used methods to identify the content of a client's thoughts and concerns. In some cases,[14] the techniques were used to identify a class of material (such as, "third house matters"), which would then presumably be narrowed down through further conversation, and the chart was then read as a specific question. In others,[15] all of the particulars of the thought as well as its outcome were interpreted seamlessly in one process. But in his *Apotelesmatics* III.4,[16] Hephaistio outlines

---

[13] See Sahl's *On Times* §12.
[14] See for instance *Search* Appendix A (throughout).
[15] *Search* I.7, the chart drawn from a work attributed to Hermes.
[16] *Search* Appendix H.

procedures for thought-interpretation which seem to pertain ambiguously to actions. The title of III.4 declares that it is on how one may *know beforehand* (thought-interpretation) the *inquiries* (Gr. *peusis*, that is, a question) of those who want to consider a *beginning* (*katarchē*). All three activities and types of chart may thus ambiguously overlap in the same consultation: for example, one might say the client is *thinking* of a lost object, and that by horary rules one knows *whether it will be found* and where to look, and then the client immediately goes home and undertakes a search. In that case, the beginning or "election" is something the client undertakes separately after having what looks solely like a thought-interpretation and interrogational consultation,[17] but the successful question chart could easily double as describing an auspicious time to undertake the search. Later, Hephaistio uses the Lot of Fortune to identify the client's thought, and in one case he says it shows that what the man wants to do will be utterly pointless. To my mind this further shows that questions, actions, and thought-interpretation could not always be easily disentangled: is Hephaistio *describing* the thought itself ("this client is thinking about a pointless affair"), or is he describing the thought ("this client is thinking about X") and *predicting* what will happen with it ("and it will be pointless")? One might well argue that this is all a case of thought-interpretation and interrogations, because Hephaistio never gets to the point of actually *electing* a time for an action. But my point is simply that, due to the intersection of thought-interpretation, undertakings, and questions, one cannot simply distinguish questions and elections on the basis that one deals with present and future things not in our control, and the other with future things which we deliberately act on.

So far, I have pointed out some puzzling things about how questions and elections relate to one another. But there is another powerful reason to connect them closely: the historical-textual fact that material on elections was repurposed by certain authors, to create question texts on those very topics. That is, some authors took material on electing the best time (say) to create a business partnership, and rewrote it as instructions for answering questions *about* what would happen in such a business partnership. Thus, many (in fact, some of the most famous) texts on questions derive from texts on elections,

[17] The *Yavanajātaka* does sometimes compare the thought-chart to the nativity, just as later horary astrologers sometimes compared the horary chart to the nativity (the "root" chart). See below.

rather than being part of an independent branch of astrology. Let me explain more about this, which will lead to considering the concept of "roots."

(5) Question texts deriving from electional texts. In a 1997 book, David Pingree had claimed[18] that some of the more important texts on questions were really adaptations from earlier electional and natal material (particularly Book V of Dorotheus, on elections or undertakings)[19]—though he did not demonstrate this in any detail. In my 2011 translation of *Judges*, I argued that Pingree was correct, and in support of that claim I began to compile citations from what I called the "Māshā'allāh group": followers (and copiers) of Māshā'allāh who wrote works on questions, especially Sahl bin Bishr and Abū 'Ali al-Khayyāt. I will describe this "group" in greater detail below. But when comparing *Carmen* V to the electional material in this book, and the works on questions in *Judges*, it seems absolutely clear to me that the basic structure and content of numerous texts on questions (as seen in *Judges* and its sources), often comes directly from *Carmen* V—whether from Māshā'allāh's translation, or 'Umar's. Throughout this book, I provide citations and comparisons which the reader may investigate.

The significance of these facts, is that questions and elections are much closer in content and style than any other branches of traditional astrology—precisely because one was often derived from the other.[20] True, many of the same rules of natal interpretation are shared with other branches; but no two branches of traditional astrology share as much in practical technique and approach (and textual readings), as questions and elections do. So again, an attempt to distinguish them in a very strict sense must fail.

---

[18] Pingree 1997, p. 47.

[19] Dorotheus of Sidon wrote a 1st Century AD work on nativities, annual prediction, and elections, which has not survived fully in Greek. It was partly excerpted and summarized by Hephaistio in his Greek *Apotelesmatica*, survived in other Greek and Arabic fragments and passages, and in an incomplete Arabic translation of an altered Pahlavi manuscript, by 'Umar al-Tabarī in the late 700s AD. Pingree edited and published al-Tabarī's Arabic version (with an English translation) under the title *Carmen Astrologicum* in 1976, which still remains the basis of Dorotheus studies today. When referring to *Carmen* in this book, I mean the Arabic version by al-Tabarī, from Pingree's edition—not the complete original which has perished, or Māshā'allāh's rival translation (see below).

[20] I say "often," because one unusual feature of *Judges* is that 'Umar's questions do not closely match the corresponding topics in *Carmen* V, while his elections here do. This suggests that perhaps 'Umar respected the distinction between elections and questions more consistently than Māshā'allāh did, since the questions and elections which derive from Māshā'allāh's Dorotheus are often virtually the same on key points.

As a matter of fact, to my mind this similarity in the texts, and the historical derivation of questions from elections and thought-interpretation material, suggests that in the mind of some people like Māshā'allāh, some questions are like elections ahead of time: i.e., a question *now* about a future event, is read just as an election for that *future time*. For instance, suppose I want to go on a successful journey. If I pose a question *now* about a future journey ("Will my journey be successful?"), the features of the chart are interpreted just as if I had asked an astrologer to elect a future time that *will be* good for travel. Likewise, we might think of event charts (i.e., interpreting charts cast for past events) as being like elections interpreted *after* the fact.

To say that questions are like elections ahead of time, and event charts are like elections after the fact, is not to exhaust the whole category of questions or event charts (although there is less to say about event charts). After all, some questions really do deal with things over which we have little or no control, and it is hard to know how anyone could make an election about them: for example, "Will X win the war?" But if we take this idea and return to the five points of ambiguity and overlap I mentioned above, we could say this:

(1) Some questions imply that an action must take place, because they state ahead of time what the necessary action is, and that it would be successful—even if one might formally elect a time later on for actually performing the action.

(2) Some elections demand a question with a favorable answer, because the question chart can indicate what features the electional chart ought to have in it. In the case of an unknown nativity, the question confirms that at least the nativity does not conflict with the action, and in lieu of the nativity the question chart acts as a proxy for it, suggesting what signs and planets need to be made fit in the later election (see §2 below).

(3) In the case of revealing information about past events, the situation is a bit more complicated. A chart taken at the time of the consultation essentially reveals what is happening *now*, in relation to a flow of events which was initiated in the past (such as what property had been stolen, and where it is now); but equally, that same chart can reveal the success of one's interest (such as whether one will recover the property) as well as how to successfully undertake an action (for instance: that the thief is fleeing and will escape soon if he is not pursued, or that the property is close to being lost unless one searches now). Nevertheless we still have a seamless analysis of the past,

present, and elective future, in the same consultation. In the case of theft, a chart cast for the past event or the current consultation, will have features describing the deliberate theft in the past; the chart at the consultation will also show the success or failure of catching the thief or recovering the property, in just the way one might ask later whether it is an auspicious time to find the thief, and so on.

(4) In the case of thought-interpretation, if the client's inquiry is about a future undertaking, the consultation chart can both reveal the thought about the future undertaking, and double as a question about its success and what must be done at a later time to bring it about.

(5) Finally, questions are like elections ahead of time, because in a textual sense they were originally electional texts which were rewritten in the form of inquiries about the future and future actions.

Roots and the logic of action

The medieval notion of a "root" was important for both the theory and practice of elections, and in fact it is relevant in all branches of traditional astrology—although it is strange to me that (so far as I know) hardly any classical Greek texts discussed it.

In the Latin West up through the emergence of English-language texts,[21] astrological works on questions were frequently interested in whether or not a question chart was "radical" (Lat. *radicalis*), and for many people in this context, "radical" is basically equivalent to "permissible to interpret." But the word simply means "rooted," and what a chart is rooted by, is a root—hence the nativity is often called a "radix," which is nothing more than the Latin for "root." For centuries, Arabic and Latin texts were concerned with the "root" chart, which provided the *context* and *basis* for other kinds of charts. In questions, some astrologers considered God's will as the ultimate root or foundation for a question's validity;[22] but in a strictly astrological sense a root or root chart is the chart for the beginning of something which has relative independence and being, and other charts are in turn dependent on it. For instance:

---

21 I am not familiar with German, French, or other vernacular works on astrology in the early Modern period.

22 For example, see *BOA* Tr. 5, Considerations 1-2, and my discussion of them in the Introduction to *BOA*.

- A really thorough election should have features which enhance or downplay features of the nativity (root).
- A question often has features which are reflected in the nativity (root).
- The transits of the planets in the solar revolution are generally considered in reference to the nativity (root).
- Annual Aries ingress charts are often considered in reference to previous ingresses or charts of Saturn-Jupiter conjunctions (root); likewise, the charts for the lesser conjunctions of Saturn-Jupiter every 20 years, must be considered in reference to the conjunction of the triplicity change (root).
- Weather prediction is often considered in reference to more general themes in ingress charts or the charts of New and Full Moons (roots).

The issue of roots was so important in elections, that Sahl begins to discuss them in the first sentence of *On Elect.*, in the context of whether elections are even useful to people who do not have favorable nativities. Then, al-'Imrānī and al-Rijāl feel compelled to respond in kind (which I will discuss in a later section). But for now, I want to discuss this concept of a root a bit further.

First, I want to emphasize one important lesson to be learned from examples like those listed above: almost nothing in this world has or is an absolute beginning or has fully independent being; almost everything is conditional and dependent and relative, and astrologically this is understood in the pairing of "root" charts with the other charts interpreted with respect to them. A dependent chart depends on a root chart, but even that root chart is contextual and depends on something else which acts as *its* root. I will return to this point below.

Second, it is useful to think of elections and roots in the context of what may be called the "logic of action." In antiquity, philosophers who were impressed with the concepts and procedures of formal logic, tried to adapt logical models to explain what happens in actions: thus they tried to recast the relationship of desire, circumstances, and action, in the form of a logic of action. For instance, suppose I have a belief that "cake is good." This is a value statement that implies a possible action such as eating, since people act based on what they think is good. Then if I see cake, it is as though there is a corresponding proposition in my mind, "this is cake." The general (or "universal") value judgment that cake is good (and the implied readiness to act on that), combined with the particular circumstance and recognition that cake is available, can yield an action—namely, eating the cake. This is a simple way to start connecting general attitudes and value judgments, with particular judgments about situations. Likewise, when investigating suspects, police generally try to connect a motive (universal) with opportunity (particular), to explain how someone might have committed a crime (individual action). The category of what is general or universal, appropriately connected with what is particular, yields an individual, concrete action.[23]

Abstract Terms	Logic of Action
Universal +Particular = Concrete individual	Motive/value judgment + Opportunity/circumstances = Concrete action

Figure 1: General scheme of the logic of action

Elections can be understood within this framework. Let me give a concrete example to get us started. Suppose that an airline is offering a sale on flights to Minneapolis on a certain date. You might say that this is an "auspicious time" to buy tickets. And that would be correct: a sale is a good time to buy tickets. But the sale is being offered to everyone, and people live complicated lives. Just because it is generally a good time to buy tickets, does not mean that it is good *for you* to buy tickets. Maybe you are broke and can't afford them anyway, or you have to be at a friend's wedding on those dates of travel. In order for this to be a good sale *for you*, the sale has to have certain features which will particularize it to your own needs and interests. To put it astrologically, suppose that the Moon is about to trine a Jupiter in the Midheaven: you might say that is a "good time" to act. But the Moon trining Jupiter like that is almost wholly unspecific to any particular action, and it would be equally a good time for everyone in the geographic area where those features apply. This is not to say it's useless, but for the election to be

---

[23] For those readers familiar with Kant's ethics, this is roughly the form of his analysis of action. The "categorical" (i.e., unconditional) imperative defines wholly general criteria for what actions are moral, while a maxim describes a particular type of action. If the maxim appropriately conforms to the imperative without inconsistency, the action is properly moral and permissible; if it does not, it is contrary to morality and not permissible.

about a definite kind of action, and especially for it to be tailored to your needs and interests, we need something more specific.

According to how I am thinking about it, the natal chart is the root and plays the "general" role here. It presents a variety of possibilities (and perhaps impossibilities) for actions, along with motives and interests. Suppose I want to elect a time for actions that will advance my career: I need to know that career advancement is generally supported in the chart, and especially that those features of the chart are primed for activation around this time (for instance, that a profection or solar return shows professional possibilities being relevant at this point in life). If I can find these features, then I have a good foundation or root for such advancement.

The election itself—or rather, the chart and the time chosen for it—plays the "particular" role here. Its features must describe a successful action at a particular time, and they must connect with my nativity so as to make it relevant to *me* and not just anyone at all. But within this role of particularity, the traditional astrologers clearly outlined two parts or levels: a general sub-level and a particular sub-level.[24] That is to say, even though the election itself plays the "particular" to the nativity's "general," we can distinguish two sub-levels of the election which allow it to be particularized to the root chart: a general one, and a particular one.

To make this clear, let's return to the example of career advancement. My nativity acts as the root and what is general for my life, while the election acts as the particularization of those general features. Now, in order to craft a proper election, the election chart itself has got to be both favorable as a whole or in general, as well as enhancing particular good things about my own chart or downplaying bad ones. For instance, in a general way we want the chart to look good, especially in terms of the action I want. So we might want to ensure that the Moon is favorable, as well as the tenth house, perhaps the Sun for glory. We'd probably want the Ascendant of the election and its lord (which signify me) to be in a good condition. And this would be a really good start: it would be a favorable time to advance one's career at this time. But is it a good time to advance *my* career? We have made the electional chart more narrow and specific to a kind of action, but it is still somewhat general. What if it turns out that my natal tenth house is in the sixth of the electional chart, with Saturn and Mars on it, in detriment and fall? That would actually speak *against* it being a good time for *my* career, even

---

[24] These are my terms, to make sense of the traditional authors.

though in the abstract the election has a lot of good general features. Could it wholly deny the success of my action? Maybe, maybe not. But in order to get just the election we want, and to make this time really particularized to me, my own natal positions must be made fit through the electional chart. That is what I meant before: although the election plays the particular to the nativity's universal, the election itself is complex and must not only have good universal features of its own for action, but also be particularized to the nativity we are dealing with.

Abstract Terms	Basic Rooted Election
Universal	Nativity
+Particular	+ Election (two parts:) *Universal: Fitness of luminaries, Fortune, etc.* *Particular: Fitness of natal positions*
= Concrete individual	= Successful undertaking

Figure 2: The logic of action as a basic rooted election

The texts in this book describe these two sides of an election, with greater and lesser complexity (in fact, I have even simplified matters somewhat). We can let al-'Imrānī stand as our model. In chapters such as I.1.2 and I.2.0, al-'Imrānī provides several views on what the general sub-level of the election should consist of: for example, al-'Imrānī believes (I.1.2) that one should make the following things fit[25] in every election: the Moon, the Sun, the planetary significator of the matter (such as Venus for getting engaged), and signs that generally indicate the matter (such as watery ones for sea travel). Then, al-'Imrānī has a kind of intermediary particular stage (I.1.3), in which one must adapt the house signifying the matter (such as the tenth for honors), both in the election and the nativity: thus if the natal tenth is Capricorn, and the electional tenth is Virgo, one should make both Capricorn and Virgo fit at the time of the election. Finally, in Treatise II, al-'Imrānī describes all of

[25] Throughout this book, I will use the phrase "adapt *X*" or "make *X* fit" to translate the Latin *adapto*. To adapt something or make it fit, means to find a time in which it is in a good condition, either in general (such as making a planet aspect the benefics) or in the context of a specific action (such as putting the Moon in fiery signs for actions pertaining to royalty or glory).

the extra details that would go into making a truly complete and particularized election: for instance, that in electing for surgery, the Moon should be in certain signs and in aversion to Mars. It is not always easy to tell whether an author is describing more general conditions or particularized ones, but these categories should work well for understanding how to approach a standard, "complete" election.

§2: Epistemological and moral issues in elections

The texts in this book share a lot in common, because the same material was often being transmitted from one to the other. But in some respects they should be viewed as engaging in a dialogue, since over the centuries the authors reflected not only on the nature and use of elections, but on certain epistemological and moral issues which were raised especially by Sahl (though probably originally by Māshā'allāh). Let me first describe a little bit about the transmission issue, and then discuss the other topics.

The most important astrological author for the material in this book, is Dorotheus. His 1st Century Greek poem was used extensively by Hephaistio in the 5th Century for his own *Apotelesmatics*, as well as being translated into Pahlavi by the Persians (with some additions and changes here and there). In the latter half of the 8th Century, both Māshā'allāh and 'Umar al-Tabarī translated this Pahlavi version into Arabic.[26] 'Umar used his own translation for at least some of his elections,[27] while Māshā'allāh's was passed on to Sahl bin Bishr and Māshā'allāh's student Abū 'Ali al-Khayyāt, and thence on to others—but not, it seems, as a stand-alone work. Instead, Sahl and al-Khayyāt seem to have copied from a book on choices which Māshā'allāh crafted from his own translation of Dorotheus Book V. Thus we get the first complete work on elections in this book, Sahl's *On Elect.*,[28] which should probably be considered *Māshā'allāh's* book of choices or elections. Then, al-'Imrānī drew on al-Khayyāt and Sahl as well as al-Tabarī (among others), so that many of his elections are Dorothean in spirit or approach, if not word-by-word: that

[26] See below for some comments on what I have called the "Māshā'allāh group" or "Māshā'allāh transmission."

[27] 'Umar's *Book of Choices* has not been translated out of Arabic, but passages attributed to him in this book do match *Carmen.*

[28] For my purposes I omit the fact that this was translated into Latin. I have translated this work from the Latin, but with reference to the Arabic edition by Crofts.

is to say, al-'Imrānī first got two doses of Dorothean material via al-Khayyāt and Sahl, and then a third via al-Tabarī. Finally, al-Rijāl copied many of his elections from al-'Imrānī but added important passages from Sahl. In this way, Dorotheus has gone through many hands and undergone several transformations and restatements, and for the most part these authors are working within the parameters laid down by him. Of course, by the Arabic period there had been much reflection about roots and many other issues: later writers were not simply unthinking, slavish copyists. Nor did they always agree with each other or with their own sources, as the reader will see.

I think the best way to start would be with al-'Imrānī, who opens his book with an argument justifying elections. After outlining the structure of the book, Treatise I begins with a review of an important point in Ptolemy's *Tetrabiblos* III.2. There, Ptolemy says that conception is the original beginning (*archē*) of the human being, while the nativity is a secondary beginning, relative to and dependent on it (*katarchē*).[29] It is true that the nativity will show the unfolding of life insofar as the native is separated from the mother, but even the conception would have showed everything (including life in the womb)—if only we knew the time of conception. But most people don't know the time of their conception, so the nativity is a wholly suitable beginning—it is wholly suitable because the separation from the womb is still the beginning of the complete human being who is ready to experience life, even if it has already devolved from the process of conception and gestation. Al-'Imrānī uses these statements by Ptolemy to justify elections: the fact that conception charts can act as beginnings instead of nativities, means that if we could *plan* a conception using natal rules (which would make the conception an election), we could know fully how the life will unfold—and so on with other kinds of undertakings.

Now, al-'Imrānī's argument here is a bit incomplete. For elections are normally taken to be secondary and relative to a root of some sort (such as a person's nativity), but here he makes the conception itself an election, when Ptolemy had claimed the conception was an *original* beginning, not a relative one. Moreover, conception is followed by a second, relative beginning (the nativity)—but what normally follows an election is simply the successful action itself, not some second beginning. So it might seem as though al-'Imrānī

[29] Remember, this is the traditional Greek astrological term for a beginning or undertaking, what we now call "elections."

has made a misstep in laying the model of elections and roots onto the conception chart. But I think we can rely on Ptolemy's naturalism to fill in the missing parts here. In Ptolemy's naturalistic, causal theory of astrology, even conception is rooted in the charts of the parents and their transits, *etc.* So, the conception can be viewed as a second beginning (*katarchê*) relative to the parents, but an original beginning (*archê*) with respect to the nativity, and the birth is a second beginning (*katarchê*) relative to conception. After reading all of al-'Imrānī, I believe that what he really wants is to use Ptolemy to make an epistemological and moral point: that *deliberate* elections are *good* because there is value in knowledge about the future and in our ability to use that knowledge to increase happiness. (Ptolemy himself argues for this in *Tet.* I.2-3.) With respect to conception, we normally want to choose the best life for our children, or at least to present them with the best opportunities. Therefore, being able to deliberately choose a conception promotes both knowledge and goodness.

What al-'Imrānī then should have done but did not, was to supply an argumentative bridge to elections proper as a branch of astrology. He could have done it by saying roughly the following: "But there is a difference between nativities and elections. Elections are indeed relative beginnings or *katarchai*, because just as nativities are relative to conceptions, complete elections are relative to nativities. But they are not quite like nativities, because an election all by itself does not reliably indicate the future to the extent that a nativity can. For, a single isolated action such as putting a boat in the water or making a business deal, is not a complete, substantial being in the way that a birth is. Elections are more like annual solar revolutions or questions, which are indeed relative beginnings but are limited in time and scope (which also makes them more varied and flexible). Moreover, while a nativity may be indirectly chosen by electing the time of conception, it does not have to be; but elections are always deliberate and closely linked to knowledge and goodness. Therefore, elections by themselves have their own astrological roles to play apart from the fact that both they and nativities happen to be relative beginnings."

After these preliminary justifications, al-'Imrānī (along with the other authors) places limitations on what elections can do—precisely because they are not complete roots on their own. Elections cannot make something happen that is astrologically contradicted in the nativity (such as electing a great marriage for someone whose chart shows terrible marriages),[30] or for events which are impossible due to various natural circumstances, like electing for a prepubescent boy that he should have a child of his own.[31] Rather, elections can only do things like mitigate or enhance already-existing indications in some root,[32] or provide generally favorable circumstances, such as good times to hunt. Indeed, in Ch. I.2.13, al-'Imrānī gives a list of possible combinations for nativities and elections: for instance, how effective a good election will be if one has a poor nativity.[33]

But our authors also pursue two related issues which pertain to professional practice and ethics: first, whether and how one ought to elect for someone whose nativity is unknown; second, whether one may use the features of a successful question chart in lieu of an unknown nativity.

Unknown nativities and using question charts

In *On Elect.*, Sahl begins[34] by pointing out that elections are weak, as compared with nativities. They are only particularly strong for kings (or perhaps, all powerful and successful people), because by definition their nativities (which are often known) already suggest success: so elections are effective at *enhancing* their actions. That is, a good election for a good natal chart will easily bring success—and in fact we might assume that in many cases such a successful person will rarely need a special election to ensure it.

But if so, we need to make a decision about electing for middle and lower-class people, especially since not many of them know their own nativities.[35] The nativities of such people often show only middling success or speak against success, so that an election might not be of much help; and if the nativity is unknown, the risk of making a pointless or even harmful election

---

[30] See al-Rijāl's *Prologue of the Author* in Book VII.

[31] Al-'Imrānī I.2.0, II.6.1. This point is actually rather interesting. Astrologers occasionally point out that one must know something about the real conditions surrounding a nativity, so that we do not predict kingship and vast wealth for a poor person—except insofar as he or she may be well-respected and better off than the rest of the poor. But here (and especially in II.6.1), al-'Imrānī even suggests that things like medical knowledge are useful for the astrologer.

[32] *On Elect.* §§1-4; al-Rijāl VII, *Prologue*; al-'Imrānī I.1.4, I.2.0.

[33] See al-Rijāl's version in his *Prologue of the Author.*

[34] *On Elect.* §§1-5c, 7-9.

[35] Obviously Sahl is writing at a time in which the time of birth was not regularly recorded. Actually, in many countries and places today the birth time is not noted.

is even greater, since one does not know exactly what in the nativity to enhance and adapt in the election. So, Sahl says, we ought to elect for such people only if we have one of the following: (1) a nativity *and* a solar revolution chart showing success at that time, or (b) a question chart for the matter, showing that it will be successful. In the latter case, we see the doctrine of roots at work in a new way. For the nativity is a root for the election, but here the question chart acts as a proxy which indirectly reveals something about the nativity: that is, a successful question indicates that the real root, the nativity, is not contrary to the action. For if the nativity *were* wholly against the action, then the question chart could not indicate success.

Sahl underscores the importance of these options, because if we went ahead with an election either for an unknown nativity (and therefore no solar revolution, either), or in the face of an *unsuccessful* question (which would put the nativity's indications into question), we might end up emphasizing bad natal features when crafting our election chart. For instance, we might emphasize Jupiter in the election, not knowing that the natal Jupiter is in fall in the 12th, squared by both malefics. In such a case, the election would either do no good or would actually do harm.

Sahl's text frames the general problem and provides a set of possible answers. But before moving on to the responses of others, I must make two points. The first concerns an ambiguity in Sahl. On its face, Sahl's text only seems to mean that we should *note the fact that* one has a successful question chart, before going on to craft a separate electional chart. But al-'Imrānī and al-Khayyāt[36] seem to understand the issue differently: that is, that one might *adapt the particular features* of the question chart, in the election chart itself. These are two very different things. For example, suppose that a client lacking a nativity wants to elect a time to travel. The astrologer duly casts a question chart along the lines of "will the trip be successful?" Suppose furthermore that the Ascendant of the question is Gemini. Sahl seems to mean that once we know the trip will be successful, we do not have to pay attention to Gemini or Mercury (its lord), because all we need to know is *that* the trip will be successful; then we simply need to do our best in crafting a suitable election using the rules in the book. But al-'Imrānī and al-Khayyāt seem to take the question's role as a substitute root more literally: namely, that the election chart would have to suitably adapt Gemini and Mercury themselves,

---

[36] See al-'Imrānī I.4.

because the features of the question chart must play an *active role* in the election.

The second point is that, despite these ambiguities, we can divide our authors up into roughly three positions. At one extreme is Sahl,[37] who allows for elections based on unknown nativities as well as questions, although he is wary of them. At the other extreme stands al-Khayyāt (as portrayed by al-'Imrānī), representing a more naturalistic view: one should not elect for unknown nativities, nor use questions at all. In the middle stands al-'Imrānī, who believes we ought to find ways to elect for everyone, but that (a) we should only use questions if we must, and (b) we should *not* use the features of a question chart in the election itself. (Instead, al-'Imrānī wants to use the many other electional strategies he lists, in order to find the best hour for an undertaking.)

So far we have seen the two extremes represented by Sahl and al-Khayyāt—which is itself interesting, since in so many other cases they seem to present the same view (namely, the one derived from Māshā'allāh). Let us now turn to al-'Imrānī, who has thoughtfully considered the matter from a variety of perspectives.

In terms of strictly astrological theory, al-'Imrānī follows a roughly Ptolemaic, naturalistic standpoint. In I.4, he explains (in a rather indirect way) that electional theory relates two charts together: the nativity and the election. The election is supposed to modify the nativity by enhancing or downplaying certain parts of it. But those who use question charts in lieu of a nativity, particularly so as to adapt the features of the question chart for the election, are introducing a third kind of chart which is not really appropriate. Specifically, question charts do not belong to electional theory because they are not *natural*, whereas the relationship between the nativity and the election can be considered natural because one is harnessing the natural causes devolving from the stars, to trigger or enhance or downplay natural potentials in the nativity. So should we abandon question charts altogether? No, says al-

---

[37] Al-Rijāl also falls in this category. Al-Rijāl knows both the material from Sahl and from al-'Imrānī, but for some reason he simply ignores al-'Imrānī's arguments altogether. The only innovation I can see is that he warns us not to elect for evil people and enemies unless one has their nativities (*Prologue of the Author*). Unfortunately, he does not explain why. Perhaps he means that we don't want to accidentally strengthen something good in their nativities, so that we should use their nativities to ensure failure. But in that case, why would the astrologer intentionally elect something bad for such people, when surely they could come back and take revenge on him?

'Imrānī: we must use what we can, even a question chart—even though, he suggests, that in themselves they do not really help. Instead, we ought to use something like a recent mundane ingress chart, because it will have a general effect over the world and it partakes of the natural system of causes.[38]

So al-'Imrānī does not really think questions will help, and he moreover believes there are alternatives. Let us see how he responds to Sahl on the issue of electing for people with unknown nativities, because we will see that he views the matter in terms of professional ethics. One simple way to look at it, is that in any election we must try to have whatever good we can get, even if it is not everything we want. But al-'Imrānī actually has three responses: (1) based on practical astrological concepts, (2) in terms of professional ethics, and (3) based on the theory of elections.

(1) Based on practical astrology. Sahl and others argue[39] that if we work without a nativity (and also without a question), we might end up unwittingly strengthening something natally bad, or weakening something nominally malefic but actually important in the nativity. An example would be making Cancer feature prominently in the election, when in fact it has Saturn in it natally; or, trying to make Mars cadent and in a bad place (such as the 6th), when in fact Mars rules the natal Ascendant and should be helped and enhanced instead. Therefore, we should not elect without a nativity (or in the absence of a nativity, a successful question chart), because of the risk of highlighting or marginalizing the wrong thing. But al-'Imrānī argues that Sahl and the others are wrong. In the first place, by avoiding such elections we are acting decisively in favor of ignorance and fears of a worst-case scenario. But also, because the naturally benefic planets are more numerous than the malefic ones, it is more likely that one will strengthen and feature benefic planets, not the malefic ones. All in all, the chances of strengthening either a malefic planet or a benefic in a poor condition are less than those of strengthening something helpful. Again, this goes to al-'Imrānī's notion that it is better to do what we can, than to do nothing because we cannot have everything we want.

---

[38] I would point out there that this kind of argument is only really persuasive if one believes in a naturalistic theory of astrology. If one believed that astrology was wholly significative or symbolic or divinational, one might allow a fuller range of uses for question charts.

[39] See al-'Imrānī I.1.4.

(2) Based on professional ethics. Using a scenario borrowed from Sahl,[40] al-'Imrānī imagines that a group of people are traveling together. Sahl uses this scenario to point out that even if one elects the time of travel for the whole group, individuals' outcomes will differ based on what their own nativities indicate. In al-'Imrānī's presentation, some astrologers conclude that it is pointless to elect for such a group, precisely because one cannot guarantee the outcome for everyone. But al-'Imrānī's response is basically that this is unprofessional and borders on the immoral. Clients come to astrologers for help, but the astrologer described here throws up his hands because he cannot create the perfect election, thus putting everyone in danger: in other words, he makes the perfect the enemy of the good. For if the astrologer believes in elections at all, he must at least agree that some times are better than others, generally speaking. But the hypothetical astrologer here does not even bother to favor an hour generally known to be better: since he does not know or cannot guarantee success for every individual, he simply suggests that *perhaps* the hour of the group's departure will not be harmful. Al-'Imrānī then invokes God in an intriguing comment to the effect that humans have the power of choice, which is provided by God in order to avoid evil: if then the astrologer hides the facts about likely outcomes because he cannot guarantee success for a group, he is effectively denying people the ability to make the knowledgeable choices which in part define their humanity. Al-'Imrānī probably imagines the astrologer meeting God in the afterlife and having to explain why he practiced astrology but did not bother to help as much as he could, simply because he did not know all of the answers.

(3) Based on the theory of elections. Finally, al-'Imrānī argues that Sahl and others are wrong about refusing to elect for people whose nativities or questions promise harm. For, he says, even if we cannot remove all of the evil, picking an hour that is generally good will at least not *contribute* to the harm. Again, this is based on the theory of elections itself: for we must assume that some hours are better than others, either in a general way or in relation to a particular action or specific nativity. If so, then even if we cannot make an action wholly successful, by definition we are obliged to say that some hour is better than another, even for someone with a terrible nativity. Refusing to elect for such people is tantamount to denying the concept of elections in the

[40] *On Elect.* §§6a-b.

first place, so al-'Imrānī believes that this refusal is self-contradictory. Certainly it adds to the accusation of being unprofessional or even unethical.

This last argument (and the view of Sahl's and others to which it responds) generally assumes that clients are undertaking *necessary* actions. That is, if someone had a terrible nativity with respect to an action, it would probably be best that he or she not attempt it at all—if it were wholly voluntary and optional. The issue of refusing to elect for a bad nativity or unsuccessful question should only come into play if we are talking about some unavoidable choice. For example, if someone's nativity had terrible indications for marriage, the astrologer should probably try to dissuade him or her from marrying in the first place. But if the client was about to have a child and felt obliged to get married for the sake of the child's stability, then we have the conflict involved in al-'Imrānī's third argument above. Sahl and others might well decline to elect the time for a good marriage, while al-'Imrānī makes us professionally responsible for helping in whatever way we can.

Al-'Imrānī's ethical reflections on elections are refreshing, because it is rare in the older literature that astrologers reflect on their profession and its consequences, or engage in debate. Guido Bonatti is another notable figure in this area, albeit not exactly in the field of elections. Most of the methodological material in his Tr. 7 is actually cribbed right from al-'Imrānī, and Bonatti even felt free to change the examples slightly. But in other areas, Bonatti shows that he is sensitive to client issues and needs, and matters of professional responsibility.[41]

§3: The Māshā'allāh transmission and the relation of questions to elections

This compilation on elections allows me to advance an idea which I began to develop while translating *Judges*, and which I described a bit in its Introduction §1: the notion of the "Māshā'allāh group" (or perhaps, "Māshā'allāh transmission"), and associated proposals about the origin of some texts on questions and the true fate of Māshā'allāh's translation of Dorotheus.

As I mentioned above, in the 1st Century Dorotheus of Sidon wrote a lengthy didactic poem on nativities, predictive methods, and elections (in-

[41] In 2012-13 I will publish a paper focusing on Bonatti as a central and praiseworthy example of what it meant to be a medieval astrologer.

cluding, it seems, event charts), nowadays known by its Latin title *Carmen Astrologicum* ("Astrological Poem"). By the time of the early Arabic period in the middle-to-late 8th Century AD, it had been altered and edited and supplemented by various authors. Traditional lore reports that both Māshā'allāh and 'Umar al-Tabarī translated the Pahlavi version separately, but while al-Tabarī's version survived—and Pingree published it with an English translation in 1976—the Māshā'allāh version was largely lost. The lore was misleading in certain crucial ways, as I will explain in a moment.

Connected with these issues is the matter of how questions arose as a distinct branch of astrology, given that there is no clear developed approach to them in ancient Greek texts (unlike the systematic treatments we find in Arabic ones). Pingree claimed,[42] though did not explain at length, that questions arose from a conscious rewriting of ancient electional material. For although the standard medieval texts on questions display a distinct style and approach,[43] the actual content and rules for many questions can be traced back to specific sentences in a text such as *Carmen*. In a similar way, 'Umar al-Tabarī's Arabic translation of *Carmen* V is titled "On Questions" or "On Inquiries,"[44] yet most of the material is clearly electional.

In 2009 I translated the Latin *Book of Aristotle* (*BA*), which Burnett and Pingree had argued (in their critical edition) had probably been written by Māshā'allāh, in an Arabic form now lost. In their commentary, Burnett and Pingree showed two important things: first, sentence after sentence of the book could be traced back to nearly identical ones in either the Greek Rhetorius or al-Tabarī's Arabic *Carmen*. Second, they provided parallel passages in an Arabic work on nativities by Sahl, which presented virtually a word-for-word version of Hugo's Latin. There are two consequences to these points. For one thing, it means that much of *BA* constitutes Māshā'allāh's own reorganization of Books I-IV of his translation of *Carmen* (along with Rhetorius); for another, it means that Sahl's book on nativities probably preserves not only the Arabic of most of Māshā'allāh's original, but that by definition it preserves much of Māshā'allāh's own translation of *Carmen*. This was my first

42 Pingree 1997, p. 47.

43 For instance, Latin texts which translate Arabic books on questions usually begin with sentences such as, "If someone asked you whether or not he would attain X, then look at…". This is more true in translations of the style of John of Seville, since people like Hugo of Santalla preferred another way of rendering the Arabic—but even Hugo's style is equally standardized and stylized, as the reader of *Judges* may easily see.

44 See Pingree's edition of *Carmen*, p. 106.

hint that Māshā'allāh's Dorotheus might still exist, but in a different form than an independent translation like al-Tabarī's.

Then, in my own translation of *Judges*, and prompted by some private bibliographical notes generously provided by Burnett, I began to see further outlines of what I called the "Māshā'allāh group," or rather the Māshā'allāh transmission: a group of texts which could reasonably be traced back to Māshā'allāh and his translation of Dorotheus. *Judges* is a compilation of Arabic texts primarily on questions, which Hugo of Santalla and possibly Hermann of Carinthia translated into Latin in the 12th Century AD. Among the nine sources translated for *Judges*, Hugo chose Sahl's *On Quest.*, Abū 'Ali al-Khayyāt's *Book of the Secret of Hope* or *Book of Questions* (it has gone under both titles),[45] and an unknown person called "Dorotheus." When comparing these three texts side-by-side, it was easy to see that they presented virtually the same information in exactly the same phrasing and sentence order. There were other things too: (1) the individual sentences often correlated with sentences in al-Tabarī's *Carmen*, showing that the texts had been derived somehow from Dorotheus; (2) the authors sometimes state that their material comes from Māshā'allāh, and occasionally one author will present the material unattributed, while a parallel author will attribute it to Māshā'allāh. If we include the above observation that (3) Sahl is known to have copied a book of nativities from Māshā'allāh (whose Latin incarnation is *BA*), while al-Khayyāt (Māshā'allāh's own student) clearly copies from him in places, I suggest we can make a couple of conclusions:

- Māshā'allāh's translation of Dorotheus was largely preserved[46] in the form of complete texts on nativities and questions (and elections, as we will see below). These texts represent what survives of his version of *Carmen* I-IV.
- The missing Book V of Māshā'allāh's Dorotheus is represented in part by the "Māshā'allāh group" of texts in *Judges*: Sahl, al-Khayyāt, and "Dorotheus." In fact, it is probable that "Dorotheus" in *Judges* is nothing more than Māshā'allāh's Arabic itself, but that there was confusion over Māshā'allāh's authorship of the translation and Dorotheus's original authorship of the material itself.

---

[45] Sezgin, p. 121 #2.

[46] I say "largely preserved," because Pingree 1999 presents and translates a lengthy section of what appears to be Māshā'allāh's Arabic translation of parts of *Carmen* II, not otherwise found in *BA*.

- More tentatively, I suggest that Māshā'allāh's translation was not lost because it never existed as such in the first place. It is perhaps even more likely that Māshā'allāh converted and reorganized the Pahlavi version directly into serviceable texts on natal, electional, and interrogational material, than that he wrote a separate translation which was then lost. For since 'Umar's own translation survived, why shouldn't Māshā'allāh's have as well, given his stature in the astrological world (assuming it is not lying undiscovered somewhere right now)?

To return to Pingree's original claim: the questions of the Māshā'allāh group in *Judges* often contain the same information and analysis we find in al-Tabarī's Arabic *Carmen*, on *elections*. In other words, *Judges* provides ample evidence that electional texts were indeed being repurposed as question texts, as Pingree had claimed. But strangely enough, 'Umar's own questions in *Judges* hardly ever reflect the Arabic *Carmen*: so wherever he got his question texts from, he did not convert or repurpose them from his own translation of Dorotheus Book V. However, his texts on elections (as seen in this book) *do* match *Carmen* very closely. These facts suggest that, unless other, unknown electional texts were being recycled in the form of questions, Māshā'allāh himself is responsible for this repurposing of electional material, which ultimately became so influential in the history of this branch of traditional astrology. Of course this does not mean that Māshā'allāh *invented* the branch of questions itself: for 'Umar and al-Kindī each have their own approaches, whose source material is not clearly or easily found. It is also possible that some authors developed texts on questions independently, based on general interpretive principles in other areas of astrology, while Māshā'allāh simply rewrote a number of existing electional ones.

The remaining question is: where is the rest of Māshā'allāh's Dorotheus? The texts in this book get us closer to an answer. In short, Sahl's *On Elect.* and al-Khayyāt's unnamed book on elections (quoted occasionally by al-'Imrānī and al-Rijāl) can be seen as representing Māshā'allāh's own rendering of Dorothean elections *as* elections (rather than as repurposed for questions). First of all, just as in *Judges*, individual sentences by Sahl and al-Khayyāt (as quoted by al-'Imrānī or al-Rijāl) often match. Second, some of these sentences can also be traced to other texts, such as Sahl's *On Quest.* and his *Fifty Judgments*, which again suggests that most of Sahl's opinions are really

Māshā'allāh's. Third, huge amounts of their material can be matched to al-Tabarī's *Carmen*, showing that they are really Dorothean in origin. In addition, there are the following points which help illuminate the idea of the Māshā'allāh transmission, as well as the relation of questions to elections:

- Although al-'Imrānī knows Sahl's work, he seems to use another version of *On Elect.*: for he regularly credits Māshā'allāh and al-Khayyāt for material which is also in Sahl's *On Elect.* So just as with *Judges*, virtually identical texts were published by Sahl and al-Khayyāt, which at least included references to Māshā'allāh if not actually constituting Māshā'allāh's version of *Carmen* V's elections.
- Al-'Imrānī and al-Rijāl rarely credit *Dorotheus* with these views on elections. Rather, when it comes to members of the Māshā'allāh transmission, they credit those members; when it comes to 'Umar al-Tabarī's Dorothean elections, they credit al-Tabarī himself. This means that my proposed confusion over the true authorship of "Dorotheus" in the *Judges* texts was not simply a fluke, since the same seems to have been true for al-Tabarī.
- An intriguing passage in al-'Imrānī I.2.1 shows some overlap in approaches to questions and elections. There, al-'Imrānī quotes al-Khayyāt on the subject of which planet to prefer as the most authoritative significator in an election. Al-'Imrānī criticizes this view, but does not seem to notice that al-Khayyāt is actually presenting the views of the Māshā'allāh group and al-Tabarī on choosing the chief significator for the querent in *questions*.[47] This suggests that even in the 10th Century there was some overlap when it came to texts pertaining to elections and questions. Of course, it is possible that in his own work on elections, *al-Khayyāt* did indeed want to use this rule from the practice of questions; but if so, then he would have deviated from Māshā'allāh's practice, as Sahl does not report such a view in *On Elect.*

To my mind, these considerations are good news for historians, translators and practitioners: they not only exemplify the overlap between questions and elections, and clarify some of the history of the Māshā'allāh transmission, but they make the recovery of Māshā'allāh's Dorotheus (and thereby

---

[47] See my citations in al-'Imrānī I.2.1.

more of Dorotheus himself) more possible. In a nutshell, most of *Carmen* I-IV is preserved in *BA* and a few other recovered passages, while *Carmen* V is preserved in the Māshā'allāh group or transmission of questions and elections.[48] In the future I will publish an article on the Māshā'allāh transmission which has more details, as well as an attempt at a "reconstructed" Dorotheus, using texts from Hephaistio, al-Tabarī, Māshā'allāh (i.e., *BA*) and his followers, Anubio, and others.

To give the reader a better idea of what I mean, the following table offers an incomplete list of citations from the works in this book. In the left column are passages from Sahl, al-'Imrānī, and al-Rijāl, all of which appear in more than one member of the Māshā'allāh transmission. In the column on the right are the subset of these which are demonstrably used for questions. Of course, there are many other passages which are used for questions, but which I cannot or have not yet verified are present in al-Khayyāt or others. The reader may consult the footnotes in the passages, where I make the connections explicit.

Citation		**Mash. group?**	**Questions?**
On Elect. (Sahl)			
§§118-21		X	X
§28		X	
§142		X	X
Al-'Imrānī & al-Rijāl			
I.2.1		X	X
I.3		X	
I.4		X	
I.2.8	VII.2.3	X	
I.2.11	VII.1, VII.2.5	X	
I.2.12	VII.49	X	
II.1.8	VII.70.4	X	X
II.1.11		X	
II.2.6		X	
II.2.7	VII.46	X	

[48] We must keep in mind that there are other potential members of this group or transmission, such as Hurrazād bin Dārshād al-Khāsib (see below).

II.3.4		X	X
II.5.1	VII.22.2	X	X
II.5.4	VII.25	X	
II.5.6	VII.27	X	X
II.8.3		X	
II.8.4		X	
II.13.3	VII.61	X	
	VII.2.6	X	
	VII.11.1/ VII.20.3	X	
	VII.25	X	
	VII.44	X	
	VII.47	X	
	VII.70.1	X?	

Figure 3: Select passages in the Māshā'allāh transmission

In closing, I would like to go into more detail about the work which must go into analyzing and comparing the texts within the Māshā'allāh transmission.[49] For sometimes, material from multiple members of the Māshā'allāh group helps to confirm what Māshā'allāh must have written, but in other cases it shows how the members diverged in their interpretation or copying—in this case, Sahl and al-Khayyāt. A good example of such divergence is a set of five passages about the Moon being harmed or impeded at the time of an election. We can divide these passages into two groups.

The first group attributes a view to Dorotheus (i.e., Māshā'allāh's Dorotheus):

> (*On Elect.* §28) And Dorotheus said,[50] if you saw the Moon to be impeded, and a matter is at hand which ought to come to be wholly and it cannot be put off, you should not give the Moon a role[51] in the Ascendant: and make her be cadent from the Ascendant, and put a fortune in the Ascendant, and strengthen the Ascendant and its lord.

[49] Of course I realize that for the most part I am only working with the Latin texts; ultimately we will have to translate the Arabic ones, as well.

[50] Cf. *Carmen* V.5.10-11.

[51] This would probably include any rulership, not simply that she should not be in it or aspecting it.

(al-Rijāl VII.3.5) Dorotheus says, if you saw the Moon to be harmed, and you had some hastened matter which you were not able to delay, you should not give the Moon any role in the Ascendant, but make her be cadent from it and its angles, and put a fortune in the Ascendant; and strengthen the Ascendant and its lord as much as you could.

Given al-Rijāl's own practice in using his sources, it is easy to conclude that he has simply copied this passage over from Sahl, who in turn has gotten it from Māshā'allāh's translation of Dorotheus (cf. *Carmen* V.5.10-11). There are three elements to the instructions: take the Moon away from the Ascendant somehow (perhaps forbidding her rulership there, too), put a benefic planet there, and strengthen the Ascendant and its lord. One small difference is that al-Rijāl's version has the Moon be cadent from the Ascendant (i.e., in aversion to the Ascendant) *and* from the angles: if so, then the Moon could only be in the twelfth and sixth, while Sahl's version would also allow her to be in the second and eighth. I am prepared to assume that Sahl has the accurate reading of Māshā'allāh here, especially since Arabic authors sometimes do not distinguish verbally between being cadent in the sense of aversion, and in the sense of the angles: so it might have been tempting for al-Rijāl to simply add "and its angles," as an attempt to clarify Sahl, when in fact he ended up restricting the possibilities originally given by Sahl. Nevertheless, the two passages are extremely similar and do not present any real problems.

But in several other passages attributed to al-Khayyāt and an "Utuluxius,"[52] we get the following:

(al-'Imrānī I.2.11) Al-Khayyāt [said], if it were necessary to choose for someone, and the Moon [were] made unfortunate, make this bad [planet which is making her unfortunate] the lord of the Ascendant, if it were free and in a praiseworthy condition; and if it received the Moon, it will be better. He also said, if [a benefic][53] were in the Ascendant, it will be good.

(al-Rijāl VII.2.5) Al-Khayyāt says,[54] if you had a hastened election, and the Moon went towards a planet [that is an] infortune, make that infor-

52 Probably a strange Latinized and garbled version of al-Khayyāt's name.

53 Added based on *On Elect.* §28 and al-Rijāl VII.3.5.

54 Al-Rijāl has taken this from al-'Imrānī I.2.11, but it has undergone changes.

tune be the lord of the Ascendant; and if [the infortune is] clear and in a good status, it will be better; and if it received [her] from the Ascendant, it will likewise be better.

(al-Rijāl VII.1) Utuluxius said,[55] If you were not able to avoid an election, and the Moon were unfortunate, make that infortune be the lord of the Ascendant.

The first two are similar to Sahl's versions, but delete any reference to making the Moon be cadent or in aversion to the Ascendant. Moreover, they add extra elements that may have been based on a misunderstanding. In fact, I believe that al-Khayyāt's entire approach was to emphasize what else one could do with such a malefic, especially since the election has to happen soon. Instead of strengthening the Ascendant and its lord, al-Khayyāt/Utuluxius now *makes* the malefic planet *be* the lord of the Ascendant. Utuluxius stops there, showing that something is missing in his version, but see what happens to the al-Khayyāt passages. Each of them uses the phrases "it is better" or "it is good," twice. This suggests that there is some basic situation, plus two enhancements. In the al-'Imrānī version, the basic situation is that the malefic can be the lord of the Ascendant if in a good condition, with the two enhancements being (1) receiving the Moon and (2) "it" (probably the benefic from Sahl's version) being in the Ascendant. But in al-Rijāl's version, the basic situation is simply that the malefic is the lord of the Ascendant, with the two enhancements being (1) that it is in a good condition, and (2) receiving her *from* the Ascendant. It is easy to reconstruct how al-Rijāl made the latter change: if al-Khayyāt had followed Sahl/Māshā'allāh/Dorotheus in recognizing the importance of there being a benefic in the Ascendant, but al-'Imrānī had made a mistake and simply used the pronoun "it," then to al-Rijāl the text would have the malefic planet both receiving the Moon and being in the Ascendant: but this is no different from "receiving the Moon *from* the Ascendant," which is exactly what he wrote. The following table shows the changes which have happened:

[55] According to VII.2 below, this is al-Khayyāt. See also al-'Imrānī I.2.11.

	Basic Situation	**Enhancement 1**	**Enhancement 2**
On Elect. §28	Make Moon cadent/be in aversion	Strengthen lord of Ascendant (i.e., be in a good condition)	Benefic *in* Asc.
Al-'Imrānī I.2.11	Malefic *is* lord of Ascendant, if in a good condition	Receiving Moon	[Benefic] *in* Asc.
Al-Rijāl VII.2.5	Malefic *is* lord of Ascendant	If in good condition	Receiving Moon *from* the Asc.

Figure 4: Divergence between Sahl and reports of al-Khayyāt

In other words, (a) for some reason al-Khayyāt ignored the original part about the Moon being cadent or in aversion; then (b) he applied the part about making the lord of the Ascendant strong or in a good condition, to the malefic itself; then he (c) agreed that there should be a benefic in the Ascendant, which al-Rijāl misunderstood and applied to the malefic planet; finally (d) he allowed that if the malefic planet received the Moon, it would be an enhancement. But al-Rijāl thought the malefic could be the lord of the Ascendant in any case (which does not make sense, if it was harming the Moon), and made being in a good condition and receiving *from* the Ascendant to be the enhancements.

From these passages, we can see how the same material can be used and misunderstood in various ways, even by astrologers apparently copying the text from someone else. If we put all of these elements together, we could get a more complete version of these ideas, which is in line with traditional astrological logic. In my proposed reconstruction of the passage below, the first sentence (with elements 1-3) represents the original text from Māshā'allāh/Dorotheus, and the second sentence (with elements 4-5) extra commentary and advice.

> (Dykes) If you saw the Moon being harmed by or applying to a malefic, and it was an election which you could not put off, then (1) make the Moon be in aversion to the Ascendant, (2) put a benefic in the Ascendant, and (3) strengthen the Ascendant and its lord as much as

possible. However, (4) if the malefic were in a good condition, you could make it be the lord of the Ascendant, in which case (5) it would be better if it received the Moon.

§4: Al-'Imrānī and al-Rijāl

As I began to describe above, the primary texts in this volume (by Sahl, al-'Imrānī, and al-Rijāl) often represent a line of copying and transmission from Dorotheus, with the addition of other, as-yet unknown or untranslated sources.[56] Dorotheus was translated and used by both 'Umar and Māshā'allāh, with Māshā'allāh's version passing on to Sahl and al-Khayyāt. Al-'Imrānī employs many sources, but inasmuch as he cites the members of the Māshā'allāh group and 'Umar, he is getting a lot of Dorotheus. Al-Rijāl not only copies many passages from al-'Imrānī, but inserts further passages from Sahl's *On Elect.*, adding to the input from Dorotheus via Māshā'allāh. In this section I would like to say more about al-'Imrānī and al-Rijāl in particular.

Al-'Imrānī: life and sources

'Alī bin Ahmad al-'Imrānī came from Mosul (modern day Iraq), spent his life in the mathematical sciences and in astrology, and died in 955 AD. According to the *Fihrist* by ibn al-Nadim (10th Century), he was the teacher of the well-known al-Qabīsī,[57] whose introduction to astrology I translated from the Latin version and published in *ITA*. Astrologically, al-'Imrānī's most well-known work[58] was a ***Kitāb al-Ikhtiyārāt*** or *Book of Choices*, the book translated here. The Latin translation[59] was titled *On the Elections of Hours* or *On the Elections of Praiseworthy Hours*, and was translated in Barcelona by Plato of Tivoli in 1133 with the assistance of a Jew named Abraham bin Hiyya—although the account at the end of the work in this book suggests that the

---

56 One of the other important authorities used is al-Kindī's *Forty Chapters*, although it is currently unknown exactly what most of al-Kindī's sources were.

57 See al-Qabīsī, p. 1.

58 According to Sezgin p. 166, ibn al-Qifti (a 12th-13th Century Muslim writer) claimed that al-'Imrānī had written a number of others.

59 See the Bibliography for the manuscripts I used for the translation. For the most part, I relied on Madrid and Paris BN 16204, but used Vatican and Munich for more difficult passages and questionable readings.

primary labor of translating from Arabic was done by Abraham, perhaps with an intermediary Spanish language. We know the date and approximate hour, because the date and planetary positions and Ascendant are described after the *explicit*, and I have cast the chart using modern software at the end of his Treatise II below.[60] It is interesting and refreshing to see a medieval translator who not only could cast a chart, but believed it was important to note the planetary positions when the work was complete.

Above, I described al-'Imrānī's views on elections, especially with respect to ethical concerns over unknown nativities. Here I would simply like to add that al-'Imrānī especially seemed to be discerning and analytical when reviewing various approaches to elections. First of all, we have seen that he actually makes arguments in favor of his views. Second, he makes rare criticisms of other authors, such as his statements against al-Khayyāt's views on strength in I.2.1: there, al-Khayyāt uses rules for selecting significators in *questions*, in the context of *elections*—with which al-'Imrānī disagrees. Third, instead of simply arranging elections by house topic (such as we find in Sahl and al-Rijāl), al-'Imrānī groups certain ones together as being appropriate for people in high status (as opposed to everyday people's concerns), with their own preparatory rules;[61] moreover, even in his divisions by house he distinguishes elections which pertain strictly to the body and its *healing* (first house), from those which pertain to slaves, servants, and captives (sixth house). Al-Rijāl on the other hand assigns matters of healing to the sixth house, because they derive from *illness*.

But fourthly and more interesting is al-'Imrānī's medical model of elections. In the last paragraph of Chapter I.2.13, al-'Imrānī describes three levels of complexity and sophistication when dealing with elections and books of astrology. The first level is that of (1) basic books on astrology which teach general principles, such as what the elements are and mean: this would be like the texts in *ITA*, and it is for this reason that al-'Imrānī consciously decides not to explain what the quadruplicities mean in elections—whereas al-Rijāl, following Sahl, does explain them. For al-'Imrānī, the knowledge of such things is like very basic knowledge about physiology and anatomy, "which should come first, before a doctor gets involved in putting medicines

---

[60] My thanks go to David Juste, who showed me an advance draft from his upcoming revision of Carmody, where he discusses the differing accounts of the charts in the manuscripts.

[61] See II.1.

together." The second level is represented by (2) the first Treatise of *The Book of Choices*, which explains basic and general electional procedures without real regard to the particulars of a situation. This, he says, is like a medical book which instructs doctors that patients with certain symptoms or problems need this or that medicine, along with teaching certain basic procedures. But the third level is like (3) the second Treatise in the book, which is on particular elections that are sensitive to particular situations, individuals, and their nativities. This is like a pharmaceutical manual, which tells a doctor exactly how to prepare medicines and apply them in particularized circumstances. And so, the astrologer is a consultant similar to a physician, who must apply general rules and principles to a specific individual, in order to get a specific result. In fact, this view helps to clarify al-'Imrānī's belief (see above) that we should even elect for people whose nativities are unknown, just as many doctors would agree that sometimes one must treat someone in an emergency even if one cannot perform all the tests one might want to beforehand. For example, one might argue that since only few people are allergic to certain antibiotics, it is better and more responsible to use them even if an allergy is revealed later, than to let a patient suffer because one does not know all the facts. Just so, al-'Imrānī argued that the malefics are fewer than the benefics, and so it is better to use one's skill to get the best possible chart in the case of an unknown nativity, than to let a client walk into danger on the off-chance that one might be strengthening a difficult (and unknown) natal planet. Offering a likely but small benefit or even a lack of harm through one's elections, is better than neglecting the help one might give out of fear of not being perfect.

Following are the authors used by al-'Imrānī:

- **Abu 'Ali al-Khayyāt** (d. early 9th Cent. AD), a student of Māshā'allāh, perhaps from his *Kitāb al-Masā'il* or *Kitāb al-Sirr*.[62]
- **Abu Ma'shar** (9th Cent. AD), from an unnamed text on elections (of which there are several attributed to him),[63] perhaps the source al-Rijāl uses for *Skilled* VII.101, since al-'Imrānī mentions in his I.2.13 that Abū Ma'shar wrote on electing by the Lunar mansions.
- **Al-Kindī** (ca. 801-870 AD), from *The Forty Chapters*.

[62] Sezgin, p. 121 #2.

[63] Sezgin, p. 146 #10-12.

- An ***al-Khasib*** (see II.1.8), who may be the same as the Hurrazād bin Dārshād al-Khāsib used by al-Rijāl (see below).
- **Claudius Ptolemy** (2nd Cent. AD), from the *Tetrabiblos*.
- **"Dorotheus,"** probably from either 'Umar's or Māshā'allāh's translation of Dorotheus.
- **Māshā'allāh** (d. ca. 815 AD), probably from either his translation of Dorotheus or a separate electional work which was the prototype for Sahl and al-Khayyāt.
- *Perhaps* **al-Hasan bin Sahl**,[64] although Sezgin says that his name was often confused with al-Hasan bin Sahl bin Nawbakht.[65]
- **Sahl bin Bishr** (fl. 9th Cent. AD), from *On Elect.* and *On Times* (but perhaps also *The Fifty Judgments*).[66]
- **'Umar al-Tabarī** (fl. late 8th Century), probably from his own *Kitāb al-Ikhtiyārāt* (*Book of Choices*).[67]

Al-Rijāl: life and sources

Abū al-Hasan 'Alī bin Abi al-Rijāl (fl. first half of 11th Century) is best known for his huge compilation, the *Book of the Skilled in the Judgments of the Stars*, which was written in Arabic in Muslim Spain and contained the views of most of the central authorities in Perso-Arabic astrology. It was translated into Old Castilian by Alvaro de Oviedo in the 13th Century (at the court of Alfonso X the Wise), and thence into Latin,[68] becoming an extremely popular manual. Unfortunately, not much is known about al-Rijāl's life. He was a

---

64 See the list of names for al-Rijāl below, and a possible use in al-'Imrānī I.5.0.

65 Sezgin p. 122.

66 Note however that al-'Imrānī typically seems to use al-Khayyāt's version of the *On Elect.* material, which al-Khayyāt most likely got from his teacher Māshā'allāh.

67 Sezgin, p. 113 #6.

68 I have relied on the earliest Latin edition (1485), but have sometimes had recourse to the later (and stylistically changed and embellished 1551 edition). I should also point out a couple of details about the 1485 Latin, which sometimes reveals its Castilian/Spanish roots. For instance, the text frequently uses a gerund or gerundive in the ablative, so as to indicate a present progressive just as modern Spanish does: *Luna...sit...separando se a Mercurio* ("The Moon should be separating herself from Mercury," Ch. VII.78); better Latin would have used *separans* instead of *separando*. Also, the 1485 Latin often uses a comparative adjective when a superlative is probably meant: for instance, staying that something is a "better" (*melior*) election, when the sense of the text is most likely "best" (*optima*) election (e.g., Ch. VII.79).

respected personage at the court of al-Mu'izz bin Bādīs, a ruler of the Tunisian Zirid dynasty in the 11th Century.

The best way to characterize al-Rijāl's treatment of elections is this: it is a largely verbatim copy of al-'Imrānī's individual elections (with some general material and rules), supplemented by numerous other passages (such as from Sahl's *On Elect.*),[69] and detailed treatments of timing methods, Lunar mansions, and planetary hours. Indeed, later sections[70] comprise some of the only evidence I know that the Persians had access to the later books of Valens: this is important, because while we know that a certain Persian Buzurjmihr or Burjmihr wrote a commentary on Valens entitled *Bizīdāj*, we know almost nothing about what was in it. Al-Rijāl himself reports that some of these views of Valens are found in a Persian book entitled *Endemadeyg*, and the similarity of the endings *dāj* and *deyg* are intriguing;[71] but so far I have not been able to find out what this book could be.

As a compiler, most of al-Rijāl's treatment consists of reports from other sources, he sometimes argues for his own view. It is also common for al-Rijāl to list a number of opinions, and then present his own with the phrases "But I say…" or "In sum…". Following is a list of al-Rijāl's named sources, whose names and works are definitely or probably known:

- *Abimegest.* Unknown, but note the similarity to *Almagest*, the common name of Ptolemy's book on astronomy. It is also likely that *Abimegest* is a title granted to Māshā'allāh, since it follows his name immediately in the *Prologue of the Author*: thus, something like "Māshā'allāh the Great."
- **Abu Ma'shar**, sometimes by means of al-'Imrānī's citations, but also a two-part *Book of Natures*, whence al-Rijāl gets Abū Ma'shar's views on elections by planetary hours (see VII.74 and 100).
- **Al-'Imrānī.**
- **Al-Fadl bin Sahl** (771-818 AD), the older brother of al-Hasan bin Sahl. He was a Persian Zoroastrian who converted to Islam in 805-06, and was one of the astrologers of Caliph Hārūn before being named as a vizier under al-Ma'mūn. According to Sezgin,[72] he

[69] See for instance the *Prologue of the Author*, and VII.51.1.
[70] See VII.102-03, and VII.105.
[71] Thanks go to Chris Brennan for pointing this out to me.
[72] Sezgin p. 115.

claimed to have used the books of the Persians, Greeks, and Copts (but surely not all in the original languages) in his work.

- **Al-Hasan bin Sahl** (782-851 AD). Sezgin (p. 122) says that he is often confused with another astrologer, but in al-Rijāl's case that is probably not so, since al-Hasan bin Sahl was the brother of al-Fadl bin Sahl, who is also cited (below). Al-Hasan bin Sahl was a vizier of al-Ma'mūn's, and the father of the esteemed female astrologer Būrān (807-84 AD). According to Sezgin, he was one of the people who translated Pahlavi astrological writings into Arabic.
- **Al-Khayyāt** (see above).
- **Al-Kindī** (see above).
- **Al-Shaibānī** (prob. fl. 10th Cent. AD),[73] an astrologer from Kufa and perhaps an older contemporary of al-Nadīm (d. in the 990s AD). He wrote a book titled *Book of Questions and Choices.*
- **Hurrazād bin Dārshād al-Khāsib** (fl. first half of 9th Cent. AD), an attendant or intern in the house of Sahl bin Bishr, who wrote both an *On Nativities* and *On Elections* (undoubtedly the one used here).
- **Māshā'allāh** (see above).
- **Pseudo-Ptolemy**, from his *Centiloquium.*
- **Sahl bin Bishr** (see above).
- **Theophilus of Edessa** (d. ca. 785 AD), son of Thomas and the primary astrologer for Caliph al-Mahdī (r. 775-85 AD). Theophilus translated Greek astrological material into Syriac, and is best known for his work on questions pertaining to war. Unfortunately, the Latin al-Rijāl does not identify what chapters or paragraphs actually come from Theophilus.
- **'Umar al-Tabarī**, in part due to copying al-'Imrānī, but also a work on times by al-Tabarī (see VII.102.5).
- **Vettius Valens** (2nd Cent. AD), the important Alexandrian astrologer whose nine-book *Anthology* preserves much otherwise unknown lore. As I mentioned above, the Persians had a commented version of this work, whose contents are largely unknown or lost.

---

[73] Sezgin p. 173.

- **Zaradusht**, a Persian astrologer writing under the name of Zaradusht or Zoroaster, among the first astrological authors translated into Arabic.

Following are some other names mentioned in the Latin al-Rijāl, whose identities I am unsure of:

- *Ablabeç filii çaed*, again a bin Sayyid.
- *Alaçmin*, possibly al-'Āsimī[74] or an al-'Uthman.
- *Alohaç filius Zaet*, the last part of which must refer to a bin Sayyid.
- *Bericos*.
- *Cadoros*.
- *Feytimus*. But since it only appears once after an occurrence of Valens's name,[75] and without an "and," perhaps it is an honorific or descriptive term for Valens himself.
- Ibn *Hebeteth*, whose name sounds like that of the astrologer ibn Hibinta.[76]
- *Minegeth/Nimagest*. I take these two names to refer to the same person, who could be al-Munajjim al-Qummī.[77]
- *Nufil*.
- *Utuluxius*, who is attributed a view in VII.1 which is later attributed to al-Khayyāt.

---

[74] Sezgin p. 167.
[75] See VII.47.
[76] Sezgin p. 162.
[77] Sezgin p. 174.

§5: The Moon and Lunar mansions

Part I of this book describes elections based solely on the Moon's connections with other planets by degree, and her motions in the Lunar mansions. These are the simplest and crudest of electional types.

Electing by Lunar applications

For electing by the Moon's applications, I have translated into English a short piece by al-Kindī, his *Ikhtiyārāt al-ayyām*, *The Choices of Days*, via a German translation from the Arabic by Eilhard Wiedemann.[78] These applying connections[79] by degree simply suggest periods of up to a day or so[80] in which it is good to perform actions that partake of the general theme of the planet involved, such as war (Mars) or presenting jewelry (Venus). There are some refinements based on the types of aspects that are best, and the Moon's Nodes. Since the Moon ought to be made fit and have a relevant connection or at least aspect by sign in any case, these types of elections should not be ignored. But their usefulness is limited, because (in al-Kindī's case at least) they are valid for everyone around the world at the same time. That is, since house positions and rulerships (which are sensitive to latitude and longitude) are ignored, it would theoretically be good for anyone at all to present jewelry when the Moon applies to Venus, or to make war when applying to Mars. This would be all right in certain limited cases, but surely it is not equally good for both warring parties to go to war at the same time, since armies are rarely equal in strength and skill. Only more detailed and refined elections can distinguish astrologically between two parties like that, such as we find in the "complete" elections in Part III.

---

[78] See the Bibliography. The manuscript is identified as Leiden Codex 199 (Cat. No. 1050), and is listed in Sezgin vol. 7, p. 131, number 3.

[79] For use of this word and other technical terms for planetary configurations, see *ITA* III.

[80] This greatly depends on how the connection between the planets is reckoned. If using the Perso-Arabic orbs for planets, then since the Moon's orb in that system is 12°, and her average daily motion in the zodiac is about that much, she will apply to any planet within her own orbs for about 24 hours. In *Forty Chapters* Ch. 2.1.5, al-Kindī advocates a distance of 6° between planets for an effective applying connection, which would take the Moon about 12 hours to traverse.

Mansions: history and concepts

Electing by the Lunar mansions suffers similar theoretical and practical problems. But since there are differences in understanding about just what these mansions are, it is good to review some opinions about them, and explain how I have constructed my table of mansions and stellar positions.[81]

The mansions are divisions of the zodiac which originally related the position of the Moon to various fixed stars, such that she "stays"[82] approximately one day in each mansion. According to al-Bīrūnī, the Indians had a set of 27 mansions and the Arabs 28, meaning that each mansion was either 13° 20', or 12° 51' 26", respectively.[83] In the Indian case, this is probably based on the Moon's tropical cycle (i.e., a lunar revolution or return), which is about 27.3 days. In the Arab case, it is probably based on the period of the Moon's visibility, reckoning the first day of the Lunar month from her first appearance out of the Sun's rays, until she goes under the rays again on the 28th day.[84] The difference between these two periods is less than one day.

According to al-Bīrūnī, just as the tropical signs are named after constellations, so the zodiacal mansions are named after the fixed stars which are contained (or used to be contained) in them. I say "used to be contained," because although the use of the mansions is very old and is tied to the fixed stars rather than the tropical zodiac, at some point in time the mansions were reckoned from 0° Aries in the tropical zodiac. Therefore, due to precession, the fixed star after which some mansion was named, no longer actually falls in that mansion.[85] (My own view is that if one is using the mansions serious-

---

[81] For these historical descriptions, I have relied on Bos and Burnett, De Fouw and Svoboda Ch. 8, Weinstock, al-Bīrūnī's *Chronology* Ch. 21, his *India* Ch. 56 (trans. Sachau), and his *Book of Instruction* (§§164-66). I largely ignore the Indian treatment of the mansions (*nakshatras*), because the lore is too complex and unfamiliar to Westerners to go into detail here.

[82] Lat. *maneo* ("to stay"), hence *mansio* ("a stay, stopover") and the English "mansion."

[83] The Latin al-Rijāl frequently omits the proper minutes or seconds, or adds them up slightly wrong. I have corrected the tropical positions of the mansions in the text.

[84] Weinstock (p. 48) puts it as "the twenty-eight nights of [the Moon's] visibility," which may be significant because it would be as though the Moon is staying or spending the night in that mansion as in an inn, during her monthly travels. I also note that the Arabic alphabet has 28 letters, and I imagine (but cannot yet confirm) that these letters might have been associated with mansions in magical practices.

[85] Al-Bīrūnī seems to approve of this new attribution of the mansions to the tropical zodiac. In his *Chronology* p. 338, he describes a man who associated changes in weather and so on to the mansions as related to the fixed stars themselves, while al-Bīrūnī himself argued that the mansions really refer indirectly to the seasonal changes occurring due to the movement of the Sun in the zodiac—i.e., that the fixed stars themselves are not the true

ly, one should probably use the positions of the stars and not the tropical zodiac.) In addition, there is some disagreement about what which actually define the mansions, as some names have changed over the years or the identities of certain ones have been disputed.[86] In the table I created for easy reviewing of the mansions, I supplied the modern longitudes for the chief stars which likely formed the mansions.[87] The reader will note that they are not distributed evenly and regularly: sometimes the distance between mansion stars is only 6° or so. This could be because their mutual positions have shifted over the centuries, or perhaps they were always like this, with some stars marking the beginning of a fixed span of 12° 51' 26", and others sitting somewhere in the middle of that span.

Apart from the kinds of electional topics found in al-Rijāl (such as what mansions are good for business partnerships), the mansions themselves connect calendrics and astronomy to matters of religion[88] and weather prediction,[89] and originated before the zodiacal signs. In terms of calendrics,[90] it is not hard to tell what day of the lunar month it is (since one may simply observe the lunar phases), but without a solar calendar it is hard to connect the lunar month with the seasons. So, lore about the full Moon being in such-and-such a mansion automatically tells us that the Sun is directly opposite her. This can easily be turned into lore about when to sow, what kind of weather to expect, and so on. For example, al-Bīrūnī offers[91] a short piece of poetry that was to be memorized for the sake of calendrics and temperature: that if the Moon were in the Pleiades in the third night of the Lunar month, then winter is over. He then explains that the Moon is about 40°

---

indicators of the position of the mansions. See his calendrical and seasonal interpretation of a bit of poetry, below. However, al-Bīrūnī is not wholly consistent in his approach, or at least does not tell us when he is merely reporting others' views and offering his own. For on p. 353, he describes how the Moon's relation to the actual mansion stars is favorable or unfavorable—but if we are supposed to reckon the mansions according to the tropical zodiac, then what would be the point of tracking the Moon's conjunction with those stars, since due to precession the stars are no longer even contained in the mansion?

[86] See Kunitzsch, who occasionally describes these changes.

[87] I say "likely," because not all of the star lists agree with one another. See Kunitzsch.

[88] See Weinstock on the Lunaria, pp. 57ff. Ancient and medieval lunar calendars connected all sorts of lunar phenomena with feasts, rest days, and such. But see also the description of the London Papyrus below.

[89] See below for an example from al-Bīrūnī.

[90] Weinstock, p. 54.

[91] *Chronology*, p. 336.

away from the Sun on the third day of the Lunar month,[92] so that if she were in the Pleiades, that would put the Sun in Aries, indicating the beginning of spring.[93]

According to al-Bīrūnī, there was disagreement about exactly when and how to measure the effects of the arisings of the mansion stars. The less popular opinion was that the arising of the stars marked the beginning of the mansion's period, which lasted until the next arising 13 days later: thus if the star of one mansion arose on (say) March 31st, then whatever that mansion indicated would be allotted the period from March 31st until the arising of the next mansion star on about April 13th. But the more popular opinion was that each mansion is allotted a time peculiar to it: for example, on pp. 351 of his *Chronology* are listed the days of effective influence for each mansion, both when it arises and sets. Moreover, al-Bīrūnī says that the Moon's presence on the stars marking the mansion was not considered favorable; but it was favorable if she were moving slowly and had not reached a station, or she were moving quickly and had moved beyond it. One should consult his *Chronology* for further information on this.

One textual reason to believe that the mansions are ancient, is that Coptic lists of names show no influence from Arabic, and Coptic died out as a spoken language before Arabic became prominent; moreover, Hephaistio and Maximus speak of the Moon staying in certain parts of zodiacal signs in their electional work.[94] Besides that, they were known to the Vedic-era Indians, and use a lunar month, which suggests Babylonia (since the Egyptians used a solar year): cuneiform tablets which go back to the 6th Century BC describe regions and constellations which the Moon passes through during the lunar month, though there are only 17 on the list.[95]

---

92 This probably refers to an old practice of beginning the Lunar month when she is actually out of the Sun's rays (at about 12° from him). Therefore, on the first day of the month she will be between 12° and 24°; on the second, between 24° and 36°; on the third, between 36° and 48°.

93 Remember that the sign a mansion is in, does not directly indicate the season in which it rises. That is to say, the mansion will arise *after* the Sun has moved past it. Thus, we are used to thinking of Pisces as being a winter month (in the northern hemisphere) because the seasons are reckoned by the Sun's motion through those portions of the zodiac. But a mansion in Pisces may first arise out of the Sun's rays in the east when the Sun is *already* in Aries. So although Pisces is a "winter month," the mansions *in* Pisces may only be visible in the east when it is already spring.

94 Weinstock, pp. 52-53.

95 Weinstock, pp. 53-54.

But why did the mansions not die out, once the basic problems of calendrics and the solar-lunar cycles were solved? Weinstock suggests two reasons. First, there is the "natural conservatism of our calendars, astrological prognostics, and magical texts: these often preserve traces of earlier stages of human thought;"[96] second, Islam's insistence on maintaining a lunar calendar also encouraged the mansions' survival in the Near East and West. Besides, al-Bīrūnī says that there was already a tradition among the Arabs for using the mansions for calendrics and weather prediction,[97] particularly through their rising out of the rays of the Sun before dawn. For example, if the Sun has moved in the zodiac so as to cover up one of these fixed stars with his light, then the star will have a period of invisibility (Ar. *ghaībah*); but once the Sun has moved away, the star will be visible just before sunrise, making its heliacal rising out of the rays just as its opposite mansion (the fourteenth from it) sets in the west. Since the Sun moves approximately 1° per day, and each mansion is approximately 13° long, a new mansion will make its arising about every 13 days—but of course this is only an average, since the exact positions of the stars relative to the ecliptic differ, not to mention that they will rise or set differently based upon one's latitude on earth. Since a given fixed star will only make this rising out of the rays once in a solar year, the mansions are again closely tied to the seasons, weather, and activities in human life (such as sowing).

There are two important texts describing the mansions, which Weinstock explores.[98] The first is the *Codex Cromwellianus 12* (from the 15th to 16th Centuries), which is very close to the Latin al-Rijāl's descriptions (and is probably based on a similar Arabic model if not the Arabic al-Rijāl himself), but is more complete than it. In it are included electional descriptions according to the Indians, "Dorotheus," and the Persians, along with imagery much like the images of the decans or faces, and apparently even some horoscopic charts. The codex explains which planet rules which mansion, and gives lists of what do to or avoid when the Moon is in it, based on the three traditions just mentioned. Weinstock points out that while many of the planetary rul-

96 Weinstock, p. 48.

97 Al-Bīrūnī describes some ways of predicting winds in his *Chronology* pp. 339-41, which I omit here.

98 The second text explored by Weinstock is London Papyrus 121, a more magically and religiously-oriented text, which is related to the mansions but not really appropriate for the kinds of electional material in this book.

erships are hard to understand, the mansions representing the ends of three of the weeks or the Moon's quarters (the 7th, 14th, and 21st), are all ruled by Saturn—which in Babylonian and Jewish tradition, are the end of the week.[99] These might be early versions of later nativities for individuals, as the descriptions suggest natal interpretations for births when the Moon is in them.

The mansion texts in al-Rijāl

In our Lunar mansion descriptions in Part II (taken from *Skilled* VII.100),[100] al-Rijāl provides lists of favorable and unfavorable activities from both Indian sources and "Dorotheus." As with al-Bīrūnī, the mansions are reckoned from 0° Aries in the tropical zodiac rather than from the mansion stars themselves. We can see that hardly anything pertains to Arabic-style calendrics or matters pertaining to weather and agriculture: instead, we are dealing with straightforward elections based on the Moon's position in a particular mansion. According to al-Rijāl, the Indians originally got their electional texts from "Dorotheus" (probably some related early Greek text of the 1st or 2nd Centuries AD). Weinstock suggests that the sequence of transmission occurred in the following way: first, the Indians got mansion descriptions from the Babylonians, and passed them on to the Far East; later, they got a second set of descriptions from a text related to the historical Dorotheus. In the meantime, the Arabs were already familiar with some pre-Islamic mansion lore or texts (probably from post-Babylonian Greek sources), but later on they received developed Indian texts through the Persians.

As for the contents of the lists, there are certain things to note. First, the Indian elections are a bit more evenly balanced across a greater number of topics. The most popular one is travel (26 instances), then planting and sowing (15), putting on clothing and ornaments (11), taking or making medicine (10), and seven others which are mentioned between 4-8 times. The Dorotheus material is much more concentrated on five topics, which he routinely

---

99 Weinstock, pp. 55-56.

100 These may originate in a book of Abū Ma'shar's, since al-'Imrānī (I.2.13) says that Abū Ma'shar wrote on electing by mansions in one of his books on elections.

mentions in the same order. Moreover, each of these five correlates extremely well with lists of the Moon in the signs, in the Arabic *Carmen*:[101]

- Marriage (19), compare with *Carmen* V.16.8-20.
- Buying slaves (22), compare with *Carmen* V.11.
- Sea travel (22), compare with *Carmen* V.25.1-12.
- Partnerships (24), compare with *Carmen* V.19.1-13.
- Captives (23), compare with *Carmen* V.27.1-13.[102]

The next most-mentioned election is cutting and washing one's hair and nails (9), with as many as thirteen topics being mentioned only once.

I note that the five most popular Dorothean topics can all be associated in various ways with the seventh house, since marriage, purchases, the destination of travel, partnerships, and fugitives are routinely related to the seventh in traditional treatments of questions. In *Judges* 4.5, 4.8-9, and al-Rijāl VII.22, the 7th is sowing and the vegetation on the land.

Not all of the lists of Moon-sign combinations in *Carmen* are represented in al-Rijāl's mansion descriptions. For instance, *Carmen* V.36.58-74 on finding runaways might easily have been included, but is not. Likewise, al-Rijāl regularly mentions things like cutting the hair and nails, which is not discussed in *Carmen*: but to my mind, the close relationship that does exist between the Arabic *Carmen* and the Latin al-Rijāl, suggests that Dorotheus's poem might have originally included elections on just those topics. But did the original Dorotheus use signs, mansions, or even decans? My view is that he probably used the mansions or decans, since in a couple of places he mentions specific degrees before which or after which it is all right to undertake an action.[103]

---

101 Some of the descriptions in *Carmen* are extremely close in form but say the opposite. For example, *Carmen* V.16.14 says that if the Moon is in Virgo, it is good to marry a widow but not a virgin, while mansion #13 in al-Rijāl has it the other way around.

102 This may be an election for when to capture someone, but it also reads as a kind of "event chart," so that one may consult the astrologer about the fate of a captive after the fact.

103 See *Carmen* V.25.3 and 10. Oddly enough, the al-Rijāl text does not mention these degrees.

The bust

Finally, a few comments about the *bust* or *buht*, an Arabic term which translates the Sanskrit *bhukti*, the ecliptical distance traveled in a period of time:[104] in this case, the distance or period which follows every New Moon. It seems that at least three methods were in use for electional purposes, which either dealt strictly in terms of distance, or else in terms of planetary or seasonal hours.[105] In Ch. VII.57.2, al-Rijāl presents one version of the *bust* from al-Kindī's *Forty Chapters*, and in Appendix D I present two others. They are as follows:

(1) The first (al-Qabīsī IV.23, in Appendix D) is a version attributed to the Indians, which seems to run as follows: consider whether the New Moon occurs during the day (when the diurnal sect and the Sun are in power) or night. If by day, then the 12 unequal hours which follow are ruled by the Sun, then the next 12 by Venus, and so on in the hierarchy of the planets, until after the 12 hours of the Moon the sequence reverts to Saturn, the Jupiter, *etc.* But of those 12 hours of the Sun (or whatever planet it is), the first 1/3 (or 4 hours) belong to that planet's first triplicity lord, the second 1/3 to its second triplicity lord, and the last 4 hours to the third triplicity lord. The idea seems to be that one ought to do things pertaining to the Sun when it is his hours, and then also those of (say) Venus when she is the triplicity lord, or Saturn when he happens to be the triplicity lord, and so on. This makes the *bust* something like an alternative planetary hour system. Al-Qabīsī's description suggests, but does not explain, one further point: if the New Moon were at night, we should expect that the first 12 hours belong to the Moon, then the next 12 revert to Saturn, then Jupiter, and so forth in descending order. If so, then this version of the *bust* works like the *firdārīyyāt*, which, due to their use of the Nodes as time lords, also suggest an Indian origin.

(2) The second (al-Qabīsī IV.24, in Appendix D) is the same as that described by al-Kindī (*Forty Chapters* Ch. 11.7) and al-Rijāl (VII.57.2), in which the unequal seasonal hours after the New Moon are divided into scorched/burnt and unscorched/unburnt hours (with some division of these periods into electionally-relevant periods). I have a lengthy comment on this method following al-Rijāl VII.57.2, with a table of hours.

---

[104] See for instance al-Bīrūnī, *Book of Instruction* §197.

[105] For these hours, see the discussion of planetary hours below.

(3) The third (*Book of Aristotle* II.4, in Appendix D) presents a distance-based version of the *bust,* here called the *buht.* Māshā'allāh simply says that it refers to the fact that the Moon travels about 12° in one day, so that after the New Moon the first period is described by her distance from the Sun. Māshā'allāh then refers us to Book V of *Carmen,* which in 'Umar's translation may refer to *Carmen* V.41.15, in which the distance the Moon travels is correlated with her aspects to her original position. That is, after twenty-eight days she will return to the place in which she had been at the New Moon. Now, the context of V.41.15 is decumbiture charts, meaning that once the Moon travels certain distances, we should check her aspects in order to make a prognosis about the patient. But if Māshā'allāh means that this version of the *buht* has more general application, then there are other possibilities. For instance, this twenty-eight day period is the same as her monthly visibility and the Arabic number of Lunar mansions, which suggests a reference to traveling through the mansions. On the other hand, *Carmen* explains that she reaches a square or opposition to her original position every seven days: since we are speaking about elections, perhaps Māshā'allāh/Dorotheus means that each of the seven planets will have electional rulership for one day in a Lunar quarter, during precisely that period in which she moves 12° in the ecliptic. Unfortunately, Māshā'allāh is not explicit on how he means to use it.

§6: Planetary Hours

As compared with the Lunar mansions, planetary hours are much simpler to use and imply more flexibility in electing times. The basic idea behind planetary hours is that each "hour" of the day and night is ruled by one or another of the planets, in descending order from Saturn, according to the planet's traditional distance from the earth (sometimes called the "Chaldean" order): Saturn, Jupiter, Mars, Sun, Venus, Mercury, Moon, then back to Saturn, Jupiter, and so on. I say "hour," because the hours used are the unequal, "seasonal" hours of the actual period of light and darkness that form our days and nights—rather than the equal, "civil" hours which assign 60 minutes to each hour.

So for instance, in the depths of winter the actual period of daylight is rather short, and the period of darkness is rather long. Nevertheless, the period of daylight is called the "day," and on any given day is divided equally into 12 parts, called seasonal "hours." The long, dark period between sunset and the next sunrise is called the "night," and is also divided into 12 equal parts. So on a certain day in winter, the day hours will be much shorter than the night hours. Most astrology computer programs calculate planetary hours for you, but all you need to know are the times of sunrise and sunset on the day in question, and you can figure it out by hand or on a calculator. Thus, if sunrise is at 7:32 AM and sunset is at 8:21 PM, then the day lasts for 12 hours and 49 minutes (or 769 minutes); dividing by 12 will make each seasonal or planetary hour last for 64.08 minutes. The first planetary hour will therefore last from 7:32 AM – 8:36 AM, the second one from 8:36 AM – 9:40 AM, and so on, until sunset. For the night hours, find out how long the night lasts (from that sunset until the following sunrise), divide by 12, and do the same.

Next, the first daylight hour is always ruled by whatever planet rules that day, according to a common traditional system: Sunday is ruled by the Sun, Monday the Moon, Tuesday Mars, Wednesday Mercury, Thursday Jupiter, Friday Venus, and Saturday Saturn. The next hour is ruled by the next planet in Chaldean order, and so on for the rest of the day, and on through the night. By revolving these seven planets through 24 hours, the first hour of the next day will always turn out to be ruled by the planet ruling the next day. The figures below provide the planetary hour assignments for each day:

	Sunday	**Monday**	**Tuesday**	**Wednesday**	**Thursday**	**Friday**	**Saturday**
1	☉	☽	♂	☿	♃	♀	♄
2	♀	♄	☉	☽	♂	☿	♃
3	☿	♃	♀	♄	☉	☽	♂
4	☽	♂	☿	♃	♀	♄	☉
5	♄	☉	☽	♂	☿	♃	♀
6	♃	♀	♄	☉	☽	♂	☿
7	♂	☿	♃	♀	♄	☉	☽
8	☉	☽	♂	☿	♃	♀	♄
9	♀	♄	☉	☽	♂	☿	♃
10	☿	♃	♀	♄	☉	☽	♂
11	☽	♂	☿	♃	♀	♄	☉
12	♄	☉	☽	♂	☿	♃	♀

Figure 5: Planetary hours during day (from sunrise)

	Sunday	Monday	Tuesday	Wednesday	Thursday	Friday	Saturday
1	♃	♀	♄	☉	☽	♂	☿
2	♂	☿	♃	♀	♄	☉	☽
3	☉	☽	♂	☿	♃	♀	♄
4	♀	♄	☉	☽	♂	☿	♃
5	☿	♃	♀	♄	☉	☽	♂
6	☽	♂	☿	♃	♀	♄	☉
7	♄	☉	☽	♂	☿	♃	♀
8	♃	♀	♄	☉	☽	♂	☿
9	♂	☿	♃	♀	♄	☉	☽
10	☉	☽	♂	☿	♃	♀	♄
11	♀	♄	☉	☽	♂	☿	♃
12	☿	♃	♀	♄	☉	☽	♂

Figure 6: Planetary hours during night (from sunset)

To use the example above, if the Sun arose at 7:32 AM on a Wednesday, then we know that Mercury rules the first hour of the day, from 7:32 AM – 8:36 AM; after that the Moon would rule the next planetary hour for 64.08 minutes, then Saturn, and so forth until sunset, when the Sun rules the first planetary hour of the night—for however long a night hour lasts on that day.

In this book, I have included works of "Bethen" (identity unknown) and al-Rijāl (*Skilled* VII.100). Only the first part of Bethen's piece is on planetary hours, while the rest is largely excerpted verbatim from the Latin translation of Sahl's *On Elect.*, suggesting that Bethen was really a medieval Latin. As for al-Rijāl, he presents two views: that of an *Ablabez* bin Sayyid, and Abū Ma'shar. We can establish which opinions are ibn Sayyid's and which are Abū Ma'shar's, from two facts: first, al-Rijāl mentions them in that order, and the paragraphs on the planets tend to differ in style right in the middle, creating two different paragraphs for each planet, one from each source; second, in *Skilled* VII.74 al-Rijāl mentions a view on the hour of Saturn from a *Book of Natures*, which was the title of the book on hours he attributes to Abū Ma'shar—and indeed, the second paragraph in the material on Saturn's hour expresses precisely that view (while the first paragraph, from ibn Sayyid, does not).

One might think that one *can* do things associated with a planet during its hour, but *not* things for which the nature of the planet may present problems. This seems to be largely true, but there are important exceptions and differences of opinion among the authors. For instance, Mars is associated with both blood and knives, but bloodletting is forbidden in his hour (probably because he is a dangerous plant, not conducive to health or delicate operations—at least in medieval medicine).[106] Likewise, Bethen says one may let blood during the hour of Venus, but ibn Sayyid says no. (In fact, ibn Sayyid seems to be all over the map when it comes to what is allowed or not.) None of the three sources (Bethen, ibn Sayyid, Abū Ma'shar) has enough substantial agreement to suggest any common source text or tradition for them. This makes it difficult to know whose opinion to trust. But al-Rijāl (VII.100) does not seem overly bothered by this, pointing out that "these elections of hours and mansions do not have so much virtue as the elections which we have stated before, which were taken from the places of the planets and from their accidents; however, we are able to aid ourselves with respect to them." So apparently, using them does not hurt, but they do not help in any powerful way.

§7: Times in al-'Imrānī and al-Rijāl

Traditional texts on nativities and questions often contain short statements about timing: for example, that a prisoner or slave might be freed when the Moon makes a particular aspect (*Judges* §6.40), or that prosperity will arrive during the period of the native's life when a particular triplicity lord of the sect light is in charge (*TBN* III.1.2). In the case of nativities, astrologers also developed genres of writing or particular places in their treatments which dealt solely with prediction, typically longevity in one place and annual or periodic predictions in another.[107] Likewise, one text (or related set of texts) which was often used as a collection of timing principles for questions, elections, and event charts, was Sahl's *On Times*, a pastiche of views from Māshā'allāh, al-Khayyāt, 'Umar al-Tabarī, Theophilus, and probably many others.[108] In fact, Sahl's version might have been matched by similar texts attributed to al-Khayyāt and Māshā'allāh, as part of the phenomenon of the "Māshā'allāh transmission" I described above.[109]

---

106 Bethen §1.

107 Thus Ptolemy puts longevity in his *Tet.* III.11, and annual predictions in IV.10; Māshā'allāh describes longevity in the *Book of Aristotle* III.1.7-10, and annual predictions in IV. Other authors put annual predictions in treatises all by themselves, such as Abū Ma'shar in *PN3*.

108 There are others texts on times as well, such as al-Rijāl VII.102.3, which is largely taken from Vettius Valens's *Anthology* III.12-13.

109 In fact, just as in *Judges* the texts of Sahl, al-Khayyāt, and "Dorotheus" (i.e., Māshā'allāh's translation of Dorotheus) are virtually identical, so in al-Rijāl VII.102.1 we

In this section I would like to address one part of Sahl's *On Times*, since it also appears in my translation of *Search* II.5 as well as in al-'Imrānī I.5 and al-Rijāl VII.102.1, 102.6-8, and 102.10: that is, the opening sections of *On Times*, which outline general principles of timing. I will disregard the latter portions of the work, which focus on house-specific predictions. Nevertheless it seems to me that the use of times sometimes seems to be out of place in a book on elections: in a work on questions, one might well want to know when to expect a matter to be fulfilled or change; but for elections, effort is supposed to be put into making the chart indicate success at the moment of the undertaking, not in order to predict a future event. But they would probably be more useful for event charts, as a way of predicting such things as how long a king will remain in power.

The first few sections of *On Times* can seem to be a jumble of ideas, rules, and principles. But I think the approach to timing can be divided into three categories:

(1) *Changes* in times, showing when an ongoing situation is likely to shift, take a detour, re-emerge, and so on.
(2) *Lengths* of time, referring to how long it will be until an event will manifest or even come to an end. Sometimes this leads only to identifying the number of time-units (such as "five"), without identifying which time-unit is involved (i.e., "months" as opposed to "years").
(3) *Conditioning elements*, referring to what circumstances will make the type of time-units be shorter or longer. For example, fixed signs might make the units of time incline towards years, while movable signs might indicate that number of weeks.

have list of times virtually identical to Sahl's, attributed to both Dorotheus and Ptolemy (pseudo-Ptolemy's *Cent.* #81).

(1) Changes in times

As for changes in times, following is a select list taken from three of our sources: al-'Imrānī I.5.1, *On Times* §1, and *Search* II.5.1-2:

- Moving into a new quarter or hemisphere (apparently by planetary motion, not diurnal rotation). Thus, if a key significator moves past the degree of the Midheaven from the southern quarter to the eastern one, it would indicate a change in the events.
- Changes in the planet's relation to the quarters of the epicycle or the deferent. For instance, if a planet reached its apogee and then moved beyond it, it would be a change.
- Changing from being western to eastern, and *vice versa*: so, a planet which passes under the Sun's rays and comes out on the other side would indicate a change.
- Moving from one sign to the next, such as a significator moving from Leo to Virgo.
- Changing from northern to southern ecliptical latitude, and *vice versa*. This would require passing through its Node.
- The Moon changing from one half of her monthly cycle, to the other.
- Stations and conjunctions with the Sun, including going under or coming out of the rays (probably at the standardized distance of 15° from the Sun)

(2) Lengths of time: the lists of the "ways"

More difficult to understand are the lists of the "ways" or "manner" of times, by which our authors usually mean how to determine the number of time-units until the culmination or appearance of an action's result: for example, if there were 13° between the bodies of two significators, then there might be 13 time-units (such as days or weeks or months or years). For this book, I compared the ways described in six different texts:

- Al-'Imrānī I.5.2 (eight ways)[110]
- Pseudo-Ptolemy, *Cent.*, Aphorism 81 (seven ways)
- *Search* II.5.2 (seven ways)
- Al-Rijāl VII.102.1 (seven ways)
- Al-Rijāl VII.102.7 (five ways)
- *On Times* §3 (five ways)

There are a number of reasons why these ways are difficult to understand. For one thing, different lists often have different numbers of items (but usually either five or seven), even though they generally agree on the first three and on the fifth. For example, Hermann's translation of *On Times* (in *Search*) lists seven ways, but John's translation of the same thing lists five.

Or, some items on the lists are redundant repetitions of points already stated: for example, al-'Imrānī I.5.2 #4 and al-Rijāl VII.102.7 #4, seem to be redundant versions of the second way (namely, a real-time transit between significators). Likewise, *Cent.* #7 seems to be a real-time transit version of the fourth type (from the significator to the place of the matter, assuming that the significator may be the lord of that place itself).

Again, some lists have closely related items which obviously come from the same manuscript lineage, but which do not match the others at all: the two passages in al-Rijāl VII.102.1 #5 and *Cent.* #5 are obviously related, but on their face do not match the others. However, their use of "adding and subtracting" and "gift" or "giving"[111] (i.e., what the planets grant), strongly suggests they are alternate versions (and perhaps misunderstandings) of the use of planetary years, which have greater and lesser numerical values and not simply units of time. For example, through her lesser years or units, Venus grants 8, while her greater ones grant 82: this is a change of numerical value (lesser and greater), and is not the same as taking a fixed distance in degrees, and equating it to so many years or months or days.

Moreover, when two authors seem to state the same method, they formulate it with slightly different and ambiguous language.

---

110 I divide his ways into eight, but the seventh and eighth can also be considered together, yielding only seven ways.

111 Since al-Rijāl VII.102.1 uses the word "gift," as does Holden's primary Greek text, I agree with him that the Latin and Greek texts which speak of "setting" (*occasu*, *dusis*) are incorrect.

Finally, some items seem simply to be in error, such as the fifth item in Hermann's *On Times*, which seems to be a garbled and redundant version of his fourth item. The sixth item in the *Cent.* is actually about the changing of times, not lengths of time.

An Arabic edition of these lists from across numerous authors would probably resolve some of these problems, such as identifying a foundational list of seven items, and one of five. But it might not resolve the question of how many times there really should be, based on categorical differences between them. Instead, I would like to propose that we organize the items on all of the lists into more cleanly-divided groups. I propose a scheme of five items, with the sources for each:

Proposed "way"	Source
1. Distance between two bodies or aspect—both zodiacal and by ascensions	• *Body-zodiac*: all authors #1, al-'Imrānī I.5.2 #7 (a transfer of light) • *Body-ascensions*: all authors #3, except for *Cent.* • *Aspect-zodiac*: al-'Imrānī I.5.2 #1, 7 (a transfer of light), *Cent.* #2 • *Aspect-ascensions*: al-'Imrānī I.5.2 #8 (a transfer of light), Hermann's *On Times* #6, *Cent.* #2
2. Real-time perfection of a conjunction (or aspect?) between planets	All authors #2 (but *Cent.* #3); apparently al-'Imrānī I.5.2 #4, and al-Rijāl VII.102.7 #4
3. Distance between significator and Ascendant (symbolic)	Al-'Imrānī I.5.2 #6, and both *On Times* #4
4. From significator to place of matter, both transit and ascensions	• *Transit*: Al-Rijāl VII.102.1 #4, 6; *Cent.* #4, 7 • *Ascensions*: Al-Rijāl VII.102.1 #4, 7; *Cent.* #4
5. Planetary years	All authors #5, except for Hermann's *On Times*.

Figure 7: Proposed "ways" of measuring time (Dykes)

According to my solution, all of the authors' lists fall into four of the five categories (except for al-Rijāl VII.102.7, which falls into three). Every list is missing either category (3) or (4), which are very similar to each other because they involve the distance between the significator and a place (rather than between it and another planet). Now, it would be possible to combine (3) and (4) into one category and then divide category (1) into either distances between bodies versus aspects, or zodiacal degrees versus ascensions; but in that case, the combined category of (3) and (4) would include both symbolic profections and real-time transits. I view it as more important to distinguish symbolic time from real time, as opposed to distinguishing different schemes for calculating a distance.

(3) Conditioning elements

So far, we have identified when to note changes in time, and what parts of the chart to note for indicating lengths of time (normally by time-units). After this, the texts generally indicate a number of conditioning elements, which make these time units longer or shorter. Not all of the texts list the same features, and none insists on there being only a certain number of them (as with the lists above). Following are some of the more important features to note:

- Type of planet:[112] superior planets like Saturn tend to make the time last longer, while inferior signs indicate shorter ones.
- Planetary speed or phase:[113] planets quick in their motion or eastern from the Sun, indicate shorter periods, while those slow in motion or western, indicate longer ones.
- Quadrant or angularity:[114] planets in eastern quadrants or angular, take place more quickly (but being angular makes them last longer), while planets in western quadrants or cadent take longer to manifest (but being cadent makes them last less long). There is also a difference among angles, as to how long a time they indicate.
- Quality of sign (triplicity, quadruplicity, ascensional time):[115] planets in fiery and airy signs, indicate shorter times, as do those in movable signs or those of crooked/short ascension; those in watery or earthy signs indicate longer ones, as do those in fixed signs or those of straight/long ascension.

---

[112] Al-'Imrānī I.5.1-3, al-Rijāl VII.102.6.
[113] Al-'Imrānī I.5.1, al-Rijāl VII.102.6-7.
[114] Al-'Imrānī I.5.0, al-Rijāl VII.102.6-7.
[115] Al-'Imrānī I.5.0, al-Rijāl VII.102.6.

Several passages give instructions and examples for mixing these categories:[116] thus for instance an inferior planet in an eastern quadrant, angular, and in a movable sign of short ascension, might indicate a number of time-units that last for so many hours, while Saturn in a western quadrant, cadent, and in a fixed sign of long ascension, might indicate so many years.

§8: Remoteness from angles, and house systems

In my Introduction to al-Kindī's *Forty Chapters* (§4, topic 9), I argued that while al-Kindī seemed to use something like the Regiomontanus house system,[117] in certain elections he recognized that it was important for the Midheaven to fall on certain signs. Specifically, for certain elections the Midheaven ought to fall on the tenth sign, rather than being "drawn back" or "drawn down" or "remote" (that is, being cadent, on the ninth sign. This approach was one way of reconciling the foundational character of whole-sign houses, with the fact that the degree of the Midheaven also indicates tenth-house matters: that is, the system of great circles (horizon-Ascendant, meridian-Midheaven) is made to match the angular whole signs (tenth sign-tenth domicile or house). In some cases, if the Midheaven cannot be on the tenth sign, it should at least be on the eleventh sign, because the eleventh sign is moving upwards by diurnal motion toward the tenth position rather than declining toward the western horizon (as the ninth sign does). Ascending and being angular suggests increase, presence, success, and the lastingness of a result, as opposed to decrease, absence, failure, and short-term results.

In the present book as well as *Judges*, we see further evidence that this was not only a generally recognized issue due to the existence of both whole signs and quadrant houses, but was also applicable to elections and may have come from an earlier Greek source. Following are a few examples of the insistence on making sure the Midheaven is not in the ninth sign:

---

116 Al-Rijāl VII.102.7, *On Times* §3, and *Search* II.5.1-2.

117 It is sometimes hard to tell how exactly the medieval authors practiced their astrology, since they have so many references to whole sign houses, mixed in with statements about the degrees of particular houses. A rare example of referring to house cusps within a tradition of largely whole-sign houses, is *On Elect.* §36, which refers to the "degree of the house of trust" (the eleventh house).

- *Forty Chapters* §485: that in constructing certain vertical instruments for drawing water, the angles should not be remote or cadent.
- *Forty Chapters* §490: that in constructing ships, the angles should not be remote.
- Al-'Imrānī I.2.7: that the degrees of the angles should not be remote; al-'Imrānī suggests some conditions which might override or compensate for such a situation.
- Al-'Imrānī I.2.12/al-Rijāl VII.2.6: that it is generally bad for the angles to be remote or "receding" or "withdrawing," particularly in cases where we want the result to last. But being in the eleventh is acceptable.
- Al-'Imrānī II.1.3 (citing al-Kindī §477): that in laying the foundations of buildings, the angles should not be remote.
- Al-'Imrānī II.1.6/al-Rijāl VII.21 (citing al-Kindī §482):[118] that in digging canals, the angles should not be remote.
- Al-'Imrānī II.3.1/al-Rijāl VII.9: when selling something whose income we want to keep, the angles should not be remote.
- Al-'Imrānī II.6.1:[119] that in electing a time to have intercourse to have a child, the angles should not be remote.
- *On Elect.* 125a/al-Rijāl VII.87: when electing a time to seat a new king, both the Ascendant and the fourth should be "fixed" signs. If the Ascendant were a fixed sign such as Taurus, the fourth sign would automatically be fixed (in this case, Leo), so the rule does not make sense unless it means that the degree of the IC should be on the fourth sign.

My sense of this rule is that it probably arose in the context of elections, and was later applied to questions. (An example of their use in questions is Sahl's *On Quest.* §1.7 or *Judges* §1.1, in which Sahl prefers that the axis of the Midheaven-IC fall on the tenth and fourth signs rather than the ninth and third signs, presumably so that the result of the question will be more firm and lasting.) For one thing, many question texts derived from electional ones,

---

118 In my original translation of this passage in al-Kindī, I believed that the use of the word "straight" (Lat. *directus*) meant "straight ascensions," but from al-'Imrānī and al-Rijāl it seems clear it means being on the tenth sign.

119 Al-Rijāl VII.30 reads slightly differently (that the angles should be "fixed"), but al-'Imrānī does seem to have the right meaning.

as I showed before. Next, for the angles to be upright and not remote is more relevant to a chart we can choose—in a question, one must take the chart one gets once the client arrives. But third, and more intriguingly, al-Rijāl VII.2.6 says that if the degree of the Midheaven falls on the eleventh sign, it is acceptable and is called *anafamentum.* This Latinized word invites a comparison with the Gr. *anaphora*, which refers to succeedent places—and indeed the eleventh is a succeedent place. There is another case in which our authors use words that sound suspiciously like Greek originals: in his I.2.0, al-'Imrānī warns us not to attempt elections which are impossible for certain nativities, such as electing for a little old woman who wants to bear a child. "For," he says, "the effect of the support does not appear except in things which are able to take on its signification." This word "support" (Lat. *firmamentum*), which refers to the election and its chart, sounds suspiciously like the Gr. *hupostasis* ("foundation, support, undertaking"), which is sometimes used to designate a chart,[120] again suggesting a Greek original. But until more original Greek texts are translated (and even if they are), this can only remain a hypothesis.

§9: A translation note

The reader should not have any real problem understanding the technical vocabulary in this book, especially since I have provided an updated Glossary. But there is one word which I should mention, which appears only in the 1485 Latin edition of al-Rijāl: *appodiare* and the adjective *appodeatus* (*appodiatus*). These words refer to buttressing something, i.e., supporting or strengthening it by buttressing it. In many cases it is rather unclear what is being communicated, but by comparing its use in VII.3.0 to Sahl's Arabic, it seems to refer mainly to a planet being strengthened. In some cases it seems to mean that a planet is supported by having a benefic aspecting it. Throughout the text, I will translate these words as "support/supported" or "strengthen/strengthened."

In addition, as with all of my works so far, material in square brackets [ ] has been added by me.

---

120 See for instance Valens, *Anth.* II.19.2: *hupostasin tēs geneseōs* ("foundation of the nativity," referring to the natal chart).

PART I: THE MOON & LUNAR MANSIONS

THE CHOICES OF DAYS

AL-KINDĪ

Should the Moon be connected[1] with the Sun in the trine or sextile, it is favorable for all business and requirements, above all for meetings with the king or sultan, and striving after the necessities available through them, fame, rank, the most important things existing in affairs, accepting declarations of obedience, the granting of a standard,[2] the donning of honorable clothing, laying on a crown, the collecting of taxes, the hunt, and shooting.

Should the Moon stand with Saturn in the trine and sextile (but only in these), it is favorable for all business and requirements; then it is appropriate that meetings take place with old men and subservient people, slaves, the great masses, those who are base. It is favorable for considering their affairs and striving for what they need, and for building fields and sowing, harrowing[3] [land], the cultivation of property, the building of splendid farmsteads and dwellings, the digging of water channels and canals and ushering water into them, assessing[4] things, the control of estate managers and being occupied with things which relate to receptacles.[5]

Should the Moon and Jupiter stand in a connection in any respect, it is favorable for all business and requirements, above all for meetings with nobles, judges, scholars, astrologers, and striving for necessities available through them, delegating the affairs of the sultan and of what is necessary for these; [this placement is favorable][6] for travel, for transfers,[7] taking and giving, sell-

---

[1] *Verbunden*, here and throughout. This probably refers to an applying, degree-based aspect (*ITA* III.7).

[2] That is, a flag.

[3] Ger. *Eggen*, Ar. *midammah*. That is, using implements to break up and level the earth.

[4] That is, through measurement.

[5] *Gefäße*. Unless this is a mistake by Wiedemann, al-Kindī might be drawing on the connection between Saturn and water (see *ITA* V.1), so that this indicates water channels, cisterns, and so on.

[6] Added by Wiedemann.

ing and buying, loaning, unwavering desire,[8] bloodletting, the drinking of remedies and medicines for illnesses, desiring that [a command] be fulfilled,[9] sailing by ship, learning the religious sciences, and entering the land that is aimed for.

Should the Moon stand with Mars in the trine and sextile (but only in that instance), it is favorable for all business and requirements, especially with emirs, princes, and everything which has to do with weapons and striving after what is necessary with that, attacking, standing fast and conquering, going to war, applying force by means of the army and army battalions, seeking those who are fleeing, and making violent attacks, riding on a hunt, and the striking of the club at throwing games.[10]

Should the Moon be connected with Venus in any way, this is favorable for all business, above all for meeting with women, servants, and feminine men, and activities involving their affairs, and striving for necessities which they have; further, for manufacturing rings and bowls, presenting jewelry, carrying out jokes, lust, sleeping with someone, circumcision, and what is like that.

Should the Moon be connected with Mercury in any way (if it is a favorable [connection]), it is favorable for all business, especially for the meetings of writers, those who calculate, the literate, doctors, astronomers, and for activities with their matters and the things which they need; for looking in books, sending messengers, betting, racing, playing backgammon or chess, buying instruments for writing, dealing with the things of children and younger siblings. Furthermore, it is favorable for dividing things up, surveying farmsteads, and collecting the land-tax.

Should the Moon stand in the Head or Tail, it is [in general] favorable for no business. Nor is it favorable for taming[11] animals. When she travels in the empty course, it gives an indication as to what one should preferably do,[12] and when one brings something to an end in [the empty course], one encounters what is more right.

---

[7] Wiedemann says "transport" (Ger. *Transport*), but the Ar. *taḥwīl* has more to do with handing things over, and is the word usually used for the transferring or cycling of years (i.e., annual revolutions). I think "transfers" also makes more sense in light of the terms immediately following.

[8] *Das beharrliche Erstreben.*

[9] *Das Begehren nach einem Nachkommen.*

[10] *Das Schlagen der Keule beim Wurfspiel.*

[11] *Dressieren*, which can also refer to trussing up animals used as food.

[12] Namely, one should do nothing.

The Book of the Skilled VII.101: *On Elections according to the Moon's Motion through the Mansions*

Al-Rijāl

[1] *Al-Naṭḥ*,[1] from the beginning of Aries up to the twelfth degree, 51 minutes and 26 seconds, is the first mansion.

The Indians say that if the Moon were in this mansion, it is good to drink medicines, to put beasts to pasture, to make a journey on that day, unless [it is] in the second hour[2] of the day.

Dorotheus said: it is not good to make a marriage-union when the Moon is in this mansion (nor even in all of Aries), nor to buy slaves in it, because they will be bad and disobedient or they will flee. However, it is good to buy domesticated and ridden animals, and to make a journey, especially by ship: because it signifies that he will go well and in a good way. It is not good to form an association in it, because he says that it will not last, but one [of them] will withdraw, unsubdued,[3] from the other. He even says that one who is caught in it,[4] will have a strong and bad imprisonment. And if it were asked of you about a theft, with the Moon appearing in Aries, say that the stolen thing is usually put on the head or face, or worked by hand. It is good to make arms in it, to plant trees, to cut the hair on the head, to cut the nails,[5] and to put on new clothes: and all of this with the Moon appearing free of the infortunes.

[2] *Al-Buṭayn*,[6] from 12 degrees, 51 minutes, 26 seconds of Aries up to the twenty-fifth degree, 42 minutes, 52 seconds of it.

---

1 "The butting" (Lat. *Alnath*).
2 This should probably read, "second part" or "second one-third" of the day, as the division of the day into thirds is repeated below.
3 *Impacatus*.
4 It is unclear to me whether this has to do with an election to capture someone, or the time of an "event chart" in which someone is captured.
5 *Ungulas*, which should be *ungues*.
6 "The little belly" (Lat. *Albethain*).

The Indians say that if the Moon were in this mansion, it is good to sow, make journeys.

And Dorotheus says that it is not good to form a marriage-union in it, [nor] to buy slaves; and concerning slaves, a ship, and captives, he says what he says for *al-Naṭḥ*.

[3] *Al-Thurayyā*,[7] from 25 degrees, 42 minutes, 52 seconds of Aries up to the eighth degree, 34 minutes, 18 seconds of Taurus.

The Indians say that if the Moon were in this mansion, it is good to trade and to avenge oneself on one's enemies; it is even [good] in a middling way for travel.

Dorotheus says: it is not good to form a marriage-union in it; it is good to buy domesticated beasts in it, and one who will be on a journey by water will undergo dread and dangers. It is not good to form an association in it, especially with a more powerful person, because he would not be able to be separated from him unless with labor and regret. And he says that one who will be captured or were caught in it, will have a strong and long incarceration on the occasion of assets: the assets will be taken away from him, and he will go out of prison. It is good for every thing which comes to be through fire, and for the hunting of animals, and for doing good. But it is bad for buying cows and a flock,[8] and for planting trees and sowing, and for putting on new clothes.

[4] *Al-Dabarān*[9] is extended from 8 degrees, 34 minutes, 18 seconds of Taurus, up to the twenty-first degree, 25 minutes, [44 seconds] of it.

The Indians say that if the Moon were in this mansion, it is good to sow, to dress [in] new clothes, and to take on[10] women and their ornaments, to demolish[11] every building and to begin another, [and] to make a journey, unless it is in the third part of that day.

Dorotheus says: it is not good to form a marriage-union in it, because the woman will desire to have sexual intercourse with another. And he says that

[7] "The Pleiades" (Lat. *Althoraie*).
[8] This contradicts the statement just given about buying domesticated animals.
[9] "The two buttocks" (Burnett) or the star Aldebaran (Lat. *Addavenam*); but "the Follower" (Robson).
[10] *Accipere.* This can mean to welcome, take responsibility for, *etc.* But see mansion 22, which implies taking a woman in marriage.
[11] Reading with 1551, for what seems to be *villae*.

it is good to buy captives, because they will be cheerful[12] and lawful; and a building which comes to be in it will be firm and lasting. It is good to buy domesticated beasts. And he says that one who will make a journey by water [in it] will have great waves; and an association [formed] in it is bad, especially with one more powerful than him: because he will not be separated from him unless with labor and regret; and one who will be captured in it will have a long captivity, and one who will have been caught on account of resources, he will escape because of assets, [and] in a good manner.[13] And it is good for every manner of building, and for digging canals, and buying male and female slaves, and beasts, and for standing with kings and other high lords, for receiving a dignity or rulership—in all of which Dorotheus praises [this mansion], except that he especially abhors it for a marriage-union.

[5] *Al-Haqᶜah*,[14] from 21 degrees and 25 minutes [and 44 seconds], up to the fourth degree, 17 minutes, and 10 seconds of Gemini.

The Indians say: if the Moon were in this mansion, it is good to form a marriage-union, to send boys to learn the laws or writings or [how] to write, and for making medicines, and for going on a journey, with the Moon appearing free from the infortunes and burning.[15]

And Dorotheus says that it is good for buying slaves, because they will be good and lawful; it is good for building and for going into the water, but it is not good for [forming] an association. He who will have been caught in it, will have a long incarceration; however, if he was caught because of resources, he will solve it [by paying his captors] and escape. It is good for washing the head, and for every manner of confrontation, and for cutting the hair on the head. And he says that it is good to buy slaves when the Moon or the Ascendant is in human signs, especially if the Moon were safe from the infortunes.[16]

---

[12] *Securi.*

[13] That is, if he is kidnapped for ransom, he (or another) will pay off the captors: see below.

[14] "A (white) circle of hair on a horse" (Lat. *Alhathaya*).

[15] That is, "combustion."

[16] Cf. *Carmen* V.11, esp. *ll.* 3,6,7,11,14. Al-'Imrānī II.7.1 attributes this view to Abū Ma'shar.

[6] *Al-Han*ᶜ*a*[17] (and it is [also] called *al-Taḥāyī*),[18] from the fourth degree, 17 minutes and 10 seconds of Gemini, up to 17 degrees, 8 minutes, [36 seconds] of it.

The Indians say that if the Moon were in this mansion, it is good for kings to undertake a battle, and taking action to form armies and cavalries, and for riders to change to better pay,[19] and for besieging estates,[20] and for pursuing enemies and evildoers. However, it is not good for sowing, nor for doing any borrowing, nor for depositing something for safekeeping.

And Dorotheus says that it is good for making an aquatic journey, because the ship will go towards where he wants, [and] in a good manner, but it will be slow; an association is good and profitable in it, and the associates will be in agreement, faithful, and lawful (namely, one to the other). And one who will have been caught in it: unless he were freed in three days, his imprisonment will be much prolonged. It is good to hunt in it, but you should not drink medicines nor drugs in it, nor should you treat wounds; and new clothes which are put on will be quickly torn.

[7] *Al-Dhirā*ᶜ,[21] from 17 degrees, 8 minutes, [36 seconds] of Gemini, up to its end.

The Indians say that if the Moon were in this mansion, it is good for sowing every seed, plowing, for putting on new clothes, and for the ornaments of women, and for riding beasts; it is not good for travel except in the last third of that night.

And Dorotheus says that he who made an aquatic journey in it, will go in a good manner just as he wanted to, but he will slow down on his return. And an association in it will be good and useful, and the associates will be lawful and in agreement (namely, one to the other). And one who will be caught in it, he will die in prison unless he will have escaped in three days. And one who will have done a deed which he has anxiety about and escaped, will yet fall into another [bad situation] in turn. It is good to wash the head, for cutting the hairs on the head, for putting on new garments, for buying slaves and beasts, for striking at one's enemy, [and] for making peace with

---

17 "The camel's brand" (Lat. *Alhana*).
18 Burnett suggests "the rain-bearers" (Lat. *Atabuen*).
19 Reading more clearly with 1551, for *ut mutant eorum lucre*.
20 *Villas*. Or rather, "cities."
21 "The forearm" (Lat. *Addirach*).

enemies—it is good for all of these. But it is bad for the buying of lands and for getting involved in the work of healing.

[8] *Al-Nathra,*[22] from the beginning of Cancer up to the twelfth degree, 51 minutes and 26 seconds of it.

The Indians say that if the Moon were in this mansion, it is good for employing medicines, and for cutting new garments, and for the ornaments of women, and putting them on. And they say that if it rains with the Moon appearing in it, it conveys usefulness and not loss; [but] it is not good for travel except in the third, latter part of the night.

And Dorotheus says that marriage-unions which come to be in it, will last for a little bit in concord, and afterwards they will disagree. A slave who is bought in it, will be an accuser of his own master, a deceiver and fugitive. And one who boarded a ship will be safe, and he will go where he wants to quickly and in a good manner, and he will return quickly; and for an association which comes to be in it, a fraud will be committed on each side, and one caught in it will stay long in prison, and[23] he will die [after] a long time.

[9] *Al-Ṭarf,*[24] from 12 degrees, 51 minutes, and 26 seconds of Cancer, up to 25 degrees, 42 minutes, and 52 seconds of it.

The Indians say that if the Moon were in this mansion, it is not good to sow any seed, nor to make a journey, nor to deposit some thing with someone for safekeeping, nor to inflict[25] evil on someone in it.

Dorotheus says that one who entered the sea in it, he will escape with the ship, and will go where he wanted, and will return well and quickly. If an association would come to be in it, the partners will create a fraud (namely one for the other); and one who was captured will stay long in prison. It is not good to cut the hair on the head, nor to cut new clothes, because one who put on new garments will perhaps die, drowned in water with them. It is good for strengthening gates and for making saws,[26] and for moving[27] wheat

---

22 "The tip of the nose" (Lat. *Alnayra*).

23 The rest of this this sentence is not in 1485, but I have added it from 1551.

24 "The look, the eye" (Lat. *Attraaif*).

25 *Procurare.*

26 *Serraturas.* Or perhaps, for engaging in sawing/cutting activity.

27 Or, "changing" (*mutando*). I take this to mean transporting it for sale.

from one place to another, and for making beds and fitting canopies over them.

[10] *Al-Jabha*,[28] from 25 degrees, 42 minutes, and 52 seconds of Cancer up to the eighth degree and 34 minutes [and 18 seconds] of Leo.

The Indians say that if the Moon were in this mansion, it is good to form a marriage-union, and *açucharum*[29] and what comes to be from that. It is not good for travel, nor for depositing something for safekeeping, nor for putting on new clothes, nor for the ornaments of women.

And Dorotheus says that a building which comes to be in it will be lasting, and an association good, because the associates will profit with each other. And one who will be caught, will be caught due to the command of some famous man, or for a great affair, and he will have a strong and long incarceration.

[11] *Al-Zubra*,[30] from 8 degrees and 34 minutes [and 18 seconds] of Leo, up to the twenty-first degree and 25 minutes [and 44 seconds] of it.

The Indians say that if the Moon were in this mansion, it is not good for dismissing captives, [but] it is good for besieging estates, and for sowing and planting; however, for trades and journeys it is mediocre.

Dorotheus says that buildings and foundations which come to be in it will be lasting, and in an association which comes to be, the associates will profit much. And one who was caught: it signifies that he was captured due to the command of some great man, and that he will have a long incarceration. And it is bad for new garments, and good for cutting the hair on the head.

[12] *Al-Ṣarfah*,[31] from 21 degrees and 25 minutes [and 44 seconds] of Leo, up to the fourth degree and 17 minutes [and 10 seconds] of Virgo.

The Indians say that if the Moon were in this mansion, it is good for beginning every building, and for renting out lands, and for planting and sowing, and for forming a marriage-union, and for putting on new garments,

---

28 "The forehead" (Lat. *Algebhe*).

29 1551 reads *azucharum*. The Latin looks suspiciously close to *zawwaja* (Ar. "to marry"), so probably something else related to marriage or sexual relations is meant.

30 "The mane," according to Burnett (Lat. *Açobrach*). This mansion is also called *al-Kharātān*, meaning uncertain (but Weinstock p. 50 believes this might be "Two Hares," after the Greek of the *Codex Cromwellianus 12*.

31 "The diversion" (Dykes) or "The change" (Burnett), Lat. *Açarfa*.

for the ornaments of women, for making journeys—in, however, the first one-third of that day.[32]

Dorotheus says that one who lent [something] will not recover it, and if he did recover it, it will be with great weariness and labor; and one who will have boarded a ship will have danger and labor, and after a long time he will escape. It is good for buying slaves and beasts, but [only] after the Moon will have gone out of Leo, because Leo is a great eater.[33] And if [the slave or beast] eats much, [he or it] will suffer in the stomach and in the belly, and [he or it] is powerful and bold, nor will [he or it] want to obey anyone.

[13] *Al-ʿAwwāʾ*,[34] from 4 degrees and 17 minutes [and 10 seconds] of Virgo up to its seventeenth degree and 8 minutes [and 36 seconds] of it.

The Indians say that if the Moon were in this mansion, it is good to sow, till, make a journey and a marriage-union, to free captives, and to let prisoners go, for the whole day.

Dorotheus says that it is not bad for one who will get married to a corrupted woman; however, if someone took a virgin wife, they will last a moderate time. And a slave which will be bought will be good and lawful and carefree;[35] and one who boarded a ship will delay his return much; and one who was caught will have losses in prison, [but] afterwards he will have a good end. It is good for drinking medicines and cutting new clothes, beginning a building, and getting involved in delights[36] and jokes, [and] making an entrance to the king and a famous man; and [it is] good for the washing of the head and the cutting of the hair on the head.

[14] *Al-Simāk*,[37] from 17 degrees and 8 minutes [and 36 seconds] of Virgo up to its end.

The Indians say that if the Moon were in this mansion, it is good for the marriage-unions of women [who are] not virgins, for healing, sowing and planting; it is not good for travel, nor for depositing something with someone for safekeeping.

---

32 I am not sure if this refers only to journeys, or to the whole list.

33 *Comestor.* I believe this means that the slaves or beasts would want to eat more than the owner can afford.

34 The constellation Bootes (Lat. *Aloce*).

35 *Securus.*

36 Reading with 1551 for *laetitiis.*

37 Meaning unclear, but this word does mean "fish" (Lat. *Açimech*).

Dorotheus says that if someone would be married with a virgin woman, he will not last with her for a long time; however, if she is corrupted, it is not bad. A slave who is bought will be good, lawful, and will esteem his master. It is good for the boarding of a ship, [and] if people would associate with each other, they will profit much and will have good, in concord; and he who was caught will quickly escape.

[15] *Al-Ghafr*,[38] from the beginning of Libra up to the twelfth degree, 51 minutes, and 26 seconds of it.

The Indians say that if the Moon were in this mansion, it is good to dig wells and canals, [but] bad for travel; it is good to heal infirmities which are from windiness (and not others).

Dorotheus says that a marriage-union which comes to be in it will not be lasting in concord, unless [it is only] for a moderate amount of time; and one who lent money will not recover it; it is to be abhorred in every journey by sea and land. And those who formed an association will be defrauded and disagree amongst themselves. It is good to move into a new house from another one, and from there to another, by making the second house and its lord and its place fit. It is good to buy and sell, and good to strive for an accomplishment. You should not buy beasts nor cut the hair on the head, but you should buy slaves because it is a human sign.

[16] *Al-Zubānā*,[39] from 12 degrees, 51 minutes and 26 seconds of Libra, up to 25 degrees, 42 minutes, and 52 seconds of it.

The Indians say that if the Moon were in this mansion, it is not good for travel, nor for healing, nor for any merchant dealings, nor for sowing, nor the ornaments of women, nor for putting on nor cutting new garments.

Dorotheus says that it is bad for a marriage-union, and a marriage-union in it will last for a moderate time in concord. A slave who is bought will be good and lawful and carefree, and those who formed an association will have discord amongst themselves and will be suspicious of each other. And one who was caught will go quickly out of the prison, if God wills.

---

[38] "The coat of mail," according to Burnett (*Algarf*).

[39] "The claws," according to Burnett (Lat. *Açebone*): namely, the claws of Scorpio or pans of Libra.

[17] *Al-Iklīl,*[40] from 25 degrees and 42 minutes [and 52 seconds] of Libra up to the eighth degree and 34 minutes [and 18 seconds] of Scorpio.

The Indians say that if the Moon were in this mansion, it is good to buy a flock and beasts, and to put them out to pasture; it is even good to dress with new ornaments, and to besiege estates.

Dorotheus says that if someone takes a wife, he will not find her to be pure;[41] a building which comes to be will be firm and lasting; one who boarded a ship will have anxiety and sorrows, but will escape; and whose who formed an association will be in discord. It is good for putting love between two people,[42] and love in this mansion will be wholly firm and lasting. It is always good for every medicine. You should not cut the hair on the head, nor buy slaves.

[18] *Al-Qalb,*[43] from 8 degrees and 34 minutes [and 18 seconds] of Scorpio, up to the twenty-first degree [and] 25 minutes, and 44 seconds of it.

The Indians say that if the Moon were in this mansion, it is good for every building, for renting lands and buying them, for receiving a dignity and rulership; and if it began to rain, it will be a thorough rain, useful and good; on a journey it is good for one going towards the east.

Dorotheus says that one who took a wife, and were the Moon in this mansion with Mars, he will not find her to be a virgin. It is bad for buying slaves, and buildings which come to be will be firm; one who boarded a ship will escape, an association made in it will have discord. It is good for planting, it is bad for new garments and cutting the hair on the head. And it is good for drinking[44] and using medicines.

[19] *Al-ʾIbrah,*[45] from 21 degrees, 25 minutes and 44 seconds of Scorpio, up to the fourth degree and seventeenth minute [and 10 seconds] of Sagittarius.

The Indians say that if the Moon were in this mansion, it is good to besiege estates and forts, and to litigate with enemies, and for making a journey.

---

40 "The crown" (Lat. *Alidil*).

41 Adding *puram* with 1551, which 1485 omits.

42 1551 reads, "it is good to put together lawsuits between two people, and to unite [people in] love."

43 "The heart," or *Cor Scorpionis* (Lat. *Alcalb*).

44 That is, drinking medicines, not alcohol.

45 "The sting" (Lat. *Yenla*), also called "the tail" (*al-shawlah*), *Cauda Scorpionis.*

It is not good for leaving something with someone for safekeeping, and it is good for sowing and for planting trees.

Dorotheus says that if someone took a wife, he will not find her to be a virgin. It is bad for buying slaves, and for the boarding of a ship, because it signifies that the ship will be wrecked; and those who formed an association will have discord[46] between the associates, and it is very bad for one who is caught.

[20] *Al-Naᶜāᵓim*,[47] from the fourth degree and seventeenth minute [and 10 seconds] of Sagittarius up to the seventeenth degree and eighth minute [and 36 seconds] of it.

The Indians say that if the Moon were in this mansion, it is good to buy beasts, and it is mediocre for travel; and if it rained it will be good, nor will it do evil.

Dorotheus says that it is good for buying small beasts, but it is bad for an association and for one captured.

[21] *Al-Balda*,[48] from the seventeenth degree and eighth minute [and 36 seconds] of Sagittarius up to its end.

The Indians say that if the Moon were in this mansion, it is good to begin every building and [to sow] seed, and [for] buying lands and beasts and a flock, and for buying and making the ornaments of women, and garments; but it is mediocre for travel.

Dorotheus says that a woman whom a man dismisses, or who will be a widow, will never be married [again]; it is mediocre for buying slaves, and signifies that the slave will think much of himself, nor will he be humble with respect to his master.

[22] *Saᶜd al-dhābiḥ*,[49] from the beginning of Capricorn up to the 12 degrees, 51 minutes, 26 seconds.

The Indians say that if the Moon were in this mansion, it is good for healing, and making a journey (except in the last one-third of the day); it is good to put on new clothes.

---

46 *Discors erit.*

47 "The ostriches" (Lat. *Alimain*).

48 "The place" (Lat. *Albeda*).

49 "Luck of the slayer" (Lat. *Sahaddadebe*).

Dorotheus says that if someone pledged [marriage to][50] a wife, he will dismiss her before they are joined in marriage, and the man will die before six months—or they will split up in disagreement and in a bad manner, and the woman will treat the man badly. It is bad for buying slaves, because [the slave] will do evil to his master, or will flee, or will be annoying or bad. It is good for the boarding of a ship, except that great disturbances of his mind will happen to him due to having a great will to return, and the like. It is good for an association, because there will be profit and great usefulness in it; and one who was caught will escape quickly.

[23] *Saᶜd bulaᶜ*,[51] from 12 degrees, 51 minutes and 26 seconds of Capricorn, up to the twenty-fifth degree, 42 minutes and 52 seconds of it.

The Indians say that if the Moon were in this mansion, it is good to heal and to put on ornaments and new vestments; it is not good to deposit something with someone for safekeeping, but it is good for a journey in the middle third of that day.

Dorotheus says: it is not good for a marriage-union, because perhaps the wife will treat the man badly, nor will they stay together much. It is bad for buying slaves, and for the boarding of a ship for one wanting to make a short journey, but it is good for an association, and he who was caught will quickly escape.

[24] *Saᶜd al-suᶜūd*,[52] from 25 degrees, 42 minutes and 52 seconds of Capricorn up to the eighth degree and 34 minutes [and 18 seconds] of Aquarius.

The Indians say that if the Moon were in this mansion, it is not good for wares nor for ornaments, nor for putting on garments, nor for taking a wife [in marriage]; but it is good for healing in it, and for sending soldiers and armies, [and] it is mediocre for travel.

Dorotheus says that it is not good for a marriage-union, because it will last [only] a moderate amount of time. A slave who will be bought will be strong and lawful and good. It is not good for the boarding of a ship, and it is bad for an association because it signifies great loss and discord at the end; and if [someone] were caught, he will be freed quickly.

---

50 *Acceperit.*

51 "Luck of the swallower" (Lat. *Zadebolah*).

52 "Luck of the lucks" (Lat. *Zaadescod*).

[25] *Saʿd al-ʾakẖbiyah,*[53] from the eighth degree and thirty-fourth minute [and 18 seconds] of Aquarius up to the twenty-first degree and twenty-fifth minute [and 44 seconds] of it.

The Indians say that if the Moon were in this mansion, it is good for besieging estates and forts, and for searching for quarrels and pursuing enemies and doing evils to them. And it is good for sending messengers, but it is not good for a marriage-union nor for sowing, nor for wares, nor for buying beasts nor a flock. It is good to make a journey towards the south.

Dorotheus says that it is not good for a marriage-union, because one [partner] will last [only] a moderate amount of time with the other. It is good for buying slaves, because [the slave] will be strong and lawful and good. A building which will come to be in it will be firm and lasting. And it is even good for the boarding of a ship, except that[54] it will be delayed. And [it is] bad for an association, because it signifies a bad end and loss; and a slave will escape.

[26] *Al-fargh al-muqaddam,*[55] from the twenty-first degree and twenty-fifth minute [and 44 seconds] of Aquarius, up to the fourth degree and seventeenth minute [and 10 seconds] of Pisces.

The Indians say that if the Moon were in this mansion, it is good to make a journey, but [only] in the first third of that day; and the whole rest of that day is not good for travel, nor for any commencement.

Dorotheus says that it is not good for a marriage-union, because it will last [only] a moderate amount of time. A slave who will be bought will be lawful and good, and if any building will come to be, it will be firm and lasting; it is good to board a ship, but it signifies slowness for the one boarding. It is bad for an association, and one who was caught will stay in prison much.

[27] *Al-fargh al-muʾakhkhar,*[56] from the fourth degree and seventeenth minute [and 10 seconds] of Pisces, up to the seventeenth degree and eighth minute [and 36 seconds] of it.

The Indians say that if the Moon were in this mansion, it is good to sow, and for wares, but it is not good for depositing something with someone for

---

53 "Luck of the tents" (Lat. *Sadalabbia*).

54 Reading *nisi quod* for *nisi quare*.

55 "The preceding spout" (Lat. *Fargalmocaden*), also called *al-Fargh al-awwal* ("the first spout").

56 "The following spout" (Lat. *Alfargamahar*).

safekeeping, nor for giving something as a loan. It is good for a marriage-union, mediocre for travel (unless [it is] in the middle third of that night, because in no way should you make a journey in it.

Dorotheus says that losses, dangers, and labors will happen to one boarding a ship. And if someone formed an association, he will have good in the beginning, [but] loss and discord at the end; and one who will was caught will not escape from prison. Nor should you buy a slave, because he will be bad.

[28] *Baṭn al-ḥūt*,[57] from the seventeenth degree and eighth minute [and 36 seconds] of Pisces, up to its end.

The Indians say that if the Moon were in this mansion, it is good for wares and sowing and healing, nor is it good for depositing something with someone for safekeeping, nor for giving something as a loan. It is good for a marriage-union and mediocre for travel, unless [it is] in the middle third of that night (which is bad).

Dorotheus says that a slave who will be bought, will be bad and angry, and very proud of himself,[58] and an association which will come to be will be good in the beginning, and bad at the end; and one who was caught in it will not go out of prison.

	Arabic Name	**Likely Star/Group**	**Modern Longitudes (2010)**
1.	Al-Naṭḥ / al-Sharaṭān	Sheratan (β Aries), Mesarthim (γ)	4° 06', 3° 19' ♉
2.	Al-Buṭayn	Botein (δ), ε, ϱ Aries	20° 29' ♉ (Botein)
3.	Al-Thurayyā	Pleiades	0° 07' ♊
4.	Al-Dabarān	Aldebaran (α Taurus), or Hyades	9° 55', or 7° 00' ♊
5.	Al-Haqᶜah	λ and φ Orion	23° 50' ♊ (λ)
6.	Al-Hanᶜa	Alhena (γ Gemini), ξ	9° 14' ♋
7.	Al-Dhirāᶜ	Castor (α Gemini), Pollux (β)	20° 22', 23° 21' ♋

57 "Belly of the fish" (Lat. *Bathnealoth*), also called *Baṭn al-rishāʾ*, "belly of the rope" (esp. the rope for a well).
58 *Appreciabit se.*

8.	Al-Nathra	Praesepe (nebula near ε Cancer)	7° 20' ♌
9.	Al-Ṭarf	ϰ Cancer, Alterf (λ Leo)	18° 00' ♌ (Alterf)
10.	Al-Jabha	Around ζ, γ, η, α Leo; ε Gemini	27°-29° ♌
11.	Al-Zubra / al-Kharātān	Zosma (δ), θ Leo	11° 27' ♍ (Zosma)
12.	Al-Ṣarfah	Denebola (β Leo)	21° 45' ♍
13.	Al-ᶜAwwāᵓ	Zavijava (β Virgo), Zania (η), Porrima (γ), δ, Vindemiatrix (ε)	27° ♍ – 10° ♎
14.	Al-Simāk	Spica/Azimech (α Virgo)	23° 58' ♎
15.	Al-Ghafr	Maybe ι and ϰ Virgo	3° 56' ♏ (ι)
16.	Al-Zubānā	Zuben Elgenubi (α Libra) and Zuben Eschemali (β)	15° 13' - 19° 30' ♏
17.	Al-Iklīl	Prob. Acrab/Graffias (β Scorpio), Dschubba (δ)	2° 42' - 3° 19' ♐
18.	Al-Qalb	Antares (α Scorpio)	9° 54' ♐
19.	Al-ᵓIbrah / al-Shawlah	Shaula (λ Scorpio), Lesath (υ); maybe Acumen & Aculeus (in sting of Scorpio)	24° - 28° ♐
20.	Al-Naᶜāᵓim	Near Ascella (ζ Sagittarius)	13° 46' ♑
21.	Al-Balda	Maybe π Sagittarius	Near 13° ♑
22.	Saᶜd al-dhābiḥ	Algedi (α Capricorn), Dabih (β)	3° 54' - 4° 11' ♒
23.	Saᶜd bulaᶜ	Albali (ε Aquarius), μ, ν	13° ♒
24.	Saᶜd al-suᶜūd	Sadalsuud (β Aquarius), ξ; 46 Capricorn	23° 32' ♒ (Sadalsuud)
25.	Saᶜd al-ᵓakhbiyah	Sadachbia (γ Aquarius), π, ζ, η	6° 51' ♒ (Sadachbia)
26.	Al-fargh al-muqaddam / al-Fargh al-awwal	Maybe Markab (α Pegasus) and Scheat (β)	23° 37', 29° 30' ♓

27.	Al-fargh al-muʾakhkhar	Maybe Algenib (γ Pegasus), Alpheratz (α Andromeda or β Pegasus)[59]	29° ♓ - 9°/14° ♈
28.	Baṭn al-ḥūt / Baṭn al-rishāʾ	β Andromeda[60]	0° 32' ♉

Figure 8: Arabic 28-mansion system, with the likely stars comprising them

[59] According to Kunitzsch and Smart (pp. 15, 47), there was some confusion between the names and stars for α-γ Pegasus and α Andromeda.

[60] According to Kunitzsch and Smart (p. 50), this mansion originally involved a faint curve of stars meant to be like a rope, connecting to the Square of Pegasus.

PART II: PLANETARY HOURS

	Sunday	Monday	Tuesday	Wednesday	Thursday	Friday	Saturday
1	☉	☽	♂	☿	♃	♀	♄
2	♀	♄	☉	☽	♂	☿	♃
3	☿	♃	♀	♄	☉	☽	♂
4	☽	♂	☿	♃	♀	♄	☉
5	♄	☉	☽	♂	☿	♃	♀
6	♃	♀	♄	☉	☽	♂	☿
7	♂	☿	♃	♀	♄	☉	☽
8	☉	☽	♂	☿	♃	♀	♄
9	♀	♄	☉	☽	♂	☿	♃
10	☿	♃	♀	♄	☉	☽	♂
11	☽	♂	☿	♃	♀	♄	☉
12	♄	☉	☽	♂	☿	♃	♀

Figure 9: Planetary hours during day (from sunrise)

	Sunday	Monday	Tuesday	Wednesday	Thursday	Friday	Saturday
1	♃	♀	♄	☉	☽	♂	☿
2	♂	☿	♃	♀	♄	☉	☽
3	☉	☽	♂	☿	♃	♀	♄
4	♀	♄	☉	☽	♂	☿	♃
5	☿	♃	♀	♄	☉	☽	♂
6	☽	♂	☿	♃	♀	♄	☉
7	♄	☉	☽	♂	☿	♃	♀
8	♃	♀	♄	☉	☽	♂	☿
9	♂	☿	♃	♀	♄	☉	☽
10	☉	☽	♂	☿	♃	♀	♄
11	♀	♄	☉	☽	♂	☿	♃
12	☿	♃	♀	♄	☉	☽	♂

Figure 10: Planetary hours during night (from sunset)

ON THE HOURS OF THE PLANETS

BETHEN

[§1: Planetary hours]

On the hour of Saturn

If it were the hour of Saturn, it is good to buy things of a heavy nature, such as iron, tin, lead, and all metals, and stone, and black fabrics, and to begin to dig gardens, and to devise some frauds against enemies. And it is not good to let blood, nor to take medicine, nor to speak to an authority, nor to speak to a prelate, monk, mime, nor to a fisherman,[1] nor a hunter, nor to any friend, nor to establish or build a wall; what is more, it is good to undertake [something with][2] no man, nor to form any association, nor to take a wife (because they will never be in agreement), nor is it good to cut clothes, nor put on new ones.

On the hour of Jupiter

The hour of Jupiter is good for buying and exchanging silver, and to deal in all business matters which pertain to silver, and to trade in fabrics of azure color, and bridges, and houses due to prayer;[3] and it is good to undertake a journey because of a master, even because of business; it is good to undertake a journey of navigation, and to take medicine, and it is good to let blood, and to speak of concord and peace and friendship, and power, and to buy horses of a chestnut color, and it is good to buy arms of *azaro*,[4] and begin [to work on] a loom,[5] and to till a field, and to sow, even to dig a well, to establish and build a wall: in short (you may say), it is good to undertake all good works in the hour of Jupiter.

---

[1] Here is an example of puzzling instructions for planetary hours: since monks, mimes, and fisherman can reasonably be associated with Saturn, why is it bad to talk with them at this time?

[2] *Nullum quidem hominem incipere* [sic?] *est bonum.*

[3] *Pontes et domos orationis causa.* I take the bridges to be separate from houses of prayer.

[4] I currently believe this is an unknown Arabic word. The Prague 1466 MS seems to read something like *dicacuo* or *de cacuo.*

[5] *Telam ordiri.*

On the hour of Mars

In the hour of Mars it is good to buy arms, and to shoe horses (and all horses fitted for war), to arm galleys, to undertake a journey because of war (whether by land or by sea), and to buy all fabrics of a red color; but it is not good to take medicine and to let blood, [or] to undertake a journey on account of some business dealing. Moreover, it is good [to undertake] all works which pertain to fire, such as those of craftsmen, cooks, bakers, [and] tile-makers. And just as we have said about the hour of Saturn, it is not good to undertake an association nor to get engaged to or marry a wife.

On the hour of the Sun

In the hour of the Sun it is good to buy gold and all things of a golden color, and golden horses. And it is the best in that hour to speak to the king and all powerful people, and it is good for authorities to undertake a journey because of war, and to begin a war; and it is good to trade in fabrics of a saffron color. But it is neither good nor bad to take medicine, let blood, or to undertake a journey because of business, or to take a wife, or carry on or make or contract an association.

On the hour of Venus

In the hour of Venus it is good to buy women, pearls, and all ornaments of a woman, and golden rings, and to embrace all womanly things, to get engaged, and it is most perfect to take a wife, also to buy white horses and white vestments, and to take medicine, and to let blood, and it is good to speak to queens and noble women.

On the hour of Mercury

In the hour of Mercury it is good to buy all painted [or] written things, wheat, millet, Italian millet, and all garments of a varied color which pertain to human use [and with] a beautiful appearance:[6] silk,[7] [other silk],[8] Chinese

---

[6] *Species.*

[7] *Bombacem.* Now follows two other words which mean silk, but I am not completely sure of the difference between them.

silk,[9] and all works which come to be from Chinese silk. And it is the best to undertake to make a decision,[10] also to take a wife and form an association, even to take medicine [and] to let blood; also to make a journey because of business, also to buy horse with white marks on the head or feet,[11] and arms of two colors (saffron and golden), and to buy vestments of a green color; [and] it is good to begin [to work on] a loom.

On the hour of the Moon

In the hour of the Moon it is good to buy honey, olive oil, figs, chestnuts, nuts, almonds, wool, linen, hemp, barley, the meat of pigs and of all animals except for sheep; it is even good to buy birds pertaining to trade, and all beasts which pertain to butchers.[12] It is good to steal[13] [and] to make deceptions, betrayals, frauds, and [do] clever things. Also, it is not good to undertake works whose stability you want, but it is good to undertake those whose quickness you want.

[§2: Triplicities, when on the Ascendant]

On the arising of the triplicities, and first on the arising of the first triplicity

If it were in the arising of Aries, Leo, or Sagittarius, since these signs are fiery it is good to undertake those things which pertain to fire under their arising: such as firing a kiln, to color gold, silver, lead, tin, [and] yellow copper[14] and on the other hand works of craftsmen.[15] And [it is good to undertake] every work whose quickness you want, to sail, to have a horse

---

8 *Setam* (*saetam*). Normally this referred to stiff bristles, but medievally it meant silk: perhaps a soft fabric made from fine animal hairs?

9 *Sericum*.

10 *Placitum*. This can also refer to an agreement to meet at a certain place or time, in order to conduct negotiations or engage in a conflict. Elsewhere in al-Rijāl (such as VII.11.1), it refers to conflicts.

11 *Baleianos*.

12 Following the medieval meaning for *macellus* rather than the classical "grocer."

13 Reading *furari* for *furare*.

14 Or, "brass" (*auricalcum*).

15 *Fabricalia*.

race, send a messenger, to raise sails, to dig a well, find treasures, and many things which it is not possible to count.

On the arising of the second triplicity

If it were in the arising of Taurus, Virgo, or Capricorn, because these are earthy signs it is good to do all works which pertain to the earth under that same arising: such as to till the land, buy lands and houses, measure land, and distribute vestments, and to buy wood from which you want to make ships and all buildings, and to do all works whose stability, perseverance, and durability you want to have.

On the arising of the third triplicity

But if Gemini, Libra, or Aquarius ascended, since they are airy signs it is good to do things which pertain to air under their ascension: such as to put a mast on a ship, and to raise [the mast] on it, and to prepare and extend yard-arms and sails. And it is good to undertake all works which pertain to a ship, the racing of horses and galleys, and travel.

On the arising of the fourth triplicity[16]

But if the Ascendant were Cancer, Scorpio, or Pisces, since they are watery signs it is good to do all things which pertain to water under their arising: such as to cast nets into the water, and to practice every kind of fishing, bathing, and constructing baths, and to make the enclosures for a water-mill, and to direct the course of water, and many things which cannot be enumerated.

[§3: Quadruplicities, based on Sahl's *On Elect.*][17]

On[18] the knowledge of the natures of the signs. The first of them are the movable signs. Know that the movable signs signify the mobility of matters,

---

[16] This section originally appeared near the end of the entire text, but I have replaced it here where it belongs.

[17] This section is taken verbatim from the Latin of *On Elect.* §§12a-17, so I have copied my revised translation of Crofts' critical edition (see below) and put it here, complete with the section numbers by Crofts.

[18] From here until §20c, cf. al-Rijāl VII.3.1.

quickly [so], and there is nothing lasting in them, nor is their time prolonged. But it is good to sow seed in them, to buy, sell, and to be betrothed to[19] a woman (all of these are successful under them),[20] (§12b) and an infirm person will be freed quickly; also, a contention will not be prolonged in them, and a fugitive will turn back quickly. Even foreign travel is useful in them; and if someone promised something in them, what is promised will not move forward.[21] Pronouncements, dreams, and rumors will be false in them; a doctor should not cure under them, nor should any planting be planted under them, and a foundation should not be laid down under them, because it is bad. (§12c) And everything which you might begin in them (whose stability you want), will not be stable; but every unstable work (and hurried things) which you wanted to do, begin under them. (§13) And the faster [of] the movable ones are Aries and Cancer, for they have more crookedness and more mobility. But Libra and Capricorn are the stronger and more balanced.[22]

(§14a) Next, the fixed ones are appropriate to every work whose stability and prolongation is sought, and what its author wants to be lasting. (§14b) And it is good and useful to build in them, and to celebrate a wedding—after the engagement was in the movable ones.[23] And if a woman were divorced by her husband in them, she will not return to him. But for judgments and

---

19 *Firmare.*

20 This parenthetical comment belongs to the translator or a later editor.

21 That is, it will not be successful or work out (*proficiet*). The Ar. says the promise will not be kept.

22 Here and below, we must take each of the signs in context of their ascensional times. The crooked signs have the shortest ascensions and so pass by the Ascendant faster; the straight signs have the longest and ascend more slowly. In the northern hemisphere, Pisces and Aries have the same, shortest ascensional time, and the times get longer as we fan out in each direction: Aquarius and Taurus have the same time, a bit longer than Pisces-Aries; likewise Capricorn and Gemini have the same time, and so on with Sagittarius-Cancer and Scorpio-Leo, until Virgo and Libra have the longest times. In the southern hemisphere, Pisces-Aries are the longest and straightest, and Virgo-Libra the shortest and most crooked. What Sahl means here is this. Movable signs are presumed to indicate quickness, but there is a difference in their actual quickness, based on the ascensional times: longer ascensional times will even out and balance the quickness of a movable sign. So, of the movable signs, Aries is the fastest crooked one, Cancer the fastest straight one (so that it is more like a crooked one); but Libra is the longest straight one, and Capricorn the longest crooked one, so their longer ascensional times balances out their movable qualities. But Sahl might also have the domicile rulerships in mind (as he seems to with the fixed signs below).

23 That is, we want the engagement to be quick (movable signs) but the celebration after the marriage to last (fixed signs).

inceptions[24] in them, there will not be confidence afterwards, unless the testimonies of the fortunes would be multiplied in them.[25] (§14c) And he who was conquered[26] in them, his imprisonment will be prolonged; and he who grows angry in them, will not be able to be appeased quickly.[27] But contracts and claims[28] in them will be useful, and it will be good to build and lay foundations. (§15) But Scorpio is lighter than all the fixed [signs], and Leo more fixed; Aquarius is slower and worse, but Taurus is more even.[29]

(§16a) The common signs are useful in partnerships and brotherhood, and whatever might be worked in them often will be repeated. But to buy and to celebrate a wedding in them will not be useful nor advantageous, and there will be trickery[30] and deception in them; and he who is charged of something in them, will escape and be relieved of that which is charged against him. (§16b) And he who is imprisoned in them will not be fixed in place (except in Pisces,[31] on account of the rarity of its appearance and emergence). And he who goes out from prison, returns to that place; and he who is taken as a fugitive in them, returns a second time to his flight; and he who goes off to a judge in them, neither an opinion nor judgment is settled

---

24 That is, questions and elections.

25 For this last point Crofts reads, "There is no satisfaction after making a judgment or starting an enterprise, unless the testimonies of the benefics are manifold." The idea seems to be for most actions, we want quick results, so one must be careful in using the fixed signs.

26 Reading *victus* for *vinctus*.

27 Crofts says the reverse: that he *with whom* one is angry, cannot be *controlled*. Perhaps this refers to elections in which we want to provoke an emotional response, such as §§129a-c below.

28 Reading with Crofts for *mercedes* ("wages, rents").

29 Here Sahl is using domicile rulerships to help distinguish the fixed signs, as he does in *On Times* (in which the domiciles of superior planets represent more time than those of inferior planets). For example, since Aquarius and Taurus have the same ascensional times (and likewise Scorpio-Leo), we need a different way of distinguishing them. Aquarius is already fixed, so being ruled by Saturn makes it even more fixed; Venus as the lord of Taurus will loosen it up quite a bit; Scorpio and Leo are somewhere in the middle, but it seems that the rulership of Mars makes Scorpio more mobile than Leo. Really, the scheme doesn't make sense. Taurus should be fastest because it is crooked and ruled by an inferior; then perhaps Leo (straight, ruled by Sun), then Scorpio (straight, but ruled by more superior Mars), then Aquarius (crooked, but ruled by most superior Saturn).

30 *Ingenium.* This is a broad word that often refers to mental skills and character in general; but the Arabic Sahl means this in the sense of clever trickery.

31 Substituting with al-Rijāl VII.3.2, for "except through his own fear." Crofts's Arabic lacks this statement, but does not make sense without it. Sahl means that (in the northern hemisphere, at least), Pisces has the shortest ascensional time of all the common signs, so it passes across the horizon very quickly.

for him.[32] (§16c) Nor [should] someone go away on a ship in them, for he who goes will be changed from one [ship] to another. To whom something is promised in them, it will be dissolved and something of it will not be completed for him; and an infirm person will be healed in them, then will incur a relapse [of the infirmity]. (§17) Therefore, all of the good and evil which comes to a man in them is doubled upon him; and if someone dies in them, then after him another person near him[33] will die in that place. And alteration,[34] and the washing of the head and the beard, and the purification of gold and silver are appropriate in them, and sending boys [to learn their] letters.

[§4: General instructions and planetary significators, from Sahl's *On Elect.*][35]

(§18) If[36] however you wish to begin something of those things which I told you, then put the Moon and the Ascendant in those houses[37] agreeing with that which you want, and conjoin the Moon with the fortunes receiving [her] in that sign. And the signs of the day are stronger in an operation of the day; and make the Ascendant diurnal [and put the Moon in diurnal signs].[38]

(§19a) The airy[39] signs are in conformity with hunting by land and sea; and the royal signs are in conformity with kings; and the signs which have voices are in conformity with him who plays the pipes and little songs;[40] and

32 Crofts says he "will not receive a firm decision or judgment."

33 *In proximo*; following Crofts, signifying a neighbor or someone related, hence the evil is doubled in relation to the *first* dead person.

34 According to Crofts, this is resettling one's home from one place to another.

35 This section is taken verbatim from the Latin of *On Elect.* §§18-21c, so I have copied my revised translation of Crofts' critical edition (see below) and put it here, complete with the section numbers by Crofts.

36 Cf. *Carmen* V.4.5.

37 Reading *et ascendens in illas domos* with Crofts, for *in ascendente illarum domorum*.

38 Adding with Crofts. *Carmen* adds that we should put the Moon and the Ascendant in nocturnal signs for nocturnal elections.

39 Crofts reads "watery," but al-Rijāl VII.3 and normal astrological logic suggest the airy signs.

40 Omitting *cum crudo et voci alhool.* This phrase has something to do with playing or singing crudely, but it does not match the Arabic (and seems incomplete), and the Arabized word *alhool* does not correspond to anything in the Arabic. Crofts says, "for those who play the nay and for lute-playing and singing."

the fiery signs are in conformity with everything which is with fire; (§19b) and the signs of equality (in which day and night are made equal)[41] are in conformity with truth and speaking truthfully and with him who works with scales; and the changeable signs[42] (and they are those in which night and day begin to be changed) are in conformity with change and with him who wants an alteration from thing to thing.

(§20) And consider,[43] for every work which you want to begin, what is the nature of that sign from the orbs;[44] and conjoin the Moon and the lord of the Ascendant with that essence; and the root[45] of that nature and its virtue is in the hour of the undertaking. (§21a) Which if you want that which is connected with[46] lords and princes and great men, and those put over cities, and visible people,[47] and the masters of fights and wealth,[48] then it is for you [to work] through the Sun; (§21b) and what is connected to lofty people, then it is for you [to work] through Jupiter; and that of farmers and the lowest people, then it is for you [to work] through Saturn; and that of generals and the masters of fights, then it is for you [to work] through Mars; and what is connected to women, then it is for you [to work] through Venus. (§21c) But[49] purchases, and sales, and contentions, and matters of writing, and businessmen, are for Mercury; and, of women, in the commingling with queens and the inquiry into those things which are among them, through the Moon.

---

41 The equinoctial signs, Aries and Libra.

42 The tropical signs of Cancer and Capricorn.

43 Cf. *Carmen* V.30.

44 That is, of the circles of heaven: see al-Rijāl VII.3.

45 Crofts reads, "and *with* the root and strength of that nature...". Both the Latin and Arabic readings make the instructions repetitive.

46 *Ex parte.* I have followed Crofts's translation. One should take this to mean elections *on behalf of* such people's actions, or matters merely *concerned with* them: e.g., one should strengthen the Sun both if a prince is the one undertaking the action, and if he is a lowly person going to see the prince.

47 *Spectabilium*, lit. "people who can be looked at." In other words, celebrities of every sort.

48 *Pugnae et largorum.* Crofts reads "executioners and amnesty," and says the Latin is a mistranslation. Executions and amnesty pertain to public justice.

49 Omitting the following redundant passage: "And that of buying, and selling, and exchanges, and the matters of writers and businessmen, then it is for you [to work] through Mercury. In the mixing with mistresses (of women) and an inquiry into what is connected to them, it is for you [to work] through the Moon."

§5: On the hour and sign of Saturn, and his Ascendant

This must be attended to very diligently: which if it were in the hour of Saturn, and a sign of Saturn ascends, it is wonderful to do all things which were said about the hour of Saturn; and understand the same about all the other hours and signs. And if you can, make the hours agree with the signs, because it is best. And what we have said about Saturn, understand thusly about all the other planets.

The Book of the Skilled VII.100: *On the Significations of the Hours*

Al-Rijāl

These are the significations taken from the book of *Abablez* bin Sayyid,[1] and from the book of Abū Ma'shar which is called *The Book of Natures*:[2] and I have put them here so that our book would not seem to be defective in any of the statements which the sages said.

And after the hours I have likewise spoken [about] the elections of the Moon according to mansions,[3] because the majority of the Arabs work and operate through them, and [their] roots are accepted by the Indians (namely from[4] the books of Dorotheus). However, these elections of hours and mansions do not have so much virtue as the elections which we have stated before, which were taken from the places of the planets and from their accidents;[5] however, we are able to aid ourselves with respect to them.

On the hour of the Sun[6]

The hour of the Sun is unfortunate[7] in every matter, except for an entrance to the king; however, you should not make an entrance to him when the Sun was setting, nor should you put on a new vestment in it, nor should you drain [a vein], nor give someone assets for the purpose of doing trade, nor for making some thing; nor should you begin any buildings, nor buy beasts; however, you should seek sages in it, [and] rulership and teaching; and you should not lie down with a woman. However, you should buy arms and ride a horse, and go out from your land to go hunting (but if you were outside [your land] you should not enter your home).

---

[1] *Ablabeç filii çaed* (1551: *Abablez filii Zaëd*). See the list of al-Rijāl's sources in the Introduction.

[2] Probably the *Kitāb al-Tabā'i'* (Sezgin p. 149, #28).

[3] See *Skilled* VII.101, in Part I of this book.

[4] Omitting a redundant *acceptae sunt de ipsis.*

[5] That is, everything in the rest of Book VII, on complete elections (in Part III of this book).

[6] In what follows, the first paragraph in each section is from *Abablez* bin Sayyid, the second one from Abū Ma'shar. See *Skilled* VII.74, where al-Rijāl credits this book of Abū Ma'shar's with a specific statement about sea travel in the hour of Saturn, showing that Abū Ma'shar is represented by the second paragraph.

[7] Reading *infortunata* for *infortuna.*

And this hour is good for receiving a dignity, and for having [something] to do with the king or with a lord, and for getting [a sense of] security by reason of resources which are never sought for yourself,[8] and for making profit. And if you gave capital[9] in that hour, he who accepts it will die, and he[10] will lose the capital. And he who was infirm in that hour will suffer a strong fever, and many times will half-die, in a manner which will do harm to him.

On the hour of Venus

It is good to ride a horse in it, but you should not board any ship; seek rulership in it, and get involved in joking around and comforts, play chess in it, and go [to have] comfort with women, and you should go out from your own land (if however you were outside [your own land], you should not enter your home). And you should contract a marriage-union with a woman, and drink medicines and drugs.[11] You should not be drained through a vein, nor through cupping. You should not plant trees nor sow any seed, nor should you strike your male or female slave, nor[12] should you cut vestments, nor should you sleep if you would be able to abstain [from it].

One who will begin a journey in that hour, will have good and usefulness from the direction of women, or what is like that. It is good to do whatever pertains to women in it, and [to wear] all painted and beautiful fabrics, and to lie down with women, and to be bold and of comfort.[13] And he who receives capital will disperse it with women, vices, and delights. And if someone will be taken infirm, he will have that infirmity on the occasion of anxieties or some error which happens to him, or some evil deed which a woman has inflicted upon him, or what is like this.

On the hour of Mercury

Ride every beast, mule, and donkey in it; and write a paper and send messengers, and you should give your assets over to trade, and you should

[8] Tentatively reading for *tibi*.
[9] Here and below, "capital" (Lat. *capital*) refers to money given in loan.
[10] Probably the first person who gave it.
[11] *Species*.
[12] 1485 omits this "not," but I have added this with 1551.
[13] *De solatio* [*solacio*]. 1551 has *proterus*, "brash."

borrow whatever you wanted to borrow, and you would receive what is owed to you. And drink medicines, and plant trees, enter in upon the king. However, you should not make a marriage-union with a woman, nor should you buy real estate nor land, nor should you enter your home if you were outside [it], nor should you buy slaves, nor should you change from one home to another, nor should you extract anyone from prisons. But you should begin every building, you should dig wells and ditches, you should seek a thing from no one.

It[14] will be good for one undertaking a journey, and he will have good and usefulness from thence; you should send a boy to every teaching, such as for writing [one's] letters and the like. It will be good to engage in commerce, send messengers, make a legal claim, give and receive. One who will accept capital, will pay it off well and in a good way; he who will give it will be contented about it and about the other person.

On the hour of the Moon

You should not begin any building in it, nor should you buy any medicine for healing, you should not cut fabrics, nor should you buy heads of cattle, pigs, nor what is like these. You should cut down trees, buy produce, you should dig ditches and wells, ride horses, honor women, give your child over to learning letters and writing, you should pursue your enemy, go out from your own land (but do not enter into it [if you had been outside it]).

And it is said that one who makes a journey in the hour of the Moon will have good on the occasion of the death of some man of his own association; however, if the Moon were in an earthy sign, this judgment is condemned. He who will give capital in this hour, will have great labor in recovering [it], until he despairs for its recovery; afterwards he will recover it, but not all [of it].

---

[14] This originally appeared as a continuation of the previous sentence, but the third-person statements begin here (with the exception of the recommendation to lead a boy to teaching).

On the hour of Saturn

You should not drink medicine in it, nor should you cut nor put on new clothes, nor shave your head, nor trim[15] the hair on your head, nor should you board any ship. However, you should go out from your home if you wanted to return on that day. And you should search for your enemy and a fugitive, you should buy arms, [but] you should not buy male nor female slaves. Assemble your associates, and you should write papers, ride every kind of donkey or mule, cast no stones nor barbs,[16] you should not seek a murder, nor should you make an agreement with anyone, nor should you drain yourself from a vein nor by cupping. You should buy every rented thing[17] and every foodstuff, you should receive a gift.

He who will go out to make a journey, will have a great danger of prisons or many anxieties, or slowness on the journey. And if the journey were by sea, he will have many waves and diverse winds, which will cast him forth to other places known to him. It is good to rent lands, to hollow out ditches, to till. He who accepts capital will lose the assets, and perhaps he who accepts it will die, or the owner of the assets will kill him; and he who will be made infirm in it, his infirmity will be prolonged, and afterwards he will die.

On the hour of Jupiter

Honor kings in it, and contract a marriage with women. You should not strike your male nor female slave; [but] you should cut fabrics in it, ride [one's] mounts. You should not drink bad drugs,[18] [but] you should go from out of your own land. You should not buy arms, you should beware of fire and its flames. You should not dig ditches, [but] sow every seed, and plant every tree, begin every building. Make it so that you sit with kings. You should not buy beasts but you should buy birds, you should not board a ship, nor should you cast stones [against] anyone.[19] You should speak with the king; you should not drain yourself from a vein nor by cupping.

---

[15] Lit., to cut "in a circle."

[16] That is, do not get into quarrels.

[17] *Conductum*. This seems to be derived from the previous point, that one should not make an agreement. In other words, try to own everything you can outright.

[18] Or, "medicines" (*species*).

[19] Again, getting into quarrels.

He who will have gone out to make a journey, will have good profit in assets and his business dealing, usefulness from a direction which he will not expect, and joys. It is good to enter upon the king, magistrates and judges. He who gave capital will have good and profit from thence, and love with his associate [or] partner; he who will become infirm, will be healed quickly.

On the hour of Mars

The hour of Mars is to be abhorred in every matter, and in every beginning and deed.[20]

---

[20] But cf. al-'Imrānī II.2.8, where Abū Ma'shar says Mars is to be abhorred *except* in matters such as bloodletting.

PART III: COMPLETE ELECTIONS

ON ELECTIONS

SAHL BIN BISHR

[For whom we should elect]

(§1) All are agreed that elections are weak, except [those] for kings. For these people (even should their elections be weakened) have a root—that is, their nativities—which strengthen every weak planet in the course.[1] (§2) But you should not elect anything for the low-class and for merchants and for those who follow [in social status], unless [it is based] upon their nativities, and the revolutions of those years, and on the nativities of their children.

(§3a) However,[2] [for] those of whom these things are not known,[3] questions should be taken for them, and the effecting of their matter may be known from those—afterwards it should be elected for them according to this.[4] (§3b) Because if someone asked you about himself, it has already arrived at the good or evil from out of his own nativity (that is, in the hour in which someone comes to you), because it is he who has asked[5] you.

(§3c) And if it is one whose quaesited matter will not come to be, or if the man who asks you (or who goes away to war) will die, beware therefore this kind of election.[6] (§4) For how would you elect for him whose root is

---

[1] That is, even a bad election will be able to take advantage of a strong nativity, and even put weak natal planets in such a strong nativity to good use.

[2] In this paragraph, Sahl is making the following argument. Normally, we prefer to use a client's nativity as the root, because it shows the general promise of success or failure in the action he wants to undertake. But if we lack such a nativity, we may substitute the chart of a *question* as to whether or not it will be successful: because a successful question chart indirectly affirms that the action is not contrary to his nativity. So, the nativity is the preferred root, and a valid, successful question chart is a second-best root. Actually, the Latin is a bit clearer than the Arabic here (at least, in Crofts's own translation): the Arabic in this sentence suggests that one should not even bother electing for someone who needs to ask a question, even though in §5a below Sahl expressly allows elections based on question charts.

[3] That is, if someone did not know his own nativity.

[4] That is, for people whose nativity is not known, we can cast a horary chart as a substitute for the nativity.

[5] Reading *quia ipse est qui te interrogavit*, omitting the extra *et est.*

[6] That is, if the querent has no known nativity, and the horary question shows bad results, consider the matter closed and do not proceed to an election.

destroyed, especially if in addition the first beginning and the old root on which one relies, is [also destroyed]?[7]

(§5a) Therefore, beware of electing for him whose root of the nativity or question signified something horrible. (§5b) [For] if it came to this,[8] [even] if you put all the fortunes in stakes,[9] and made the bad ones and every planet which did not agree with the lord of his Ascendant be cadent,[10] it would not profit the man anything, (§5c) and especially for those who are low- and middle-class: because you do not know whether you might elect an Ascendant or star which is inimical to him in the root, or there were a bad one in that same ascending sign which you have elected for him.

[The importance of the root]

(§6a) In fact, this is to be warned against[11] for those who sail by sea, or for those who go on a foreign journey in one hour (whose intention is on [just] one foreign journey): but certain ones of them suffer shipwreck, indeed certain ones escape it, and certain ones of them discover assets (but certain ones discover nothing). For the condition[12] of certain ones cannot be likened to the conditions of others of them. (§6b) And I[13] have already tested this many times in the gathering together of certain people who went out from a place in one hour, and they arrived at another region at one hour: but certain

---

[7] The Latin text reads as though we are still speaking about a low-class client who has a bad nativity (the first or ancient root), and the substitute root (the question) is also bad or "destroyed." But in the more succinct Crofts version, it is unclear what chart is being referred to as the root: the nativity or the question. Either way, the point is taken.

[8] That is, if you were somehow coerced into crafting an election for such a person.

[9] Ar. *watad* (sing.), also meaning "tent poles" or something stuck into the ground. In Latin this is the usual "angles" (lit. "corners," Lat. *anguli*), but since the Arabic is available for this text I have used a better rendering of it. It translates the Greek *kentron* ("pivot," among other words), and refers to the angles. But it is sometimes unclear whether Sahl and other Arabic writers are referring to the whole-sign angles from the Ascendant (the ascending sign, tenth sign, seventh sign, fourth sign), or the regions of power or stimulation which follow the axial degrees (e.g., from the degree of the Midheaven to the eleventh-house cusp). This is a problem related to house systems, and so points to more fundamental problems and issues in understanding ancient and medieval practices.

[10] Reading based on Crofts, for the Latin's more awkward "and made the bad ones be cadent from them, nothing will profit him; and every planet which did not agree with the lord of his Ascendant would not profit the man anything."

[11] The idea is that if you choose one election for a group of people, some of those people will inevitably have a better or worse relation between the election chart and their own nativities: therefore they will encounter different things on the journey.

[12] *Esse.*

[13] This may in fact be Māshā'allāh: see Introduction.

ones of them went back more quickly with the best assets, and certain ones took it slow in the same place; but certain ones of them perished before [they could] return to their own homes. For this happens to them because of their nativities and because of their distribution[14] in those years themselves.

(§7) We even see certain people rejoice and drink on a bad day and on a day to be feared (namely [a day] of many impediments), and quarrels come together and enter upon them on a good and praiseworthy day. (§8) And perhaps you will see the significator[15] joined to a bad one from a square aspect or the opposition (or it will be with it in one sign), but he will discover good in it: this does not happen unless perhaps the bad ones are more agreeable to it because they were the first lord of the Ascendant[16] or the lord of its distribution, or the lord of the Ascendant of the revolution of the year.

(§9) If however you elected [based] on the Ascendant of a question or a nativity which you knew, or on the lord of the Ascendant (that is, the sign of the profection of the year), your election will be more worthy, because you would know what (of the stars) is in accord with it,[17] and what his Ascendant would be. Therefore be careful in this chapter, and let your work[18] be like your election.

[More on the theory of elections: natures and benefics/malefics]

(§10a) And know that the All-powerful and Highest has created every creature (namely the world and whatever there is in it) out of the four natures—that is, out of the four elements—and[19] He put the earth in place and

---

[14] That is, the direction of points through the bounds of the natal charts, indication time-lord periods. I am not sure whether Sahl is referring to the distribution/direction of the natal longevity releaser, or of the Ascendant, or what. But the point is that if the natal predictive methods already indicate good or bad for that specific time in an individual's life, it is likely to override a very general election made for an entire group.

[15] This may refer to the Moon, who is sometimes simply referred to as "the significator" or "the indicator" in texts on questions (see throughout *Judges*).

[16] Reading singular with the Arabic (here and in the rest of the sentence). In this first phrase, Sahl probably means the lord of the Ascendant in the nativity, just as he has referred to the nativity as the "first beginning" and the "old root" in §4 above.

[17] Reading *ei* for *eis* (with Arabic).

[18] Crofts's Arabic reads this as "action," so it could mean that the client's deed should be carefully undertaken just as the election is carefully chosen.

[19] The Ar. is subtlely different for the rest of this: "And He joined the earth and her rational and irrational, movable and immovable beings to the heavens, and placed between them insensible things, of which the learned men are cognizant…".

every thing which is above it (of what is rational and irrational, and of what is movable and immovable) in a circle; and between this and the circle He put subtle things which the wise know, (§10b) like that subtle circumstance[20] which He put between the stone of a magnet and iron, and the one that is between a father and a son, and between the one eating and food. Know this and understand it.

(§11a) Therefore from the concord which is between each of the two essences (namely the superior and the inferior), matters are combined properly; and they are destroyed by adversity.[21] And the fortunes are balanced[22] (that is, of a temperate nature), but the bad ones of a harmful nature (and therefore they wish to impede);[23] (§11b) but if they were received,[24] their [malefic] essence will not wholly be absent, [nor] the malevolence of their imbalance;[25] and they are like thieves, and, of men, the citizens of evils, and from them comes adversity and discord, alteration also and the confusion of matters. Understand all of this.

(§12a) The Ascendant and whatever is in it concerning elections[26]

[Quadruplicities][27]

On[28] the knowledge of the natures of the signs. The first of them are the movable signs. Know that the movable signs signify the mobility of matters, quickly [so], and there is nothing lasting in them, nor is their time prolonged.

---

[20] *Occasio*. This word really means "occasion" or "pretext," i.e., the circumstance that allows something to happen. Crofts says "relation," which is easier to understand; but perhaps the Latin translator chose this word judiciously: instead of merely positing a relation, he wanted to emphasize that this relation is the *precondition* for there to be interaction between the parts of the cosmos.

[21] Crofts reads: "*when* there is harmony between the two essences, the higher and the lower, things are balanced, and when there is disharmony, they are upset" (emphasis mine).

[22] *Aequales*.

[23] Cf. Sahl's *Fifty Judgments* #2 and 32, or *Tet.* I.5: the malefic planets are harmful because they are more extreme in their natures.

[24] Following Crofts (for *reciperint*).

[25] Reading with Crofts for "cunning of hostility." Cf. *Fifty Judgments* #25.

[26] This heading must have been added by a later editor or translator. The section title in Crofts is actually the first sentence below (rendered in Crofts as: "The science of the natures of the signs").

[27] For this subsection on the quadruplicities, cf. *Carmen* V.3-4.

[28] From here until §20c, cf. al-Rijāl VII.3.1.

But it is good to sow seed in them, to buy, sell, and to be betrothed to[29] a woman (all of these are successful under them),[30] (§12b) and an infirm person will be freed quickly; also, a contention will not be prolonged in them, and a fugitive will turn back quickly. Even foreign travel is useful in them; and if someone promised something in them, what is promised will not move forward.[31] Pronouncements, dreams, and rumors will be false in them; a doctor should not cure under them, nor should any planting be planted under them, and a foundation should not be laid down under them, because it is bad. (§12c) And everything which you might begin in them (whose stability you want), will not be stable; but every unstable work (and hurried things) which you wanted to do, begin under them. (§13) And the faster [of] the movable ones are Aries and Cancer, for they have more crookedness and more mobility. But Libra and Capricorn are the stronger and more balanced.[32]

---

[29] *Firmare.*

[30] This parenthetical comment belongs to the translator or a later editor.

[31] That is, it will not be successful or work out (*proficiet*). The Ar. says the promise will not be kept.

[32] Here and below, we must take each of the signs in context of their ascensional times. The crooked signs have the shortest ascensions and so pass by the Ascendant faster; the straight signs have the longest and ascend more slowly. In the northern hemisphere, Pisces and Aries have the same, shortest ascensional time, and the times get longer as we fan out in each direction: Aquarius and Taurus have the same time, a bit longer than Pisces-Aries; likewise Capricorn and Gemini have the same time, and so on with Sagittarius-Cancer and Scorpio-Leo, until Virgo and Libra have the longest times. In the southern hemisphere, Pisces-Aries are the longest and straightest, and Virgo-Libra the shortest and most crooked. What Sahl means here is this. Movable signs are presumed to indicate quickness, but there is a difference in their actual quickness, based on the ascensional times: longer ascensional times will even out and balance the quickness of a movable sign. So, of the movable signs, Aries is the fastest crooked one, Cancer the fastest straight one (so that it is more like a crooked one); but Libra is the longest straight one, and Capricorn the longest crooked one, so their longer ascensional times balances out their movable qualities. But Sahl might also have the domicile rulerships in mind (as he seems to with the fixed signs below).

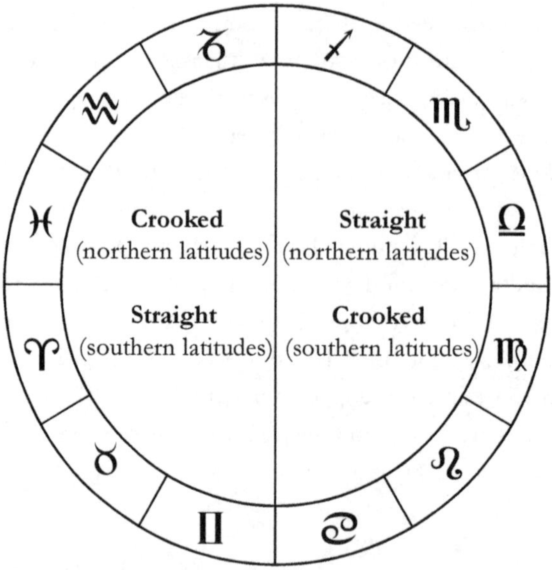

Figure 11: Straight and crooked signs, in northern and southern hemispheres

(§14a) Next, the fixed ones are appropriate to every work whose stability and prolongation is sought, and what its author wants to be lasting. (§14b) And it is good and useful to build in them, and to celebrate a wedding—after the engagement was in the movable ones.[33] And if a woman were divorced by her husband in them, she will not return to him. But for judgments and inceptions[34] in them, there will not be confidence afterwards, unless the testimonies of the fortunes would be multiplied in them.[35] (§14c) And he who was conquered[36] in them, his imprisonment will be prolonged; and he who grows angry in them, will not be able to be appeased quickly.[37] But contracts

---

[33] That is, we want the engagement to be quick (movable signs) but the celebration after the marriage to last (fixed signs).
[34] That is, questions and elections.
[35] For this last point Crofts reads, "There is no satisfaction after making a judgment or starting an enterprise, unless the testimonies of the benefics are manifold." The idea seems to be for most actions, we want quick results, so one must be careful in using the fixed signs.
[36] Reading *victus* for *vinctus*.
[37] Crofts says the reverse: that he *with whom* one is angry, cannot be *controlled.* Perhaps this refers to elections in which we want to provoke an emotional response, such as §§129a-c below.

and claims[38] in them will be useful, and it will be good to build and lay foundations. (§15) But Scorpio is lighter than all the fixed [signs], and Leo more fixed; Aquarius is slower and worse, but Taurus is more even.[39]

(§16a) The common signs are useful in partnerships and brotherhood, and whatever might be worked in them often will be repeated. But to buy and to celebrate a wedding in them will not be useful nor advantageous, and there will be trickery[40] and deception in them; and he who is charged of something in them, will escape and be relieved of that which is charged against him. (§16b) And he who is imprisoned in them will not be fixed in place (except in Pisces,[41] on account of the rarity of its appearance and emergence). And he who goes out from prison, returns to that place; and he who is taken as a fugitive in them, returns a second time to his flight; and he who goes off to a judge in them, neither an opinion nor judgment is settled for him.[42] (§16c) Nor [should] someone go away on a ship in them, for he who goes will be changed from one [ship] to another. To whom something is promised in them, it will be dissolved and something of it will not be completed for him; and an infirm person will be healed in them, then will incur a relapse [of the infirmity]. (§17) Therefore, all of the good and evil which comes to a man in them is doubled upon him; and if someone dies in them, then after him another person near him[43] will die in that place. And alteration,[44] and the washing of the head and the beard, and the purification of

---

38 Reading with Crofts for *mercedes* ("wages, rents").

39 Here Sahl is using domicile rulerships to help distinguish the fixed signs, as he does in *On Times* (in which the domiciles of superior planets represent more time than those of inferior planets). For example, since Aquarius and Taurus have the same ascensional times (and likewise Scorpio-Leo), we need a different way of distinguishing them. Aquarius is already fixed, so being ruled by Saturn makes it even more fixed; Venus as the lord of Taurus will loosen it up quite a bit; Scorpio and Leo are somewhere in the middle, but it seems that the rulership of Mars makes Scorpio more mobile than Leo. Really, the scheme doesn't make sense. Taurus should be fastest because it is crooked and ruled by an inferior; then perhaps Leo (straight, ruled by Sun), then Scorpio (straight, but ruled by more superior Mars), then Aquarius (crooked, but ruled by most superior Saturn).

40 *Ingenium.* This is a broad word that often refers to mental skills and character in general; but the Arabic Sahl means this in the sense of clever trickery.

41 Substituting with al-Rijāl VII.3.2, for "except through his own fear." Crofts's Arabic lacks this statement, but does not make sense without it. Sahl means that (in the northern hemisphere, at least), Pisces has the shortest ascensional time of all the common signs, so it passes across the horizon very quickly.

42 Crofts says he "will not receive a firm decision or judgment."

43 *In proximo*; following Crofts, signifying a neighbor or someone related, hence the evil is doubled in relation to the *first* dead person.

44 According to Crofts, this is resettling one's home from one place to another.

gold and silver are appropriate in them, and sending boys [to learn their] letters.

[General advice on elections]

(§18) If[45] however you wish to begin something of those things which I told you, then put the Moon and the Ascendant in those houses[46] agreeing with that which you want, and conjoin the Moon with the fortunes receiving [her] in that sign. And the signs of the day are stronger in an operation of the day; and make the Ascendant diurnal [and put the Moon in diurnal signs].[47]

(§19a) The airy[48] signs are in conformity with hunting by land and sea; and the royal signs are in conformity with kings; and the signs which have voices are in conformity with him who plays the pipes and little songs;[49] and the fiery signs are in conformity with everything which is with fire; (§19b) and the signs of equality (in which day and night are made equal)[50] are in conformity with truth and speaking truthfully and with him who works with scales; and the changeable signs[51] (and they are those in which night and day begin to be changed) are in conformity with change and with him who wants an alteration from thing to thing.

(§20) And consider,[52] for every work which you want to begin, what is the nature of that sign from the orbs;[53] and conjoin the Moon and the lord of the Ascendant with that essence; and the root[54] of that nature and its virtue is in the hour of the undertaking. (§21a) Which if you want that which is

---

45 Cf. *Carmen* V.4.5.

46 Reading *et ascendens in illas domos* with Crofts, for *in ascendente illarum domorum.*

47 Adding with Crofts. *Carmen* adds that we should put the Moon and the Ascendant in nocturnal signs for nocturnal elections.

48 Crofts reads "watery," but al-Rijāl VII.3 and normal astrological logic suggest the airy signs.

49 Omitting *cum crudo et voci alhool.* This phrase has something to do with playing or singing crudely, but it does not match the Arabic (and seems incomplete), and the Arabized word *alhool* does not correspond to anything in the Arabic. Crofts says, "for those who play the nay and for lute-playing and singing."

50 The equinoctial signs, Aries and Libra.

51 The tropical signs of Cancer and Capricorn.

52 Cf. *Carmen* V.30.

53 That is, of the circles of heaven: see al-Rijāl VII.3.

54 Crofts reads, "and *with* the root and strength of that nature…". Both the Latin and Arabic readings make the instructions repetitive.

connected with[55] lords and princes and great men, and those put over cities, and visible people,[56] and the masters of fights and wealth,[57] then it is for you [to work] through the Sun; (§21b) and what is connected to lofty people, then it is for you [to work] through Jupiter; and that of farmers and the lowest people, then it is for you [to work] through Saturn; and that of generals and the masters of fights, then it is for you [to work] through Mars; and what is connected to women, then it is for you [to work] through Venus. (§21c) But[58] purchases, and sales, and contentions, and matters of writing, and businessmen, are for Mercury; and, of women, in the commingling with queens and the inquiry into those things which are among them, through the Moon.

[Impediments of the Moon]

(§22a) Therefore, if you wished to begin some work, adapt the Ascendant and its lord, and the Moon and the lord of the matter.[59] And in the beginning of works, beware of the impediment of the Moon, just as Dorotheus[60] (and the rest of the sages) said—and there are ten ways:

> (§22b) The first way[61] is that she is burned up under the Sun by 12°, and likewise after him (but it is easier after him).[62]
>
> The second, that she is in the degree of her own descension.

[55] *Ex parte.* I have followed Crofts's translation. One should take this to mean elections *on behalf of* such people's actions, or matters merely *concerned with* them: e.g., one should strengthen the Sun both if a prince is the one undertaking the action, and if he is a lowly person going to see the prince.
[56] *Spectabilium*, lit. "people who can be looked at." In other words, celebrities of every sort.
[57] *Pugnae et largorum.* Crofts reads "executioners and amnesty," and says the Latin is a mistranslation. Executions and amnesty pertain to public justice.
[58] Omitting the following redundant passage: "And that of buying, and selling, and exchanges, and the matters of writers and businessmen, then it is for you [to work] through Mercury. In the mixing with mistresses (of women) and an inquiry into what is connected to them, it is for you [to work] through the Moon."
[59] One should probably also make the lord of the Moon fit, as al-Rijāl reads in this place (VII.3.4): cf. *Carmen* V.5.21.
[60] Cf. *Carmen* V.5.3-9, and compare to Sahl's *Introduct.* §5.16, as well as *ITA* IV.5 and *Search* I.5.
[61] Cf. *Carmen* V.5.3-4.
[62] That is, after she has passed him and he is behind *her*.

The third,[63] that she is in the opposition of the Sun.

(§22c) The fourth,[64] that she is joined to bad ones, or in the light of their square aspect or the opposition.

The fifth,[65] that she is with the Head or the Tail, from a degree to 12° (which is the boundary of an eclipse).

The sixth,[66] that she is in the last degrees[67] of the signs (which are the bounds of the bad ones).

(§22d) The seventh,[68] that she is cadent from the stakes, or in the burnt path (which is the end of Libra and the beginning of Scorpio)—and this[69] is the worst that there is of the impediments of the Moon, and especially if it were the inception of a marriage or something concerning the matters of women, or buying, or selling, or foreign travel.

(§22e) The eighth, that she is in the twelfth sign[70] from her own house (that is, in Gemini), with a bad one, or were she in the opposition of her own house, or absent from it.[71]

(§22f) The ninth,[72] that the Moon is slower in course: and this is what the sages call a similarity to the course of Saturn, so long as her course

---

63 Cf. *Carmen* V.5.5.
64 Cf. *Carmen* V.5.29.
65 Cf. *Carmen* V.5.5.
66 Cf. *Carmen* V.5.8.
67 Reading *gradibus* for *gradus.*
68 Cf. *Carmen* V.5.8.
69 I do not know whether both of these count as the worst, or just one of them (and if so, which one).
70 The Arabic has "in a twelfth-part with a malefic." But that suggests a bodily conjunction by sign or degree, which was already described above. The Latin al-Rijāl (VII.3.4) suggests that the sign represented by the Moon's twelfth-part has a malefic on it, which is precisely the sort of thing described by Paul of Alexandria (Ch. 22, and the Olympiodorus commentary with examples). Then, *Carmen* V.5.5 has the Moon being in the sign indicated by a malefic's twelfth-part, also the type of thing described by Paul. I suggest that we should use the twelfth-part interpretation or Paul or al-Rijāl, not the "twelfth sign" of the Latin.
71 That is, in aversion to Cancer (as Crofts explains, and also al-Rijāl in his VII.3.4).
72 *Carmen* V.5.6.

in a day is less than 12°, and [even] if it was one minute less (this is if her course in the day were less than her average course in one day), which is written in the *Canon*, that is, in the *Book of Courses.*[73]

(§22g) The tenth, which Māshā'allāh and the sages of our time have said: this is if the Moon were empty in [her] course.

[More general advice]

(§23a) And make the Moon fit, according to your ability; and you should not put her waxing in any Ascendant, because this is to be feared on account of what happens to [the election's] owner[74] because of infirmities in the body, unless the lord of the Ascendant or a fortune[75] are aspecting the ascending [degree]:[76] (§23b) because a planet which does not aspect its own house is like a man absent from his own home, who cannot repel nor prohibit anything from it. (§23c) But if a planet did aspect its own house, it is like the owner of a home who guards it: for whoever is in the home, fears him, and he who is outside fears to come to it.[77] (§24) And if the lord of the Ascendant were a bad one, make him aspect[78] from a trine or sextile aspect.

---

[73] The Arabic does not add this statement about a *Book of Courses* (which must be a book of tables and ephemerides like the *Zij*), but gives a description in terms of *kardajas*: "when your calculation for the moon is in the first *kardaja* of its *kardajas*, so that the *kardaja* is from one to fifteen degrees." According to Crofts (p. 157) and Sarton (pp. 420-22), a *kardaja* was originally the sine value of 1/96 of the circle (or 3° 45'), equivalent to 1/24 of 90° (a quarter of a circle), namely .0654. But later, it was thought to derive from 1/24 of the *whole* circle, equivalent to 15°. So, Sahl is assuming this later view, which not all authors used even in later time. At any rate, I do not really understand what Sahl means by this.

[74] I.e., the one undertaking the action.

[75] Crofts reads, "and the lord of the house of the moon." But notice that the Latin nicely parallels the use of the malefics in §24.

[76] Crofts herself has added *[gradum]* because the Latin reads *ascendentem* (implying a masculine subject) as opposed to its usual *ascendens*. But the Arabic itself does not specify the degree, implying only a whole-sign aspect. Crofts helpfully notes (p. 158) that if the Moon is in the Ascendant and the lord of the Ascendant aspects the Ascendant, then both the Moon and the Ascendant will have their lords/dispositors aspecting them, which is often recommended by Sahl.

[77] In this context, it suggests that the lord of the Ascendant can check the tendency of the Moon to create infirmities while she is in the Ascendant.

[78] Crofts states in a footnote and annotation (pp. 102, 158) that the malefic is supposed to aspect *the Moon or* the Ascendant, but I do not see where she gets the Moon from. To me it seems that only the Ascendant is pertinent here.

And beware lest you put the lord[79] of the Ascendant or the Moon (if there were bad ones aspecting the Moon) in a stake, and that you do not put them in the stakes of the Ascendant.[80]

(§25a) Nor[81] should you make the Lot of Fortune, in all beginnings or questions, be cadent from the aspect of the Moon or her conjunction; and you should not look at the lord of the Lot of Fortune, nor should you care if the Lot is cadent from the Ascendant, *if* the Lot aspected the Ascendant and the Moon. (§25b) And strive to put the lord of the Ascendant with the Lot, because this is more useful and of greater profit. And you should never put the Moon in the second, or the sixth, or the eighth, or the twelfth from the Lot, because this is horrible.[82]

(§26) And[83] always set up the Ascendant and the Moon, in all beginnings, in signs of straight ascension, because they signify ease and progress; and you should not put them in signs of crooked ascension, because they signify complication or hardship and slowness.

Also, the Ascendant and the fourth [sign] from it[84] signify what happens to that election.

(§27) Therefore, look at the fortunes and the bad ones from the places, both the strong and the weak,[85] and speak about the beginning of that matter and its end, from that strength and weakness.

(§28) And Dorotheus said,[86] if you saw the Moon impeded, and a matter is at hand which ought to come to be wholly and it cannot be put off, you should not give the Moon a role in the Ascendant: and make her be cadent from the Ascendant, and put a fortune in the Ascendant, and strengthen the Ascendant and its lord.

---

[79] I take this to mean *a malefic* lord of the Ascendant. Crofts gives the following: "if there are two malefics in aspect with the moon from an angle, place it from the angles of the ascendant."

[80] The Arabic is vaguer and unclear about what we are supposed to do or not do: "beware of placing the lord of the ascendant or the moon, if there are two malefics in aspect with the moon from the stake, place it from the stakes of the ascendant."

[81] The first part of this paragraph bears a resemblance to the later *Forty Chapters* §241.

[82] Cf. *Carmen* I.5.3-5.

[83] Cf. *Carmen* V.2.2-5. But *Carmen* says the opposite: signs of direct ascension show difficulty and slowness, those of crooked ascension will be faster.

[84] The Arabic adds the lord of the fourth sign, as well.

[85] I take this to refer to the strong and weak places, not planets that are otherwise made strong or weak by other considerations.

[86] Crofts (p. *xi*) says that this is based on *Carmen* V.5.10-11. See my Introduction for a discussion of this passage.

(§29a) The second sign from the Ascendant, and whatever is in it, in terms of elections

[Borrowing and lending]

If[87] you wished to choose the hour for the lending[88] of money, let the Moon be in Leo or in Pisces, or in Scorpio or Sagittarius, or in Aquarius, and let her be defective in light, and let both fortunes be deficient[89] and aspecting the Moon or Ascendant. (§29b) And[90] let Mercury be cleansed of Mars, and [let] the Moon be with Jupiter or Mercury; and beware lest the Moon be impeded by any one of the bad ones; nor let Mercury be joined to them [by bodily conjunction] or in their square aspect; nor let the fortunes be cadent: (§29c) because if the Moon were with Mars, he will fall into labor, and worry, and [bad] business dealings, and harshness or contention. And if she were impeded by Saturn, he will fall into something prolonged, and delay, and he will get out of it after distress and fatigue.

(§30a) If[91] however you wished to conceal the lending, so that no one would be able to perceive it, let the Moon (while you take it or seek it) be under the rays, going toward the conjunction of the fortunes after her separation from the Sun: for this is easier for the owner [of the election], and more concealed, and it will not be made public. (§30b) For if the Moon were in her exit out of being burned up, going out toward the conjunction of Mars, this will be made public and it will fall into the mouths of men, and in the mouths of those whom you do not want that they should know it. (§30c) And beware lest the Moon be in the circle of the signs (without latitude, that is, in the Head or Tail)[92] or in the burnt path, because this is horrible.

(§31) And Dorotheus said,[93] you should not take what is loaned, nor should you loan something to someone, while the Moon is in the first degree of Leo or Gemini or Sagittarius, or [if] these signs[94] were ascending: because this is hateful for a loan especially. (Know this.)

---

87 For this election, cf. *Carmen* V.20.

88 Omitting "taking and," with Crofts: borrowing is described below.

89 *Carmen* V.20.7 has the Moon deficient, but does not make the benefics so.

90 Through the rest of this paragraph, cf. *Carmen* V.20.2-4.

91 For this sentence, cf. *Carmen* V.20.5.

92 This parenthetical remark is by the Latin translator.

93 See *Carmen* V.20.6.

94 *Carmen* does not fault the entire sign, but only the degrees mentioned.

[Business partnerships]

(§32a) And[95] if you wished to partner with someone in assets or in a work, it is better for this that the Moon be cleansed of the bad ones and joined to fortunes, and that she be in common signs (so that it would be multiplied),[96] or the Moon should be in Leo or in Taurus. (§32b) And it is to be abhorred in these things that the Moon should be in the lower signs[97] (and worse than the rest is Libra because the burnt path is in it; likewise abhorred is Aquarius). (§33) And let the Moon be received from a trine or sextile aspect, so that [the partners'] separation is good: because in the square aspect and the opposition there will be words between them (that is, a quarrel in the separation). Also, an aspect of esteem signifies the goodness or honesty of their separation, and their faithfulness and good will. (§34) And beware of the presence of the bad ones in the stakes, because the Ascendant belongs to the one of them beginning the partnership, or him who is of lesser age;[98] but the seventh [sign] belongs to the other partner; and the tenth [sign] signifies what will be between them, and the multitude or scarcity of wealth; but from the fourth is known the conclusion of their matter. (§35) And beware lest the lord of the Ascendant does not aspect the Ascendant, or that the lord of the house of the Moon does not aspect the Moon: because if it were so, one of them[99] will delude his partner, and their matter will be made worse in the separation.

[Investing money for profit]

(§36) And if you wished to send forth [your] assets,[100] seeking its wealth, adapt the Moon and Mercury, and the lord of the house of assets, not to

---

[95] Cf. *Carmen* V.19.1-14, which lists each sign individually, but Sahl has tried to shorten things and makes a few changes. Sahl omits Aries, which *Carmen* says is bad; he makes Taurus good, which *Carmen* says is bad; he makes Capricorn bad, which *Carmen* says is good; and Sahl makes it ambiguous as to whether Pisces is good or bad—*Carmen* says it is good.

[96] That is, so the experience is repeated, for ongoing profit and cooperation.

[97] That is, the signs of southern declination.

[98] As though the querent is a junior or inexperienced apprentice seeking to partner with a master.

[99] Crofts says "both."

[100] *Mittere*, a fair translation of the Arabic "channel." The text refers to investing your money in some activity in order to make a profit.

mention the lord of the degree of the house of trust.[101] (§37a) And let the Moon be joined to Mercury, and make Mars be cadent from each of them just as you are able; also make Mercury fit and purge him of defects. (§37b) If however Mercury were retrograde, adapt the Moon and the degree of the house of trust, and make Mercury be cadent from the light of Mars; and you should not make [Mercury] be cadent from the aspect of Venus and from the lord of the eleventh. (§38) And let your trust (in the channeling[102] of assets and in the search for wealth) always be in Mercury, and the Moon, and the degree of the house of trust, and their lords, and make Mars and his light be cadent from [Mercury and the Moon].[103]

[Sales and purchases]

(§39a) And[104] if you wished to elect the hour of a purchase, make the Lot of Fortune fit, and let it be in the houses of Jupiter, joined to fortunes: because this will be better for the one buying than for the one selling. (§39b) And the Moon, if she were in signs of straight ascension, increased in light and number, and joined to the fortunes, whatever he would buy in that same hour, its owner will lose in it:[105] for this is better for the one selling than for the one buying. (§39c) And let Mars be cadent from the Moon and Mercury, because in a sale and purchase Mars impedes, and he is the one who signifies labor and contention. (§39d) Likewise the Tail—therefore make it be cadent from the Moon especially (and it is below Mars [in malice]).[106]

(§40) And if you wished to sell, put the Moon in her own exaltation or triplicity, separated from the fortunes and aspecting the bad ones, but do not let her be joined to them.[107]

---

101 The eleventh.
102 Following Crofts, for the Lat. *directione*.
103 Following Crofts, who clarifies this.
104 For this paragraph, cf. *Carmen* V.9.1-7.
105 By "it," Sahl means what is bought: the new owner will lose money on it, or lose the object itself.
106 Adding the words in brackets, based on al-Rijāl VII.11 on the same topic.
107 This seems to mean that she should be in a sign-based configuration, not a degree-based connection.

[Alchemical works]

(§41) And if you wished to perform a work of alchemy, or a work which you wished to repeat, let this come to be [with] the Moon in common signs, cleansed of the bad ones, and let the Ascendant be likewise—therefore adapt it. And if your work were in gold, strengthen the Sun and make him fit in its inception.[108]

(§42) [The third sign and whatever is in it concerning elections]

And whatever there is in the third sign concerning elections, a portion of it falls[109] in the ninth and another portion in the house of friends: we will state it then, if God wills.

(§43) The fourth sign and whatever is in it, in the manner of elections

[Building a house]

If you wished to elect so that you might build a house, adapt the Moon and her lord, the Ascendant and its lord, also the Lot of Fortune and Mercury. (§44a) And make Mars be cadent from these significators which I have named for you, and you should never give him a role in anything concerning the building of houses. (§44b) And if it could not come about but that he did have a role, make Venus strong in her own place, and give her strength over Mars, and join her to him from a trine or sextile aspect: because Mars does not impede a matter of Venus, in view of the greatness of her friendship toward him. (§44c) And make Saturn be cadent from Venus according to your ability (on account of his enmity), with Mars and with the Moon, if they aspect each other from esteem.[110]

(§45a) And[111] let the Moon be increased in light and number, and joined to Jupiter from a square aspect, because this is better than the opposition:

---

[108] See *On Quest.* §13.12 for more on alchemy.
[109] Reading the indicative with the Arabic, for *ceciderit.*
[110] Both the Arabic and the Latin seem to be missing the operative *and*, so that Saturn should be *both* (a) cadent from Venus *and* (b) in a good aspect with Mars and the Moon. But see also al-Rijāl's alternative report from "Nufil" in VII.20.3.
[111] For this paragraph, cf. *Carmen* V.6.

and this signifies the beauty of the building and its perfection. (§45b) And beware lest the Moon be with Saturn or the Tail, or Saturn be in the Ascendant or in the fourth: because this signifies slowness and duress in the work, and that it will not be erected; (§45c) or if it were erected or were inhabited, its inhabitants will not cease to suffer fears in it, and infirmities, and robbers, and tribulations from death, and the building will split open, and perhaps it will fall down. (§45d) And if Mars aspected [the Moon],[112] and it[113] was ascending (in the circle of the apogee or the short one),[114] burning up and falling down will be feared for it; and let the Moon be then increased in light, because then it will be useful for its owner. (§46) And let the lord of the house of the Moon be aspecting her, likewise let the lord of the Ascendant be aspecting the Ascendant (and they should be cleansed of the bad ones): because if they did not aspect, its owner will not stay in it.

[Destroying a house]

(§47a) And[115] if you wished to destroy a house, let this be when the Moon descends in her own circle, and she were separated from the bad ones and joined to the fortunes; and let the fortune itself be eastern or ascending direct, (§47b) or let the Moon be joined to the lord of her own house out of esteem (that is, from the trine or sextile aspect), so that its destruction will be easier; but in the square aspect and the opposition, its destruction will be more difficult.

[Buying and occupying land]

(§48) And if you wished to buy lands and to enter into them with someone,[116] or you wished to own land so that you might get from someone what

---

112 Reading *eam* for *eum*, following Crofts.

113 Crofts uses "it" for all planets, so it is unclear whether the Moon or Mars is meant. But it is probably Mars, due to the reference to burning and falling down later in the sentence.

114 This parenthetical remark is by the Latin translator. Crofts understands this notion of "ascending" as simply meaning the left-hand side of the chart, i.e., from the IC to the Ascendant, to the MC.

115 Cf. *Carmen* V.7.

116 Crofts reads, "to occupy them with someone."

it renders,[117] let Saturn be in his own exaltation or in his own triplicity or bound, and let Jupiter be in his aspect from a stake[118] or a trine aspect, and make Mars be cadent from them. (§49a) And let the Moon be in the beginning of [the Lunar] month, aspecting Saturn from esteem, increased in number, also in the aspect of Jupiter: this signifies the populating of that land and its renderings. (§49b) Which if you were not able to have the aspect of Jupiter with Saturn, make it Venus instead of Jupiter, and you will make the watery signs fortunate: because if you made them fortunate with the fortunes, they will be better than the airy signs. (§49c) And let the Moon be in her own exaltation or in the Midheaven, and the lord of the Ascendant aspecting her; also, let the Moon and the Ascendant be cleansed of the bad ones and from defects.

[Digging: rivers and wells]

(§50a) And if you wished to divert[119] a river or dig a well, let this be when Saturn is eastern, and the Moon under the earth in the third or fifth, free from the bad ones, made fortunate and received; (§50b) and beware lest there be one of the bad ones in the Midheaven: because this is to be feared, lest the well tumble down or the river flow off.[120] (§50c) And let Saturn be in the eleventh from the Ascendant, and the Moon be joined to a fortune in a fixed sign, and the fortune itself ascending in the circle.[121] (§50d) And the better of the fortunes is Jupiter. Which if you were unable to do this, put Jupiter[122] in the Midheaven, because this is more lasting for the river and more stable for the well.

---

117 This is according to the Latin version, which suggests the rent, either as a portion of what is grown on it or as a portion of the proceeds after the crops are sold. Crofts reads, "you want to take a land or receive it from someone."

118 My sense is that this refers to one of the whole-sign angles from Saturn, not from the Ascendant. Cf. §61a below.

119 *Deducere*. Crofts reads, "make a river flow."

120 Or, "run dry" (Crofts).

121 Crofts reads, "let the benefic be joined to the moon in a fixed, ascending sign."

122 Omitting *(fortunas, id est)*. My reading matches Crofts.

[Planting]

(§51) And if you wished to plant palm trees, or fig trees and the rest of trees, let this be when the Moon is in a fixed sign, and the lord of her house is aspecting her from the watery signs. (§52a) And let the Ascendant be a fixed or common sign, and the lord of the Ascendant [be] ascending and eastern.[123] (§52b) Because if it were ascending and it were not eastern, they will sprout faster but they will make a delay in producing fruit; (§52c) and if it were eastern, descending, they will sprout slowly and produce fruit quickly (and if it were eastern, ascending, they will sprout quickly and produce fruit quickly); (§52d) and if it were western, descending, both [processes] will be slow: namely their arising and the fruit. (§53) And let the lord of the Ascendant and the lord of the house of the Moon be aspecting them,[124] and let them be free of the bad ones and from burning.

[Sowing]

(§54) And if you wished to sow seed (or something [which you never want to lose]),[125] let the Ascendant be a common sign, and its lord in a movable sign, aspecting the lord of its own house, and itself[126] free from the bad ones: because if a bad one aspected it, the seed itself will encounter impediment. (§55a) Therefore, let the Moon be increased in light and number, because if the Moon were under the rays and defective in number, the seed itself vanish and nothing will sprout from it. (§55b) And if it were as I have told you before, with the Moon increased in number, the seed will sprout thinly, according to the quantity of that which is sown.

---

123 It is hard to know which sense of easternness/westernness is meant here. The al-Khayyāt version quoted in al-Rijāl VII.25 specifically mentions latitude ("ascending in its latitude"), but al-'Imrānī's version of the same chapter (II.5.4) simply says "ascending eastern." Certainly the lord of the Ascendant should be outside of the Sun's rays, if not actually rising before him.

124 That is, the lord of the domicile of the Moon aspecting the Moon, and the lord of the Ascendant, the Ascendant.

125 Reading with Crofts for the awkward *quod ultra volueris exercere.*

126 That is, the lord of the Ascendant.

(§56) The fifth sign and whatever is in it in terms of elections

[Conceiving a child]

If you wished to elect the hour of conjoining [sexually], namely so that you would generate a male child, let the Ascendant and its lord, and the Moon and the lord of the house of children, be in masculine signs or in a masculine part of the circle at the hour of conjoining; and you should not put any but a masculine planet in the Ascendant of that same hour or in the sign of children. (§57a) And if you want that it be female, let these significators be in feminine signs and in a feminine part of the circle. (§57b) Which if you could not do this and these significators were diverse (that is, if certain ones of them were in masculine signs, but certain ones in feminine ones), let the lord of the hour and the planet receiving the Moon's disposition be partners with those who had more testimony in the masculine signs and in a masculine part of the circle, and the child will be according to this.

[Miscarriage and abortion]

(§58a) And[127] if there were a dead child in the uterus and you wished to take it out, let this be when the Moon is defective in light, descending from the [belt toward the south],[128] aspecting the fortunes from a trine or square aspect with the aspect of Mars. (§58b) And better and more worthy than this is if the sign of the Moon and the Ascendant were of the feminine signs which are of straight ascension, and not in crooked signs.

[Educating children]

(§59a) And if you wished to hand a child over for training, or to send him to a place in which he might be taught some profession[129] or mathematics,[130] let your election be for this: and let the Moon be aspecting Mercury, and let

---

[127] Cf. *Carmen* V.18.

[128] Reading with *Carmen* V.18.1. Both the Latin and Arabic have her descending from the Midheaven toward the seventh, with the Arabic also calling this "descending from the belt." But *Carmen*'s text makes it clear this means moving southwards in ecliptical latitude, or perhaps even in equatorial declination into the southern signs (i.e., Libra through Pisces).

[129] That is, a trade skill.

[130] *Numerum.*

them be free from the bad ones. (§59b) And let the Ascendant be Gemini or Virgo, and let Mercury be eastern, ascending—and do not let him be descending, nor retrograde, (nor in his own first station),[131] nor in his own descension, nor let him be impeded—and let the lord of the house of Mercury be likewise. (§59c) And you should not make the Moon be descending and deficient in light, because it makes the training slow down; and let the lords of their houses be aspecting them.

(§60a) The sixth sign and whatever is in it in terms of elections

[Exorcisms]

If[132] some devil or an infestation of evil inhabitants were in some place or house, or some terrible thing which is to be feared had followed him (namely the inhabitant), or there were some phantasm appearing, and you wished to remove it from its place or from some man by means of a song[133] or some entreaty[134] or trick, (§60b) beware lest the Moon or the Ascendant be in some one of these signs: namely in Leo and Cancer, in Scorpio and Aquarius. But let the Moon be in the rest outside of these, separated from the bad ones and joined to the fortunes.

[Taking medicines for bowel and digestion problems]

(§61a) And[135] if you wished to elect for taking medicine for [the bowels],[136] that is, those who have [bowel] spasms, or for taking medicine for a pain of the belly, or to make a plaster, let this be when the Moon [or] the Ascendant is in Libra or in Scorpio (and the Moon in it), joined to the fortunes, and you should not put one of the bad ones in the stakes of the

131 This phrase is in the critical Latin edition, but not in Crofts.

132 Cf. *Carmen* V.37.

133 Or more likely, a spell or incantation, following Crofts. That is, an exorcism.

134 Reading with Crofts for *inquisitione* ("search, examination").

135 Cf. *Carmen* V.38.2. Note that §§61a-63 present the first of three schemes for the body: §§65a-d present the second, and §§66a-b the third. See also al-'Imrānī I.2.9 for a little more discussion of this topic.

136 Reading with Crofts, for *ad eos qui mali fuerint*. *Carmen* includes the management of diarrhea and using enemas.

Moon.[137] (§61b) Which if it could not happen but that this does take place, let this be by a trine or sextile aspect, without the opposition and without the projection of the two rays,[138] or the entrance under the rays [of the Sun]: because if it were so, it will make pain and impediment.

[Taking medicines affecting different parts of the body]

(§62a) If[139] however you wanted a cure for the head and whatever comes down from [out of] it (like gargling and vomiting), let the Ascendant[140] and the Moon be in Aries or Taurus, [and the Moon] defective in light and joined to the fortunes. And beware of the aspect of the Sun from the square aspect or the opposition in Aries especially, on account of the heat of the Sun.

(§62b) But for remedies which are projected into the nostrils (like suffumigations[141] and sneezing-powders and so on), let this be when Cancer or Leo or Virgo is ascending, and the Moon is joined to the fortunes; and do not let her be joined to the bad ones, nor to a retrograde planet, nor to an impeded one.

(§63) And if you wanted a cure for the body (namely the hands and feet), let Capricorn or Aquarius or Pisces be ascending, and let the Moon be in them, joined to the fortunes.

[Curing old diseases]

(§64a) And if you wanted a cure for some old disease, let your election for doing this be when the Moon is in her triplicity (and the better one is Taurus, because it is of the diseases of the earth).[142] And let the Moon be cleansed of the bad ones, and let the fortunes be in the stakes of the Moon from Taurus, and it will be stronger and better. (§64b) [And take care] so that the old infirmity goes away and does not return to him who suffers it, and beware

---

[137] That is, in the Moon's whole-sign angles.

[138] Crofts believes this refers to the orbs of the planets, but that does not make sense to me. It probably refers to besieging.

[139] For this paragraph, cf. *Carmen* V.38.1.

[140] Omitting the redundant *Aries*.

[141] That is, smoke or other odors inhaled through the nose (as when we inhale eucalyptus fumes to clear the sinuses). Crofts reads, "snuff."

[142] I am following Crofts's interpretation here, that Sahl wants either the watery or earthy triplicity (since she is a triplicity lord of each), and that the earthy one (of which Taurus is a member) is better.

lest the Moon be joined to Saturn in particular, because it signifies the prolonging of the illness.

[The Moon in signs and regions indicating limbs]

(§65a) And Māshā'allāh said: look, in every cure which you wanted, at the place of the infirmity in the body: which if it were in the part of the head or throat or chest, cure it when the Moon is in Aries, and Taurus, and Gemini (which is the upper part); (§65b) and if it were in the part of the belly and lower in the pubic area and the navel, cure it when the Moon is in Cancer and Leo and Virgo: and this is the middle part; (§65c) but if the disease were in the lower part, namely in the anus and in the lower part of the body, cure it when the Moon is in Libra and Scorpio and Sagittarius. And let the Moon be joined to the fortunes, increased in light and number. (§65d) And if it were a disease from the knees below, up to the feet, cure it when the Moon is in Capricorn and Aquarius and Pisces.

(§66a) And it is even said[143] that every pain which is from the head up to the navel ought to be cured when the Moon is between the stake of the earth, ascending up to the Midheaven, through this ascending part of the circle: and this is the place which is called the "upper part of the circle." (§66b) And if it were from the navel to the lower part of the feet, you will cure him when the Moon is between the tenth, descending to the stake of the earth, which is the "lower part of the circle." (§66c) And let there be a fortune in the Ascendant: because if it were so, it signifies that he would be healed and progress.

[Eyes, touching with iron, cupping, letting blood]

(§67a) And[144] if there were some blister[145] in the eye, or some thing, and it were necessary that it be touched with iron or scarified, and there were a covering[146] over it, or it were in some place of the body for which it is necessary that it be touched by iron (like the cutting of a vein), let this be when the

---

143 That is, by Māshā'allāh (confirmed by al-Rijāl VII.44): it must come from his translation of Dorotheus (see *Carmen* V.27.26).

144 For this set of topics, cf. *Carmen* V.39-40. For §§67a-c in particular, cf. *Carmen* V.40.1.

145 *Vesica.* Or, a pustule (Crofts) or cyst.

146 *Coopertorium.* Crofts reads "film." This probably refers to cataracts.

Moon is increased in light and number, (§67b) unless, however, [it is] in drawing away [fluids] by cupping: because then you will make the Moon defective in light and number, joined to the fortunes. And let Jupiter be above the earth in the Ascendant, or the eleventh, or the tenth or ninth;[147] and beware of [the Moon's] conjunction with Mars if the Moon were increased in light and number. (§67c) If however you were unable to put Jupiter in these places, let him be aspecting the Ascendant. And beware lest the Moon and the Ascendant be in the earthy signs, and lest the Nodes[148] be commingled with Mars (that is, having some communion with Mars); (§67d) and beware then, in the Moon's rising [out of the beams]—that is, when the Moon passes by the Sun through 12°; likewise in the prevention; or that Mars be in the Ascendant when [the doctor] cuts this off; and likewise Saturn, unless Saturn is in the beginning of the [Lunar] month and the Moon is increased in light and number. (§68a) Because if he cut something off from the body, or punctured it, it will putrefy, and the draining or puncturing will not profit the one suffering the infirmity. (§68b) And[149] you should not cut a vein nor extract a tooth if the Moon were in a movable or common sign, clothed by (that is, commingled with) the bad ones, unless the Moon is cleansed of the bad ones or there were a strong fortune with the Moon, or she were joined to it[150] from a trine or sextile aspect.

(§69a) But pains which are in the eyes, like an inflammation and whiteness[151] and the rest of the infirmities which are cured by iron, let this be in the increase of the Moon's light and her number, according to what I told you [above], before this heading. (§69b) And let [the Moon] be cleansed of Mars in the curing of the eye in particular, because if he aspected, let him be held back[152] in this. But if Saturn aspected then, if the Moon were increased in number and light in the beginning of [the Lunar] month, it impedes less. (§69c) If however she were remote from the prevention,[153] make the Moon aspect Mars from a trine aspect, and let her be joined to a fortune. And do not give strength to Mars in any curing of the eyes, because the sages agree

---

[147] The ninth does not appear in the Arabic.

[148] Following Crofts, for "beware lest the Moon and the Ascendant be in earthy signs and *in Gemini*."

[149] Cf. *Carmen* V.39.9.

[150] I believe this means "the benefic."

[151] *Phlegmon et albedo.* Crofts reads, "tumours and leucoma."

[152] *Abstineatur.* That is, do not let the doctor perform the procedure. Crofts reads, "...[Mars] will become more vehement in this."

[153] That is, after the Full Moon has passed.

concerning the impediment of Mars in the head. (§69d) And they even said:[154] everything which is cured with iron, look at its sovereignty in terms of the body,[155] and you should not put the Moon nor the Ascendant in this sign, nor should you touch anything with iron if the Moon were in a common sign nor in a movable one.

[Removing hair]

(§70a) If you wished to shave hairs with ***nūrah***[156] (this is to remove hair with a certain kind of remedy), and so on, let this be when the Moon is in feminine signs, defective in light. (§70b) Which if you were unable to do this, you should not put her in hairy signs (as Aries is, and Leo, and the rest of the bestial signs), and let the lord of the Ascendant be descending from the Midheaven to the stake of the earth.[157]

[Buying slaves]

(§71a) And[158] if you wished to make a purchase of slaves, beware lest the Moon be joined to bad ones, or that there be a bad one below the earth, nor let the Moon be in a movable sign: (§71b) because it signifies that the slave will be unfaithful to [his] master, and he will not be stable in one condition; or he will be fleeing if the Moon were separated from bad ones (except for Libra, which is more useful for this). (§72) But in fixed signs he will be enduring and supportive, and honoring his own master—except for Scorpio, because then he will be a whisperer,[159] and an accuser, and weak in words; and in Leo he will be desiring,[160] and on account of the gluttony of his belly a pain of the belly will happen to him; and he will be a robber. (§73) And let the Moon be in common signs, because this will be praiseworthy (except for Pisces, because he will consider betrayal in his own mind, and unfaithfulness toward his own masters, and he will be absent from them). And fear the con-

---

154 Cf. *Carmen* V.39.8-9.
155 That is, see which sign rules the afflicted part of the body.
156 A depilatory paste (Lat. *annora*).
157 That is, the IC.
158 For this paragraph, cf. *Carmen* V.11.
159 Reading *susurrator* for *susurro*.
160 Or, ambitious. Crofts reads "greedy."

junction of the Moon with the bad ones, because if she were joined with bad ones, it signifies that the slave will be sold.

(§74) And if you wished to [gain something from slaves],[161] beware of the presence of the Moon in the twelve signs,[162] just as it is in the fifth book of Dorotheus.

[Freeing slaves]

(§75a) And if you wished to render a slave free (a freedman), let this be when the Moon is cleansed of defects, increased in light and number, and joined to the fortunes. (§75b) And let the fortune itself be eastern, increased:[163] because if it were western [and] increased, he will find good but pains will happen to him, and he will not cease to have the defect[164] until he dies. (§75c) But in the increase of the Moon's light, he will be sound in body; and in the increase of number, it will signify the discovery of assets. (§76a) And let the Sun and the sign of the Midheaven[165] be cleansed of the bad ones: because if they were impeded, the master will find impediment according to the nature of the sign. (§76b) And let the hour of liberation be when the luminaries aspect each other from a trine or sextile aspect, so that there will be concord and esteem between the slave and master, and he will find good from him: (§77a) for the square aspect is the middle, and the aspect of the opposition signifies that the slave will contend with his master. (§77b) And he who made a slave a freedman when the Moon was impeded, slavery will be better for him than freedom: therefore put the Moon in fixed signs.[166]

---

[161] Reading based on Crofts, for the Latin "make a slave free." The Ar. says "if you want to *gain anything* from slaves from the presence of the Moon in *the twelve signs*, it is in the fifth book of Dorotheus." This is a reference back to *Carmen* V.11, which speaks about the individual signs in purchasing a slave.

[162] Reading with Crofts for the Latin "twelfth sign."

[163] Perhaps increasing in latitude, as with §§51ff (according to al-Rijāl VII.25).

[164] *Deficere.* This verb generally means to be lacking, to fail, to run short, to be weak.

[165] Crofts reads, "the sign *in* mid-heaven" (emphasis mine). This must mean the sign on which the degree of the Midheaven falls, since that sign will be crossing the meridian.

[166] This "therefore" (*ergo*) is misplaced, since the Moon's being unimpeded does not entail that she be in fixed signs. In the Arabic these are two separate statements: slavery is better for someone if the Moon is impeded, *and* one should put the Moon in fixed signs.

(§78a) The seventh sign and whatever is in it in terms of elections

[Marriage][167]

If you wanted the election of a marriage, beware lest the Moon be in the twelfth, and beware lest she be in signs which are not useful for this (which are Aries, Cancer, Capricorn, Aquarius). (§78b) And beware of the signs in which the bad ones and the Tail were, if you wished to be engaged to a woman. And let this be when the Moon is joined to fortunes and she is in a movable sign—and better than all of them together is the sign of Libra.

(§79a) And beware, in getting engaged, lest the Moon be in a fixed sign.

(§79b) But[168] in the [sexual] conjoining (that is, when someone goes in to his wife in order to use her), beware lest she be in a movable sign or in a common one: but let this be when the Moon is in a fixed sign:[169] (§79c) and better than the rest are Leo and Taurus (but Scorpio and Aquarius are not useful for the woman). (§80a) And the middle of Taurus is better [than] its beginning and end; but the first half of Gemini is worse, and the end is good; also, Aries and Cancer are bad, but Leo is praiseworthy (except that each of them will not cease to destroy the assets of his partner). (§80b) And Virgo is useful for a woman who already had been married, but not for a virgin; Libra, too, is bad; but the beginning of Scorpio is useful, and its end bad, because it signifies that their partnership will not be prolonged. (§80c) Also, Sagittarius is bad, and likewise the beginning of Capricorn (its middle and end is good); Aquarius too is bad, and likewise Pisces.

(§81a) And[170] there is no usefulness in marriage if Venus aspected the bad ones. And let this be when Venus is in the houses of the fortunes and their bounds, joined to the lord of her own house. (§81b) If however the lord of her house were a bad one, let her be separated from it, and let Jupiter be elevated over[171] her, or Venus be joined to him from a trine aspect; (§81c) and let the Moon and Jupiter and Venus be aspecting each other by a trine or sextile aspect, and the better of these is the trine aspect (and especially the

---

167 This election in Sahl seems to be a jumble of material on engagement, having sex, and marriage; it is not always clear to me which of these topics Sahl is describing in a given sentence, or why he deals with them in the (uncertain) order he does.

168 See *Carmen* V.16.8-20.

169 Undoubtedly so the sexual intercourse will last a long time.

170 Cf. *Carmen* V.16.21-24, and perhaps V.16.5.

171 That is, overcoming or in the tenth sign from her position (see *Carmen* V.16.22).

triplicity of water). (§81d) And[172] let the Moon be increased in light and number, free from the bad ones, and let Venus always be in her own house or exaltation, or triplicity, or her own joy, or in the conjunction of Jupiter or Mercury, and Mercury made fortunate and strong.

(§82a) Likewise,[173] make the Sun fit just as I have told you before, because from the Sun and the Ascendant is known the being of the man;[174] and from Venus and the Moon and the seventh sign is known the being of the woman. (§82b) Therefore, beware of the aspect of the bad ones to them from the conjunction or the square aspect or the opposition.

(§83a) And[175] if it were a woman [getting] married, let the Moon be in common signs and the work be according to what I have told you before. And let the Ascendant at the hour of the marriage[176] be of the signs which I told you before, so that the Moon would be in them. (§83b) And you should not put any of the bad ones in the Ascendant, nor should one aspect it from enmity; and let one of the fortunes be in the Midheaven.[177]

(§84) And Dorotheus said,[178] "Because then a child will be granted to them in that same year in which they are joined; which if [a watery sign][179] were in the degree of the Midheaven, the woman will become pregnant in the first conjoining."

[Going to war]

(§85) The knowledge of the hours of going out to war.[180] It is necessary that you should make the Ascendant one of the houses of the higher planets, of which the stronger is the house of Mars, if he were in a sextile or trine aspect of the Ascendant. (§86a) And let the lord of the Ascendant be in the

---

[172] Cf. perhaps *Carmen* V. 16. 36-37.
[173] Cf. *Carmen* V. 16. 1-4.
[174] Crofts says "child," indicating the man whose nativity it is. Cf. *Carmen* V.16.1.
[175] For this paragraph, cf. *Carmen* V.16.3.
[176] Lat. *coniugii.* Crofts says "consummation," i.e., the first sexual intercourse after the marriage. *Coniugium* can have this connotation.
[177] That is, in the Midheaven of each nativity: this is a kind of synastry consideration, not an election. See the following footnote.
[178] This must refer to *Carmen* V.16.25-26. Here *Carmen* makes two statements, both in a synastry context: (a) if a benefic is in the Midheaven of each of the nativities of the man and woman, then they will conceive in the year of their first sexual intercourse; (b) if the tenth domicile of each is a fertile (watery) sign, they will conceive at their first sexual intercourse. Al-Rijāl VII.54 has the longer and more correct version.
[179] Following Crofts.
[180] For this topic, cf. Sahl in *Judges* §§7.160 and 7.167.

Ascendant or in the eleventh or the tenth;[181] and beware of the fourth or the seventh and the eighth. And it should not be burned up nor cadent, nor joined to a cadent planet who does not receive it.[182] (§86b) And make the lord of the seventh be joined to the lord of the Ascendant, or put it in the Ascendant or in the second. (§87a) If you wished that they be joined, [then] put Mars[183] in the stakes, so that they would encounter each other and war will fall between them. And join a fortune having a role in the Ascendant, to Mars, so that it might bar him from the Ascendant. (§87b) And you should not go to war unless Mars is in an aspect of friendship to the lord of the Ascendant, like if he himself is the lord of the Ascendant[184] and he is strong and in a good place, and not impeded, nor burnt up, and he is in signs of straight ascension. (§87c) And beware that you do not put him [anywhere] except in the domain[185] of the Ascendant, so that his help will be toward him whom you are sending to war and him who sends the soldiers to war, because they will be saved,[186] by the command of God. (§88a) Even adapt the second and its lord for the soldiers[187] of the one initiating [the conflict], and the eighth and its lord for the soldiers of the enemy; and you should not put the lord of the eighth in the seventh, nor in the eighth, but put the lord of the eighth in the second.

---

[181] The Arabic omits "the tenth."

[182] Crofts makes it sound as though one should avoid the fourth, seventh, and eighth only *if* the lord of the Ascendant is in one of these bad conditions. But this is against normal astrological practices and the logic of passages like §88a below.

[183] Reading with the Ar. The Latin was garbled, putting Mars with the lord of the seventh as part of the previous sentence, and making the lords of the seventh and the Ascendant be conjoined in an angle, in this sentence. Al-Rijāl VII.55 confirms this reading.

[184] Crofts reads, "Only go to war when Mars is in command in his course, that he can be the lord of the Ascendant," with the rest of the conditions following. (Still, it is a good idea for Mars to be in a good aspect to the lord of the Ascendant.) Al-'Imrānī II.1.8 is closer to the Latin Sahl here, while al-Rijāl VII.55 matches Crofts.

[185] Ar. *ḥayyiz*. That is, Mars *should* be in the domain of the Ascendant. This word is used in several ways in medieval astrology. In Arabic it is sometimes a synonym for "sect," but in other cases it refers to a specific sect-related rejoicing condition (*ITA* III.2): a diurnal planet above the earth by day or below it by night, and in a masculine sign (or a nocturnal planet below the earth by day or above it by night, and in a feminine sign). However, this use of *ḥayyiz* may simply mean that Mars should be in the eastern side or hemisphere of the chart: note the following statements about Mars helping out the one going to war (which is represented by the Ascendant), and al-Rijāl, who refers to the "side" (*pars*) of the Ascendant.

[186] Reading with Crofts for "freed."

[187] That is, the *allies* of the one undertaking the action (and the eighth for the opponent's allies). See Crofts, "supporters."

(§88b) And put the Lot of Fortune and its lord in the Ascendant or in the second, and you should not put them in the eighth nor in the seventh. (§88c) And you should not make the Ascendant and the lord of its house impeded, if you began a matter; likewise the dignity of the twelfth-part of the Moon.[188] (§89a) Because it is necessary in the matter of war to make the stars of war fit (that is, Mars and Mercury), also the Moon and the lord of her house. Therefore, look, in the fitness of these things, and you should not be neglectful in this (nor should you hand it over to forgetfulness).

(§90a) And know that if you brought both armies forth[189] for war wisely, just as I have said above, he will gain the victory who, of them, was born at night and in whose nativity Mars had a role:[190] because Mars is the master of wars, and wars are committed to him. (§90b) And perhaps they will enter into an agreement or will give up the war (that is, if the place of their departure to war were good).[191]

[Military actions: buying arms, destroying forts and arms, and ending the war]

(§91) And if you wished to buy arms and the instruments of war, let this be when Mars is in his own house or in the exaltation or his own triplicity, at the end of the [Lunar] month: because the sages were careful lest the Moon be with Mars at the beginning of the [Lunar] month (and at its end, it is more useful).[192]

(§92) And if you wished to overwhelm fortresses,[193] let the undertaking of this work be when the Moon is impeded, without strength.

---

188 This may mean that the sign of the Moon's twelfth-part, and its lord, should be in a good condition and not have malefics in it.

189 *Produxeris.*

190 The Latin is more specific than the Arabic, which reads "who had Mars in his nativity." Al-Rijāl VII.55 describes one who was born at night or who had Mars "in a better place" in his nativity. A nocturnal nativity with a powerful Mars is obviously chosen because Mars belongs to the nocturnal sect and will therefore be of the sect in power. Sahl must be recommending that we look to other favorable sect conditions and rulerships and placements: like Scorpio rising and Mars in the eleventh (and in a masculine sign), in a nocturnal chart.

191 Crofts reads, "if the position of the departure to battle of both of them works favorably." Per al-Rijāl's reading (VII.55), this refers to having a favorable chart on each side of the conflict.

192 Sahl is implying that the Moon should be joined to Mars, which is precisely what al-Rijāl VII.56 says (though he differs from Sahl in certain respects).

193 Crofts reads, "demolish forts," but the idea is the same.

(§93) And if you wished to destroy some instrument of war,[194] begin this when Mercury is impeded and without strength.

(§94) And if you wished to spoil the fighting,[195] let this be when Mars is impeded and without strength.

[Destroying land, idols, and evil places]

(§95) And[196] if you wished to destroy land, begin when the Moon is made unfortunate, not having strength.

(§96) And if you wished to destroy a place of idols and the place in which it is prayed to a devil and not to God, begin this when Venus is impeded and without strength.

(§97a) The eighth sign and whatever is in it in terms of elections

If[197] some man wished to make a will, he should not begin this when the Ascendant and the sign of the Moon are movable, because this would signify[198] that the will's recommendation[199] will be changed. (§97b) But let it be committed [to writing] when the Moon is defective in number and increased in light, and the Moon should not be joined to a planet under the rays (because this signifies the quickness of death). (§98) And more cunning[200] than this [is if] the Moon were with Mars or in his square, or in his opposite, or Mars were in the Ascendant or aspecting it from enmity: because this signifies that the recommendation will not be changed, and the infirm person will die from the same infirmity, and the recommendation will not be perfected after his death [or it will be stolen].[201] (§99) And if Saturn were [positioned] likewise from the Moon and the Ascendant [as Mars was], the life of the man will be prolonged, and the recommendation will be perfected after him, and

---

194 That is, instruments belonging to the enemy.

195 Reading with Crofts for "destroy the opposition of the war."

196 Cf. *Carmen* V.7.1, and al-'Imrānī II.1.5.

197 Cf. *Carmen* V.42.1-7.

198 Reading *significet* for *significat*.

199 Lat. *commendatio*, referring to something entrusted to someone else to carry out. This election is concerned with whether the decedent's wishes will be carried out.

200 *Callidius*. But Crofts reads "worse," which is also suggested by al-Rijāl VII.67. The Latin might be a misread for *certius*, "more certainly so."

201 Adding missing phrase from Crofts.

it will not be changed in his life, nor after his death. (§100) And if Venus and Jupiter were in a like manner from the Moon and the Ascendant, the owner of the recommendation will live longer and change the testament.[202]

(§101) The ninth sign and whatever is in it in terms of elections

[Foreign travel in general]

You[203] should not neglect to direct the foreign travels of men based upon their nativities (namely, upon the Ascendant[204] of every nativity and its stakes). (§102a) And let the Moon be in its Ascendant or in its Midheaven; and adapt the lord of the matter which you seek, and adapt the lord of the year, and the lord of the Ascendant of the root and of the year.[205] (§102b) Which if you did not know what I said,[206] look (for him who came to you) from the lord of the matter which is sought, to see where its place is from the lord of the Ascendant.[207] (§103a) After this, indicate to him the hour suitable to his nativity or question (that is, you should not make the Ascendant of the question and its lord cadent from the Ascendant of his departure). (§103b) And let the Ascendant of the departure be the tenth [sign] of the Ascendant of the question or nativity, if he sought a kingdom; and if he sought a business deal, the eleventh [sign] from the Ascendant of the question; and likewise in every matter which you sought, make that sign the Ascendant for him. (§104a) And let the Moon be in the stakes and in the succeedents of the stakes, if she were free from the bad ones; and let her be aspecting the Ascendant. But if she were impeded, make her be cadent from the Ascendant. (§104b) And let the lord of the Ascendant and the lord of the house of the Moon be in stakes, and let the Moon aspect the lord of her own house. (§105a) And beware lest you put the Moon with the bad ones, or

---

202 Reading with Crofts (and al-Rijāl VII.67) for the garbled and incorrect Latin, "will end his life and the recommendation will follow."

203 Cf. *Carmen* V.21-22, though there are not a lot of clear parallels here.

204 Reading with Crofts, for *ascensiones* ("ascensions").

205 So we must adapt: (a) the lord of the matter in the election chart; (b) the profected lord of the year of the nativity; (c) the lord of the natal Ascendant; (d) the lord of the Ascendant in the solar revolution.

206 E.g., if the traveler did not know his own nativity, so that one could not adapt its features or that of the solar revolution.

207 That is, simply look at the lord of the matter and the lord of the Ascendant in the election chart itself.

in their aspect from the square aspect or the opposition, because the aspect of the bad ones to the Ascendant is easier than their aspect to the Moon[208]— (§105b) and this especially in foreign travel, because her conjunction with Mars in the beginning of the [Lunar] month signifies robbers, or a king,[209] or fire. (§106) And always beware lest you put the Moon in the fourth, but put her in the fifth (if she were made fortunate in this place, there will be less absence in the foreign travel, and more profit in his matters, and more success in it, and also less loosening[210] of his body, and easier for his journey, and more for the safety of him who was with him). (§107) Even the presence of the Moon in the Ascendant in his entrance and departure is horrible, because infirmity will be feared for the one on foreign travel in his journey, or heavy labor in his body.

[Journeys to particular people]

(§108a) If however it was a journey to the king, make the Moon be joined to the Sun or to the lord of the Midheaven from a trine or sextile aspect, and let the Sun be in a good place in the Ascendant, or in the eleventh or in the tenth; (§108b) because if he were cadent, he will not find good from him;[211] and if he were in the ninth, or in the third and the fifth, it signifies labor and middling success. Likewise the western stake and the fourth [stake] signify a scarcity of good, with labor and slowness. (§109) And if you sought nobles and judges, or the leaders of sects (that is, bishops and the rest such), let there be a conjunction of the Moon with Jupiter from the stakes, or in a good place from the Ascendant. (§110) But if your departure were to the leaders of battles, let there be a conjunction of the Moon with Mars from a trine or sextile aspect, and beware of his conjunction and the stakes;[212] and let Mars be in the ones following the stakes.[213] (§111) And if your departure were to those who are of mature age, or to ignoble people, let her conjunc-

---

208 This is an interesting claim I have not read elsewhere.

209 *Regem*, but this should read "tyrant" with Crofts, which makes more sense.

210 Crofts reads, "strain." The Latin idea seems to be that his body will not fall apart under the strain of travel.

211 The Latin reads as though this means, "the traveler will not find good from the king." But Crofts reads as though the *astrologer* will find no good in the *Sun*. In practice it will not make a difference.

212 This probably means Mars should not be in the whole-sign angles of the *Moon*.

213 This suggests the angles of the *Ascendant*.

tion be with Saturn from friendship, and let Saturn be in the succeedents of the stakes. (§112) But if your departure were to women, join the Moon to Venus and let Venus be in a masculine sign; and if you could [make it] so that she is in the places which I told you before for a partnership, do so. (§113a) And if your departure were to writers and merchants and the wise, let the conjunction be with Mercury. And beware lest Mercury be then under the rays, or retrograde, or the bad ones aspect him: (§113b) because[214] as often as the star to whom the Moon is joined, or a planet which is in conjunction with[215] the Ascendant, or the lord of the seventh were slow or impeded, it signifies complications and duress in those ways.

[Sea travel]

(§114a) If[216] however it were a foreign journey by water, let the Moon be in signs of water, and beware of the conjunction of the Moon with Saturn from a stake in foreign journeys of water. And beware of [the malignity of] Saturn, so that he is not in a watery sign, and lest he be fixed in the Ascendant[217] of the departure, or with the Moon. (§114b) Which if it would not come about but that it were so, let the Moon be joined to him with a strong fortune (or in its[218] aspect) from a trine or sextile aspect, or from a stake, so that it would take away the malignity of Saturn due to shipwreck or impediment or a severe tempest.

(§115a) For[219] in sailing the sea you should not make the luminaries impeded, because if they were adapted and safe from the bad ones, and if they were not[220] made fortunate by the fortunes, they signify safety and prosperity. (§115b) But if they were impeded, the man will be dead or lost on his foreign journey. And you should not sail the sea when the Moon is between the old

---

[214] For the rest of this sentence, cf. *Carmen* V.21.7. Reading some of the clauses with the Ar. and al-Rijāl VII.70, as they are clearer.
[215] Reading with the Ar., for "in the opposite of."
[216] For this paragraph, cf. *Carmen* V.25.16-18, and 39.
[217] Crofts reads, "with command over the Ascendant of the departure or the Moon," which probably means being the lord of the Ascendant or the lord of the Moon's domicile.
[218] This probably means "the benefic's aspect."
[219] For this sentence and the next, cf. *Carmen* V.25.34.
[220] This seems counterintuitive: one would expect things to be better if they *were* made fortunate. But *Carmen* V.25.34 does say that the luminaries are free of both the infortunes *and* the fortunes.

Moon and the new,[221] because this is horrible. (§115c) If[222] however he sailed the sea on account of a business matter, adapt Mercury and the Moon especially, and let it[223] be aspecting Jupiter from Cancer or Pisces: (§115d) for Scorpio is horrible in sailing the sea on account of the place of Mars and his enmity against those sailing the sea. (§115e) And fear the bounds of the bad ones in sailing the sea—wherefore in sailing the coast [or traveling over mountains][224] there is less impediment than in sailing the sea.

[Land versus sea travel]

(§116) And[225] if it were a foreign journey by land, the Moon should not be in watery signs, [but should be] cleansed of the bad ones. And beware of the aspect of Mars in a foreign journey on the land,[226] just as I have warned you to beware of Saturn when sailing the sea. And beware lest the foreign journey be of any kind when the Moon is in Scorpio. (§117a) And know that the healthiest [signs] are the earthy signs for him who wished to ride by land, and the watery ones for him who wished to sail in the water of the sea. And Saturn is of greater impediment in the sea, and more strongly so if he did not aspect Jupiter. (§117b) And beware, in a foreign journey on land and by sea, if the Moon is in the last image[227] of the sign of Libra. (Know all of this.)

---

221 *In interlunio.* Crofts reads, "when the Moon is absent." I take this to mean the period when the Moon is under the rays of the Sun.

222 For this sentence, cf. perhaps *Carmen* V.25.33.

223 Mercury or the Moon. This sentence in Crofts says we are to adapt Mercury *or* the Moon, not *and* the Moon.

224 Filling in missing phrase, with Crofts.

225 For this paragraph and the next, cf. *Carmen* V.25.39, and 42-43.

226 Reading with Crofts for "coast."

227 Normally I would take this to mean "face" or "decan," but Crofts provides an argument (based on Arabic usage, p. 184) that this means "paranatellonton," extra-zodiacal constellations rising at the same time. I am unsure about this. At any rate, the last portion of Libra is in the burnt path, so it would be bad no matter what the meaning of "image" is here. But see *Carmen* V.25.7.

[Entering a land or region]

(§118) And[228] know that it is necessary (should you wish to) to adapt the region into which you are entering, so that you adapt the second from the Ascendant while you enter any kind of region which you wanted to: and if you did this, you have already adapted the region. (§119a) And you ought to adapt the Ascendant, and its lord, and the Moon and the lord of the second, if you can; therefore make it be a fortune and let it be above the earth in the ninth or in the tenth or in the eleventh; (§119b) and never should you put it below the earth (namely in the fourth or fifth or sixth), because this is horrible in a foreign journey and in a work which you seek in that region; and let it be above the earth, whether it were a fortune or a bad one. (§120a) And strive so that the lord of the house of the Moon is with the lord of the second above the earth, and you should not put him under the earth, because this is not praiseworthy (unless that which you seek in that region is a matter which you wish to conceal, so that it does not appear until it is perfected). (§120b) And let the Moon then[229] be between 12° and 15° from the Sun—and better yet if the Moon, when she goes out from under the rays up to 3°, is made fortunate. For this is better and more praiseworthy than everything which you need in the concealment.[230] (§121) And if you sought a kingdom in that region, make the Midheaven and its lord fit, with the second from the Ascendant, and the Moon.

[The Moon in the signs for travel]

(§122a) After this,[231] look, in foreign travels (according to what Dorotheus said for foreign travels by water), at the place of the Moon in the signs. Which, if she were in the first face of Aries and the planets aspected (or they did not aspect), it signifies the ease of his matter; (§122b) and if she were in Taurus, the impediment of Mars will be less for her, but if however Saturn aspected, it will impede [the client] and will make a shipwreck for him;[232] and

---

[228] Cf. *Carmen* V.22.7-13, and 2; also Sahl in *Judges* §9.12 (*On Quest.* §9.2). In the Latin of 'Umar's book on nativities (see *PN2* App. A), this is attributed to Māshā'allāh and is a question, not an election.

[229] That is, if you *do* want the matter to be concealed.

[230] In other words, this is the best thing to do in matters of concealment.

[231] Cf. *Carmen* V.25.1-13, and al-Rijāl VII.76.1.

[232] *Carmen* and al-Rijāl do not distinguish the malefics here, simply saying that there will be losses if they aspect the Moon in Taurus.

in the second face of Gemini it signifies slowness, [but] after this safety; but in Cancer, safety from every impediment; (§122c) but in Leo, say impediment—and more strongly so if a bad one aspected; and in Virgo, say prosperity and slowness, and turning back;[233] and in Libra, if she had crossed ten degrees, you should not go on a foreign journey by land nor by sea;[234] and in Scorpio, say sorrow; (§122d) and in Sagittarius, say before the journey is perfected he will turn back;[235] and in the beginning of Capricorn a little bit of good; and in Aquarius, say slowness and safety; and in Pisces say impediment and difficulty. (§122e) And if a bad one aspected, the detriment will increase; but if a fortune aspected, the impediment will be made better and the good will be strengthened. (Know this.)

(§123a) The tenth sign and whatever is in it in terms of elections

[Traveling with a king or prince]

If you wished to set out with a king or prince to a region over which he was already in charge, let this be when Jupiter is in the Ascendant or in the seventh,[236] because this signifies that he who goes will find good and joy in that journey, and he will see what pleases him. (§123b) And beware lest you put Jupiter in the fourth, because this is horrible; and let the Moon and Venus testify to him from one of the stakes. And beware lest Saturn and Mars[237] be in the Ascendant or in one of the stakes. (§123c) And you should not put the Moon under the rays; and beware lest she be with the Tail or with the bad ones, because there is no good in this: for if he went on a foreign journey, he will not return; and if he became infirm, he will die; and if he went off to war, he will be killed or overcome.

---

233 Crofts reads, "safety *but* a slow return" (emphasis mine).
234 But see *Carmen* V.25.7.
235 Crofts reads (with express puzzlement), "say that he will remove its colours." *Carmen* says, "calamities and misfortune from the waves will reach it" (*Carmen* V.25.9-10). Again, *Carmen* is speaking about journeys by sea.
236 The Latin adds, "or in the ninth."
237 Following the Arabic by omitting Venus.

[Attaining a dignity]

(§124) And if you wished to be raised up and moved to a kingdom,[238] let this be with the ascension of Leo,[239] and let the Sun be in Taurus in the Midheaven and the Moon in the Ascendant, joined to fortunes or to the lord of the Midheaven.

[Accession to the throne]

(§125a) And if you wished to introduce a king into the seat of his empire, let the Ascendant be a fixed sign, and likewise the fourth,[240] (§125b) and let the lord of the Midheaven be free from the bad ones, and the lord of the Ascendant in a good place, received, and the lord of the tenth should not aspect the eleventh from enmity. (§126a) And let the Moon be aspecting the lord of her own house from friendship; also the lord of the fourth sign should aspect the fortunes. (§126b) If however you were unable to do it based on what I have told you before, let the Moon be received and the lord of the fourth in a strong place, aspecting the fortunes. (§126c) Which if you could not do this, make it[241] be cadent from the Ascendant and its aspect, and make the fortunes be aspecting the fourth sign and the Midheaven.

[Particular dignities]

(§127) And if you wished to elect the hour so that you would be set over the [tax] revenues,[242] let the Moon be joined to Saturn out of friendship, at the beginning of the [Lunar] month, and let her be in the house of Saturn, and the fortunes aspecting her: because this signifies stability (and that the work will be stable); and let the Midheaven be a fixed sign, so that it will be one work.

---

238 Crofts reads, "enhance your reputation to the ruler." The Latin clearly assumes that the increased reputation has an official post as its goal.

239 That is, Leo should be the ascending sign.

240 This must refer to the degree of the IC, which should be on the fourth sign, a fixed one.

241 This seems to mean the lord of the fourth.

242 Crofts reads, "to supervise levying taxes."

(§128a) And if you wished to secure [military] standards,[243] let the Moon be in the houses of Mars, made fortunate, and let her be aspecting Mars from esteem, with the fortunes, at the end of the [Lunar] month, [with her] joined to them. (§128b) And the confirmation of those standards which are below the king[244] will be more worthy than this if the Moon is cleansed [of the bad ones] and she is not in the houses of the bad ones, nor in Cancer, (§128c) unless it is the standard of the master of the war: and let *this* be in the houses of Mars (and the better and more useful of them is Scorpio, on account of the strength of Mars, and his stability in it).

[Making an enemy of the king]

(§129a) And if you wished to make an enemy of the king, and you yourself were the one being inimical, let this be when the Moon is increased in light, and let the Moon and the Ascendant be cleansed of the bad ones, (§129b) and let the lord of the Ascendant be in an optimal place from the Ascendant, in one of its own dignities, direct and safe from the bad ones (whether it was a fortune or a bad one). (§129c) And let the lord of the seventh be in a bad place from the Ascendant, not aspecting a fortune nor the luminaries.

[Approaching an inimical king]

(§130) But if he were angry with you, you should not appear to him unless the Moon is defective in light, and let [the Ascendant and its lord, and the Moon, be impeded; and let][245] the lord of the seventh be made fortunate in a good place from the Ascendant, so that it is stronger for your own matters.

---

243 These are the flags and standards used on the battlefield to make announcements and give commands.

244 That is, of those who are not of royal status.

245 Adding based on Crofts.

(§131a) The eleventh sign and whatever is in it in terms of elections

[Making friendships]

If you wished to make a friendship with someone, let the Moon be cleansed of the stakes of the bad ones, and let the lord of the eleventh be aspecting the Ascendant from friendship. (§131b) And[246] make the Moon be joined to the essence of the planet which you seek: like Venus for women, and Mercury for writers, and all the circles according to what that brings.[247]

[Seeking something hoped for]

(§132a) And[248] if you wished to seek some thing from any man, let the lord of the Ascendant be aspecting the Ascendant from friendship, and let the Ascendant be a fixed sign or a common one; and let the Moon be in [the Ascendant],[249] or in its triplicity[250] or square aspect; (§132b) and beware of the opposition, nor let [the Moon] be joined to bad ones, or [beware] lest she is not aspecting the lord of her own house. If however the Moon did not aspect the lord of her own house, the matter will not be perfected. (§132c) Therefore, seek things always when the Moon is increased in light and number, and the lord of the Ascendant direct, and the Moon joined to fortunes; if however the fortune were direct and the Moon joined to increased fortunes, it will be increased. (§133) And beware lest Mercury be in a bad condition: because if he were impeded and he were received, it signifies inconvenience and duress, and a second return in the seeking.[251]

---

246 According to Crofts (p. 187), this sentence belongs in the next paragraph, on seeking things from people. Indeed, *Carmen* V.14 (on seeking things from people) does begin with statements about the Moon and then combines her with different planets for different types of people.

247 Reading with Crofts for "will come for this." Sahl means we should pick the natural significator of the type of person that pertains.

248 For this election, cf. *Carmen* V.14, which however does not match it closely.

249 Following Crofts, instead of having the lord of the Ascendant be in the Ascendant—which would have contradicted the previous instruction.

250 I.e., in a whole-sign trine.

251 This last clause seems to be rendering the Arabic, "it indicates displeasure in the request and a mean refusal." The Latin (and not the Arabic) seems to mean that he will be rebuffed once and have to try again.

(§134) And make the Moon be joined to the planet to which your matter pertains: like the Sun for a king and Mars for generals and those making war (likewise regarding the remaining lords of the circles).

(§135) The twelfth sign and whatever is in it in terms of elections

[Buying animals]

If[252] you wished to buy a beast, let this be when the Moon is joined to fortunes and they are direct and eastern, ascending; and beware the conjunction of the bad ones, because then it is to be feared concerning the beast. (§136a) And if it were tamed and already ridden, buy it when the Ascendant is a common sign and the Moon in a fixed sign (except for Aquarius and Scorpio). (§136b) And let the one to whom she is joined, be direct [and] ascending, so that the beast might increase in price and body: because if it were retrograde ascending, there will be diminishment in the body of the beast but the price will be increased; and if it were direct descending, it will be increased in body and the price will not be appropriate for it. (§137) But if the beast were untamed, that is, not ridden, let the Ascendant be a common sign and the Moon in a movable sign, joined to a fortune; after this, do just as I told you before in the first heading.[253]

[Hunting and fishing]

(§138a) And if you wished to go out to hunt, go out under a common sign, and let the lord of the seventh be defective[254] and descending, and let it be in the succeedents of the stakes: because if it were cadent, it signifies that the prey will escape after he caught it. (§138b) And let the Moon, in every departure to hunt, be separated from Mars, made fortunate in an optimal place from the Ascendant. And you should not go out to hunt if the Moon

---

252 *Carmen* V.12 is a short chapter on buying animals, but bears little resemblance to this. To my mind there is ambiguity in this election, because it recommends that the planet to which the Moon applies be ascending (probably in its epicycle or apogee), which increases the price. But the increase in price should benefit the seller, not the buyer.

253 This must mean in the first sentence of this chapter, i.e., §135, using the same criteria of ascending, descending, *etc.*

254 Crofts reads, "decreasing."

were at the end of the signs, nor void in course, nor in a movable sign. (§138c) And beware lest the lord of her own house does not aspect her: because if it did aspect her, it will signify ease for him in the matter.

(§139a) And make Mercury be cleansed of the bad ones in a hunt by water; if however you wanted a hunt in the mountains, let the Moon be in Aries and its triplicity; (§139b) if but it were a hunt for birds, let the Moon be in Gemini and its triplicity, joined to Mercury or separated from the same Mercury, [with] him descending: because this is better.

(§140a) And if you wanted a hunt by sea, let this be when the Ascendant is a common sign, and its lord in a watery sign; and beware lest the Ascendant be a fiery sign. And let the Moon be aspecting the lord of her own house. (§140b) And know that the impediment of the Moon with Mars in a hunt by sea will be worse and of more scarce profit: therefore beware of the impediment of Mars in a hunt by sea (and beware of the impediment of Saturn in a hunt by land). (§140c) Also, were you to make Venus and the Moon fit, and Mars did not impede them in a hunt by sea, the catch will be doubled (by its owner)[255] and multiplied, and its owner will gain the greatest wealth, and the hunt will prosper by means of its owner: (§140d) therefore let the Moon be joined to Venus, and let Mercury be with her; and if however Mercury were impeded by Saturn, it will not impede this. And beware lest Mars be in a watery sign and the Moon be joined to him, or Venus be joined to Mars.

[Fleeing or performing concealed actions]

(§141a) If[256] however you wanted to take flight or perform a concealed work, and [for] everyone who wished to flee or be hidden: let this be when the Moon is separated from the bad ones and joined to the fortunes. And let the Moon be joined to Saturn under the rays, and let her be joined to the fortunes at the time of her exiting from under the rays.[257] (§141b) And the

---

255 That is, the one undertaking the action. Arabic authors frequently speak of the client as the "master" or "owner" of the question or election.

256 Cf. *Carmen* V.5.3-4.

257 Crofts makes this last clause pertain to *Saturn*, not the Moon: "when he is joined to a benefic on emerging from the rays." But it seems to me that the statement applies better to the Moon. This was also mentioned before in §30a-b with specific reference to the Moon.

luminaries, if they were to arise[258] over some matter, they will uncover it and make it appear: therefore beware of their aspects in a like way.

[Pursuing fugitives]

(§142) And[259] if you sought someone fleeing, let this be when the Moon is joined to the bad ones or she is going out from under the rays: and in her going-out [from the rays] let her encounter a bad one from the square aspect or the opposition or conjunction;[260] and you should never put the Moon nor the planetary receiver of the disposition[261] in the fourth.

(§143) On that which is not in the twelve signs in terms of elections

And[262] if you wished to write a letter, let this be when the Moon is joined with Mercury, cleansed of the bad ones; and let Mercury be strong and made fortunate, not retrograde, nor impeded, and let him and the Moon be cleansed of the bad ones.

The *Book of Elections* of Sahl bin Bishr ends.

---

258 *Orta fuerint.* See the version of this statement in al-Rijāl VII.73. It must refer to the notion (in *On Quest.* §7.13 and *Carmen* V.35), that a luminary in or aspecting important places indicates the discovery of a thief or recovery of goods.
259 Cf. Sahl in *Judges* §7.72 (*On Quest.* §7.10). This is probably based on Māshā'allāh's translation of *Carmen*, as both al-Khayyāt and "Dorotheus" have similar passages (*Judges* §§7.77 and 7.78, respectively).
260 The Arabic omits the conjunction.
261 That is, the planet to which she (or any other planet) applies.
262 Cf. *Carmen* V.15.

THE BOOK OF CHOICES
AL-'IMRĀNĪ

[Prologue]

IN THE NAME OF THE LORD. 'Ali bin Ahmad al-'Imrānī said: You have asked me, my dearest, that I should compose a book for you on choosing hours according to the methods of the astrologers in every beginning of works. And therefore I have compiled this book, one better than all of those in which the ancients agreed.[1] And I have put two treatises in it:

> The first treatise is on the advantages of the elections of hours, and how one must choose for those whose nativities are known, or how [you must choose] for those who make interrogations about those things which they want to undertake, and what are the hours in which whatever was undertaken, is ended.[2]
>
> The second treatise [is] on particular elections, such as entrances into estates[3] and departures from them, or beginning a journey, and what is like these. And I have organized it in a clear order, to the extent that we may discover whatever we want to find.

Now, this book (namely, of elections) is not like a book on nativities: in [nativities], we are able to put off [certain topics] until we review [our] books.[4] But in this science, it sometimes happens that the haste to choose [a time] is so great that it is not permitted to look in one's books. And I believe that this method of treating [the subject] will please you not a little, after it has been made evident to you.

---

[1] *Convenerint.* Throughout the book, al-'Imrānī highlights disagreements (or at least, multiple opinions) among the older authorities.

[2] That is, prediction: see I.5 below.

[3] *Villas.*

[4] *In quibus differe possumus donec libros revolvamus.* This sentence must be read with the next one. Al-'Imrānī seems to mean that with nativities, many topics will not be relevant until much later, or we have lots of opinions to review, and we can wait until later to advise a client on some area of life; but in elections, a client tends to have a pressing need, and we must be able to give clear guidance quickly.

TREATISE I

The first treatise has five sections,[5] the first of which is whether elections are useful; the second, on the elections of all undertakings; the third, on the elections of men whose nativities are known; the fourth, on the knowledge of whether what is asked about will be ended well or badly, and on his election after an interrogation that is made; the fifth, which hours we trust so that what was begun, would be perfected.

Chapter I.1.0: Whether elections are useful

Through evident reasoning, it has been proven by Ptolemy the king[6] that the works of the judgments of the stars are certain. And I have added certain proofs in my own book, while I have laid out the words of Ptolemy. Therefore, it is necessary that a portion of this wisdom (namely, that of elections) be useful, if we concede that the work is true. For from this work it is agreed that if we knew the hour of the impregnation of some woman or of an animal, we will know through it what would become of this seed until it receives breath,[7] and what [would happen] until it would go out of the uterus, and what could become of it up until the day of death, just as he says in [his] work on astrology: but astrologers did not judge through nativities [in this way], since they could hardly be certain of the hour of impregnation. However, Ptolemy says the hour of the nativity signifies a second[8] beginning.

---

[5] *Differentiarum.* In my own treatment, I will label these as "chapters."

[6] In this paragraph, al-'Imrānī is referring to the discussion of conception charts and birth charts in *Tet.* III.2. Ptolemy suggests that while the conception chart might be called an original beginning (*archē*), the birth chart may be considered a kind of inception (*katarchē*) which builds upon it. Since *katarchē* is the standard Greek word used for what we call "elections" or "choices," the thrust of al-'Imrānī's discussion is to say that electional astrology has as much validity as natal astrology—and he wants to use Ptolemy to prove it. Moreover, this use of Ptolemy suggests a reliance on naturalism or physical causes to explain why certain times have various qualities. I explain this argument a little bit more in my Introduction.

[7] *Inspiretur.* Al-'Imrānī seems to mean the traditional view that the soul or living-giving breath enters the fetus sometime during the pregnancy. See for example Abū Bakr I.2 (in *PN* 2).

[8] Reading *secundum...initium* with Paris 7413-I for *omne* (Madrid) and *iudicium* (Paris 16204). Ptolemy considers the nativity to be a *katarchē*, a beginning *relative to* or *deriving from*, the true *archē* or beginning: conception.

Since this is so, when we elect the hour of conception for someone by following the judgments of the books of nativities, good things will befall the native, which the astrologer will have pronounced according to the books of nativities; and in the same way we will speak about the planting of trees, and about sowing seeds, and also in the building of cities, and also in every inception.

[Chapter I.1.1: For whom one must elect]

All astrologers[9] are agreed that one should elect for no one whose nativity is unknown—which to me does not seem consistent.[10] Know that it is good to elect according to nativities, but in every [case of] two good works, if it is impossible that what is best should be had, one must not overlook the other good which is possible to have. For those doing this[11] are likened to a certain traveler who, though he was able to go by horse, since he was not able to mount on a golden sedan chair, nor [have] a tent which would protect him from the heat of the Sun's rays, after dismissing the horse the stupid man went along on his journey [on foot]. In the same [way], one must have confidence with respect to the election of those whose nativities are unknown, and those whose nativities are made clear, except that there are certain things necessary for those whose nativities are made evident with us.

[Chapter I.1.2: Universal features of elections]

And[12] the root which is necessary in each [kind], and about which we have confidence with respect to those things which we undertake in them, is that we must undertake to adapt the universal things: that is, [1] the Moon (who has a signification in every beginning, place, time, and for every man), and [2] the Sun (who is in charge in the circle, like a king),[13] and [3] the star which signifies the matter which we want to undertake (as is Venus in getting be-

---

[9] This opening hearkens back to Sahl's *On Elect.* §1, which also speaks of other unnamed astrologers who prefer not to elect for unknown nativities. But like al-'Imrānī, Sahl (§§3a-5a) believes that we can use the chart of a question as a root for proper elections. (Al-'Imrānī also believes that certain general things can be done for people with unknown nativities, as we will see.)

[10] *Congruum.*

[11] Namely, those who overlook the next-best option.

[12] For this paragraph, cf. Sahl §§20-21c.

[13] That is, the Sun is in the middle of all of the planets, in the order from Moon to Saturn.

trothed, Jupiter for assets), and likewise [4] the sign which signifies that nature which we are undertaking, so if we want to enter the sea, one must adapt a watery sign (that is, if [the sign] were cleansed of the bad ones and their aspects, let it be made the Ascendant, or let the Moon or the lord of the Ascendant be in it, and other things like these).

However,[14] things which are not extremely necessary (but some must be considered), both for those whose nativities we knew, and for those whose [nativities] we do not know, are namely these: that we should choose a masculine sign in masculine matters, and a feminine one in feminine matters, and what is like these.

[Chapter I.1.3: Particular features of elections]

And if we set forth[15] the fitness of these universal things (that is, the Sun and the Moon, also the star which naturally signifies the matter to be commenced), then one must adapt the particulars.

The first of them is that we adapt the house which signifies the matter about which it is asked. And for those whose nativities we knew, one must adapt the house which signifies that in the root of the nativity as well as the house which signifies it at the hour of the election.[16] But for those whose nativities are not known, we will adapt the house signifying the matter at the hour of the election.

But [one must also] adapt the Ascendant and the fourth and their lords:[17] not so much that the matters may be perfected, but even so that the body and soul would be made fit, and the end—whether the nativity is known or not.

But which house[18] is said to be the one signifying [the matter] at the hour of the election and in the nativity, is established as being not of the universal things, and here is such an example: the second house from the Ascendant signifies assets in this hour and in that same land; and in this same [land] and

---

[14] Cf. *Carmen* V.4.5, and Sahl §18.

[15] *Praemiserimus.*

[16] For instance, suppose it is a fifth-house election, and the client has Capricorn in her natal fifth. But, for some reason at the time of the election, it is best to have (say) Cancer on the fifth. In that case, we should make sure that both Capricorn and Cancer are made well fit at the time of the election.

[17] Cf. Sahl §26.

[18] Al-'Imrānī, means "which domicile," or "exactly which degrees of a sign."

in this same [hour] it will be the house of brothers in another land; and this same house, in another hour in this same land, signifies travel or another thing different from this. But Jupiter is the significator of assets in every hour and land, [and] so Venus even [signifies] women. Also, the houses of the planets signify the same thing that their lords do, and by the same reasoning for the rest.

[Chapter I.1.4: Two objections based on unknown nativities]

[1] Against this, the sophist says: "It is possible that one of the bad [planets] will rule over an unknown[19] nativity, and [if] we are always making the bad ones cadent and in a bad place, in this way adversity will befall the owner of this election."

We respond to [the sophist]: "We cannot listen to what you are saying. For it is possible, on the other hand, that good planets rule. Which if we [instead] would make [both] good and bad ones strong in his elections,[20] evil will germinate, and thus we will be the cause of death and adversity for him.

"And another thing: those whose nativities are ruled by bad ones are few, for there are five fortunes, but [only] two bad ones.[21]

"Look: many[22] men are going to enter the sea,[23] and they have consulted an astrologer so that he may elect their hour. On account of what we have said before,[24] the astrologer denied counsel to them, [so that] all of them going away were endangered, and thus the one who denied them counsel was the cause of their death: and perhaps if he had elected for them, they would not have been endangered. For God, creating evil, has given a remedy: he has barred us from giving ourselves over to death."[25]

---

19 Reading *ignotae* with Madrid for *in nocte* in many other *mss.*

20 That is, if we took the objector's implicit advice and made the malefics strong as well, on the chance that they ruled the nativity.

21 Obviously Mars and Saturn are naturally malefic, and al-'Imrānī is viewing the rest of the planets as benefic (even though Mercury is not necessarily benefic in himself).

22 The various *mss.* use inconsistent numeral designations or demonstrative pronouns, so it is impossible to tell how many al-'Imrānī means.

23 Cf. *On Elect.* §§6a-b.

24 That is, if we refuse to elect for people with unknown nativities, for fear of denigrating a malefic planet.

25 I am not sure what the role of this sentence is, though it certain suggests that it is our duty to do what we can to avoid facing death senselessly. The theological bit about God creating evil is also troubling. But Paris 7413-I reads, *concedens* ("granting"). So, it could mean, "granted that there is evil, God has given a remedy…".

[2] To[26] those who deny that elections are useful, we would say: "If someone asked you to elect an hour for him which was the worst in every way, and you know that after one or two hours or more you could choose an hour for him which is most certainly good, and you say, 'We are not choosing that future hour for you (which is most certainly good), but go out in this hour because perhaps it will not harm you,'" the error of this is clear to all. For if they say [to themselves], "*perhaps* it will not be harmful," there is already a doubt as to whether it is good or bad. Put another way, there is no doubt but that [an election] is useful and secure to all.[27]

They are similar to one of whom it was asked which of two paths was more secure, and there were always wolves in one, but with respect to the other he was uncertain as to whether there were wolves in it or not. And he said to the querent that he [should] enter the one in which he knew there were always wolves, saying "go here, because perhaps you will not find wolves." And we have opposed this, since we have agreed with their own words:[28] for one must say that it is not to be doubted but that a bad hour is always a bad hour.

But among the hours which are chosen, certain ones are of perfect good, certain ones of less perfect good, and certain ones give perfected good, certain ones mediocre good.[29] But if we chose a perfect election for someone, for what he wants to begin, with which his nativity agrees, and while the revolution of his year is prosperous, all things will come out as prosperous on every side. But if on the other hand the nativity or the revolution (or each) do not testify to that good, it is possible that the election is so strong by nature, that he can wholly destroy that malice, like an antidote[30] destroys all poison; and it is possible that it would diminish the evil, just like [a medicinal] syrup does; and it is possible that he would incur neither good nor evil (and this on account of the strength of [his] nativity). Finally, however, it is impossible but that a good election should take away from evil, however small.

---

26 This paragraph is a statement of professional responsibility.

27 That is, by agreeing in principle that there is such a thing as a good or bad time, astrologers who rely on their ignorance of a birth chart to refrain from making an election, are insincere and unprofessional.

28 Reading *consensimus* with Madrid and Paris 16204, for *concessimus* ("we have yielded to") in other *mss.*

29 This seems redundant. Al-'Imrānī seems to want these categories to match the scenarios below, but to my mind something might be wrong with the Latin text.

30 *Tyriaca*, from the Ar. *tiriāq*.

But if his nativity and revolution was known to us, and we knew that it would only be adverse for him, and that he wholly could not avoid what would happen, it is better that we choose a good hour for him, just as it is for certain people growing ill, to whom we offer medicine: for if did not profit the sick person, [at least] it will not harm.

Which if the nativity and revolution signified much good in what he wants to do, and he began to work in a bad hour and in a bad election, it is possible that the hour is so bad that the whole goodness of the nativity and the revolution is destroyed, or perhaps is diminished by that, or it will profit nothing.

It is clear therefore from what has been set out, that a good election cannot hinder, and equally a bad one cannot profit. And from this we will know that a good election should absolutely not be overlooked, by the aid of God.

Chapter I.2.0: On the general works of elections for every man

An election is nothing but a beginning for all undertakings, not [something] after an undertaking: like the hour of building a home, the beginning of which is when the foundation begins to come to be or be measured.[31] And an election is according to nobility and position, and time, place, and age, and according to the things themselves which must be chosen. For an election by a king is not to be likened to an election by a merchant, nor that of a boxer to an election by a scribe, nor that of builder to be likened to that of a peasant, nor will we elect in the month of March for one wanting to sow in the winter, and we will then elect for the same man wanting to sow in the mountains. And in the same way, one must not elect for a man of complete age, that he should beget a son, nor for a sterile or [very] young man that he should beget [a child], nor for a little old woman, nor for those like these. For the effect of the support[32] does not appear except in things which are able to take on its signification.

But a perfect election for beginning every matter, is the adaptation of: [1] the Ascendant and of [2] the fourth and [3-4] their lords, [5] the Moon and

[31] Bonatti criticizes al-'Imrānī here, pointing out that although measuring and such "are preparatory for building, still they are not *of* the building" (*BOA* Tr. 7, Part 1, Ch. 6). Bonatti believes the proper beginning of a building (and where the election should come in) is in the laying of the first stones or the beginning of the actual building process.

[32] *Firmamenti.* That is, the electional chart (or rather, the conditions described in it). I suspect that al-'Imrānī or his sources may have come from a Greek text which used the word *hypostasis* here.

[6] her lord, [7] the Sun too, and [8] the Lot of Fortune and [9] its lord, and [10] the planet which naturally signifies that for which [the time] is chosen, and [11] the house signifying it[33] and [12] its lord. If however you wanted rather to make a matter fit so as to destroy it, we destroy its significators with such a destruction that it agrees with destroying a thing, such as will be explained in what follows.

[1] The Ascendant and [3] its lord, and [5] the Moon, and [8] the Lot of Fortune, signify the manner of the thing which we are beginning; however, the Ascendant and its lord in particular signify the body of the one undertaking [it], and [his] soul.[34] Therefore, the signification of the thing to be begun is just as we have said: that is, if the Ascendant were good or bad, or its lord, there will be what it signifies according to their condition, and the Moon will participate with them in this, and the Lot of Fortune, according to what their condition was. And if the Ascendant and its lord were void in course from a good one or bad one,[35] and the lord of the Ascendant was middling in between each (that is, between strength and weakness), then the signification will belong to Moon according to her condition in terms of fortunes and the bad ones—and the Lot of Fortune will participate with her. But if the Moon were void in course just as we said about the Ascendant,[36] the signification will belong to the Lot of Fortune according to the signification of all.[37] And I view it that the significations of all (a reminder of which preceded) will always be mixed together, and of them we prefer [them] and make [them] fortunate just as we have set forth in the reminder of them.

And [7] the Sun signifies kings and nobles and lasting things, and we should very concerned with his fitness and strength in what we have said before. And [10] the planet which signifies the matter being chosen, will manage that matter according to its own condition—and likewise [11] the house of the matter and [12] its lord.

---

33 Omitting *in ascendente* ("in the Ascendant"), which makes no astrological sense. The Ascendant and its lord were already covered.

34 Cf. Abū Ma'shar on the Ascendant (of the solar revolution) as signifying the body, and its lord the soul (in *PN3* II.2).

35 I believe this means that it has equal influence from benefics and malefics; but it could also mean that no planet aspects the rising degree within orbs.

36 If we go by the statements before, this means that the Moon has equally benefic and malefic influences.

37 I take this to mean that the Lot will *take on* the signification of everything.

[Chapter I.2.1: Chief significators according to al-Khayyāt]

Al-Khayyāt the astrologer said,[38] "One must consider the lord of the Ascendant and the Moon: and the one of them which we find to be stronger, we will make it the significator of the beginning. And this is an opinion which we should consider, and what would follow from that.[39] For if the lord of the Ascendant were weak and made fortunate, and conjoined to fortunes, and the Moon strong and not made fortunate, and joined to the bad ones, I would make the significator the Moon,[40] and we will judge evil."

But this is an error. For we ought to be judging good and prosperity, and the partnership given to the Moon is moderate. But if the Ascendant had been strong at that same hour, we would not have looked at the Moon in any way. And therefore we prefer the Moon to be with the bad ones in hunting [a fugitive],[41] and we make the lord of the Ascendant fortunate.[42]

[Chapter I.2.2: Chief significators according to Abū Ma'shar]

Abu Ma'shar said, five things signify the end of the matter. The first of these is [1] the lord of the fourth house; the second, [2] the lord of the house of the Moon; third, [3] the planet with whom the Moon will be joined last, from the sign in which she is;[43] fourth, [4] the lord of the house of the Lot of Fortune; fifth, he indicates [5] the fourth from the sign in which the Moon is.

---

[38] This view actually expresses the opinions of what I have called the "Māshā'allāh group" (Māshā'allāh, Sahl, al-Khayyāt) and 'Umar in choosing the significator of a *question*: see *Judges* §§A.130, 1.1, and its Appendix C from Māshā'allāh's *On Reception* Ch. 2. I am not sure that al-Khayyāt ever intended it to apply to elections, but we will see that al-'Imrānī criticizes just that application.

[39] In other words, al-'Imrānī wants to be very careful about the difference between strength and benefic/malefic quality. He believes that favoring strength (such as being angular) over quality is wrong, and is about to explain why.

[40] That is, *if* we follow al-Khayyāt's advice.

[41] I have added this material in brackets because the hunting material does not refer to making the Moon weak—but the material on hunting a fugitive does (see II.13.2-3, and Sahl §142), and al-'Imrānī himself repeats the point in the Preface to Treatise II below.

[42] Al-'Imrānī has perhaps been overly brisk here. He does in fact think the Moon is highly important, but she is not the or a chief significator of the *client* or agent of the action. But because al-Khayyāt does treat her this way, it is possible that he will not even look at the Moon at all if the lord of the Ascendant had been strong. Rather, al-'Imrānī believes that the Moon signifies the course of the matter itself, so that in some instances we will want to make her weak or strong no matter what the lord of the Ascendant is doing.

[43] That is, before she finally leaves the sign in which she is. After connecting with that planet, she will be void in course.

(And a certain one of the moderns[44] says that one must add the lord of the fourth from the place of the Lot of Fortune.)

But if the Ascendant were the significator of the matter chosen (in the way we have set it out), the significator of the end of the matter will be [1] the lord of the fourth from the Ascendant, if however it aspected the fourth; if not, then [2] the lord of the house of the Moon will signify the end, if it aspected the Moon. Without that, the significator of the end will be [3] the planet to which the conjunction of the Moon arrives last, from the sign in which she is. But if she were void in course, the significator will be [4] the lord of the Lot of Fortune, if it aspected the Moon. But if it did not aspect [her], it will be the lord of the fourth house [from the Moon],[45] if it aspected the Moon. But if not, [2] the lord of the house of the Moon will signify the end, and we will commingle with it all of the other significators of the end.

And if the Moon were the significator of the chosen matter just as we said before,[46] the significator of the end of the matter will be [2] the lord of the house of the Moon, if it aspected her; and if it did not aspect, we would follow through in the order which we set forth before [3-5].

And if the Lot of Fortune were the significator, [4] the lord of the Lot of Fortune will be the significator of the end of the matter, if it aspected the Moon. [And] the signification will always return to [2] the lord of the house of the Moon.

But according to the one who wanted to attribute the signification to the lord of the fourth from the place of the Lot of Fortune, we should give it a signification after [4] the lord of the Lot of Fortune.

And if the Moon were in a sign, conjoined to any planet, degree by degree, [3] that planet itself will be the significator of the end, before [2] the lord of the sign of the Moon.

[Chapter I.2.3: Chief significators according to al-Kindī]

And al-Kindī said,[47] make the Ascendant and its lord fit, and the lord of [the lord's] house, and also the Moon and her lord, and the lord of the house

---

[44] This person's identity is currently unknown.

[45] I have added this because it follows the logic set forth in the previous paragraph, and because we have already looked at the lord of the fourth.

[46] See I.2.0 above.

[47] For this paragraph, al-'Imrānī primarily has *Forty Chapters* §§141-43 and 552 in mind. For al-Kindī, the place of the Ascendant or Moon or Lot signifies the beginning of the

of *her* lord, and likewise the house of the Lot of Fortune, and the house signifying the matter for which you are choosing, and their lords, and the lord of their lords.

And he said[48] that the Ascendant signifies the beginning of the condition of the one from whom the interrogation comes, but its lord [signifies] the middle, and *its* lord the end of the matter.

And[49] in the same manner, he used to favor significators from the Lot of the matter.

He[50] even often used to attribute a signification to the stronger planet in the places—for example, the releasing [places], which are the Sun and the Moon and the Lot of Fortune, and the Ascendant, and the place of the conjunction or prevention [which preceded the chart]. And he used to make that one the significator of the one who was asking.

And[51] he used to make the planet [which was] stronger in the place of the matter, the significator of the matter.

Sometimes[52] he even used to make the planet ruling in the ascending degree, the significator of the one asking.

[Chapter I.2.4: Chief significators according to 'Umar al-Tabarī]

But the consideration of 'Umar al-Tabarī[53] was not so subtle as was that of al-Kindī and Abū Ma'shar. For he used to adapt everything which we said before ought to be made fit, and he used to make [*all* of them] partners in the signification.[54] But to the fourth house and its lord, he used to give especially the signification of the end of the matter, and likewise to the house of the Moon—and in this the majority of the astrologers who have spoken about elections, agreed. However, we cannot make matters fit according to [all] opinions. Therefore, we ought to adapt what we can, after we have adapted those things which are very much necessary.

---

affair for that matter; the lords of these places represent the development or middle of the matter; the lords of those lords, the end. See also al-Rijāl VII.2.1.

[48] *Forty Chapters* §143.

[49] *Forty Chapters* §141.

[50] *Forty Chapters* Ch. 3.2.

[51] *Forty Chapters* Ch. 3.1.

[52] This would seem obvious; I am not sure what section in *Forty Chapters* al-'Imrānī might mean.

[53] Source unknown at this time.

[54] Adding in brackets, and adding emphasis, to bring out al-'Imrānī's point: 'Umar simply said to use everything.

Abu Ma'shar said,[55] it is impossible for us to make all twelve houses fit, for the malefic planets cannot be removed from the heavens; but we ought to make the degree of the Ascendant and its lord fit, and the degree of each luminary. For if these were impeded, there will be no remedy.

Therefore,[56] it appears that the fitness of the house of the end of matters is very necessary *after* the adaptation of the aforesaid, then the Midheaven,[57] then the Lot of Fortune (and these belong to the body of the one beginning); but so that the matter would be perfected, one must adapt the planet which signifies the matter,[58] and the house which signifies that matter, and its lord.

Chapter I.2.5: On the fitness of a sign

Also, the fitness of a sign (when it will not be said to be bad, and that it is far from every impediment) is that the sign be free of the bad ones[59] and their aspects (the square and the opposition), nor is it besieged between the two bad ones (and this is that there would be a fortune or its trine or sextile ray in it):[60] it will be increasing the good. And by how many more those fortunes were, its good will be that much greater (and if, in addition to this, the sign were cadent from the angles, or besieged between the two bad ones, it will harm not at all or [only] a little bit). And if the good planets aspected it from a square or opposite, it will not useful (and especially from the opposite). But if the good ones and bad ones aspected it, we will commingle their significations, and the one which was stronger will obtain the victory. Which if they were equal in strength, the sign will be as if a fortune or infortune did not aspect it [at all]. And if the planet aspecting the sign had some dignity there, it will be better.

---

55 Source unknown at this time.

56 This seems to be al-'Imrānī reflecting on the passage from Abū Ma'shar immediately above.

57 But he has not mentioned this before, and this may be an error. On the other hand, al-'Imrānī may be referring to the importance of putting the Midheaven on the tenth sign.

58 By general signification, such as Jupiter for wealth or Venus for love.

59 That is, by their bodily presence in the sign.

60 Besieging may happen by degrees or by sign (see *ITA* IV.4.2). Here, al-'Imrānī is saying that a sign will be besieged if the malefics fall on either side of the sign, with the benefics being in aversion from it; but the sign will be rescued from besieging if a benefic casts a sextile or trine ray into it. See the figure below.

And the lord of the sign must be made fit, for the reason that it has two significations: namely the signification of the place in which it is, and its natural one.[61]

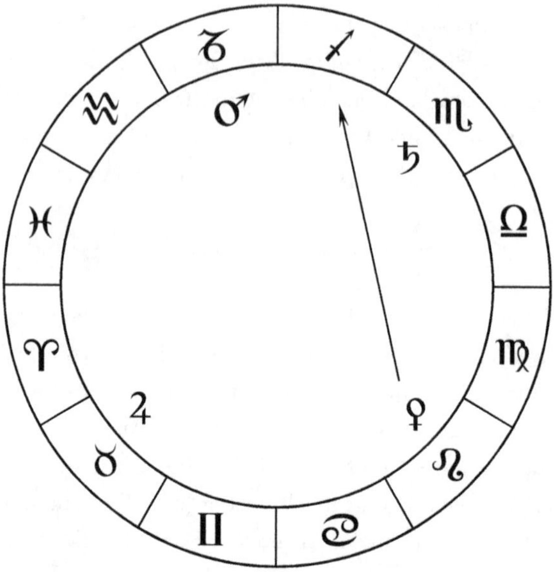

Figure 12: Venus rescuing Sagittarius from besiegement by body

Chapter I.2.6: On the fitness of a planet[62]

The fitness of a planet is when nothing bad is said about it, [and] every impediment is removed from it: so that it is cleansed of the bad ones, direct, and not weak, nor is it in a cadent nor impeded sign. And if it were cleansed of the bad ones and [also] made fortunate,[63] the place of the end will not

[61] I don't quite think this means its natural significations in the normal sense (such as Jupiter indicating wealth and Venus love): I think al-'Imrānī is referring to the planet's rulership *over* the house we are interested in. In that case, the planet's two significations are: the place it is in, and the place it rules. These are always the two key elements of delineating a planet, beyond what the general meaning of the planet is. But, perhaps the Latin is a little clumsy, and al-'Imrānī *does* mean its natural signification and its location.
[62] For similar lists of these conditions, see *ITA* IV.3-5.
[63] For example, being aspected by benefic planets.

impede it, whatever it was;[64] nor must one say that it is in a bad place, on account of the fortunes which are aiding it. And if it were cleansed of the bad ones, and made fortunate, and strong, and in a good place, then it is said to be virtually of perfect goodness. But if the other fortune assists it, its good will be increased; and if the aspects of the fortunes were to the right, it is more praiseworthy and better (likewise, the right aspect of the bad ones is praised less).[65]

If therefore we have made the sign and the significator-planets fit just as we have said before, the hour of the election will be good and perfect according to what that fitness was.

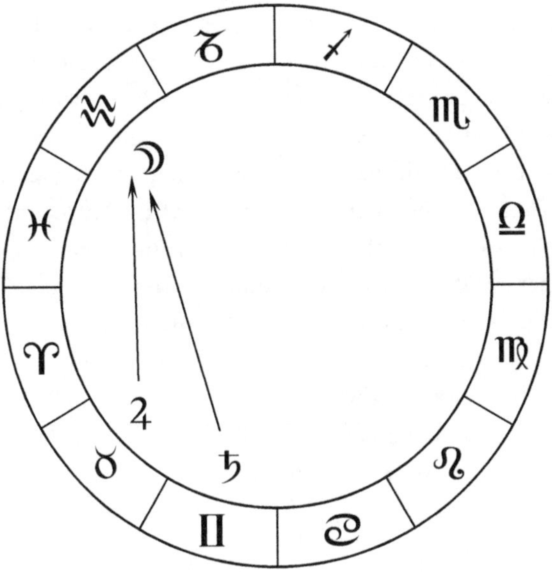

Figure 13: Jupiter and Saturn sending right aspects to the Moon

---

64 Reading *impediet locus* with the other *mss.* for Madrid's *impediet locum*, though I am not quite sure what this means—perhaps that if the place of the end (the fourth) is in a bad condition, it will not matter.

65 Right aspects (sometimes called "dexter") are those cast by a planet to places earlier in the zodiac, to its right as we look at it. Left aspects (sometimes called "sinister") are those cast later in the zodiac, to the left as we look at it. So if the Moon is in Capricorn, Mars in Scorpio will aspect her with his left sextile, while Venus in Taurus aspects her from a right trine. Right aspects are generally considered more powerful, which is why al-'Imrānī suggests the right aspects of benefics are more helpful than their left ones, while right aspects from malefics are more harmful than their left ones.

[Chapter I.2.7: Increasing the fitness][66]

And there are some things which increase and decrease the fitness. But those which increase, are that the sign from which we begin signifies the matter to be chosen, by nature: this is that it be a watery sign in elections of waters, and an earthy one in earthy things (and thus with the rest [of the elements]); and movable in elections of matters which we want to happen quickly, and four-footed in elections of four-footed things—even if[67] we may not be able to take it in the strict sense (and taking it in the strict sense is that we would take the sign having fixed claws for four-footed [animals] having fixed claws, and thus for the rest). And likewise there are certain signs which are appropriate for kings and magnates, such as Aries, Leo, [and] Sagittarius (but especially Leo). If therefore we want to elect for a king, we should make Leo the Ascendant or the tenth. And if we could not, let us return to the class of signs and put Leo, Aries, or Sagittarius in the place. And one must do it in the same manner with the place of the Moon, and the place of the lord of the Ascendant, also the place of the lord of the house of the matter, and the place of the planet naturally signifying the matter. And we ought to consider the proper quality, or, if we could not, the class.[68]

And the houses of the planets signify what their lords do: so the house of Venus[69] signifies taking a wife and nuptials, just like Venus herself, and one must speak in this way about the rest.

This even increases the good: so that the lord of the house of the matter is signifying what the house or its nature does;[70] which if [that] could not

---

66 This subchapter is al-'Imrānī's own version of *Forty Chapters* Ch. 4 (which al-Rijāl has in his own VII.2.1). The first two paragraphs deal with what al-Kindī calls "likeness" or "suitability." The third paragraph deals with what al-Kindī calls the "good fortune" of the significators.

67 *Ita tamen si.*

68 Al-'Imrānī seems to be referring to his example of the royal signs: if we cannot get the best and most precise sign we want (the "proper quality," *proprietas*), we should at least use one from its general class.

69 That is, the domiciles of Venus: Taurus and Libra always indicate nuptials, simply because they are ruled by Venus. Al-'Imrānī probably does not mean that they indicate nuptials directly and immediately, but that such things are included in their typical class of possible significations. If Taurus were the twelfth house, then it would first of all indicate earthy things because it is an earthy sign; but it would also indicate enemies, by actually being in the twelfth house. Indicating nuptials would be one of the possible additional meanings because it is ruled by Venus.

70 I believe al-'Imrānī means the following: that in an election for marriage, let Venus (who naturally signifies love) rule the 7th, or for seeing the king, let the Sun rule the 10th.

happen, let it be signifying the same thing that the Ascendant and its lord do;[71] and they should aspect each other with an aspect of friendship; and likewise, the Ascendant and its lord, or all of them, should be thus, or [at least] some of them. And one must beware lest there be any difference between these two and the other two, or contrariety between the Ascendant and its lord, and between the house of the matter and its lord.

It even increases the good for the Ascendant to be of the sect of the hour,[72] and likewise the place of the significators. And a planet should wholly be in a place of its sex, and in [its] other proper qualities.

And[73] let the Ascendant be a fixed sign if we wanted that [the matter] be strong and lasting; and in the same way let the Moon[74] be in one of these signs. And if we wanted the matter to pass by quickly, nor to remain a long time, let the Ascendant be a movable times, and let the significator (namely, the Moon) be in one of the aforesaid. And the two-bodied signs are in between the movable and fixed, and they signify change and alteration.

And[75] let the Ascendant be a sign of the signs of straight ascension in every matter which we want to make fit, so that we may investigate truth and justice: and these wholly alleviate the investigation of matters. And if the Moon and the other significators were in these, it will be good.

And one which has dignity in their places, should aspect the significators with a good aspect. And if the others did not aspect, at least let the lord of the bound aspect, and especially [let one aspect] the Sun: for it is good that one who has dignity in its own place should aspect him.

And let the Lot of Fortune and its lord, or one of them, be in the house of the matter or in the Ascendant, or in the tenth or eleventh.

But the angles should be fixed,[76] and they should not be remote (and especially in those things which we want to last). But if the angles were remote, and the lords of each (namely, of that sign in which the angle falls by equal degrees, and the one where the angle falls by degrees of ascension) were as-

---

71 I am not quite sure what this means.

72 *Ex ayz horae*. This sentence is very close to *Carmen* V.4.5, which says that the Ascendant and the Moon should be in signs of the sect of the chart (diurnal ones for diurnal activities, nocturnal ones for nocturnal ones).

73 Cf. Sahl §§12a-17.

74 Adding *luna* with Paris 16204, as Madrid omits it.

75 Cf. Sahl §26.

76 That is, in a fixed sign. Sahl (*On Quest.* §1.1, *Judges* §1.1) says that the common signs are next-best.

pecting each other, it will be good and praiseworthy, and especially if they aspected the Ascendant; and if these aspects were from an angle, it will signify exaltation and a great name. And we will be able to commingle the significations of these two signs, if their lords did not aspect each other.

Moreover, what increases the fitness is that one of the fixed stars which is likened to the fortunes, and is of their nature, is in the degree of the Ascendant itself, or in the degree of the Midheaven, or in the house signifying the matter, and especially if it were of the nature of the planet which signifies the matter.[77]

Abu Ma'shar said, if you chose the hour for someone, whether [it was] a foreign journey or something else,[78] and you found the sign in which its lord or the lord of [its] exaltation was, to be strong,[79] one should not have any suspicion about it; or if the Sun or Moon is there, or it receives the Sun or Moon, it is better than any other [sign] in which none was. And he said, let there be a planet in it which has some dignity there, if it were a bad planet; if it were a good one, one does not need to consider whether it has any dignity in it or not. But the reception[80] of the Moon is that the Ascendant not be the sign of her detriment, nor the sign of her fall, and we should speak in the same way about the reception of the Sun.

---

[77] For example, if a prominent fixed star of the nature of Venus and Jupiter, were on the Ascendant, and it was a money (Jupiter) or love (Venus) question.

[78] Reading with Paris 16204, for Madrid's "if you chose all things so that something would be begun, whether it is a foreign journey or something else."

[79] Reading the more correct *forte* for *fortis.*

[80] The idea here is that if a planet casts a ray in to the sign of its fall or detriment, the influence is in some way rejected or of no use. Al-Kindī describes something of this situation in *Forty Chapters* §102.

[Chapter I.2.8: The Moon in the Ascendant][81]

Al-Kindī said[82] that he does not allow the Moon to be put in the Ascendant, for the reason that the Ascendant is contrary to her, and [that] the Sun is not contrary to the Ascendant, but makes a matter appear and be manifest, and loosens a matter which is bound up.[83]

But the opinion of Abū Ma'shar agrees more with the opinion of Ptolemy:[84] for according to [Ptolemy], the Moon is hot and a fortune, like Venus—which Abū Ma'shar testifies to,[85] when he talks about foreign journeys.

However, Māshā'allāh and his associates[86] said that the Moon should not be in the Ascendant for foreign journeys: and Abū Ma'shar did not favor this

---

81 This subchapter must be read along with al-Rijāl VII.2.3. At first the passage seems disorganized, but al-'Imrānī's discussion (and al-Rijāl's response) can be boiled down to six points. (1) Māshā'allāh and al-Kindī (and 'Umar: see al-'Imrānī II.13.2) agree that the Moon should not be in the Ascendant, and especially for travel, because the Moon's qualities are contrary to the Ascendant's (which is hot). Al-Kindī also adds that the Sun is not a problem in the Ascendant. (2) Now, Abū Ma'shar disagrees with this prohibition about travel, but his opinion is inconsistent. Because on the one hand, when discussing travel in one of his books, he seems to approve of the Moon being in the Ascendant, and agrees with the well-known view of Ptolemy (from *Tet.* I.4) that the Moon is warming: this means that her qualities are *not* contrary to the Ascendant, so she is not prohibited from being there. The problem is that in other places (such as the quotes in *ITA* V.7), he says that the Moon is *cold*, not warm. (3) Not only that (adds al-Rijāl), but when talking about natal longevity procedures, he says that the Moon is one of the "cutting" planets which takes life away (probably when the Ascendant is directed to her): again, this suggests contrary qualities. So Abū Ma'shar's views are again inconsistent. (4) Because of this inconsistency, al-Rijāl agrees with the others that she should be prohibited. (5) But al-'Imrānī and al-Rijāl may be making different conclusions from all of this, or at least al-Rijāl's conclusions are a garbled version of al-'Imrānī's. (5a) Al-'Imrānī concludes that since she has a signification for every beginning and that she makes the Ascendant fortunate, she may be put there—which he says is an "appropriate place." (5b) But al-Rijāl, with very similar language, begins by saying the Moon signifies "few" journeys (perhaps he meant "short" journeys), *no matter* what she might otherwise mean for beginnings, and specifically says that the "appropriate place" for her is one in which she aspects the Ascendant. (6) Finally, both al-'Imrānī and al-Rijāl simply point out that there is disagreement about the role of the Sun in the Ascendant (which was mentioned by al-Kindī), but they do not discuss it further.

82 *Forty Chapters* §147.

83 Reading with al-Rijāl VII.2.1 for "divides a conjoined matter." Hugo's al-Kindī says the Sun will remove a delay, while Robert's version says he will uncover hidden things.

84 Ptolemy says that the Moon is somewhat heating but largely moistening, in *Tet.* I.4.

85 Source unknown at this time.

86 See *On Elect.* §23a for the general prohibition, and 107 for the prohibition related to travel.

opinion. [In addition], he himself used to say:[87] the Moon is cold and moist, and the Ascendant hot—and so they[88] do not agree.

Also, she has a signification over every beginning, and particularly over the beginning of foreign journeys: for that reason she is to be put in an appropriate place, and in addition to all of this she makes the Ascendant fortunate.

They say that the Sun is not good in the Ascendant, because he is an infortune in the conjunction and prevention:[89] and in this opinion, all do not agree.

[Chapter I.2.9: 'Umar al-Tabarī on benefics in the Ascendant]

If some fortune were in the Ascendant, not impeded, and prosperous, it will be very good. And what 'Umar al-Tabarī commended[90] more is that it be in the first one-third of the house of the Ascendant: because he said this hastens the matter. But to me, it seems that if it were in the ascending degree itself, or it would ascend a little after the ascending degree (because it is going toward the Ascendant), it is better, and makes the Ascendant more fortunate.

[Chapter I.2.10: The conjunction and prevention prior to the election][91]

Those[92] things which even increase prosperity, are that the place of the preceding conjunction or prevention[93] which was before the election be cleansed of the bad ones, and made fortunate; likewise the lord of the place

---

[87] See *ITA* V.7, which contains Abū Ma'shar's views from both his *Abbreviation* and the *Great Introduction*.

[88] If we stick to the Latin, there are two disagreements here. First of all, since the Ascendant is hot, this latter statement by Abū Ma'shar about the Moon being cold means that their qualities disagree. But the other disagreement is that Abū Ma'shar does not agree with himself: in one place he agrees with Ptolemy that the Moon is hot, but in the other texts he says she is cold.

[89] Reading with Madrid for Paris 16204's "he has strength there in the conjunction or prevention," because Madrid agrees exactly with the parallel statement in al-Rijāl VII.2.3. But I do note that Paris 7413-I seems to read as Madrid does.

[90] Source unknown at this time.

[91] Cf. al-Rijāl VII.2.4.

[92] From here until the quote from Abū Ma'shar, al-'Imrānī seems to be doing a more organized and fleshed-out version of stray statements by al-Kindī in *Forty Chapters* §§478-79, 483, 488-89, 494-95a, and 536.

[93] Al-'Imrānī (or rather al-Kindī) is referring to whether the time of the election comes after the most recent New Moon (conjunctional) or Full Moon (oppositional, sometimes called "preventional").

of the conjunction or prevention. (But[94] the place of the prevention is the place of the luminary which was above the earth. If the place of one were in the degree of the east and that of the other in that of the west, that of the east is the place of the prevention.)

For al-Kindī said the conjunction has a signification over all things which come to be up to the prevention, but things that would be done between the prevention and the conjunction, are signified by that prevention. And for that reason, it is necessary in every beginning and every nativity, to consider attentively all things of the conjunction and prevention, so that we may know whether it was in an angle or one following an angle, or cadent, and what is on that very degree of the conjunction or prevention or in that sign itself, with respect to the fortunes or bad ones, and their aspects; and who they are which aspect it degree by degree, or by any other aspect;[95] and likewise the lord of the place of the conjunction or prevention, namely whether it is under the rays or in its own light.[96] For if these were impeded, whatever was begun will be weak or unstable. If conversely [they were] safe, they will signify the perfection of the matter, and its goodness.

And[97] one must beware lest the Moon, when she is separated from the conjunction or prevention, would be joined to the bad ones (and it is good that she be joined to the fortunes).

And[98] let the place of the conjunction or prevention be in one of the angles, with the fortunes, and the Moon should be going to a conjunction of

---

[94] I have read this paragraph with Paris 16204, but Madrid contains the extra phrase: "is the lunar place" (*est locus lunaris*). Traditionally, there were two views about which place to use for the New Moon (the prevention). One view was that we always use the Moon's place (attributed to Māshā'allāh and the Indians and some Muslims by ibn Ezra in *Search* App. F). The other view (*Tet.* III.3, and endorsed by 'Umar al-Tabarī in *TBN*) is the one expressed here, although Ptolemy does not speak about what to do if the prevention is exactly on the horizon.

[95] This statement seems to concede that whole-sign configurations to the sign of the conjunction/prevention can be considered, and not simply those which are close by exact degree.

[96] That is, it is far enough away from the Sun to be visible on its own.

[97] For the following paragraphs, cf. *Forty Chapters* §§483 and 495a. For al-Kindī, these statements have to do with elections for digging canals and constructing ships, but he probably would have agreed with observing the fitness of the conjunction or prevention in many different elections.

[98] Now al-'Imrānī considers four combinations of the conjunction/prevention and the Moon's application: good-good, good-bad, bad-good, and bad-bad.

the fortunes: for this is a signification of exaltation and the perfected fortune of things, even those whose end will be praised.

But if the place of the conjunction or prevention was [good] as we said before, and the Moon (when she was separated from them–namely the conjunction or prevention) were joined to the bad ones, it signifies the beginning of things will be praiseworthy, but the end bad.

If however the place of the conjunction or prevention were (as we said), joined to the bad ones, but the Moon (when she was separated from one of them) was joined to the fortunes, the beginning will be unpraiseworthy, but the end praiseworthy.

And if the place of the conjunction or prevention was (as we said) with the bad ones, [and] even the Moon (when she was separated from any of them) were joined to the bad ones, all things will be bad, at the beginning and end.

If, at the hour of the conjunction or opposition, its lord[99] were eastern,[100] and in its own house or exaltation or triplicity, the owner of the things which were undertaken, will be clever [and] prudent, so that through his cleverness and prudence he will escape from the aforesaid evils. For the lord of the conjunction or prevention signifies the essence[101] of the matters which were undertaken in it. If the lord of the conjunction were to the contrary, it will happen contrarily to the matter.[102]

If the place of the conjunction or opposition were even in one following the angle, what we said about his cleverness and prudence will happen to the owner of the things at the end of the matters.

If the place of the conjunction or prevention were even cadent from the angle,[103] the matters which were undertaken in it will be bad, and without any favorable end. And this is the knowledge of al-Kindī.

Which,[104] if we have understood his words just as they seem to sound, we will say that all things having a beginning within one and the same conjunc-

---

[99] The lord of the sign in which it occurs.

[100] I have chosen "eastern" with Paris 16204 over Madrid, because the final paragraph below also has the lord of the conjunction/opposition being eastern—albeit at the hour of the election itself.

[101] Reading *substantiam* with Paris 16204, for Madrid's *distantiam.*

[102] Reading with Madrid, as Paris 16204 immediately jumps into the following paragraph but mixes it with this one.

[103] Al-Rijāl VII.2.4 takes this to mean, cadent relative to the Ascendant of the *election*, and likewise for the previous statements about being angular and succeedent.

tion or prevention, would arrive to good or evil in one and the same way: and we see the matter happens otherwise. For we see two things of the same type undertaken on one and the same day, be ended in different ways: for one has good, but the other the contrary. But we ought to understand from his words just as we stated it at the beginning of this chapter:[105] that if the elections of matters which we begin were good according to the elections (even those things which al-Kindī said were good), the good will be increased and will come to be quickly, without delay. Were the election bad, but the things which al-Kindī said [were made] good, it will diminish the good. If however each (namely, the election and what al-Kindī said) were bad, the evils will be doubled and will happen quickly.

What increases the good (if even [the previous things] are made clear) is that in every election we should adapt the place of the lord of the quarter of the year,[106] just as we do the conjunction or prevention. But the fitness of the conjunction or prevention in this work is more individualized[107] than the lords of the quarters of the year, and the fitness of the place of the lord of the quarter of the year [more individualized] than the lord of the year of the world. However, if we could adapt all, it will be better.

Abu Ma'shar said, if the lord of the election[108] were the lord of the sign of the Moon at the hour of the revolution of the year, or the lord of the Ascendant of the year, and it was fortunate at the hour of the revolution and the election, it signifies the increase of the honor of the one beginning [the matter], and the praiseworthy end of the matter begun.[109] And he said, if the

---

104 Now al-'Imrānī proposes an objection to al-Kindī, which he will then refute. The objection is that, since the conjunction or opposition is relevant for about two weeks, it would make every undertaking for everyone either good or bad for that entire time (which is absurd). His response is that an election cannot make something happen absolutely, but it can only ever enhance or detract from something.

105 Now al-'Imrānī means to go through four more combinations of the election and al-Kindī's extra significators, in terms of goodness and badness. But the manuscripts seem to only list three, and have them listed in different order. Nevertheless it is clear what al-Kindī is trying to do.

106 In this paragraph, al-'Imrānī is suggesting that an ideal election should be viewed in the context of the mundane ingresses of the year and quarters (and why not the profected lord of the year of the nativity as well, or the lord of the Ascendant of the natal revolution?), much as al-Kindī suggests we do for weather prediction (*Judges* §Z.8, *Forty Chapters* Ch. 38).

107 *Proprius.*

108 Probably the lord of the Ascendant of the election.

109 Omitting a clause in Madrid: "that is, were it not in the Ascendant of the election nor did it aspect."

lord of the Ascendant of the year did not testify,[110] nor the places of the luminaries, nor the place of the Midheaven, the matters will be [only] a little bit refined.[111]

Al-Tabarī said, if the degree[112] of the conjunction or prevention, and their lord, were in a praiseworthy place, the matter will be firm and praiseworthy, and likewise if someone were born or ordained in that hour, and put in charge over some office.[113] And he stated the praiseworthy places at the hour of the inception,[114] and I believe this opinion to belong to the ancients.

Al-Kindī said,[115] if the lord of the conjunction or prevention which was before the election [were] eastern, in its own house or aspecting it with a trine aspect at the hour of the election, it signifies the effecting of the matter; and if it does not aspect, there will be no usefulness in it.

[Chapter I.2.11: Other considerations]

And they[116] take testimony (in the fitness of a matter to be done) from the lords of the triplicity of the Moon at the conjunction or prevention, for they are the guardians of the nativity and every undertaking: and if they were received and made fortunate at the hour of the election, it signifies good; but if to the contrary, evil.

It even increases the good that the Ascendant of the election be a sign made fortunate in the revolution of the year. And let that fortune be in any angle (and particularly in the Ascendant or in the tenth), or let it be in a following angle,[117] or in the house of the matter.

And the let the significators be in good places, agreeing with them. And let them be strong at the hour of the election: and the strength of the planets

---

[110] This is perhaps where we should put Madrid's clarifying statement that it is not in the Ascendant of the election, nor does it aspect it.

[111] *Subtiles.* Al-Rijāl puts this more strongly, saying that the matter will be low-quality and despised.

[112] *Pars.*

[113] *Praepositurae.* This medieval word refers to a number of positions of authority, from being a provost, to a priory or monastery, an archdeaconate, royal bailiff, and so on.

[114] Probably the Ascendant, Midheaven, and eleventh.

[115] Exact source unknown, but it is similar to ideas in *Forty Chapters* §§483 and 495a. Vatican and Munich do not attribute this view to anyone.

[116] Source unknown, but cf. *Carmen* V.5.30.

[117] That is, a succeedent; al-'Imrānī probably has the eleventh especially in mind, the succeedent to the tenth.

is that they be ascending in the north[118] (and sometimes it is necessary that they be ascending in the south).[119] And let the Moon be in the angles, increased in light and number[120] in matters which we want to be increased, and the contrary for the contrary. In matters which we want to be quick, the significators should be quick in motion and even,[121] and let them be going under the fortunes, above the bad ones.[122]

But the Moon is the significator of a matter above the earth (and this [is] in every matter which we want to be revealed), and under the earth in every matter which we want to be concealed.[123]

And the lord of the Ascendant [should be] eastern,[124] and likewise the other significators, [as many] as we could [make them].

And[125] let the planet to whose conjunction the Moon goes, be good: for this signifies what is going to be with respect to the matter undertaken.

Al-Kindī said,[126] if each of the luminaries aspected each other by a praiseworthy aspect, it signifies the strength and force of the matter which was undertaken in [that hour], and especially if the Moon were "at the beginning of her joy"—and that is the sign in which the Head was.[127]

Māshā'allāh said,[128] the planets are said to be strong when they are western from the Moon, just as they are when they are eastern of the Sun;[129] and the Moon rules in the night, just as the Sun does in the day.

---

118 That is, in northern ecliptical longitude.

119 For examples of this, see al-'Imrānī II.2.10 and al-Rijāl VII.9.2.

120 *Quantitate.*

121 *Aequo.* I am not sure exactly what al-'Imrānī means here.

122 This could mean that they should have benefics overcoming them from the superior square, and they should be overcoming the malefics from the superior square.

123 That is, she should be in those hemispheres of the chart for these types of matters.

124 This probably means rising before the Sun and being out of the rays, prior to the retrograde station.

125 Cf. *Carmen* V.28.4.

126 Source unknown, but Paris 7413-I reads *Alchimenides* or *Alchimemdes*, here and below, while the Latin al-Rijāl reads *Alaçmin* for each, suggesting a name such as 'Uthman.

127 This may have been an idiosyncratic phrase of al-Kindī/Alaçmin or his sources. Being in that sign would indicate that the Moon is or is about to be in degrees of northern ecliptical latitude.

128 Source unknown at this time.

129 This is related to ancient definitions of bodyguarding (*ITA* III.28). Māshā'allāh means that the planets' bodies should be in an earlier degree of the zodiac relative to the Sun (so that they rise before him by diurnal motion), but they should be in later ones relative to the Moon (so that she moves towards them by planetary or zodiacal motion).

Al-Tabarī [said],[130] if we could not make the Moon and the Ascendant fit [at the same time], and the election were in the day, one must first adapt the Ascendant, and especially if the Moon were under the earth. But if the election were nocturnal, one must first adapt the Moon, and especially if she were above the earth. If we are able to defer the beginning from the day until the night (or conversely), one must consider which is the better adaptation—namely that of the Moon or of the Ascendant—and we will do what seems best to us. And[131] the being of the Moon in the day above the earth, and in the night below the earth, is wholly good, and increases the strength of the Ascendant. And[132] if it were necessary for us to elect for someone, nor could we make the Moon fit, we should put Jupiter or Venus in the Ascendant or the tenth, for these will adapt a good inception with great fitness.

And one of the ancients said: this[133] must be done if we want the matter undertaken to last for a long time. But in the matters which we want to last a long time (as are nuptials, the building of cities, and what is like these), the fitness of the Moon is preferable. And if the Moon were weak, she must be removed from the angles and the followers of the angles, and if she could not be removed from the angles of the matter, do not let her aspect the Ascendant nor its lord,[134] nor the planet which signifies the matter chosen. And if we cannot remove her from all of the aspects, let her be removed from those she can be.

And al-Kindī said,[135] if we could not adapt all the significators, it is sufficient to make the Moon fit, [although] it does not make us secure about the matter being destroyed.[136] And[137] the fitness of the significator pleases him more than that of the Moon.

---

[130] These first two sentences derive from *Carmen* V.5.32-33.

[131] This sentence goes contrary to the spirit of the sect rejoicing condition known as *ḥalb* (*ITA* III.2) in which nocturnal planets always want to be in the hemisphere opposite the Sun.

[132] This sentence is based on *Carmen* V.5.10-11.

[133] Probably referring to the previous view by al-Tabarī.

[134] This probably means a degree-based aspect, since if she is in the angles she will of course be aspecting the rising sign itself.

[135] See my footnote to the previous statement by "al-Kindī."

[136] Reading with Paris 7413-I because it matches al-Rijāl more (especially since it mentions the Moon). Paris 16204 reads, "it will be good to adapt in a sufficient way, but it does not make us secure unless the matter should be destroyed."

[137] Adding this sentence from Paris 7413-I.

And[138] al-Tabarī used to prefer the fitness of the lord of the matter to the fitness of the Moon and the lord of the Ascendant, and that of the rest of the significators. But what he said is useful [only] for this, that the matter which we have begun would be perfected; [however, it is] better to guard the body and spirit than the perfection of the matter.

Which[139] if the Moon were ponderous, so that she would go less than 12° (a motion which is like the motion of Saturn), it signifies slowness and difficulty.

Al-Khayyāt [said],[140] if it were necessary to choose for someone, and the Moon [were] made unfortunate, make this bad one the lord of the Ascendant, if it were free and in a praiseworthy condition; and if it received the Moon, it will be better. He also said, if [a benefic][141] were in the Ascendant, it will be good.

And[142] one must note that praiseworthy matters increase the good, but unpraiseworthy matters increase evil. Therefore, what he said was sufficient.

[Chapter I.2.12: Things to beware of][143]

But, however, so that I might speak more perfectly, let me explain those things which one must beware of.

You[144] must beware, in a conjunction of the bad ones, lest that conjunction be with any significator in the same sign, or in the opposite, or from a square aspect. It is not bad that it should be from the trine or sextile, and especially if there were any reception between them. For then, according to Māshā'allāh,[145] they will be fortunes. And I say to you that then they do not impede.

---

138 Reading this paragraph with Paris 7413-I, because it is longer and better matches al-Rijāl VII.2.5.

139 Adding this paragraph with Paris 7413-I.

140 Cf. *On Elect.* §28, which is rather different. This sentence also appears in different forms in I.3, and in al-Rijāl VII.1 and VII.2.5.

141 I have added this along with *On Elect.* §28 and al-Rijāl VII.3.5. See my Introduction for a discussion of this passage.

142 This seems to be by al-'Imrānī.

143 Many items in this list can be traced to ideas expressed in Sahl's *Fifty Judgments*, even if they are not stated in precisely the same way.

144 For this paragraph, cf. *Fifty Judgments* #2, 5, and 31, and the footnote below.

145 Cf. Sahl's own *Fifty Judgments* #2, which might therefore be taken from a work of Māshā'allāh's; that judgment is itself related to *Carmen* V.5.13, but it seems it has undergone some changes. 'Umar's version simply says that an action will have "no strength"

And beware lest the bad ones be in places from which we take the significators (nor in the fourth, nor in the opposite, nor in their pivot),[146] nor that the significators should be cadent or weak.

And you should beware of an eclipse, and especially in the sign in which there was a luminary at the hour of the nativity[147] of the one for whom we are electing.

Nor should the Moon be under the rays of the Sun, and she must wholly be removed from every impediment.

And beware lest one of the fixed stars which are of the nature of the bad ones be in the Ascendant or in the Midheaven, or in the house of the matter chosen.

And do not let the significator[148] be joined to the Sun (nor he joined to it).[149] And one must beware the square aspect of the Sun, and the opposite. If however there were reception between them, it will be a little bit better. And always, the opposite gives quarrels and contrarieties.

And the bad ones should not be in the angles, and particularly not in the Ascendant or the tenth, and especially if the bad ones were lords of the houses signifying evil (such as the sixth and the eighth): then they signify what their houses do.

And the Ascendant should not be a sign such that its lord is about to enter burning in that same year. Nor let the Ascendant be a sign which is impeded in the revolution of that same year.

You[150] should even take precautions lest the Moon be slower[151] in motion nor subtracting in number (if she would be going less than 12°) in any matter

---

(that is, it will be nullified or neither good nor bad) when it is in various aspects or in an assembly with a malefic. But Sahl's judgment #2 (again, which must be from Māshā'allāh) says that malefics restrain their malice when in a sextile or trine. But Sahl does *not* say that sextiles and trines from malefics will be fortunate or turn them into fortunes, as al-'Imrānī understands him to say here.

[146] Adding with Madrid.

[147] Adding with Paris 7413-I.

[148] I believe this is actually the Moon (who is sometimes referred to in Arabic sources as "the significator"), and that this little paragraph probably derives from *Carmen* V.5.5 and V.43.6.

[149] Reading the parenthetical statement with Munich. The distinction being drawn here is evidently between the inferior planets and the superior ones, respectively.

[150] Cf. *Carmen* V.5.6-7, *On Elect.* §22f, and *Fifty Judgments* #13.

[151] Reading with Paris 7413-I, for *calidior.*

which we want to come to be quickly, for then she delays the matter, and renders it difficult, unless the significators were many.[152]

And[153] the movable signs should be removed in every [matter] whose stability and durability we want. And in the same way, the fixed signs [should be removed] in every matter which you wanted to pass by; [and] the common ones from everything which you wanted to come to be just as he desires:[154] for these render whatever comes to be in them, difficult.

It is[155] bad that the angles would be remote, falling in [their] remoteness:[156] this is that the tenth according to number,[157] be the ninth according to the calculation of the houses.[158] And there are some who call this removal "receding."[159] But the receding of their ascending is good and praiseworthy, and especially in matters which we want to last a long time—but the remoteness of the ascending is that the tenth by number be the eleventh in the calculation of the houses.

Even beware lest the lord of the Ascendant nor the lord of the house of the matter, nor the planet signifying the matter, nor the lord of the house of the Moon, nor the planet to which the Moon is being adjoined, be "in senility": this is if it were near the setting Sun in the evening:[160] for then it signifies the uncleanliness of the matter. Which if we cannot remove all of the aforesaid from this, one must at least remove the lord of the Ascendant and the lord of the matter. And if a planet were in senility, setting in the evening and far away[161] from the Sun, it will not be bad, but it will signify the effecting of the matter with delay and slowness.

---

152 Reading *nisi* with Paris 7413-I. Perhaps it means that a slow Moon can be counterbalanced by other significators which indicate speed.

153 Cf. *Fifty Judgments* #36, especially because the statement about the common signs is close in meaning there: namely, that something else will be attached to the matter (rather than it going just as the client wants).

154 That is, without any changes or repetitions or complications.

155 The *mss.* seem to read *dominus enim* or *domini [unclear]* (Munich) here, but it seems to be an error.

156 Reading for *remotione cadenti.* See my Introduction for this topic. Unfortunately, the Latin here is rather confusing in its presentation of the concept.

157 Reading with Paris 7413-I and Munich, for *recedentem.*

158 That is, the tenth quadrant-based house be on the ninth sign.

159 Reading with Paris 16204 for Madrid's "advancing." Al-'Imrānī is probably referring to al-Kindī, in *Forty Chapters* §§477, 485, 490.

160 That is, if it sets after the Sun and is close to it. For the superior planets, this would mean at the end of their synodic cycle, being near to his rays as he is about to conjoin with them. For the inferiors, it must mean retrograding so as to be going under the rays.

161 *Procul.*

But if it were necessary to begin something in the praiseworthy hours which we have said before, and the Moon [were] joined to Mars or Saturn, and the matter to be begun were of the things which are signified by the fortunes (such as the commerce and merchandise which Mercury signifies), begin under these because it [will] be perfected: but something of the nature of that bad one will be mixed together there. And[162] the better condition which the bad ones could be [in] is if they were received, and the worst is if they were horrible.

And if the Ascendant and its lord were in the aspect of the Sun, and the Sun [was] good, aspecting the Ascendant with a good aspect (and likewise the Moon),[163] and the luminaries aspect each other by a good aspect,[164] the matter will be made public (and [even][165] to the king). And if it were a fugitive, he will be caught. But[166] if the aspect were a bad one, it will be uncovered, but not as it ought to be. But if the significators were above the earth or in the Midheaven, it will be uncovered, and the matter will be made manifest.

And if the lord of the Ascendant or the Moon were under the rays of the Sun, or the luminaries were cadent from the Ascendant, not aspecting each other,[167] or the Moon and[168] the significators were under the earth (and especially in the fourth), it signifies that the matter will not be uncovered but will be hidden. And if the lord of the Ascendant were a bad one,[169] evil will follow from it being covered up, and especially if the luminaries were[170] impeded. And if they were made fortunate, he will escape from the aforesaid evil.

---

[162] Cf. *Fifty Judgments* #25, and *On Elect.* §11b.
[163] Cf. *Carmen* V.36.51. The *mss.* have *luna* (the Moon) in the nominative, as though she is aspecting the Ascendant, too; but *Carmen* has the Sun aspecting the Ascendant and *her.*
[164] Cf. *Carmen* V.35.8.
[165] The *mss.* seem to have variants of *non poterit/potius/potus.*
[166] Cf. *Carmen* V.35.2-3.
[167] This should probably read "it," meaning that they are in aversion to the Ascendant.
[168] Paris 16204 says "or" (*aut*), but that might be a misread for "and" (*et*).
[169] This may mean "made unfortunate," rather than being a malefic.
[170] Omitting *non* ("not"), since it does not make sense astrologically, and the next clause clarifies that they are then made fortunate.

[Chapter I.2.13: Other advice on fitness and roots]

But all of the things which we have said before, in terms of praiseworthy and unpraiseworthy things, must not be considered except after we have adapted the roots which we mentioned at the beginning of this Treatise:

[1] If the fortunes would rule in the aforesaid roots, one does not need to consider those things which follow,[171] even if they are bad.

[2] If however the fortunes were strong and they were ruling,[172] we need not look at those things which follow, even if they are praiseworthy.

[3] If each were praiseworthy, the [good] fortune will be doubled.

[4] But if the roots were bad, but the things which follow were praiseworthy, they do not help much; if however [the things which follow] were bad, they increase the evil.

[5] And if it were necessary to begin something, and the bad ones were in charge[173] in that hour,[174] one must adapt the things which follow: for they will subtract from the evil, even if [only] a little bit. And one must beware lest the things which follow are bad.

Which if someone asked of the astrologer that he would elect an hour for him to do something, and there was a doubt on the part of the astrologer as to which planet and what house would signify it, one must make the Ascendant and its lord fit, also the luminaries, and the house of the end of the matter and its lord, so that it would guard the body and soul[175] of the one undertaking it, and the end of his matter, whether it would come to an effect

---

171 See I.3 below, where the "things which follow" are secondary roots such as the solar revolution, but not the election itself.
172 Reading *dominantes* for *dominante.*
173 Reading *praefuerint* with Madrid for *fuerint* in the other *mss.*, which would make it read "and there were bad ones in that hour."
174 This might actually mean, "in the nativity."
175 Adding "and soul" with Madrid.

or not.[176] And one must do likewise if someone asked to elect for a matter which he does not want to reveal to the astrologer. And in such things it is good to begin them in the hours in which Jupiter, Venus, and the Sun rule, for these will make the matter fit, whatever it is.

But if the nativity of the querent were known, and it was necessary to weaken one of the significators (such as the lord of the seventh if we wanted to go on a hunt or to a fight, and what is like these), no planet should be weakened which has a strong testimony in the nativity, and especially the victor over the nativity[177] (and it is evident enough that this is not to be weakened): and these are in harmony with every beginning.

And for certain men, we ought to do certain things of the following, which should not be done for others. For an election of kings, we ought to make the Sun and the tenth and its lord fit; and in elections for kings this should not be said in terms of the things which follow, but in terms of the necessary things and the roots.[178] But for scribes, one must make Mercury fit in all things which are going to be undertaken. And we make Mars fit for all those things of which he is the significator, such as are boxers, blacksmiths, butchers. [And we adapt] Jupiter for judges and merchants, but Venus for women and delightful people;[179] Saturn for farmers, old men, and widows. And generally we adapt the planet signifying his people, and the land, also [his] sect[180] and work and age, even the sign and the hour (thus a feminine sign for women, and of the hours, the hours of night; for men a masculine sign and the hours of the day); and for every man, the sign signifying his people and fatherland: such as Aries for the *Accumuedi* and *Alcordi*,[181] Scorpio for the Arabs.[182]

---

[176] This seems to mean that if we do not know the correct house or general significator, then the best we can do is protect the client's health and prevent a disaster in the events, even if he does not get what he wants in the end.

[177] For medieval methods of determining this, see *Search*.

[178] Al-'Imrānī seems to mean that in elections for certain types of people, the fitness of certain planets and houses should be counted *as being* one of the fundamental and necessary things, no matter what particular type of election they want: so in an election for a king, the Sun is made fit no matter what the particular action will be.

[179] Reading *amabilibus* with Munich for variations such as *arabilibus* (Vatican, "plowable things") and *oratoribus* (Madrid, "orators").

[180] That is, his religious or philosophical sect.

[181] These two words probably refer to Hamadhān and the Kurds, which are however attributed to Taurus in *ITA* I.3.

[182] One rationale for attributing Scorpio to the Arabs is that the Saturn-Jupiter conjunction of 571 AD, which preceded the rise of the Muslims (who were originally mainly

Sometimes it even happens that many houses must be made fit: such as if we want to buy slaves or animals, we will adapt the house which signifies the matter (as is the sixth, in this example), and we will likewise adapt the second for assets, for slaves and animals are counted among assets. And thus too, we can adapt many planets for one thing: just as when we elect for dyers so that they may dye in red, one must adapt Mars (who signifies redness), and we will make him be aspecting the Moon and the Ascendant and its lord, by an aspect of friendship. And if it were the fabric of a woman, one must [also] make Venus fit; and for that of Slavs or slaves, Saturn; or Mars if it was pertaining to war (as is a military banner) or increasing [the war];[183] and if it were a fabric which is used by all, we should adapt from however many we can, and particularly the one which signifies [its] color.

At the beginning of this Treatise, we said that if we needed to weaken some significator, we should weaken it just as it is right to: for example, in the search for a fugitive, our intention is to destroy the condition of the fugitive and his adversary, and for that reason we will make the Moon weak and impeded by the bad ones, because she signifies every beginning.[184]

And for one taking a purgative,[185] [we make it] so that the Moon is impeded by an impediment matching this matter: this is that we should put the Moon in her own descension:[186] for we loosen it so that the harmful humors (which we are taking the antidote for, in order to expel them) traverse through the lower part [of the body]. And the Moon should not be impeded by the bad ones, lest the humors and the antidote be impeded before it should be, and this evil would happen to the one taking the medicine: for Saturn would pack it together and prohibit its exit, [while] Mars would expel it with excessive sharpness: and I say these two would harm the one taking

---

Arabs), was in Scorpio. But it could also be due to the fact that the Arabs were desert people (see *ITA* I.3).

183 Reluctantly reading *augens* with Vatican and Munich for *algensem* (Madrid) and *aligens* (Paris 16204), although these might be transliterations for the Arabic *al-jān* ("evildoer, criminal"), or perhaps even something like *jināzah* ("funeral").

184 Following Madrid. Paris 16204 reads, "our intention is to destroy his condition and make [the fugitive] weak: we will make the Moon be impeded by the bad ones, because she signifies every beginning." But as Bonatti points out in a comment on this passage (*BOA* Tr. 7, Part 1, Ch. 12), being impeded or unfortunate is not the same as being weak.

185 *Catarticam*. Here al-'Imrānī seems to mean a laxative.

186 Reading the rest of this sentence with Paris 16204, for Madrid's much more abbreviated version. See for instance II.2.10 below.

the antidote. And it happens in this way [and] in these matters (namely with an impediment).

But the Ascendant and the other significators should not be impeded by the infortunes in any manner, but one must labor so that the Ascendant its lord would be made fit; and we will make them be made fortunate as much as we can, if we are choosing in hours in which the Moon was impeded. And if the lord of the Ascendant were made fortunate, it will not impede, even if[187] the Ascendant were in the burnt path (or whatever the ascending sign was).

And we will speak thusly of the impediment of the lord of the seventh, if we came out for a battle or hunting. This is a universal opinion in elections, both for those whose nativities are known, just as for those whose [nativities] are unknown. And for that reason there are examples to be introduced with respect to particular elections, so that what has been said before will shine forth brightly. And we will put them in the following Treatise. And whatever was necessary [for elections in general] must not be repeated in every election, as is the custom of many who intend to make a sprawling Treatise, but we will put in every chapter what will be necessary to do.[188]

Moreover, we will lead your memory back to those five things[189] which we said before (just as when we gave a purgative to someone): so that the Ascendant and the Moon should [sometimes][190] be in the burnt path, and likewise we praise the descent of the Moon in the south, and in the same way we will say that one should beware of certain things which we have praised [before], just as we spoke about the taking of a purgative: so that one should beware of the aspect of the bad ones, whatever kind of aspect it was. And we have already stated that their trine and sextile aspect is not bad, and especially if they were received.[191] But if you were asked why that is [so], you would be able to understand [that] through what has been set forth before, nor will it be difficult except for one for whom this knowledge is not in use.[192]

---

[187] Reading *etsi* for Madrid's *et si* and Paris 16204's *et non.*

[188] That is, he will not repeat all of these general points about benefics, malefics, and so on, but only review what is peculiar to the type of election at hand.

[189] Probably referring to the list to which I assigned numbers, at the beginning of this subchapter.

[190] In this paragraph, al-'Imrānī means that sometimes a particular election will require planetary positions that would otherwise seem bad according to the general rules.

[191] Cf. *Fifty Judgments* #2 and 25.

[192] That is, for someone who has learned these rules but has not bothered to put them to use as *active* knowledge.

And we have already omitted many things whose usefulness is excessive[193] in this work, and their justification[194] weak. Because if we considered them, the praiseworthy hours would on that account be so few, that we would not be able to elect for anyone except for after a long time: such as is a consideration of the hours which the Indians call "burnt,"[195] and days which are called "days of the diminishment of water" by sailors and the Egyptians,[196] and also the things which Abū Ma'shar mentioned in his own book on elections, concerning elections for the mansions [of the Moon] (and even his statement was excessively prolix).[197]

And likewise, we have omitted many things about which other people have handled in their books on elections: just as are the fixed signs, the common ones, and the movable ones; even those ascending straight and crooked, and many others which pertain to introductions, not to this work.[198]

Among the books on astrology, this book is just like a book on antidotes is, among the books of physic;[199] and this Treatise is just like a book which teaches practitioners of physic about the what, the how, and how much they should offer to the sick. But the second Treatise of this book is just like a book in which preparations (such as pills, electuaries, *etc.*)[200] are contained, and so on. But to deal with the fixed, common, and movable signs in books of astrology is like dealing with simple medicines in books of physic, the knowledge of which should come first, before a doctor gets involved in putting medicines together.

---

193 *Nimia.* What al-'Imrānī means is that it is too much to ask for people to take them into account, whatever their usefulness is.

194 *Ratio.*

195 That is, the hours of the *bust* or the "scorched hours." For a standard version from al-Kindī and the Sanskrit word this comes from, see al-Rijāl VII.57.2 below. In *ITA* VIII.4, al-Qabīsī gives a different version. See also Māshā'allāh's *Book of Aristotle* II.4 (in *PN* 1), and Appendix D below.

196 I am not sure what these are.

197 For elections using the mansions, which may or may not be taken from a book of Abū Ma'shar's, see Part I of this book, taken from al-Rijāl VII.101.

198 Al-Rijāl, apparently disagreeing with al-'Imrānī here, takes just such passages from *On Elect.* for his own book: for instance, see al-Rijāl VII.3.1.

199 Physic is an antiquated term for medicine, based on the idea that the four elemental "natures" (fire, earth, air water) and their mixtures play the key role in health and illness. The word "physics" or "physic" (Gr. *phusis*) means "nature."

200 An electuary is a medicine designed to melt in the mouth through sucking, rather than being drunk or swallowed (such as sucking on a medicinal tablet to treat thrush in the throat).

Chapter I.3: On the elections of those whose nativities are known

But the roots which must be considered for these are three, namely:

[1] That we should look at the victor over the nativity,[201] and we should put it in an angle or one following an angle; it is even better that it be above the earth,[202] free from the bad ones and joined to the fortunes.[203] If however the planetary victor were a bad one, we should put it in a follower of the angles, outside the angle: because perhaps it would destroy the matter, and the destruction would come to be from the direction of the owner of the matter.[204] But what follow this root, and increase the fitness, are that the lord of his revolution of the year is just as we said about the victor over the nativity, and likewise the lord of the Lot of Fortune in the root[205] and the revolution. And according to certain astrologers, [we should adapt] the lord of the sign of the profection,[206] and the lord of the orb.[207]

[2] The second root is that the Ascendant of the root (or the Midheaven) be the Ascendant of the election, if it were free of the bad ones. But if there were a fortune in it or one aspected it with an aspect of friendship, it will be better. But if it could not be that the Ascendant or the Midheaven of the root would be the Ascendant of the election nor [its] Midheaven, let it be the eleventh. If however [we could not do this], instead of it we should put the sign of the profection or of the Lot of Fortune of the root or of the revolution [there], if they were free of the bad ones (as we said before).

> Al-Khayyāt said, you should make the house of that matter in the nativity, the Ascendant of the election; and let the Moon be aspecting the Ascendant, if a bad one did not aspect her.[208] But if she were in the aspect of a bad one, and that bad one were the lord of the nativity, [209] it will not impede [her]. And in no way should the Ascendant of the election be the house of infirmities in the root, nor that of death, nor of

---

[201] See my *Search* for various methods on finding this, especially the table of victors in the introduction.
[202] Adding this point about being above the earth, with Vatican and Munich.
[203] Madrid adds, "strong" (*fortis*), but this might have been a redundant misread for *fortunis*.
[204] That is, from the client, since it is his or her own victor.
[205] That is, the nativity.
[206] Also known as the lord of the year.
[207] Perhaps referring to the "lord of the turn" (Ar. *dawr*): see *ITA* VIII.2.3.
[208] Cf. *On Elect.* §28, which probably inspired this statement.
[209] This should probably be the "victor" over the nativity, as al-'Imrānī describes above.

enemies.[210] And the place of the Ascendant of the election should be in a good place from the Ascendant of the root, and if it is possible for the same to be so for the Ascendant of the revolution, and for the sign of the profection, as well as the place of the Lot of Fortune of the root and [the Lot of Fortune] of the revolution, it is good. But lacking that, [adapt] as many of them as we could, and especially the Lot of Fortune in the root of the nativity.[211] And the strength of the significators, and the aspects of the fortunes, annuls every evil.

Then,[212] if we were able to put the lord of the matter (in the root of the nativity or the revolution or the profection)[213] either in the Ascendant of the election or in the Ascendant of the revolution, free from the bad ones, it brings about the matter without difficulty. And if in addition to this it were free from the bad ones, strong, and made fortunate, the matter will reach a perfection better than anything [else] of this kind. And if the lord of the Ascendant of the root or the lord of the Ascendant of the election or of the Ascendant of the revolution, were in the house of the matter in the nativity or the election or revolution, it will signify the perfection of the matter with labor, and searching into the matter: and this will be if it were strong and[214] free from the bad ones. And if we were not able [to do it] so that the planets would be as we have said before, but they aspected that sign with a friendly aspect, it will be good; and if the lords of the two aforesaid places were aspecting each other with a friendly aspect, it will be good.

[3] The third root is that we should look at a nativity which signified evil for him in that year:[215] you should not undertake any grand work in that year,

---

210 That is, the natal sixth, eighth, and twelfth, respectively.

211 This seems to mean that the sign of the natal Lot of Fortune should be in a good place in the electional chart.

212 This paragraph refers to a basic principle in questions, such that if the lord of the matter is in the Ascendant, then the matter comes to the querent (or, here, the client); but if the lord of the Ascendant is in the place of the matter, the client must do more work to bring it about. See examples of this in *Judges* §10.1.

213 Reading *profectionis* with Paris 16204, for Madrid's *electionis*.

214 Paris 16204 reads, "or."

215 Al-'Imrānī seems to mean that the nativity in question (by profection or revolution) suggests a general quality of evil, such as a malefic in bad condition in the sign of the

and especially a work which would pertain to that evil which is signified. If, however, it were necessary for him to undertake it, let us make the planet signifying [the evil] be cadent, and we should make the Ascendant fit, as well as we would be able to—and likewise the lord of the end of the matter, and their lords. One must even place a fortune in the place where that bad one was in the root, or [put that natal place] in the rays of a fortune. Which if that could not be, we should then remove all the bad ones,[216] and especially that bad one which is introducing the present fear.

> If[217] however the nativity did not signify evil in that year [generally], but in that year[218] it signified the destruction of the matter to be undertaken, we should adapt the sign in which the planet naturally signifying the matter was at the root of the nativity and the revolution, and also the sign in which it is at that hour of the election, and their lords—and especially that sign in which it was at the root [of the nativity] and at the hour of the election.

> Which if the nativity signified the fitness of that matter in that year,[219] one does not have to labor much so that the matter would be perfectly good: for the matter will be perfected, nor will it be hindered, even if the election is not perfectly good.

And whatever we say in this chapter must be considered after we have adapted all things which we have set forth in the preceding chapter,[220] for they must not be overlooked.

However, there are certain hours in which no work must be begun, such as is the hour of an eclipse, and especially if the hour of the eclipse were in

---

profection. He does not mean that it specifically indicates problems for the elected matter—for that, see the next paragraph.

216 This probably means, "make the malefics in the election, be in aversion to the key places."

217 Reading this paragraph with Paris 16204, as it is clearer and contains the extra clause at the end. Here, al-'Imrānī seems to mean that something about the particular matter itself has bad qualities: such as if the election were about children, but there is a malefic in poor condition transiting the fifth at the solar revolution.

218 Reading *anno* for *hora* ("hour").

219 Reading *anno* for *hora* ("hour").

220 I am not exactly sure which chapter al-'Imrānī means.

the sign of the Ascendant of the root [of the nativity], nor in its triplicity,[221] nor in its square aspect.

'Umar said, the seventh aspect[222] belongs to Saturn, because his houses are opposite the houses of the luminaries. But in this manner the trine belongs to Jupiter, the square to Mars, the sextile to Venus. But if one of these [planets] were impeded in the nativity, we should not make the Moon in the election be aspecting any of the planets (whether it were a fortune or a bad one), by the aspect of [that] impeded planet—and with such an example: if Venus (whose aspect is the sextile) were impeded in the root of the nativity, the Moon should not be made to be aspecting Jupiter or [any] other planet at the hour of the election, by a sextile aspect. However, it pleases me[223] enough to consider this for bad planets: to me it does not seem it must be considered for good ones; in fact, it will perhaps subtract something from the good, but not as much as it will [subtract from the evil], with respect to the bad ones.[224]

And one must note that if we wanted to hinder any significator (such as the lord of the seventh, in going out to do battle or for hunting), we should not hinder anything which was strong in the nativity, and especially the victor over the nativity. But if we would turn ourselves to another,[225] and if it were possible that we would not weaken any significator of the revolution, it will be good.

---

[221] That is, in the whole-sign trines of the natal Ascendant.

[222] That is, the opposition. This paragraph refers indirectly to the *Thema Mundi*, which illustrates the relationship between the domiciles and aspects. See *ITA* III.6.2, and al-Kindī's own explanations in *Forty Chapters* Ch. I.1.8. The domiciles of Jupiter aspect Leo and Cancer from the trine, those of Mars from the square, those of Venus from the sextile.

[223] This seems to be al-'Imrānī commenting on 'Umar's view.

[224] That is, it is better to observe this rule in avoiding greater harm from the malefics, since even a difficult benefic will at least still be a benefic: therefore if we observed this rule for benefics, we risk taking away even the little good they may still indicate.

[225] *Divertamus nos ad alium.* I am not quite sure what this means. If it meant to do a different election, we would expect *aliam.*

Chapter I.4: On elections after an inquiry has been made, whether the matter is perfected or not[226]

Certain ones of the astrologers,[227] when they want to elect for someone, used to take an interrogation from him about the matter which he was wanting to undertake; and they used to treat[228] the Ascendant of the interrogation just like the Ascendant of a nativity, and the planet which is in charge of [the interrogation] and its lord,[229] be just like the lord of a nativity, and likewise the Lot of Fortune—and afterwards, they used to elect just like for one whose nativity is known. But if they perceived through the interrogation that the matter would not be perfected, or they feared some adversity, they did not make an election. And if such a great necessity demanded that they be unable to put it off, they used to elect for him just like it is if a nativity reveals or introduces terror. And if the interrogation signified the effecting of the matter, they used to elect for him just like we said before about those whose nativities declare good.

Al-Khayyāt said, in a certain book of his, that one should elect for no one whose nativity is unknown, nor by means of an interrogation. And in this opinion all do not seem to agree, nor [do they disagree] in vain. For, many wise astrologers used to elect for every man; if however one of those sages did not want to elect for someone without an interrogation, for that reason he used to do [the interrogation] so that his election would be perfected—not because it was necessary in *every*[230] election.

But how will we deny the effecting of the matter (on the grounds that the interrogation will not signify it), when all the astrologers say that the evil which is signified by a nativity can sometimes be changed, sometimes be annulled, through a good election?[231] For that reason, it was necessary to look

---

226 This chapter has to do with using the details of a successful question chart, as the basis of the election: e.g., making the Ascendant of the *question* the Ascendant of the *election*. Al-'Imrānī has no problem with using the *fact* of a successful question to put the astrologer at ease *about* the election, but he does not want to use the details of the question chart as roots. And apparently, al-Khayyāt had agreed.

227 Namely Sahl, in *On Elect.* §§3a-5a.

228 *Ponebant.*

229 Al-'Imrānī is not describing two planets here: the "planet in charge [of the interrogation]" and the "lord [of the interrogation]" are the same planet.

230 Emphasis mine.

231 What al-'Imrānī seems to mean is this. The theory of elections says that a nativity's features may be enhanced or annulled through an election. But those who use question charts and adapting the features of the question chart in the election, are introducing an

at the nativity. For, with this being removed,[232] no usefulness will be found in books of judgments, and Ptolemy shows all of this perfectly in Chapter Two of the first book of [the *Tetrabiblos*].[233] Moreover, the judgments of interrogations are not established[234] as are judgments of a nativity. For nativities *are* natural things, [but] interrogations are *like* natural things.[235]

And for those among whom this opinion[236] flourishes, they do not contradict the roots, but they limit the work:[237] an example of which is that they consider the Ascendant of the year of the world, and the Ascendant of an interrogation: and where there were fortunes and bad ones in each, they make the Ascendant of the election be one of the signs in which there were fortunes at the hour of the revolution of the year of the world, and in the interrogation. And instead of the Ascendant of the interrogation, *we* use the Ascendant of the nativity for one whose nativity we know. But for one whose [nativity] we do not know, we have faith in the Ascendant of the revolution of the year [of the world]. And we do not put ourselves in so much anxiety that we look at matters which do not help, nor do they harm if we did look.[238]

And according to what they say, one must consider that the Ascendant of that same hour be made fortunate, and there is no impediment to the Ascendant of the conjunction or prevention which was before the revolution, and before the interrogation, and before the hour of the election. And they even said that if the lord of the revolution of the year had testimony in the interrogation, you should give it a role in the Ascendant of the election, and make the Midheaven of the interrogation be the Ascendant of the election or

---

external chart—namely the question—which contradicts the theory. Instead, we ought to have recourse to the nativity instead of this third chart.

232 That is, without a nativity.

233 *Alharbaha* [Paris 16204] or *Alarbaa* [Madrid], "that is, the *Quadripartitum*." Al-'Imrānī seems to be referring to Ptolemy's causal and naturalistic view of astrology: according to Ptolemy, all of the native's future events will be a result of external causal influences after birth, and internal causal influences which are in turn caused by mixtures of elements and such which are due to the planets' natal configurations.

234 *Rata*. This can also mean, "settled, certain, fixed."

235 This is an interesting point, but would only be forceful for someone who already believed in a naturalistic theory of astrology.

236 That is, those who believe one may use an interrogation as a root.

237 *Constringunt opus*. I am not sure what is limiting about this opinion.

238 Reading *nec tamen nocet* with Madrid and both Paris *mss.*, for *nec tam nos* (Vatican, Munich). In other words, the view here is that interrogations do not help at all, but they don't necessarily harm—nevertheless one should not use them *instead* of nativities.

the house of the matter to be chosen: for this grants it so that it would be perfected quickly.

And for those whose nativities they did not know, they used to look to see if something great (whether good or evil) is happening to them,[239] such as if they had been put in charge over some high office,[240] and especially if it was the first dignity over which they were in charge, or any matter over which they were not used to being in charge, or [if] any great adversity happened to them, like captivity or shipwreck: and they used to look at the Ascendant in that same hour, and they took it as being just like the Ascendant of a nativity: and they revolved their years just as it comes to be in nativities, and they used to judge by that figure just as they do nativities—and this is not far removed from the truth.

And if we proved for some man that his condition would be made fit (if some planet were strong) and his condition would be destroyed (if that same planet would be hindered), we are able to suspect that that planet would have some rulership in his nativity, and it can be said thusly about the signs. For if a sign befell [him] thusly with respect to prosperity (or adversity if it were hindered), we should suspect that it is the Ascendant of the nativity, and we will make the planet and sign fit in every beginning of his, just as we do with a nativity. But one must not rely on it.[241]

And in this way, the sages of the stars were able to judge which planet or what sign would rule over climes and cities.[242]

Chapter I.5.0: In what hours we may have trust that what was undertaken in them, would be perfected

In[243] what was set forth before, it was explained [by al-Kindī] that if the significators were in the angles or those following the angles, and in a good aspect of the luminaries (and especially that of the one which rules the time),[244] and were in a praiseworthy aspect of those which rule in their plac-

239 What al-'Imrānī is about to describe is what we would call an "event chart" today.
240 *Praepositurae.*
241 That is, this may be a least-bad option for an election, but do not rely on it for any further natal analysis.
242 Cf. al-Rijāl VII.20.
243 For this paragraph and the next, cf. *Forty Chapters* §§132-35.
244 That is, the sect light (the Sun in a diurnal chart, the Moon in a nocturnal chart).

es,[245] the matter which was begun will be perfected, if it were of those things which you wanted to last. Al-Kindī said,[246] if the matter to be begun were of those things which we want to pass by quickly, the cadent [places] will be significators of the effecting of the matter if they were made fortunate, because the fit places are contrary to these.[247]

But[248] knowing the hour of the end of the matter, and its quickness and slowness, is taken from the signs and their places, also from the planets and from the significations and natures of each of them. But the quickness and slowness of the matter in this place is a function of[249] the matter which we begin: for there are certain things which are ended after a month, and they are said to be ended quickly, and certain things which are ended on that same day but are said to be ended slowly. However, we should take the signification from the signs if a sign were the house of the matter, or the Ascendant, or there were some [planet] in it which would signify the hour. We even take the signification from the signs according to their nature, such as quickness from the movable ones, delay and slowness from the fixed ones, [and] what is in the middle between each, from the common ones (and they present weakness to the matter, and their signification is not very strong nor safe). And if the Ascendant were of the signs of straight ascension, it signifies slowness; one of crooked [ascension signifies] quickness. Fiery[250] signs [signify] quickness more so than the others, the airy ones less quickness, earthy ones [the most] slowness, watery ones less [slowness].

But[251] the signification is [also] taken from the places of the signs, and according to what it was in terms of the houses: for the Ascendant and the tenth signify quickness (namely, days and hours); the seventh, not great slowness (such as a month); the fourth delays the matter, and perhaps signifies years. But the succeedents of the angles signify what their angles signify, except that they delay the matter which was begun, more moderately than [the angles] do. However, the seventh delays the matter more so than the

---

[245] That is, their lords.

[246] *Forty Chapters* §133.

[247] Reading with Madrid and Munich, for "the contrary places are fit for these." That is, the normally fit places (angles, succeedents) are contrary to the cadents.

[248] This paragraph seems to be broadly based on *Forty Chapters* §134-35.

[249] *Relata ad.*

[250] Cf. al-Hasan bin Sahl in al-Rijāl's VII.102.6, and Māshā'allāh's *On the Knowledge of the Motion of the Orb* §3.

[251] Cf. *On Times* §2.

fourth.[252] The cadents [signify] slowness. And generally, all things that are above the earth signify a quicker speediness than what exists under the earth.

Moreover,[253] the eastern quarter (which is from the Ascendant to the Midheaven) signifies quickness; the southern one ([which is from the Midheaven to the seventh]), mediocre quickness. The western one (which is from the seventh to the fourth) signifies a middle slowness; the northern one ([which is from the fourth to the Ascendant]), slowness. And if it happened that a sign signifying quickness is in the fourth, it signifies the quickness of matters; and if a movable sign would be the Ascendant or the tenth, this will be the fastest quickness that we could have from the signs.

[Chapter I.5.1: Planetary significators for signs]

But[254] the planets from which we take the signification of the hour, are the lord of the Ascendant and the lord of the matter, if they aspected each other. Which if they did not aspect each other, we will take the Moon—if, however, she were not cadent. For if she were cadent, we should take the planet to which the Moon is being joined. Which if there were no [such planet], we will take the Sun.

And to me, the luminaries have a not-small signification for times. But it pleases certain people that one should look at all of the planets which we stated before; and whichever one they found to be the victor over the Ascendant and [over] the house of the matter, they give that one the signification of the time.

And a light planet signifies more lightness than slowness. If a planet were quicker in course, it signifies quickness; and if it were in [its] average speed, it signifies being in the middle; in [its own] slow [course], slowness.

And if it happened that planets which signified quickness in every way, were significators in that hour, [and] in places signifying quickness in every way, this situation will be faster for every matter of that same type. Which if they signified slowness in every way, and their places were ones signifying slowness in every way, it will be slower for every matter of that same type.

---

252 This probably means that the *succeedent* of the seventh (namely the eighth), indicates more slowness than that of the fourth (namely, the fifth) does.

253 Cf. *On Times* §3.

254 Cf. *On Times* §3.

But[255] planets signifying a time in which a matter begun will be perfected, will give their own signification (both of the good and of the bad), according to what we will judge through them, if they changed condition, either in a weak change or in a stronger one. But a change of the weaker ones is that a planet is in some quarter (of the quarters of the circle), and it changed its own condition through the motion of the firmament: namely, one which goes from the east to the west, to another quarter, or it was under the earth and it will change itself to be above the earth, [or] it will descend from the upper [region] to the lower one. But a strong change is if it were eastern, [and] it would become western, or the other way around; [or] it will be changed from one sign to another sign (and especially if the change would happen to a sign in which it had some dignity).

[Chapter I.5.2: Lengths of time from Sahl's On Times §3][256]

And[257] we have already taken many things with respect to the distinction of hours,[258] of which [the first] is that we should look at [1] the number of degrees which are between a planet and the one to which it is being adjoined,[259] among the significators of the hour.[260] And we put that number as being hours or days or months or years, according to what the places signified in terms of quickness and slowness, [or] according to what the planetary significators signified from the quickness or slowness of their motion, and the rest of the things which we set forth before, and according to the nature of the matter begun (whether it is of those which can be ended in hours or days, or more slowly), and in this way whatever we count by the number of degrees, comes to be. And here is an example of that: let the Moon be the significator, and she is in the fourth degree of Aries, going toward the con-

---

255 Cf. *On Times* §1.

256 For a discussion of these times, ask the Introduction.

257 For this paragraph, cf. *On Times* §3.

258 That is, in the list of several predictive approaches in *On Times* §3.

259 *Adiungitur*. That is, a connection by degree. Al-'Imrānī's example below allows for aspects, but the other versions of this passage (which do not contain an example) suggest only a connection by body.

260 That is, the significators of the chart for the election—even though these rules should really pertain more to questions.

junction of the Sun (who is in the tenth degree of Leo). And there are six degrees, which we put down as the number of hours or days or months.[261]

[2] And after this, is that we should look to see when a planet going to the conjunction of another planet will arrive in the sign in which it is, [precisely] to the number of degrees in which the heavier planet is, and this is the hour sought.[262] An example of this matter is the Sun and the Moon just as we said before, so that we should see when the Moon would reach the tenth degree of Aries (since the Sun was in the tenth of Leo). We find that the Moon reaches there in about 12 hours,[263] and we will say that the matter would be ended then, if it were of the matters which can be ended in such a short space of time.

[3] And after this, that we should look to see what [distance] there is between a lighter planet and the planet to which it is being joined—namely, in terms of the signs and fractions of the signs. And we put down the number of their degrees as the number of hours or days or months in which the matter is ended, according to what we said before.[264] An example of this is the conjunction of the Moon with the Sun, between which there are 126°, which we put down as being [that many] hours or days or months, as the matter itself demands.

[4] And after this,[265] is that we should look to see when the conjunction itself will be perfected, and this will be the hour. And in the same example, we have found about 6 ½ hours,[266] for this is the hour at which the conjunction will be perfected by degree and minute.

[5] And after this, that we should look at the years[267] of the planet which signifies the beginning, if there were reception between it and the other one to which it is being joined: and we put their number as being years or months or days or hours, just as we said. And according to their strength we will put down their greater or lesser or middle years.[268]

---

[261] That is, according to the criteria of the quickness and slowness of the place: in the Ascendant, it might be hours; in the fourth, a longer unit of time.

[262] That is, when they will perfect their assembly or aspect by transit in "real time."

[263] Reading for Madrid's *8*, and what appears to be Paris 16204's 5. Since the Moon travels about 12° per day, it will take her about 12 hours to travel 6°.

[264] That is, the actual number of degrees and minutes between them will translate into a number of time units. The other versions of this paragraph equate each degree to days, not to the other units as al-'Imrānī has it here.

[265] This item is really a variation or repetition on item #2 above.

[266] I believe this should be 12 hours, not 6 ½.

[267] Reading *annos* with Madrid and *On Times*. Paris reads *gradus* ("degrees").

[268] See the table of years in al-Rijāl VII.102.3.

[6] And sometimes,[269] a day is put down for each degree, of those which are between the degree of the Ascendant and the degree of the one who receives the disposition:[270] and in this manner every sign will be signifying a month.

[7] Moreover,[271] if the one which bears away the disposition between them, reaches the other to which it transfers it, either by its body or by rays, we will take the degrees which are between them and will put them down as being days or months.

[8] Moreover, if the one who bears it away between them, arrives at the other to which it bears it away (whether by body or by aspect), we will give months or days according to the number of degrees which are between them, by ascensions of the sign in which the one who bears it away.

[Chapter I.5.3: More on planets signifying times]

In every matter, the Moon signifies the hour, and particularly in quick matters. And likewise the Sun, but particularly in those things which come to be slowly. However, the lord of the Ascendant and the lord of the matter, if they were conjoined, will signify the quickness of the effecting of the matter. If however other things were testified to, and especially if the lord of the Ascendant were heavier[272]...

And[273] if the Moon dismounted in[274] the Ascendant or the house of the matter, or she aspected any of them[275] (and especially from the square or opposite), it will be the hour—and likewise for critical days. And the Sun is stronger in this work than the Moon is, if he were just as we said before

---

269 Reading *quandoque* with Paris for Madrid's quinque ("five").

270 That is, the one who receives the "management," the planet being applied to. Other variations on this paragraph allow the counting to go either way, from the planet to the Ascendant or the Ascendant to the planet.

271 This item and #8 below each involve transfers of light; #7 has to do with real-time transits and symbolic times using zodiacal degrees, while #8 has to do with the same distance in ascensional degrees.

272 This seems to be an incomplete thought, and something must be missing in the Latin *mss.*

273 This paragraph seems to be a rough version of the last paragraph in *On Times* §3; cf. also *Search* II.5.2.

274 That is, "was in."

275 That is, the places.

about the Moon.[276] And likewise, when the Moon will have arrived to the place of the significator, it will be the hour.

And[277] perhaps we will make the victor over the beginning be the significator of the hour, and we will look at its situation with the victor over the house of the matter.

And we have already found certain people[278] who extracted a releaser from this matter just as in nativities, and they direct its degree to the places of the fortunes and the bad ones, and they make every degree by ascensions into a year or month, according to the nature of the matter. And if it arrived to a fortune (namely, before a [bad one]), the matter will be perfected with prosperity; but if [it reached] a bad one first, the contrary. But Mars signifies quickness, namely so that something of Martial things will be commingled with the matter. And in the same way, they direct the ascending degree and the degree of the house of the matter to the good ones or bad ones. And[279] sometimes they direct the degrees of the house of the matter to the degree of the Ascendant.

But[280] they trust in the Lots, [and] they direct the Lot of the matter just as they do the releaser; then they commingle the significators.

And sometimes they[281] revolve the Ascendant of the election, just as the Ascendant of a nativity is revolved.

---

276 Paris 16204 omits the part about the Sun being "stronger." What Madrid seems to mean by this strength is that the Sun takes a longer time, or perhaps will have a more momentous indication.

277 This possibility is so generic it could come from any number of sources.

278 Such as al-Kindī, in *Forty Chapters* Ch. 3.3.

279 Reading the rest of the paragraph with Munich.

280 *Forty Chapters* §141; Hermann mentions this in *Search* II.5.1.

281 This probably refers to *On Times* §12 (attributed to Māshā'allāh), which casts solar returns for event charts.

TREATISE II

[Preface]

Now that we have set forth general[282] rules on elections in the preceding chapters, in the present one we ought to remember the examples of what we have set forth, so that they seem easier. And if it were necessary to choose something, nor could we scrutinize everything which we set forth before, we will find it described in this Treatise.

In the first place, we have preached[283] that a perfect election (in every matter which we want to make fit) [demands that we] adapt the Ascendant and the fourth, and their lords, and also the Moon and her lord, also the Sun and the Lot of Fortune, and the lords of all of these, and the planet which naturally signifies the matter to be chosen, and even the house of the matter, and its lord[284] [should be] in the Ascendant of the election.

And one should not make any of the significators which we ought to weaken in any beginning, be a planet which has a strong testimony in the Ascendant of the nativity of the one for whom we are choosing (if his nativity were known)—and especially the victor over it,[285] nor [should the weakened planet be] the significator of the revolution of that year.

And these are the roots which we ought especially to adapt in elections. Of course, perhaps there will be an adaptation of matters (which we will remind [you of] in their own places [below]), such that we should weaken one of them—just as the Moon must be weakened when searching for a fugitive, since we do not want[286] *his* fitness.

And in this book are 13 chapters, in which there are 64 sections.[287] And one must not wonder if, in any of these, we recall anything which is in another. For there are certain things which are under one category, in another

---

[282] Paris 16204 reads, "useful" (*utiles*).

[283] In I.2.0 above.

[284] The *mss.* read *dominum*, indicating that it is also something to be made fit; but the rest of the sentence does not make sense unless we also assume (as al-'Imrānī has advised) that the lord of the house of the matter is in the Ascendant.

[285] This may be the Ascendant, but perhaps refers to the victor over the whole nativity: see I.3.

[286] Reading *nolumus* with Madrid for *volumus* ("we *do* want") in other *mss.*

[287] That is, there are 64 subchapters distributed among the 13 chapters which follow.

manner than they are under another. And this is the number of all things,[288] with God's praise.

Chapter II.1.0: [Electing for powerful people][289]

The first chapter is the path of matters which particularly pertain to kings and princes (for the most part).[290] The first section [is] on the confirmation of dignities; the second, on the removal of dignities; the third, on the building of cities and forts; the fourth, on the building of houses and the rest of what is in a city and fort; the fifth, on the destruction of the buildings of enemies; the sixth, on the rerouting[291] of rivers and springs; the seventh, on the building of ships for defeating enemies; the eighth, on going out to battle or something else; the ninth, on the reconciliation of enemies; the tenth, on returning; the eleventh, on the hunt; the twelfth, on racing horses; the thirteenth, on games.

On the beginning of things pertaining to kings and princes

In every beginning for kings or princes or what is for their sake, at the beginning one must make the Sun, and the tenth, and its lord, fit. According to Dorotheus and others,[292] the Sun should not be conjoined to a bad one nor [in] its square or opposite aspect, but he should be in the aspect of the fortunes, in an angle or a follower of an angle, or he should be in his own sign, or one which has dignity in his place should aspect him (but not from the opposite or square),[293] and it should not be with him in one sign.[294] And he

---

288 This seems to be a numerological statement, perhaps referring to 64 as being the square of 8.

289 In what follows, my chapter designations provide the Treatise, Chapter, and Subchapter for each part, and I have retained the section titles below in my headings. The division and titling of sections and chapters is a bit uneven at the beginning in the manuscripts, with two different paragraphs vying to be the first chapter, and the later section headings differ slightly from their descriptions here.

290 *Secundum maiorem partem.* This can also mean, "according to the majority," suggesting that al-'Imrānī is going to report a set of majority opinions. But I favor my interpretation, since although most of the elections in this first part pertain to powerful people, others may have enemies or want to bet on horses, *etc.*

291 Reading *eductione* with Madrid for *edificatione* ("building") in other *mss.*

292 Source unknown at this time.

293 Adding "or square" with Madrid.

294 Probably because of the threat of the Sun's rays.

should be in a masculine quarter and in a masculine sign, and if he were in a place in which he would have dignity, it will be better. Nor should he be in a sign in which there is going to be an eclipse in that year.

And each luminary should be in the bound of a fortune, aspecting each other with a praiseworthy aspect. Even the lords of their bounds [should be] in some dignity of their own, aspecting the luminaries. And generally, we should make them fit as much as we could, in strength and good fortune.

And if there were an unfortunate conjunction or prevention, one should not begin anything which pertains to powerful people, unless after 15 days: and after that we should make the election fit just as we said before.

Chapter II.1.1: On the confirmation[295] of dignities

[First], one must adapt all the things which we said before in the preceding [section] on royal undertakings.

Therefore,[296] let us begin with those who are confirmed [in a dignity] so that they may be in charge of wars. Let the Ascendant be one of the houses of Mars, and Mars should be made fortunate, aspecting the Ascendant or[297] its lord with a trine aspect.

But if it were not a confirmation for war, let the Ascendant be one of the houses of Jupiter (which are even useful for warriors). And let Jupiter be aspecting the Ascendant or its lord with a praiseworthy aspect.

And know that the fixed signs (and the common ones) are more praiseworthy and better than the movable ones, in the elections of matters which we want to last for a long time. It is even good that the Moon be joined to the Sun by aspect, and the Sun to Jupiter with a regard of friendship.[298] Which if the Sun were in the triplicity of Aries, it will be good.

And it must also be done thusly in the election of kings and their children, and in every great matter which we want to last for a long time.

But if it were the dignity of a scribe, let Mercury be aspecting the Ascendant and its lord by an aspect of friendship, namely so that he would be

295 Reading with the earlier description of this chapter, for *electione*.

296 Cf. *On Elect.* §128a.

297 Paris 16204 reads, "and." Surely it would be best to aspect both.

298 Following Munich and Vatican (*amicitiae respectu*) for "in an aspect of friendship, received" (*aspectu amicitiae respectus*). But surely being received by the Sun would be a fine thing.

faithful in his dignity. And if it were the dignity of a treasurer,[299] one must make the second house and its lord fit, and it should not be impeded.

Chapter II.1.2: On the removal of dignities

If we want to deprive those whom we have confirmed of a dignity, and it was our intention that, considering their usefulness, after the removal they would be restored in that same dignity, we should put the Moon in a sign of two bodies,[300] in some angle. And also, let the Ascendant and its lord, and also the lord of the house of the Moon, be in a sign of two bodies. But the Moon and her lord[301] should be increased in light and number,[302] and they should be ascending in the north;[303] and observe here whatever we said about rank.[304]

But if you did not want to stand in the way of depriving [him of it],[305] let the Moon be made unfortunate, burned up, in the sixth or in the twelfth, in a fixed sign, in the dignity of a fortune, with the soundness of the Ascendant and its lord. And let them be fortunate, and so on.

In the instructions written above,[306] one should not think that we are contradicting what we said in the first book, in which we said that the Moon is the significator of an interrogation, since there was no signification [for her] in the Ascendant.[307] In this chapter, since we have made the Ascendant safe and fortunate, therefore the Moon will have signification over the matter itself which we want to make fit or destroy. For she is the significator of eve-

---

299 *Camerarii.*

300 That is, a common sign.

301 But Munich and Vatican say, "and the lord of the Ascendant."

302 Paris 16204 reads, "computation" (*compoto*).

303 Probably in northern ecliptical latitudes, but perhaps even declination.

304 *Ordinatione*, probably referring to the general instructions in II.1.0 above.

305 Reading *nolueris/nolueriмus* with Munich for *volueris/voluerimus*

306 Namely, the previous paragraph.

307 I believe this refers to I.2.1, in which al-'Imrānī criticized al-Khayyāt for assuming the Moon could act as the chief significator for the client. Al-'Imrānī is pointing out that since we are taking away someone's dignity, it is all right to put the Moon in a poor condition, since the Moon signifies the overall situation, not the client himself. The client (who is taking away the man's dignity) is represented by the Ascendant, which is made strong here.

ry *undertaking*: and understand whatever we are going to say in this book, according to this method.[308]

Chapter II.1.3: On the building of cities and forts

If[309] you wanted to build cities or forts, one must make the Ascendant a fixed sign, earthy, and likewise a sign in which the Moon is, and the lord of the Ascendant.[310] And the Moon should be increased in light and number, going toward her own exaltation, and toward the conjunction of a fortunate fortune in its own exaltation or the exaltation of the Moon, received. However, we do not say it is harmful if it[311] were in a watery sign. It is even useful that she[312] be ascending in northern declination. And let her be waxing, in more than one-half of her light.[313]

Al-Tabarī said that she should be in crooked signs, because they signify augmentation.[314]

Al-Kindī said[315] the Lot of Fortune should be in any angle, and the angles should not be remote.[316] The Tail [should be] in the twelfth, but the lord of the conjunction or prevention quick in its own motion, in its own dignity. And this opinion is good and authoritative.

But sometimes it is impossible to make all things fit. And we praise it the Moon is under the earth, and being joined to a planet appearing above the

308 That is, the Ascendant signifies the *client* who is removing the man from his dignity or raising him up to one; the Moon signifies the action or situation itself. Therefore, we make the Ascendant good to make his efforts as an agent successful, while we harm the Moon to harm the position of the man in the office or dignity. Al-'Imrānī had already addressed this type of situation in I.2.13.

309 For this paragraph, cf. al-Rijāl VII.20.3.

310 By definition this would make the Ascendant Taurus, with Venus and the Moon in it (although, if one were using quadrant-based houses, I suppose the Moon and Venus could also be in Gemini if the span of the house was large enough).

311 The Ascendant.

312 The Latin does not specify, but in context I take this to be the Moon.

313 That is, between her first quarter and the Full Moon.

314 Al-Tabarī is probably getting this from something like *Carmen* V.43, which describes the Moon's relation to prices and commerce (see al-'Imrānī II.3.2-3, and al-Rijāl VII.11.2). When the Moon is in the crooked signs (in the northern hemisphere, but the straight ones in the southern), she will by definition be increasing in her declination.

315 See *Forty Chapters* Ch. 15 for a fuller discussion of this.

316 Al-Kindī means that the degree of the Midheaven should not fall into the ninth whole sign, but should be in the tenth sign. But he may allow it to be in the eleventh sign.

earth. And we should make Saturn fit, as a significator of the building of cities and the populating of lands: and what is more praiseworthy in this is that he would be aspecting the significators with a trine aspect, with reception. And we should adapt the planet whose exaltation is [in the] Ascendant, and the lord of the exaltation of the place of the Moon.

And 'Umar al-Farrukhān [al-Tabarī][317] said, the lord of the exaltation is to be preferred to the lord of the house, in buildings and everything which we want to be elevated above the earth. And this opinion is good.

And one must labor in the adaptation of all things which we set out before in the chapter on rank.[318] But if it were a building of ignoble men,[319] we should adapt however many things we could, after we have adapted the rootable things in elections.

Chapter II.1.4: On the building of houses and the rest of what is in a city and fort

And if it were a building in which we want drinking and games or other things which pertain to being merry, let Venus be aspecting the Ascendant with a praiseworthy aspect, she being fortunate, of a good condition. And if it were a house of study, let it be Mercury instead of Venus. If it is a prison,[320] let it be Saturn instead of her.

Chapter II.1.5: On the destruction of the buildings of enemies[321]

One must note that destruction is contrary to building: therefore, we must do the contrary in that case.[322] We should make the Ascendant a fiery or airy sign, and let the Moon and the lord of the Ascendant be in signs just like that.

---

[317] Both Madrid and Paris 16204 suggest al-Farghani (*afargani*, *alfragani*, respectively), but al-Farghani has no 'Umar in his name. So, I take this to be a mistake for al-Farrukhān, which is indeed part of 'Umar al-Tabarī's name.

[318] *Ordinationis*. This seems to refer to the specific instructions for important people, in II.1.0 above.

[319] That is, regular people rather than kings, princes, and nobles.

[320] Reading *carcer* with Madrid for what seems to be *sectitus* in Paris 16204.

[321] For this chapter, cf. al-Rijāl VII.58.

[322] See II.1.3-4 above.

Al-Tabarī said,[323] the Ascendant should be a sign of straight ascensions, and the lord of the Ascendant western,[324] ascending after the Ascendant, diminishing[325] in course, going toward the conjunction of a planet just like that. And it should be going toward the sign and degree in which it falls;[326] nor should it be slow nor retrograde; and it should be cadent from the angles.

The Moon[327] should not be western,[328] and she should be cadent from the angles, diminishing in course and light, conjoined to a cadent planet and to one going toward the degree in which it falls, or to the degree in which the Moon falls.

But if she were above the earth, she should be[329] conjoined to a cadent planet which was under [the earth],[330] and she should be southern in declination and latitude, nor should she be joined to a retrograde planet, nor should the lord of the Ascendant be retrograde. And this work should happen in the last quarter of the Lunar month, nor should the Moon aspect her lord, nor the Sun.

And this election is for the destruction of a building whose re-building we do not want.[331] But if we did not intend it for that, the work will be easier. And in every matter, one must adapt the roots which we stated before.

Chapter II.1.6: On the rerouting of rivers and springs[332]

In this work,[333] let Saturn be eastern, and also the lord of the Ascendant, free from the bad ones.[334] But the Moon [should be] under the earth, namely

---

323 I am not currently sure how much of the following really belongs to al-Tabarī.

324 This probably means that it should be about to "sink" under the rays of the Sun. Being "western" and "sinking" is the same word in Latin and Arabic.

325 *Minuens*, which might also mean "subtracting" (see also below).

326 That is, its fall, here and below.

327 Cf. perhaps *Carmen* V.7.1.

328 That is, rising after the Sun: for she would then be waxing, which suggests increase rather than destruction.

329 Reading *sit* for *sitque*.

330 Or perhaps, "joined to a planet *falling* under [namely, *being* under] the earth," which is how the Latin al-Rijāl understands it.

331 Reading *nolumus* with Madrid for Paris 16204's *volumus*.

332 Cf. al-Rijāl VII.21.

333 Cf. *On Elect.* §§50a-d.

in the third or in the fifth, in a fixed sign;[335] and if she were above the earth, let her be in the eleventh; and it is even good that Saturn be in the eleventh, [though] he should not be joined to the Moon by body. And we should make Jupiter fit, nor should there be a bad one in the Midheaven.

Al-Kindī said,[336] the Moon should be in the first square from the Sun, made fortunate, increased in number, in an angle; nor should the angles be remote.[337] And the lord of the Ascendant should be eastern, in its own dignity, in an angle or one following an angle, and the Ascendant a watery sign, made fortunate by a strong fortune (and likewise the Moon). And the Lot of Fortune must be made fit, and the degree of the conjunction or prevention.

Chapter II.1.7: On the building of ships for defeating enemies[338]

Let[339] the Ascendant be made a fixed sign, and if all the angles were in fixed signs, it will be better. But the Moon and the lord of the Ascendant should be in an angle; however, a strong fortune should be put in the Midheaven, and let it be strong (that is, let it be eastern, and by dignity, and by quick motion). And let the Moon be in her own greater motion.

We should also make Mars fit, if it were because of war. But if they were ships on account of transportation, let the Moon be in her own average course, ascending in her own circle.[340]

And[341] in all of these things, if we have made the lord of the conjunction or the prevention fit, it will be good. And let the Moon, when she was separated from either of them,[342] be joined to a fortune.

---

334 Madrid suggests that Saturn should also be free from the bad ones or from evils, but the text is ungrammatical and may be an error.

335 Reading with Sahl and al-Rijāl VII.21 for manuscript variations such as "under the earth, namely in the third or fourth" (Madrid) and "under the earth, namely at the beginning or in the fifth" (Paris 16204, misreading *initio* for *tertio*).

336 Cf. *Forty Chapters* Ch. 16.1, §§482-483. Al-Kindī himself adds more information than is found here, and Hugo's al-Kindī differs in a few details.

337 See my Introduction.

338 Cf. al-Rijāl VII.59, though most of this chapter is from *Forty Chapters* Ch. 17.

339 Cf. *Forty Chapters* Ch. 17, §§490-92a. Al-'Imrānī has changed this paragraph somewhat, because al-Kindī assumes the ship is for transportation, and so warns against Mars. But al-'Imrānī instructs us to adapt Mars, and then uses al-Kindī's statement about the Moon's apogee after that.

340 That is, in the apogee (either of her epicycle or deferent).

341 Cf. *Forty Chapters* Ch. 17, §494-95a.

342 That is, after her separation from the most recent conjunction or prevention.

We also praise it if the lord of the Ascendant is going toward an angle. And one must consider[343] the fourth house: this is the place of ships and what is like that. Therefore, we should adapt it, and make it a watery sign.

But some people[344] claimed it is useful that the Moon be in Taurus or Gemini, for there is a river;[345] and we ought to beware of the aspect of Mars.

Also we judge the condition of the Moon above the earth to be useful.

But to launch ships into the water is like this.[346]

Chapter II.1.8: On going out to battle or something else[347]

It is necessary to make Mars fit, and to make him be aspecting the Ascendant by a trine aspect. After that, he should have[348] the greatest dignity in it (and it is better that it be his house), and he should even aspect the lord of the Ascendant by a praiseworthy aspect. And let the lord of the seventh be weak, made unfortunate, cadent, and what is better is that the one which makes it unfortunate be the lord of the Ascendant.

And let the lord of the Ascendant be eastern, going toward an angle, in one of its own dignities, elevated over the lord of the seventh, from the tenth [sign from it].[349] It is even useful that the lord of the Ascendant be an infortune,[350] crossing over[351] the lord of the seventh. But if the lord of the Ascendant were above the earth, and also the lord of the seventh under the earth, it will be good. And if the lord of the seventh [is] being made unfortunate by the lord of the Ascendant, we will have trust that the king of the rebel enemies will be captured, with the aid of God.

And we ought to make the second house and its lord fit, so that the condition of assets is adapted, and that of the allies. And it is good that the lord of the Midheaven be aspecting the Ascendant, and it has a dignity (namely

343 Al-Rijāl reads that the lord of the conjunction or prevention should *aspect* (i.e., look at, consider) the fourth.

344 Cf. *Carmen* V.23.3-4.

345 This must be the long constellation Eridanus (a river), which does indeed overlap the early signs (and would have done so more in past centuries).

346 Cf. *Carmen* V.25.

347 Cf. al-Rijāl VII.55.

348 Reading *habeat* for *habuit.*

349 That is, overcoming him (see the Glossary).

350 Reading *infortuna* with Paris 16204, for Madrid's *fortuna.*

351 *Transiens.* This suggests that it is transiting over the body of the lord of the seventh.

house or exaltation, or another) in it; and it should not aspect the degree of the seventh, nor should it have any dignity [there].[352] Which if that could not happen, let it have a greater dignity in the Ascendant [than in the seventh].

And one must work with the Moon in the same way as with the lord of the Ascendant.

Al-Kindī said,[353] it is good that the prince (against whom the [rebel] army goes out), never begin to do battle with them while the Moon is made fortunate; but if a battle is demanded when she is not fortunate, [he should not flee].

[Also],[354] it should be hateful for the combatants to begin a war in the hours which are said to be "burnt up." And this must be done after we have adapted the rooted things in elections, and the rest of the things which we have set out before in this chapter.

On the beginning of departing on any journeys not pertaining to war

And[355] it is necessary that this precede an election for a departure to war: it is good that the ascending sign be earthy, if however the journey were by land. But if by water, watery. And let the Moon be above the earth, going toward an angle. And one must beware of Mars on land, and Saturn by water. And we should make the ninth and its lord fit.

Al-Khasib said,[356] the third and its lord are adapted just like the ninth and its lord.

---

352 Paris 16204 reads that *if* it aspects the degree of the seventh, it should not have a dignity there.

353 Cf. *Forty Chapters* Ch. 11.6, §§406b-07a. Al-'Imrānī's version here is unnecessarily cramped, and is explained better in al-Rijāl VII.57.1. The point of this is to say that the Moon governs the action which is undertaken: here, the rebel has initiated the conflict, and al-Kindī assumes the king or prince is responding by going out to meet him. So, if the rebel (the initiator) has begun the conflict under a fortunate Moon, it will go better for him than for the king, though al-Kindī suggests that this is not a reason to flee if the king really must fight. Likewise, anyone initiating a conflict under an unfortunate Moon, should think twice and "refuse the war."

354 Cf. *Forty Chapters* Ch. 11.7, and further explanation by me (with an example table based on al-Kindī) in al-Rijāl VII.57.2.

355 Cf. *On Elect.* §§116-17a, and *Carmen* V.25.39-42.

356 I currently believe this is probably Hurrazād al-Dārshād al-Khasib (see introduction), who seems to be quoted again below. For the fitness of the third, note al-Khayyāt's instruction below (related to *On Elect.*) that the Moon should aspect from the ninth or the third. The manuscripts spell his name as: *Achacib, Alchabib, Alkabith, Alkab, Alchabit,* and so on.

Abu Ma'shar adapts the lord of the hour at the beginning of departing on the road.

Al-Tabarī and a certain other person[357] [say] the Ascendant and its lord signify the place from which someone is withdrawing, but the seventh and its lord the place to which he goes. However, the Midheaven and its lord [signify] the journey and its condition, [and] we will signify the end by the angle of the earth. Therefore, we must make the angles fit, and their lords, and especially the seventh (which is the place of the matter), [and] the fourth (the end of the matter).

And the Moon should be increased in light and number, nor should she be cadent [from] the Ascendant.[358] But the lord of the place of the Moon and the lord of the Ascendant [should have] gone out from under the rays, and be movable—but a "movable planet" is said when it is in an angle or in one following an angle. And the increase of the Moon signifies that he would quickly reach the place to which he goes. Also we praise that Mercury, having gone out of burning, would be joined to a fortune: for this is good for those going due to buying or selling, since Mercury signifies roads and merchandise.

Al-Khayyāt said,[359] it is good that the Moon be joined to a planet signifying the matter, or that she be in its house: so that if the journey were to the king, she would be joined to the Sun; if to soldiers, to Mars; and it happens to the rest according to this method. Finally, each one (that is, the Moon and the planet signifying the matter) should be safe. And this opinion is good.

Māshā'allāh said,[360] if there were an infortune in the second house, who had no testimony there, it signifies that some hindrance would happen in those things which he left behind, of the nature of that bad one. And if it were received, the hindrance would be diminished; but if not received, or it would be in a place in which it falls, the impediment will be increased, and especially if it were retrograde. And one must speak in this manner about a fortune. And[361] if the lord of the seventh were in the Ascendant, it signifies

---

357 Perhaps al-Kindī Ch.8.3, but for this paragraph and the next see also Sahl's *On Quest.* §9.1 (*Judges* §9.1); cf. also the source text in *Carmen* V.21.1-4, and al-Rijāl's use of it in VII.70.4.

358 Reading *cadens* with Paris 16204 in addition to Madrid's *ascendens*, with *Carmen* V.21.2. *Carmen* specifically mentions the sixth and twelfth.

359 Cf. *On Elect.* §§108a-13b, and *On Quest.* §9.1 (*Judges* §9.1).

360 Cf. *On Quest.* §9.3 (*Judges* §9.12).

361 The first part of this sentence is from *On Quest.* §9.2 (*Judges* §9.12).

that it will occur to him on the road where he goes; and likewise if the Moon were joined to a retrograde planet impeding[362] her.

And *ibn al-Khasib*[363] said, and one must defer a journey so long as the Moon were in the second face of Libra.

And al-Khayyāt said,[364] the aspect of the bad ones to the Ascendant, is easier than that to the Moon. For the Moon has been given the signification of travel, for she particularly has the signification over every beginning. Therefore, her signification in journeys is doubled, and for that reason she is stronger. But if the nativity of the traveler were known, let the Ascendant of the journey be the tenth[365] of the nativity, and the Moon be in the ninth house of the nativity, increased in light and number, or let her be joined to fortunes from the ninth or the third. And if his journey were to the king, let the tenth of the nativity be ascending, and the Moon be joined to the Sun; however, if he went to those doing battle, let the Moon be joined to Mars; and thus with the rest. But if the Moon were impeded, nor however could we put off the journey, let the Moon be cadent from the Ascendant, and likewise the planet which impedes her, and we should adapt the entrance [into the region to which he goes], and be concerned with that.

And al-Tabarī said,[366] whoever desires a quick and prosperous return, should put Venus and Jupiter in the square of the Sun and the Moon, and let the Moon be between the two fortunes, separated from one and joined to the other. And let the Moon be increased in light and number.

And generally, if the Sun were in the opposition of the fortunes, it will signify the quickness of the return. And the infortunes make the return slow down, and they impede with the greatest impediment. And if a fortune were with them, prosperity will follow. If the Moon were in the fourth, it will signify a long stay.

---

362 Reading *impediet* or *impedienti* with Paris 16204 for Madrid's *recipienti* ("receiving").

363 Cf. *On Elect.* §122c, but see *Carmen* V.25.7 and the beginning of this section. This is probably Hurrazād al-Dārshād al-Khasib, just as Hurrazād (a follower of Sahl's) is quoted in al-Rijāl VII.20.3. But the manuscripts of al-'Imrānī give the names as: *Abnalchasib, Abnalcadib, Albualchacib*, and so on.

364 Cf. *On Elect.* §§101, 103b, 104a, 105a, 110.

365 Reading with Munich and *On Elect.* §103b, although Sahl himself (like al-Khayyāt below) says this should only be if the man is traveling for tenth-house business.

366 Cf. *Carmen* V.22 (on which this is loosely based) and al-Rijāl VII.72.

Chapter II.1.9: On the reconciliation of enemies

Seeing[367] that after bringing war to mind one should remember concord, let us follow through with that. And so, let it be that the lord of the seventh be weak and made fortunate,[368] and let it[369] be joined to the lord of the Ascendant by a trine or sextile aspect, or aspecting the Ascendant by a good aspect.

And let the lord of the twelfth, too, be weak and cadent; and if the twelfth house itself were impeded, it will even be good. And we should make the eleventh and its lord fit, and one must do thusly with the twelfth and its lord as with the seventh and its lord.[370]

And the lord of the Ascendant should be in the Midheaven, or going toward it; let the Ascendant and its lord be as strong as we could [make them], in strength and good fortune.

But if the lord of the twelfth were friendly to the lord of the Ascendant or in its aspect of friendship, it will be better. And if the degree of the Ascendant and the degree of the twelfth were two degrees of one strength (that is, so that the days of one would be equal to the days of the other, or their ascensions were equal),[371] that is the best that it could be in the fitness of the houses.

And if the one who makes the peace is the king, we should adapt those things which we have remembered at the outset of this chapter.[372] And let the lord of the Ascendant be crossing over the lord of the twelfth.[373] If the signs from which we are taking the significations were fixed or ascending straight, it will be better.

---

367 Source unknown from here to the quote by al-Tabarī below.

368 Reading *fortunatus* with Paris 7413-I. Other *mss.* have *fortuna* (though Paris 16204 has *unfortunatus*). It makes sense that it would be made fortunate (suggesting good will and openness), but weak (suggesting that the enemy is less powerful and more amenable to reconciliation).

369 Reading *iunctus* with most of the *mss.* (though Paris 16204 reads *Luna iuncta*, "let the Moon be joined").

370 That is, make them both weakened but somehow made fortunate.

371 Cf. *ITA* I.9. But it is highly unlikely that, in a quadrant-based house system, both of these degrees would be related in this way. Al-'Imrānī might simply mean that the degrees of the *signs* for these houses have this relationship (such as if the twelfth were Gemini, and the Ascendant Cancer).

372 Or perhaps, from II.1.0.

373 This is probably a reference to overcoming.

If however this concord were by the hands of legates coming together or through letters, we should make Mercury fit. But if it were by the presence of each [of the combatants], we should make Jupiter fit. And the lord of the Ascendant should be in a commanding[374] sign, but the lord of the seventh and twelfth in obeying signs.[375]

Al-Tabarī said, if you wanted to lead or draw enemies out from their own places by fraud or cleverness, let the Moon and the Ascendant be in Aries or Taurus or Gemini or Virgo or Sagittarius or Capricorn or Pisces; let the Moon be joined to one of the fortunes, or one of them should be in the Ascendant. And the lord of the Ascendant should not be cadent from an angle, [and should be] aspecting the Ascendant by an aspect of friendship—and let it be in the aspect of a fortune. And it is good that the lord of the twelfth be weak.

Chapter II.1.10: On returning

After we have made mention of withdrawing [from a conflict], we must remember returning from a journey. The adaptation of this is making the second house and its lord fit.

Of course the entrance of the prince and of every one who rules in that same city is the hour at which he enters the gate of the city; and the entrance of those who are of lesser dignity is the hour at which [each] enters the gates of his own palace, or of the place in which those subject to him show respect [for him].[376] But the entrance of any foreign traveler about to pass through the city is not that, because they have neither authority nor dignity in it.

Abu Ma'shar [said], the entrance of the king into the city is the hour at which he first enters it. If however he were to withdraw afterwards and return again, we will not be concerned with his return in the way that we know universal matters, but in the way that we know lesser matters. For it is just like a revolution in nativities: for whether the nativity were good or bad, the revolution will increase or diminish [that] only a little bit.[377]

---

374 *Praeceptorio.*

375 Again, cf. *ITA* I.9.

376 Reading *venerantur eum* for *veneratur eos*. This verb can also mean to beg, worship, and so on: obviously, where the greatest respect is shown to him.

377 Abū Ma'shar seems to mean that more care should be taken with the return from an entire campaign or major journey (which is being likened to a nativity here), not a tempo-

Therefore,[378] in every entrance, we must make the second and its lord fit, and this will suffice for us after we have adapted the rooted things in elections. And if the lord of the second were in the Ascendant, safe and fortunate, it will be better; and if it were not in the Ascendant, let it be in the tenth or in the house of trust,[379] and in no way should it be put under the earth. But if it happened that the Moon would be with the lord of the second, she being made fortunate, it is better. And let the Ascendant be a fixed sign, and the lord of the Midheaven removed from the infortunes, nor should it aspect the eleventh with an unfriendly aspect. But let the fourth house be a fixed sign. If however we were not able to make the Moon fit, let her be banished from the Ascendant, and let us make fortunes be aspecting the house of the end of the matter and the Midheaven. And let us beware of the lord of the second, lest it commit its own management[380] to the lord of the sixth or twelfth or fourth or eighth; and what is worst is that it would commit its own management from these places to their lords, and if these same places in the revolution of the year of the world[381] were evil. And it is good that the Moon be increased in light and number.

Which if you wanted that the one who enters, should depart without delay [but] with prosperity and profit, one should make the lord of the eighth be eastern and quick in its own motion, increased in number, and likewise the Moon. And let the planet with which the Moon is being joined, be quicker in course.

Chapter II.1.11: On searching and hunting

For every search and hunt,[382] it is good to make the seventh house be a sign which is likened to the hunted thing. That is, if we wished to hunt four-footed things on land, let it be an earthy sign; if flying things, an airy one; and

---

rary return which is only part of the whole journey (likened here to a solar revolution, which is only valid for one year).

378 Cf. *On Quest.* §9.2 (*Judges* §9.12), and *On Elect.* §§118-20a. This paragraph might also be continuing the opinion of Abū Ma'shar above, since it bears a similarity to many passages and may represent Abū Ma'shar's amalgam of them.

379 That is, the eleventh.

380 *Dispositionem.*

381 This should probably be in his *natal* solar revolution.

382 Madrid reads, "for every search for a fugitive, and a hunt." Source unknown at this time.

if it were by sea, a watery one. We even say it is good that the lord of the seventh be in corresponding signs, and the lord of the Ascendant should be strong and fortunate, but the lord of the seventh weak and unfortunate. And if the lord of the Ascendant or Mars were the one to make it unfortunate, it will be good. But the planet from which the Moon is being separated should be aspecting the one to which she is being joined. And we should make the Sun fit, because he signifies hunting.[383] Also, one must make fit all the things which we said before in the chapters on wars. And if the hunt were in rivers, the Ascendant should be a sign of two bodies. And in every way let the lord of the seventh be diminished, descending, cadent, remote.

Al-Khayyāt said[384] that [the lord of the seventh] should be in one following an angle: because if it were remote, [the prey] would escape from the hands of the hunters. But if the lord of the seventh did not aspect the lord of the Ascendant, one must have fear that we will not find the prey. And the Moon should be increased in light, and the one to which the Moon is being joined should be cadent. But the lord of the Ascendant [should] be elevated above[385] the planet to which the Moon is being joined.

Chapter II.1.12: On racing horses

A certain person said, it is good for the one who begins this, that he should go out of his own home with the lord of the hour appearing in the Ascendant. And this is the counsel of al-Kindī.[386]

Wherefore,[387] the first [lord of the hour] will come before all of those who come ahead.[388] And if it were in the Midheaven, [the horse] will come in se-

---

383 Probably because hunting parties (at least, for large game and not sustenance) is often an upper-class pursuit, and in many cases was a noble or royal privilege. Remember that in this part of Treatise II, al-'Imrānī is largely discussing elections for kings and nobles.

384 Cf. *On Elect.* §138a for the first two sentences of this paragraph.

385 That is, overcoming (see Glossary).

386 This is not so, based on *Forty Chapters* §649, though it does make sense. In Hugo's translation of al-Kindī, all of the angles are important (but especially the Ascendant), and the lord of the hour at the moment (probably at the time of the race) signifies the winner, the next lord of the hour the next one, and so on. It may be that al-'Imrānī or this other "certain person" combined these two ideas as an election, so that the lord of the hour would be in the Ascendant when leaving for the race.

387 This is Sahl (and probably ultimately from Māshā'allāh), *On Quest.* §12.1 (*Judges* §12.1).

388 Omitting a statement in Paris 16204 that one must also adapt everything else one can in the chart, since that is not in Sahl.

cond. But if in the seventh, he will likewise come in third. And lastly, its presence in the fourth will render him last. And we must beware lest it be in a place in which it falls, for one will especially have to fear for him.

And he said[389] that the Moon should be in Sagittarius or in the middle of Libra.

Chapter II.1.13: On games

A certain person said,[390] he who intends to undertake this should leave his home under a movable sign, because there is no usefulness in fixed signs. And by his words it seems that the common ones are between each. And if the Moon were joined to Mars from a trine,[391] it will be good, and one should beware of Saturn. And he sees it that [the client's] face and chest should be against[392] the Moon. And he praised it that the Moon should be above the earth.

Chapter II.2.1: On works whose significations are taken from the Ascendant, [and first on breastfeeding][393]

It is necessary that as the wet-nurse begins to give the boys' milk, [that] the Moon be joined to Venus by body, and let each be safe; and it will be better if Venus were descending.[394]

And it is right in everything which we recall to mind, that we first make the rooted things fit.

---

389 Source unknown at this time.

390 Probably Māshā'allāh, as al-Rijāl VII.64 credits him with the statement about facing the Moon.

391 But see al-Rijāl's alternative reading in VII.64.

392 That is, facing the Moon."

393 Cf. al-Rijāl VII.31.

394 Probably in ecliptical latitude, as al-Rijāl says.

Chapter II.2.2: On taking boys away from the breast[395]

It is good that the Moon be far away from the Sun, joined to the lord of her own house, and the Ascendant should be one of the houses of the fortunes, even though the house of Venus displeases certain people: for they used to fear that the mother of the one would not draw another boy from the breasts.[396]

And a certain person said, if we were separating boys from wet-nurses, if the Moon were in *al-Ṣarfah*,[397] the twelfth mansion (it is in Leo),[398] boys will not care to nurse from another.

But certain others said, let the Moon and the lord of the Ascendant be in signs of seeds (such as are Virgo, Taurus, Capricorn), so that the boy would desire the eating of crops and herbs.

Chapter II.2.3: On the cutting of the nails[399]

Let the Moon be increased in light and number, in an angle or one following an angle, nor should she be in Gemini nor in Sagittarius,[400] nor even joined to their lords—for it will be feared that they will not grow back.

But let her be in the house of Venus or Mars or in Cancer or in Leo.

Chapter II.2.4: On cutting the hair of the head or the body[401]

Let this be when the Moon and the Ascendant are in signs of two bodies. However, certain people commended Virgo, nor did they condemn Aries nor Libra; nor do they esteem Capricorn nor Taurus. And if the Moon and the Ascendant were safe [and] in signs of seeds, the growth will accelerate.

---

395 Cf. al-Rijāl VII.32.

396 Reading tentatively for *ne genetrix alterius* [*ulterius?*] *alium puerum ab uberibus non subtrahet.* The meaning might be different if, instead of *genetrix* ("mother"), we read it as *nutrix* ("nurse"). This seems to mean that the nurse or mother will be reluctant to wean another child later on.

397 Lat. *Acarfa.* See al-Rijāl VII.101, in Part I of this book.

398 Reading the correct constellation, for *Libra.*

399 Cf. al-Rijāl VII.8.

400 Al-Rijāl reads, "Pisces."

401 Cf. al-Rijāl VII.6.

And we should beware of the aspect of Saturn, and especially if he aspected with an aspect of enmity,[402] for one must fear lest worms would follow. And if Mars aspected with a bad aspect, it is feared lest he would be cut with the razor or an abscess would arise, and the like.[403]

Chapter II.2.5: On entering a bath[404]

It is good that the Moon be in one of the houses of Mars, joined to the Sun or Venus or Jupiter, from a trine or sextile aspect; and they do not praise the conjunction of Venus nor the aspect of Saturn.

Which if she were not in a house of Mars, let her be in the house of the Sun or in her own [house]. Nor do they want the house of Mercury nor Venus nor Saturn. And beware lest the Moon be joined to one of the aforesaid degree by degree in the same sign. But[405] if he were not there for being anointed with *nūrah* (that is an ointment by which [people] are anointed in the bath, for removing [hair]), we do not condemn the other signs, if however they were safe.

Chapter II.2.6: On healing the sick

If we undertook this, it is good that the Moon not be in the opposition of the lord of the sixth nor that of the eighth, even if they would be fortunes. But if they were infortunes, she should not be in any aspect of them. Which if that could not be [so], do not let them aspect with a bad aspect, nor should the Moon be descending.[406] Also, one must adapt the planet which signifies the sick limb (like Mercury, who signifies the ears); but the Ascendant signifies the whole body.

---

402 Reading *inimicitiae* with Madrid for Paris 16204's *amicitiae*.

403 Weinstock p. 59 suggests that elections for cutting the hair or nails must have been for special ritual occasions, not for everyday trimming. Still, one wonders what they must have been doing for such frightful things to be possible.

404 Cf. al-Rijāl VII.5.

405 Reading with Madrid, in comparison with *On Elect.* §70a. The manuscripts vary wildly here, probably because of the similarity of *iunctio* and *iuncta* (joining, joined) with *unctio* (anointing). But note that *On Elect.* has very different instructions for this.

406 Probably in ecliptical latitude, but possibly in declination.

Chapter II.2.7: On remedies pertaining to surgery[407]

Al-Khayyāt said,[408] the Moon should be increased in light and number, and let her be made fortunate by Venus and Jupiter.

However, one must beware of every aspect of Mars. For when the Moon is in the increase of her light, she is more severely impeded by Mars. And if she were decreasing, she is more severely impeded by Saturn.

And the Moon should be in a fixed [sign]. And beware lest the Moon aspect the sign signifying a limb being cut by iron, by any aspect; nor even should the lord of the Ascendant be in it.

And the Moon should not be cadent. And it is good that the lord of the Ascendant be in the Ascendant or in the Midheaven.

And it should be likewise in the treatment of the eyes, on account of an abscess or blemish.

And adapt the planet signifying that limb, and even the sign.

Chapter II.2.8: On the letting of blood by phlebotomy or cupping[409]

It is good that the Moon be in the defect of her light, in a masculine sign, and joined to Mars; nor should they fear Mars unless he is ascending in latitude and in the circle of his apogee. And the lord of the house of the Moon should be aspecting him with a praiseworthy aspect.

And a certain person said[410] that one must beware of Taurus and Leo in this work, and he testifies that the signs of two bodies are not to be feared (and especially if there were a fortune in it). And he even said, if it were necessary to let [only] a little bit of blood, let the Moon be in Libra or Scorpio, and the Moon should be not in the conjunction of Mercury, nor of Saturn; and they hated Capricorn and Virgo and Pisces. And they used to put the Moon in the defect of her light, nor should there be an infortune in the second house from the house of the Moon. They also hated the movable signs, unless they were in the aspect of the fortunes.

---

[407] Cf. al-Rijāl VII.46 for some of this. This chapter is a jumble of statements by al-Khayyāt, which largely parallel *On Elect.* §§67a-b and d, and 69a and d.

[408] Cf. *On Elect.* §§67a-d, based on *Carmen* V.39-40.

[409] See also al-Rijāl VII.7.1, which has a number of other views.

[410] Source unknown at this time.

Abu Ma'shar said, Mars is an infortune in every work, except in those things which pertain to blood and the opening of the veins, and to the letting of blood by cupping, or in the healing of the sick.

Al-Kindī said,[411] it is necessary that the Moon and the Ascendant be in airy signs or fiery ones, and even their lords. Nor should you touch any limb while the lord of the Ascendant was in the sign whose limb it was. Also, we praise it that the lord of the Midheaven be a fortune, aspecting the Moon or the lord of the Ascendant, and that the lord of the Ascendant and the Moon are not in the fourth house. And cupping[412] is better after the prevention. Also, letting [blood] is praised more at the beginning of the month. Beware even the conjunction of the lord of the eighth with the Moon.

Chapter II.2.9: On the circumcision of boys[413]

The Moon should be elevated above Venus,[414] and joined to Jupiter. And we should beware of the Ascendant and its lord, and also Venus and the Moon, and Saturn, lest [Saturn] aspect any [of them] by a bad aspect, and especially the Ascendant[415] and the Moon. For Saturn signifies a repetition of the incision, also poison and rottenness. The lord of the Ascendant should be ascending, but the Moon and her lords northern, going toward an angle. And Mars should not be in an angle; however, the Ascendant and the Moon should not be in the sign of Scorpio.[416]

---

[411] Cf. *Forty Chapters* Ch. 32.

[412] Reading with al-Kindī for *aerea*. Al-Kindī believes the air-based suction of cupping is better after the Full Moon, while bloodletting by veins is better after the New Moon.

[413] Cf. al-Rijāl VII.33.

[414] Probably by overcoming (see Glossary).

[415] Reading *ascendens* for *ascendentis*.

[416] Al-Rijāl reads this as though Mars should not be in an angle *nor* the Ascendant (which is redundant).

Chapter II.2.10: On giving purgatives[417]

If[418] we were to do this, it is good that the Moon be in the last half of Libra or the beginning of Scorpio,[419] and let her lord be made fortunate and strong, and likewise the lord of the Ascendant. It is even good that the Ascendant be one of these signs, or any other of the lower signs: that is, which signifies the lower [part of the body], such as Libra and those which follow after Libra, namely [Scorpio], Sagittarius, Capricorn, Aquarius, Pisces. It is even good that the Moon be in them.)

And let [the Moon] be in a sign signifying that limb, made fortunate[420] and strong.

And if we wished to heat or chill with that medication, or to dry or moisten, let the Moon be in a sign signifying that (that is, a hot or cold or dry or moist one).

And we should beware lest one of the significators or the Ascendant be in the cud-chewing signs, for these signify vomiting.

And[421] let the Moon always be ascending in the south.

And a certain person said,[422] of the cud-chewing signs, only Capricorn[423] is hateful.

And[424] [al-Kindī] barred the Moon from every aspect of each infortune, that is, Mars and Saturn. (For Saturn binds up the medicine, but Mars leads it out, up to the flowing of blood. And let it be likewise for electuaries, except that whatever the Ascendant was, it will not harm to such a degree if it were made fortunate—and likewise the lord of the Ascendant and the place of the Moon.) And one must beware of the lord of the eighth.

---

[417] That is, laxatives administered orally. But it may also refer to medicines administered through colonics or suppositories. This chapter is almost completely taken from *Forty Chapters* Ch. 34. Cf. also al-Rijāl VII.47.

[418] For the first four paragraphs, cf. generally *Forty Chapters* Ch. 34; for the first paragraph, see also *On Elect.* §§61a and 65c-d.

[419] Omitting Madrid's *quia ista significant anima[m]*.

[420] Reading *fortunata* for *fortuna*.

[421] This is not from al-Kindī. I believe it means ascending in southern ecliptical latitude.

[422] Source unknown at this time, but cf. al-Rijāl VII.47, which allows Taurus and Virgo for purgatives.

[423] Reading with Paris 16204 for Madrid's *Scorpius*.

[424] Now we return to al-Kindī, §638, with parenthetical remarks by al-'Imrānī.

Chapter II.2.11: On binding drugs[425]

If[426] the drug were of those drugs which, [even if they are binding], tend to provoke certain people to vomiting, we should beware of signs which are called "cud-chewing." But if it were not of those which provoke vomiting, one does not have to beware of the cud-chewing [signs]. But, however, one must beware of Taurus.

And we should adapt the sign which signifies the limb on account of which the medicine is given, just as well as we could.

And let the Moon be in her own average course, in the north, and we should beware of the aspect of Mars. And if she were in the first three degrees of Taurus,[427] it will be good, and likewise if the lord of the Ascendant[428] were going to its own exaltation.

Chapter II.2.12: On sneezing [drugs] and gargles and vomiting, through potions or any other [means][429]

It is good that one who wanted to use one of these, make the Ascendant and the Moon and the place of the significators be of the cud-chewing signs, with everything that we said before about purgative medicines.[430]

And al-Tabarī said, let the Moon be diminished in light and course, ascending in the circle of [her] apogee.

Al-Khayyāt said,[431] let the Moon and the lord of the Ascendant be in Cancer or Leo or Virgo.

---

425 *Constipantes.* That is, medicines which prevent diarrhea or generally support the retention of fluids, as opposed to purgatives.
426 For this paragraph, cf. al-Rijāl VII.47.
427 The precise degree of the Moon's exaltation is usually taken to be at 3° Taurus.
428 Adding *ascendentis* with Paris 16204.
429 Cf. al-Rijāl VII.49.
430 See II.2.10 above.
431 Cf. *On Elect.* §62b, which has a bit more information.

Chapter II.2.13: On putting on new vestments[432]

This chapter pertains to the chapters set forth above, because it is about the body.

It is good that the Moon and the Ascendant be in movable signs, nor [is it] bad [in] signs of two bodies. And of the fixed signs, one must beware of Leo, unless it is some vestment which pertains to war.

Let the Sun be in the Midheaven, and it is good that the Moon be increased in light.[433]

And it is even praised that the second house be made fit, and its lord, and especially in the purchasing of vestments, and in their cutting.

Chapter II.3.1: On the elections of those things which particularly pertain to the second house, and first on the restoring or recovery of assets loaned to someone

[General significators in financial matters]

It[434] is right for you to give priority to certain general things in everything which pertains to assets or profit, or in anything from which we wish to make profit. So, it is necessary to make the second house and its lord fit; also Jupiter, because he naturally signifies assets.[435]

Which if the election were about profit which you never want to be lacking any longer, let the Ascendant and the significators be in a fixed sign, nor should the angles be remote. But if it were something which is to be sold, let it be the contrary,[436] after the rooted things in elections were made fit.

[Paying back a loan or getting one's own money back]

Therefore,[437] if we wanted to receive and restore assets, make the Ascendant and its lord fit, and also Jupiter, and let Mars be cadent from the Moon and from the Ascendant and the Lot of Fortune, and from the Lot of as-

---

[432] Cf. al-Rijāl VII.34.

[433] Probably because these situations suggests prominence and visibility.

[434] For this paragraph and the next, cf. al-Rijāl VII.9.

[435] Al-Rijāl also adds the Lot of Fortune.

[436] This probably includes using the common (or even movable) signs.

[437] For this paragraph and the next, cf. al-Rijāl VII.10.

sets[438] (according to those who trust Lots).[439] Let Mars even be cadent from the second house, and also from the lords of all of these. Also, the signs which give and take (and they are all airy)[440] are said to be good in the accepting of money.

And if we wished to restore something which pertains to eating, one must beware lest the Ascendant or the Moon be in signs of much eating (which are Aries, Taurus, Leo, and even the last part of Sagittarius, also Capricorn and Pisces). Nor should the Ascendant or the Moon be in the conjunction of Saturn.

Chapter II.3.2: On buying[441]

In this, let the Moon be in some feminine angle,[442] also the lord of the Ascendant, subtracting[443] in motion. But the lord of the Midheaven and Mercury should be safe. And if the Moon were with Mercury, it will be useful. If Mercury were even in his own lesser course,[444] it will be good.

'Umar al-Tabarī said,[445] the crooked signs are good for those buying, and even seem to help sellers. And if the Moon were in signs ascending [in declination],[446] increasing [her] number, it makes whatever someone then buys, dear—and contrariwise.

And a certain person said,[447] buying and selling in the first quarter of the Lunar month is useful for each; but in the second quarter, it is more useful

---

438 The Lot of assets or money or substance is taken by day and night from the lord of the second to the second, and projected from the Ascendant: see *ITA* VI.2.4.

439 This comment suggests that al-'Imrānī does not particularly favor any Lots besides the Lot of Fortune.

440 This also recalls the commanding/obeying, and seeing/hearing signs: see *ITA* I.9 for different schemes of these.

441 For this chapter, cf. the diagrams and texts in al-Rijāl VII.11.2.

442 Reading with Madrid and al-Rijāl VII.11.2 for "sign" (Paris 16204).

443 Or, "diminishing" (*minuens*).

444 This probably means he is going very slowly.

445 *Carmen* V.43.2 does not say it is good for buyers, though perhaps it is better when she is still in southern declination, from Capricorn to Pisces. See al-Rijāl VII.11.2.

446 Omitting "straight," as it would not make astrological sense and is contrary to *Carmen* V.43.2, the very sentence on which it is based.

447 Cf. *Carmen* V.43.4-8, and al-Rijāl VII.11.2.

for the seller; however, the third quarter [is] most useful for [the buyer];[448] but the fourth, on the contrary, is asserted to be very useful for the buyer.[449]

And certain people deny that the Moon should be in the aspect of Saturn.

Chapter II.3.3: On the selling of seeds and other things which pertain to open fields, and anything for sale[450]

Let[451] your election be in the first quarter of the Lunar month, and let the Moon be increased in her motion, in increasing signs (and these are the crooked ones).[452]

And[453] let her be in[454] the Ascendant, in one of the two increasing quarters (and these are the masculine ones), and the lord of the Ascendant in one of these places. Also, the Midheaven and its lord [should be] free of the bad ones.

The Moon [should] even be with Mercury, and he eastern, quick in his motion, free of the bad ones.

Chapter II.3.4: On lending money[455]

The Ascendant[456] and its lord belong to the debtor, but the seventh and its lord belong to the one whom he owes (that is, who lends [the money]). But Mercury and the Moon signify the debt itself.

---

448 Reading with *Carmen* V.43.7, although the Latin suggests that it is still more useful for the seller.

449 Perhaps al-'Imrānī believes that the price will go sharply down in the last quarter of the Lunar month, but the general scheme in *Carmen* (and al-Rijāl VII.11.2, and *ITA* V.7, al-Qabīsī) suggests that the last quarter may be slightly better for the buyer, but will be fair to both.

450 For this chapter, cf. the diagrams and texts in al-Rijāl VII.11.2.

451 Cf. al-Rijāl VII.11.2, and especially *Carmen* V.43.2, 5. The first quarter of the Moon brings a fair price and profit, and moving fast in signs increasing in declination will be good for sellers and profit.

452 The crooked signs (in the northern hemisphere, from the beginning of Capricorn to the end of Gemini) do have shorter ascensional times, but they are also the signs which move northward in declination, from the lowest (Capricorn) to the highest (Gemini). See al-Rijāl VII.11.2.

453 Cf. al-Rijāl VII.11.2.

454 Reading with Paris 16204 for Madrid's *ab*.

455 Much of this chapter is based on *Carmen* V.20 or *On Elect.* §§29b-31.

If therefore there were concord between the lord of the Ascendant and the lord of the seventh, and the Moon and Mercury were in the Ascendant or with its lord, made fortunate, it will be perfected with ease.

But if the Moon were under the rays of the Sun, the Sun will be signifying the assets themselves instead of the Moon.[457] And[458] if the Moon were in the burnt path or descending in the south,[459] or in the first degrees of Leo or Gemini or Sagittarius, or if those degrees themselves were ascending, they do not signify good for the one giving, but they convey usefulness to the one taking.

And a certain person said,[460] by no means do we say it is useful when loaning, that it be the hour of Saturn or the Sun.

Chapter II.3.5: On raising the hand [to receive money][461]

One[462] must note that this is contrary to the section set out before, because it is good that the one who receives the loaned thing, receives it when the Moon is in Leo or Libra or in Aquarius or Scorpio or Sagittarius. And let the Moon be diminishing her light, in the aspect of Jupiter and Venus and Mercury. The Ascendant should even be one of the aforesaid signs. Also, the lord of the Ascendant and the lord of the seventh should be free and concordant [with each other].

And certain people[463] held the hour of Mars and the Sun to be hateful.

---

456 Cf. al-Khayyāt in *Judges* §2.14, indirectly based on *Carmen* V.20. Unlike al-'Imrānī, *Carmen* (and al-Rijāl VII.13) have the Ascendant as the lender or owner of the assets, and the seventh as the borrower. But al-Khayyāt says that the client gets the Ascendant, whatever role he plays in the transaction.

457 But *Carmen* also suggests that either the assets will be harmed (for lending that is public) or the matter will be concealed.

458 Cf. *On Elect.* §§30c-31, and *Carmen* V.20.6.

459 Probably in southern ecliptical latitudes (based on al-Rijāl, who explicitly says so); but based on the declination model of the Moon's relation to prices (see esp. al-Rijāl VII.11.2), this may refer to being in signs of southern declination.

460 Certainly Abū Ma'shar: see al-Rijāl VII.100, in Part I of this book.

461 Cf. al-Rijāl VII.14.

462 For this paragraph, cf. *On Elect.* §§29a-b, and *Carmen* V.20.7.

463 See Abū Ma'shar in al-Rijāl VII.100, but there al-Rijāl does not like the hour of Mars for anything.

Chapter II.3.6: On changing one's lodging-place[464]

This matter has to do with matters which are signified by the second house and its being, such as a traveler's entrance into cities. And we have already set forth the election for it in the first chapter of this book.[465]

However, a little thing must be added in this, namely that the fourth house should be Taurus or Leo:[466] for these designate that the house will be clean, also a good place and with few impeding animals (that is, mice, bed-bugs, lice, and fleas). Scorpio signifies creeping, poisonous things, and especially if it were in the aspect of Saturn—therefore, it is hateful. Nor should there be any infortune in the fourth, nor should they aspect it by any aspect of enmity. It is even praiseworthy that Venus should be in the fourth house.

Chapter II.4.1: On elections pertaining to the third house, and first on the reconciliation of brothers[467]

In this one must make the third house fit, and its lord, after the adaptation of the rooted things. However, the lord of the third should be in the conjunction[468] of the lord of the Ascendant, by a trine or sextile aspect with reception, and [the lord of the third] should aspect the Ascendant with an aspect of friendship. Also, it is good that the lord of the Ascendant be in the tenth or eleventh, and that the Moon be aspecting each.

And if it were our intention to pacify older brothers, we should make Saturn fit, and make him be aspecting the tenth or eleventh[469] by a praiseworthy aspect, with reception. And if our intention were about middle brothers, let it be[470] Mars instead of Saturn; but if about younger brothers, Mercury. And

---

464 Cf. al-Rijāl VII.15.
465 Probably II.1.10.
466 Paris 16204 omits Leo.
467 Cf. al-Rijāl VII.17.
468 That is, a degree-based connection by aspect, not assembled in the same sign.
469 Following Madrid, but the other manuscripts (and al-Rijāl VII.17) do not specify the place Saturn should be aspecting. If it was added later, the scribe must have assumed that the lord of the Ascendant would be in the tenth or eleventh, as recommended in the previous paragraph.
470 Reading with Paris 16204 for the rest of this sentence, as Madrid omits Mars and younger brothers, incorrectly assigning Mercury to middle brothers.

for sisters, one must make it Venus for every type: for older, younger, and middle sisters.

And let your election for the reconciliation of fathers with children be according to this method, except that one must make the fourth house fit instead of the third. And likewise with the house of children, if we wanted to reconcile them with fathers.

Chapter II.4.2: Instruction in those things which pertain to devotion to God[471]

It is good to make the third house and its lord fit, also Jupiter and each luminary; and let the Ascendant be one of the houses of Jupiter. (We even make Mercury fit if it were our intention to consider an election in a subtle way.) And let these planets each other by a praiseworthy aspect. And likewise, let each of them aspect the house of the other, in accordance with what you could do.

Chapter II.4.3: On the sending of legates[472]

Let the Moon be joined to a planet signifying the one to whom we are sending [the legate], so that if it were the king, let her be joined to the Sun, nor should they be cadent. And if it were a judge or merchant, to Jupiter; and thus with the rest. And let the planet to which the Moon is being joined, be free [of the bad ones].

---

471 *Cultum dei.*

472 Cf. al-Rijāl VII.36.

Chapter II.5.1: On those things which pertain to the fourth house, and first on the purchase of real estate[473]

In all of these, we should make the fourth house fit, after we have adapted all things which we stated about buyers.

[Buying land for purposes of construction]

Which[474] if this were a place which we want to inhabit, let the Moon be in her own house or exaltation, or in the Midheaven, aspecting the lord of the Ascendant. And banish Mars from every aspect. And[475] let the fourth house be a fixed sign. Also, the lords of the angles [should be] eastern, increased in their own motion, ascending in the north.[476]

[Buying land for purposes of cultivation][477]

But[478] in the purchase of any real estate, let the fortunes be having dignity in the angles, and especially in the Ascendant and the fourth. And let even each of the luminaries be aspecting the Ascendant and the fourth by a friendly aspect. Nor should there be a retrograde planet in any angle, nor should the lords of [the angles] be retrograde.

Al-Kindī said,[479] the bad ones should not be in the ninth nor in the eleventh nor the fifth. The fourth should not even be a fiery sign, nor should there be a fiery planet in it, and especially if they were cadent from[480] the fortunes. Also, Saturn should not be aspecting the fourth if it were a watery sign. And if the lord of the Midheaven were an infortune, it will be bad.

The[481] Ascendant even, and its lord, signify the land itself, and its [new] possessor, and its usefulness,[482] and its habitations.[483] But the Midheaven and

---

473 Cf. al-Rijāl VII.22.
474 Cf. *On Elect.* §49c.
475 Cf. *Forty Chapters* §475.
476 Probably ascending in northern ecliptical latitude, but perhaps by declination.
477 Most of this election is based on *Forty Chapters* Ch. 14.1.
478 Cf. al-Kindī §469.
479 Cf. *Forty Chapters* §§472-73, but also my notes to al-Rijāl VII.22 in his version.
480 That is, "in aversion to."
481 Cf. *Forty Chapters* §470, and al-Rijāl VII.22. In the two diagrams below, boldface indicates points of disagreement between al-Kindī and the Māshā'allāh group (and *Carmen* V.10.1)
482 *Utilitatem.* Perhaps, its value or profitability.
483 Reading *habitationes* for *habitationem.*

its lord signify whatever is raised up above the earth, such as trees and what is like these. The seventh and its lord signify its cultivators. (And certain people even testify that they signify the herbs and the rest of what sprouts on [the land].)[484] The fourth and its lord signify its goodness, and whatever is had on it, in terms of seeds. Therefore, whichever one of these were found to be good, good things must be said about that which it signifies.

Al-Tabarī said,[485] Jupiter and the planet from which the Moon is being separated, belong to the buyer. The one to which the Moon is being joined, signifies the end of the matter and whatever will result from [the sale or cultivation].

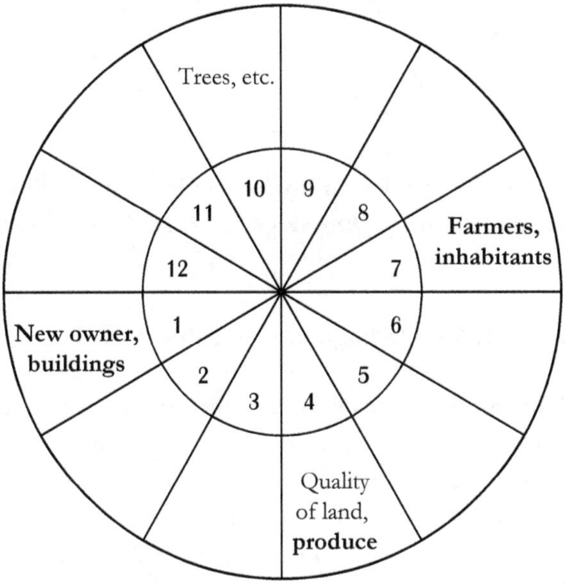

Figure 14: Angles for buying land for cultivation (al-Kindī, *Forty Chapters* §470)

[484] This is an insertion by al-'Imrānī: he is pointing out that the Māshā'allāh group (Sahl, al-Khayyāt, and "Dorotheus" in *Judges* 4.5, 4.8, and 4.9) make this attribution in questions about purchasing fields. The Māshā'allāh group's position is identical to *Carmen* V.10.1.

[485] Source unknown at this time.

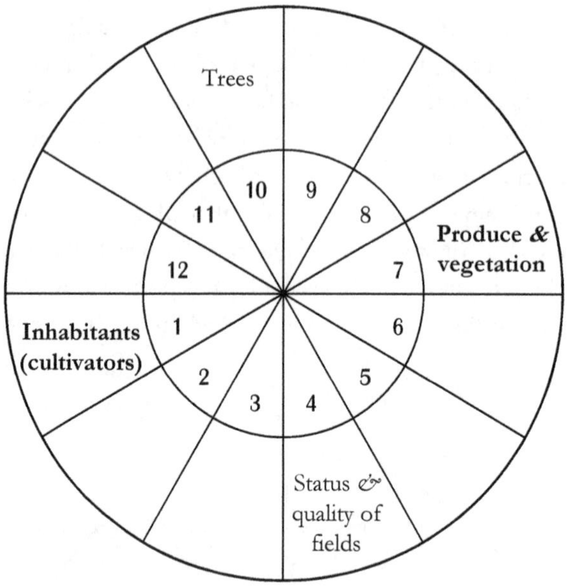

Figure 15: Angles for buying land for cultivation (Māshā'allāh group [*Judges* §4.5, 4.8-9], *Carmen* V.10.1)

Chapter II.5.2: On beginning to cultivate real estate[486]

It is good that the Moon be received by the fortunes, but she and the one who receives her should be in an angle or in one following an angle. Also, let the condition of the lord of the Ascendant be just as the condition of the Moon. One must even labor so that there is a fortune in the house of assets, free [of the infortunes], and the lord of the Lot of Fortune [is also there]. And al-Kindī said: or the Lot of assets [could be there]. He even said that the degree of the conjunction or prevention should be in an angle.

[When the Moon separates from the conjunction or prevention, she should apply to a fortune that is in an angle][487] or going toward an angle. But the lord of the conjunction or prevention should be a fortune, and also the lord of the fourth house and the lord of the house of the Moon.

---

[486] For this entire chapter, cf. *Forty Chapters* Ch. 16.4, and al-Rijāl VII.23.
[487] Adding with al-Kindī and al-Rijāl.

Chapter II.5.3: On the building of a mill[488]

Let the Moon or the Ascendant be in Aries or Libra, or in the last part of Virgo or Pisces. One must even beware lest the Moon be in Cancer or in Capricorn, because they are contrary to equality: for day and night in them are [the most] unequal. And if the Moon and the lord of the Ascendant were in the other signs,[489] without the aspect of the infortunes, it will be good.

And if the mill were suspended from ships, begin the work just as we said before at the beginning of the work on ships,[490] except that the beginning of a mill must be adapted just as it is stated in this place: for the origination of the ships is the first beginning.[491]

Chapter II.5.4: On planting trees and sowing seeds, and all things which are fruitful in that year (namely in its own season)[492]

Let the Moon be in movable signs; and if she were in Capricorn or Cancer[493] or Virgo, it will be good. And let the Moon be increased in number. It is even praised if she were in Pisces.

For trees, let the Moon be in fixed signs, and particularly in Taurus or Aquarius. And let Saturn be direct, in [a place] following an angle, even in a place where he has some dignity or testimony, or in the Ascendant. And let the Ascendant be one of the aforesaid signs. However, let Jupiter be aspecting Saturn by a praiseworthy aspect, from a place in which he has some testimony. Of course, one must beware of Mars. Certain people even preferred the lord of the exaltation to the lord of the house in the planting of trees.

Al-Khayyāt said,[494] let the lord of the house of the Moon be aspecting her from a watery sign; and if the Ascendant were not a fixed sign, let the Moon and her lord be ascending [in its latitude],[495] eastern.

---

488 Cf. al-Rijāl VII.24.

489 This seems to mean Aries and Libra (or late Virgo and late Pisces), which is how al-Rijāl reads it.

490 See II.1.7 above.

491 That is, when the ships are built: a well-elected and built mill will be no good if the ship itself is faulty.

492 Cf. al-Rijāl VII.25.

493 Paris 16204 omits Cancer.

494 Cf. *On Elect.* §§51-52a, and the version in al-Rijāl VII.25.

Chapter II.5.5: On contracting [to work] the land[496]

One must make the Ascendant and its lord fit. And let the lord of the Ascendant be going toward an angle in an earthy sign (and likewise the Moon), or let it be in the angle of the earth. But the planet from which the Moon is separated, should be free, for it signifies the land. And let the lord of the seventh be a fortune, in agreement with[497] the lord of the Ascendant as well as you could [make it happen]; and [let] the planet whose conjunction the Moon seeks, be in agreement with the one from which she is being separated.

And in the same way in electing for the contracting of rivers and in the cultivation of the land.

But the Ascendant and its lord, and the planet from which the Moon is being separated, signify the owner of these; the fourth signifies [the land] itself, and [the seventh] belongs to the one who is contracting for it, and likewise the lord of the seventh and the planet to which the Moon is being joined. Also, we should make fit whatever must be fit.

Chapter II.5.6: On the leasing out of houses and produce[498]

The Ascendant signifies the habitation of the place,[499] and the seventh the inhabitant.[500] But the Midheaven [signifies] the price which is given in the

---

495 Adding with al-Rijāl.

496 Cf. al-Rijāl VII.26. This election seems to assume that the client (Ascendant) is the owner of land, and wants to pay someone else (the contract worker, the seventh), to work it. For the opposite type of situation, see II.5.6 below and its counterpart in al-Rijāl VII.27.

497 Adding the rest of this sentence with Paris 7413-I.

498 Cf. al-Rijāl VII.27. In my own view, this election is backwards. For one thing, both this chapter and the previous one have the Ascendant signifying the owner of the land, and the seventh as the contract worker—which makes the house assignments redundant. Next, the second paragraph clearly links this election with *Carmen* V.8 (and its descendants in Sahl and al-Khayyāt, in *Judges* §§4.11-12), which has it the other way around: the Ascendant is the contract worker seeking to rent the rights to the land, and the seventh is the owner. (In fact, many of the elections and questions that have to do with leasing and business arrangements can be confusing as to who is playing what role.) So, I propose that this election is the reverse of the previous one: the client is the contract worker seeking to work someone's land for a fee (in order to gain profit), and the seventh is the owner of the property. In indented paragraphs below I have provided what I believe is the correct reading of the election, based on *Carmen* and the Māshā'allāh group.

499 On al-'Imrānī's version of the election, this is the owner.

500 That is, the contract worker.

lease. But the angle of the earth [signifies] the end of the matter. Also, adapt whatever of these was necessary to make fit.

> [*Dykes's proposed correct version:*] The Ascendant signifies the inhabitant, and the seventh the habitation of the place. But the Midheaven [signifies] the price which is given in the lease. But the angle of the earth [signifies] the end of the matter. Also, adapt whatever of these was necessary to make fit.

For if the Ascendant were made unfortunate, the owner of the habitation will lie about his faithfulness. If the seventh, the inhabitant will lie.

> [*Dykes's proposed correct version:*] For if the Ascendant were made unfortunate, the inhabitant will lie about his faithfulness. If the seventh, the owner of the habitation will lie.

The one to which the Moon is being joined signifies the one who leases [the land in order to work it], that is, the one who accepts the price;[501] and the one from whom the Moon is being separated, [signifies] him who gives the price.[502] Also, the lord of the house of the Moon signifies the end.

> [*Dykes's proposed correct version:*] The one to which the Moon is being joined signifies him who gives the price; and the one from whom the Moon is being separated, [signifies] the one who leases [the land in order to work it], that is, the one who accepts the price. Also, the lord of the house of the Moon signifies the end.

Al-Tabarī said,[503] we should make Jupiter and Saturn fit, and make them be aspecting each other by a praiseworthy aspect.

---

501 That is, it is the contract worker who accepts the terms of the owner.
502 That is, the owner, who sets the terms and charges the fee to work the land.
503 Cf. also *On Elect.* §§48-49b.

Chapter II.6.1: On those things which pertain to the fifth house, and first on the conceiving of a son[504]

It is good in this election that the Ascendant be a masculine sign, and one of straight ascension, also that the angles are fixed and not remote.[505] The lord of the Ascendant [should be] in the Ascendant or in the Midheaven or in the eleventh, and let the planet which first reaches the ascending degree through its own motion,[506] be a fortune. One must note, through those things which were set forth before, that it is necessary for each luminary to be made fit in what is like this, and especially it is very necessary to make the lord of the time fit (namely the Sun in the day, and the Moon in the night). An infortune should not be in any angle, but [only] a fortune, it being free of the bad ones and strong.

It[507] is also good that we turn ourselves to the lord of the Ascendant, and beware lest the lord of the Ascendant be a planet which would impede in the ninth month, for we often see births happen in [that month]. It is even praiseworthy to guard against this same thing (if it were possible) in the seventh and tenth [months]: for birth does tend to happen in them. And [therefore] the lord of the Ascendant ought to be strong in this hour, and made fortunate, [and] even the luminaries.

And one must be on one's guard lest the lord of the sixth or eighth (if it were an infortune) be commingled with any significator in any way; and generally, all things which are said to be unpraiseworthy in books of nativities should be avoided, and one must take what is approved of in those same books, with the roots of the elections.

Al-Khayyāt said,[508] we say it is best that the Moon be in the Ascendant, in the trine aspect of the Sun. He even said, beware of the burnt path, and we should make Venus fit. For if Venus would be impeded, the cultivation[509] (that is, the woman) is corrupted. But if the Moon [is impeded], the seed is corrupted. Also, make the fifth house and its lord fit.

---

504 Cf. al-Rijāl VII.30.

505 That is, the Midheaven should be on the tenth sign (and perhaps the eleventh), but not the ninth. See my Introduction.

506 That is, through its own motion in the zodiac. This probably includes aspectual relations as well, otherwise in most cases this planet would always be the Moon.

507 For this discussion of months, cf. Abū Bakr I.2 and I.5, in *PN2*.

508 Source unknown at this time.

509 *Cultura.* Al-Khayyāt is likening the womb to soil, and sperm to seed.

Certain people even approved it that the conception be during unequal hours (namely in the first or third or fifth, or in like ones).

Which if it happened that the Ascendant is Libra (which is a rational sign), it will be good—if however the sign of Libra and its lord were free [of the bad ones]: for then Cancer (which is a sign of many children) will be in the Midheaven. And let the rest of the significators be in male signs: for he will impregnate and conceive a male.

And let us apply natural works in matters which pertain to physic: that is, let us look lest she be drunk or her womb twisted or in any way infirm. For the circular significations are perfected according to how the matters subjected [to them] are able to receive the significations.[510]

Chapter II.6.2: On gifts[511]

In this one must make the fifth house and its lord fit, when we send[512] gifts to someone or even when we accept them.

And in sending, one must make fit everything which we said before in the chapter on the loaning of assets (namely, in the third [chapter]).[513]

And when we receive them, one must consider all of the things which we put forth before at the beginning of that treatment.[514]

Also, we should make the lord of the Ascendant fit, and let us make him be ascending above the lord of the seventh,[515] with the other electional roots.

---

510 That is, a woman with uterine problems can only be subject to a good election insofar as her uterus is physically capable of doing the things which are indicated. Al-'Imrānī has repeatedly emphasized the importance of root charts and actual physical conditions.

511 Cf. al-Rijāl VII.35.

512 Reading *direxerimus* for *dixerimus*.

513 Reading *capitulo* for *tractatu*. Cf. II.3.4 above.

514 Probably II.3.1.

515 That is, overcoming him (see Glossary).

Chapter II.7.1: On the sixth house, and first on the buying of captives

[The opinion of al-Kindī]

Let[516] the Ascendant and the Moon be in fixed signs of straight ascension, and domesticated ones (not wild ones), and likewise the lord of the Ascendant. And we should make the sixth and its lord fit, and it should be joined to the lord of the Ascendant by an aspect of friendship, and with reception; also the Moon and the lord of the Moon.[517] Al-Kindī said the lord of the Lot of captives and slaves[518] should also [be joined to the lord of the Ascendant by a friendly aspect, and received], and it[519] should be making the Ascendant and the Moon fortunate.

And it is necessary that the Ascendant or the Moon or the lord of the sixth not be in Leo. But we praise it that it be in Taurus or at the end of Sagittarius.

[The opinion of others]

Abu Ma'shar said,[520] let the Moon and the Ascendant be in signs formed in the image of a man, or in the others with fortunes (except for Aries and Scorpio, also Capricorn and Pisces). And let the sixth house and its lord be in the concord of the Ascendant and its lord.

Certain people even said,[521] the captive will be according to the nature of the sign, and according to what pertains to the animals of that type: such as Pisces, which signifies impetuous people, who do all things from impulse,[522] and like Leo, which signifies the proud, and [such] a slave will not be obedient to his master. And this opinion is praiseworthy.

And a certain person[523] testifies [that] if the infortunes were below the earth, the slave will be unfaithful.

---

516 This paragraph is based on *Forty Chapters* Ch. 19, §§512, 514, 516.
517 That is, these other planets should be well configured with the Moon and her lord, *etc.*
518 See *ITA* VI.2.20 for two Lots of slaves in the Perso-Arabic tradition.
519 Or rather, all of the aforesaid planets.
520 Cf. *Carmen* V.11, especially *ll.* 3, 6, 7, 11. But Abū Ma'shar has probably gotten this from *Forty Chapters* Ch. 19.
521 Paris 16204 identifies this as Abū Ma'shar, again. Cf. *Carmen* V.11, and *On Elect.* §§71a-73.
522 *Qui cum impetu faciunt omnia.*
523 *On Elect.* §§71a-72.

The sign of Sagittarius even indicates that the captive is a free man,[524] if it were ascending.

Chapter II.7.2: On the manumission of captives and the imprisoned, and domesticating horses[525]

In[526] all of these things which we have said before in this heading, it is necessary to make the Ascendant and its lord fit. For the Ascendant designates the one who manumits, but the seventh the one who is manumitted; the Midheaven, [the reason] for which he is manumitted; the fourth, the end of the manumission and what it will come to. If therefore the Moon were made unfortunate in the seventh, we will fear lest he be led back into captivity or prison.[527]

Chapter II.7.3: On the buying of animals[528]

It[529] is good that the Ascendant and the Moon be in the sign of that animal, or that it was particular to that kind of animal, made fortunate by the lord of that sign, or by another (if she were not received); and if the lord of that same sign were not a fortune, it will not impede afterwards [if] it were an aspect of friendship and with reception.

And[530] if the animal were masculine, let as many places of the significators [as possible] be in male signs, but if feminine, contrariwise.

But if it were necessary to make some broken or infirm limb of the animal fit,[531] let the Moon be in the sign signifying that limb, she being made fortunate.

---

524 *Liber*. But does this mean that he *will be freed*, or that he was captured as a free man?

525 The rest of the title in Madrid reads, "and on the donation of horses because of God." But al-Rijāl VII.51 clearly reads this in terms of domestication, so I have read it that way.

526 Cf. *Carmen* V.13.5-8.

527 Paris 16204 reads that this is the captivity or prison he "had been in," implying not just any captivity, but going back to the same master or jailer he'd had before.

528 Cf. al-Rijāl VII.52.2, and al-'Imrānī's comment at the end of II.13.4.

529 For this paragraph, cf. *Forty Chapters* §§578.

530 For the rest of this chapter, cf. *Forty Chapters* §§580, 582-83, and *Carmen* V.12.4.

531 Al-Kindī reads this as referring to branding or tattooing.

And we should make fit what there was of the nature of that animal, or of the nature of what is like that animal. And if the animal were not for riding, let Leo be made fit, or the end of Sagittarius.[532]

And in no way should the fitness of the sixth and its lord be abandoned.

Chapter II.7.4: On the buying of animals with which we hunt

Let this be with the Moon in Gemini or its triplicity, or in Sagittarius, or in the first half of Capricorn, because in that half is the house of a hawk.[533] And this, with the fitness of the sixth and its lord and of all of the electional roots taken together.

Also, in the buying of flying [animals for] hunting, al-Tabarī said: it is best in this that the Moon be in the last part of Gemini or in Leo or in Sagittarius (for there is a wolf,[534] which is a plundering animal, just as flying animals for hunting should be). And likewise, in the buying of hunting dogs and what is like these.

And a certain other person said the Moon should be in Cancer (and he seems to want this because it is the house of the Moon), and the Moon is[535] full (which has the quickest motion, and therefore the dogs will be fast).

Chapter II.8.1: On the seventh house

Whenever[536] anything is handled between two persons, generally the Ascendant will belong to the undertaker [of the action], and the seventh to the one who is sought; but the Midheaven [belongs] to the one who decides between each (and if it were war, it will be the significator of victory); the fourth, the end of the matter. The Moon will even signify those traversing [between them]: but the one from whom the Moon is being separated, [will signify] the one undertaking it, and the one to which she is being joined, the

---

532 Reading with al-Kindī for "the end of Leo…or Sagittarius."

533 This is undoubtedly a reference to the constellation Aquila ("Eagle"), sometimes called *Vultur volans* ("flying vulture") in ancient literature. It sits in northern declinations just above the constellation of Capricorn.

534 I am not sure what constellation this is.

535 *Est.* This should probably read "should be" (*sit*).

536 Cf. *Forty Chapters* §§150-52 and Sahl's version in *On Elect.* §34; *On Quest.* §7.8 (*Judges* §7.37 and 7.48); and *On Quest.* §7.23 (*Judges* §7.147).

one who is sought. However, the lord of the house of the Moon is the significator of the end of the matter. And so, the one which the lord of the Midheaven will favor by dignity or by aspect, if it were the Ascendant or seventh or the Moon, it will be stronger.

Chapter II.8.2: On an association[537]

Let the Ascendant be a sign of two bodies, and likewise let the house of the Moon be in a sign of two bodies, or let the Sun be in Leo (for the Sun and his house are congruent with associations).

Chapter II.8.3: On a purchase and sale

Al-Tabarī said,[538] the Ascendant and its lord belong to the one selling, the seventh and its lord to the one buying. But the Midheaven and its lord [belong to] the price, but the fourth and its lord the thing to be sold. Even the planet from whom the Moon is being separated, [belongs to] the seller, and the Moon herself to the thing to be sold, and the one to which she is being joined, the buyer.

Al-Khayyāt said, it is not bad if the Moon were in the Ascendant in a purchase or sale, and he hates her being there for journeys.[539]

Chapter II.8.4: On the betrothal of women

Let[540] the Ascendant be a fixed sign, and (as al-Khayyāt testifies) the better ones are Taurus and Leo.

But[541] the Ascendant and its lord belong to the man, the seventh and its lord to the woman. We will even look for the man from the Sun, and the

537 Cf. al-Rijāl VII.60, and *Carmen* V.19.1-14.
538 Cf. *Judges* §§7.56, 7.58-59, and *Carmen* V.9.
539 Cf. *On Elect.* §107.
540 Cf. *On Elect.* §§79b-c, which is actually for electing the consummation of the marriage, not the betrothal. As Sahl points out (§14b), we want fixed signs for the consummation, but movable ones for the engagement.
541 Cf. *Carmen* V.16.1.

planet from whom the Moon is being separated; however, for the woman [we will look] from Venus and from the planet to which the Moon is being joined. But the Midheaven will indicate what is going to be between them; the fourth, the end (and, as it pleases certain people, the dowry).

And if the significators of the man and woman were in a masculine sign, it will be better for the man; and one must speak conversely for the woman. And if the significator of the man were in a masculine one, but that of the woman in a feminine one, the condition of each will prosper.

Certain people[542] even take the significator of the one initiating, to be the planet from whom the Moon is being separated, and that of the other as the planet to which she is being joined, and [the significator] of each to be the Moon herself. But they used to give Mercury to the children, and they hated it that the Moon would be in a rational sign.

And[543] the same thing is the work of an election for the purchase of a female captive bought for the purpose of having sex[544] with her. But in the purchase of other female captives, this is not considered.

Chapter II.9: On the eighth house, and first on the fitness of an inheritance[545]

In this it is necessary that the eighth house be one of the houses of Jupiter or Venus, free; and let its lord be in one following an angle. If it were in the second, it will be good, with however its good health, and that of the [eighth][546] house and its lord.

And if perhaps it happened that the degree of the eighth[547] would be in the bound of Jupiter or Venus, it will be good.

One must even make the Moon fit, so that she aspects the lord of the eighth house with a praiseworthy aspect; and in addition we should make the rest of the electional roots fit.

---

542 Perhaps *Carmen* V.16.1 and 5.

543 For questions on this, see *On Quest.* §6.9 (*Judges* §6.61).

544 *Causa agendi cum ea*, lit. "for the purposes of doing it with her."

545 *Haereditatum.* Traditionally, what was often inherited was land: this Latin word is the same as that for "real estate." Cf. al-Rijāl VII.68. This is probably an alternative election for writing a will: see the Dorotheus/Sahl version in al-Rijāl VII.67.

546 Adding with al-Rijāl.

547 This indicates that al-'Imrānī or his source was using quadrant-derived houses at least part of the time.

Chapter II.10.1: On the ninth house, and first on moral teaching[548]

Let the Moon and the Ascendant be in a rational sign, and the lord of the Midheaven[549] be in the Midheaven or going towards it. And let the Midheaven and its lord be concordant with the lord of the Ascendant, and the Moon with Mercury or joined to him by an aspect of friendship.

And let Mercury be of a good condition, made fortunate and strong. We even praise it that Mercury be aspecting the lord of the Ascendant, nor should the Moon be diminishing [her] course, nor descending from the apogee.

And make the ninth and its lord fit. But in the instruction of writing, one must (in addition to all of these) make the tenth house fit (which signifies works): for writing is a science and work.

In this chapter we have even comprehended the paths, mention of which we made in the first treatise.[550]

Chapter II.10.2: On instruction in singing and those things which pertain to gladness[551]

In this, one must make Venus fit, and let her be in one of her own dignities; and likewise Mercury. And let him be joined to her. Let even the Moon be in one of her own dignities, or in Pisces, separated from Mercury and going toward the conjunction of Venus.

And let the Ascendant be one of the dignities of Venus. If the ascending degree were even the dignity of Venus and Mercury,[552] it will be good.

Nor should Venus nor Mercury nor the Moon be cadent. If however the Moon were in the ninth (which is the house of knowledge), made fortunate

548 Cf. al-Rijāl VII.77, and *On Elect.* §§59a-c.

549 Al-Rijāl has "Ascendant," which seems more right to me.

550 I am not sure what al-'Imrānī means by this, since most of these elections use multiple criteria.

551 Cf. al-Rijāl VII.78.

552 Reading with the other *mss.* besides Madrid, which seems to read this as being in the bound of Venus and face of Mercury. That would limit the possibilities to certain degrees in Taurus, Cancer, and Aquarius.

and strong,[553] it will be good: for it signifies the perfection of the matter. Let even the others be made fortunate.

But if the lord of the Ascendant were in the ninth, made fortunate and strong, it will be good.

A certain person said it is necessary in playing the lyre that the Moon be in Capricorn; but in striking a tambourine[554] (an instrument which the Saracens especially use in games, and it is wooden) and what is like that, let her be at the end of Leo. But for the trumpet, let her be in signs lacking voice. However, the signs having voices are good in elections for singing and playing,[555] and especially Gemini and Virgo.

And in this matter we should make the ninth and its lord fit. And if it were your intention in this, [to do] something which pertains to a work, the fitness of the tenth will be good, which we even commend in every beginning of a matter.

Chapter II.11.1: On the tenth house, and first on instruction in swimming[556]

Let the Moon and the Ascendant be in a watery sign, and let the lord of the Ascendant be in the Midheaven or going toward it, strong and made fortunate. Let even the Moon be ascending in the north,[557] in one of her own dignities, the better one of which is Cancer.

Chapter II.11.2: On instruction for fighting[558]

It is necessary that the Moon and the Ascendant be in the triplicity of Aries, and let Mars be of a good condition. And the Moon should not be in the place in which she falls, and especially in military instruction. And if the Moon were in her own exaltation, it will be good, and likewise the lord of the

[553] Through the rest of this sentence and the next, I have read a mixture of Madrid and Paris 16204.

[554] *Athabur* (Paris 16204), *attabur* (Madrid). Obviously what follows in parentheses is the medieval translator's own comment.

[555] *Modulandis.*

[556] Cf. al-Rijāl VII.92.

[557] I am not sure if this is by ecliptical latitude or declination.

[558] Cf. al-Rijāl VII.91.

Ascendant. Which if this could not happen, let it[559] be in the Midheaven or going toward it.

And certain people said, in wrestling instruction, let the Moon be in Gemini.

Chapter II.11.3: On instruction in other works[560]

One must make the tenth (which signifies works) and its lord fit; also the Moon. And we should put the planet naturally signifying that work, in one of its own dignities, made fortunate and strong: like Mars, who signifies craftsmen and butchers, and the Sun, who signifies moneychangers and goldsmiths.

And we should make Mercury be joined to it, because he has a partnership in works, and especially in matters which come to be through the subtlety of the mind, like painting and the forming of images or the construction of the astrolabe. And let Mercury be of a good condition. But it is necessary to put the Moon in her own dignity, joined by an aspect of friendship and with reception to the planet signifying the matter. And if she were in the house of the planet signifying the work, it will be good, and especially in the house which pertains to it.

And let the Ascendant and the place of the Moon be going to[561] a sign of the matter, like earthy signs for those things which are worked from earth, and watery ones for those which are worked from water.

Chapter II.12.1: On the eleventh house, and first on those things which pertain to acquiring a good name and reputation[562]

At the beginning of these it is good to make the eleventh and its lord fit. And let the Ascendant be one of the houses of Jupiter, and if it is possible that he would be put in the eleventh or in the Ascendant, or he would aspect

---

559 I take this to mean the lord of the Ascendant, as in the previous chapter.

560 Cf. al-Rijāl VII.90.

561 *Veniens*. Per al-Rijāl, this simply means that the Ascendant and Moon should be "in" such places.

562 Cf. al-Rijāl VII.94.

them with a praiseworthy aspect, it will be good. It is even good that Jupiter be strong, free. But if the lord of the eleventh were in the Ascendant or conversely, it will be good.

Let us even make the Sun be free, in the tenth, and the Moon should be joined to him from a trine or sextile aspect; and in addition if she were separated from the lord of the eleventh or Jupiter, it will be better: then the matter will even be made public and will be praised more.

And generally, let all of these significators be aspecting each other with a praiseworthy aspect, and especially the luminaries and the Ascendant and the eleventh. And let them all be received, or as many as we could, along with the other electional roots.

Chapter II.12.2: On seeking a matter, both one promised and one sought[563]

In this one must make the eleventh house and its lord fit, also the Lot of assets[564] and its lord, and let them each (or one of them) be aspecting the Ascendant with a praiseworthy aspect. And let the lord of the Ascendant and the Moon, and the planet signifying the matter, be received by the lord of the eleventh house.[565]

Now, the Ascendant and its lord signify the one who seeks the assets. The seventh and its lord the one from whom it is sought. And for that reason it is necessary that the seventh be free of the bad ones; but if not, the petition will be made in vain. The Moon is said to signify the thing itself.

But[566] if the petition to be made were to an old man or anyone who is signified by Saturn, let the degree[567] of the eleventh be in some dignity of Saturn. But if it were to be made to a scribe, let what we said be [a dignity] of Mercury: the house, namely, or exaltation or bound. And we should make that planet fit: that is, if it were an old man to whom the petition is made, we should make Saturn fit; and thus with the rest.

---

[563] Cf. al-Rijāl VII.95.

[564] Al-Rijāl reads "Lot of Fortune," which is probably right.

[565] Paris 16204 reads as though the lord of the Ascendant and the Moon should also be received *by* the planet naturally signifying the matter. Vatican creates a separate clause, reading as though the planet naturally signifying the matter should be ascending.

[566] For this paragraph, cf. *Carmen* V.14.6-7.

[567] Again, this suggests that al-'Imrānī or his source was using quadrant-based houses at least part of the time.

And al-Khayyāt said,[568] let Mercury be joined to Jupiter or to Venus, but the lord of the Midheaven should be going toward the lord of the Ascendant.

Which[569] if what is sought is money, make the second house and its lord fit, along with the aforesaid; and let there be an aspect between the lord of the house of assets and the lord of the Ascendant, nor should an infortune cut in between them.[570] Also, the lord of the eleventh and the lord of the Lot of Fortune should aspect it[571] with a good aspect.

And if it were the matter of a woman or what pertains to nuptials, [adapt] the seventh and its lord, just as was said about the second and its lord, and thus with the rest.

Chapter II.12.3: On seeking love and friendship[572]

Let the Moon (along with the fitness of the eleventh house and its lord) be received by Venus from a trine; and what is better is that she be received by house or exaltation. Which if that could not be, let [Venus] be received by the Moon from a trine, and she herself should be received by Jupiter or by the lord of her own house. And if even this were impossible, let the Moon be in some dignity of Venus, free.

But if one is seeking because of a desire to profit, let the Lot of Fortune be in the Ascendant or in its triplicity. If it is sought because of real estate or any land, let [the Lot] be in the fourth house, and thus with the rest.

---

568 Source unknown at this time.

569 I am not currently sure whether this is still al-Khayyāt or not.

570 See *ITA* III.23 for different forms of "cutting."

571 I am not sure who or what is meant by "it" here.

572 This entire election is based on *Forty Chapters* Ch. 22, §§546-49. There are some differences between the texts, so they should be compared. Cf. al-Rijāl VII.96 for his version.

Chapter II.13.1: On the twelfth house, and first if you wanted to hinder any enemy, or on the king catching his enemy or a less powerful person[573]

Let the twelfth be unfortunate, and its lord made unfortunate and weak. And it were made unfortunate by the lord of the Ascendant, it will be praiseworthy. But if it were not this at the beginning of the journey, let the Moon be made unfortunate by the Sun, and the Sun in a good place. And if she were made unfortunate by one other than the Sun, it will be better.[574]

Chapter II.13.2: On searching for a fugitive[575]

But if a prince or anyone else wanted to hinder someone who is under his authority, al-Tabarī said, let the Moon be in the conjunction or prevention or in the burnt path, or with the Head or with the Tail or in the Ascendant (because the Ascendant is contrary to the Moon, according to his opinion),[576] or she should be in the aspect of the bad ones, or she should be before or after the Lunar eclipse by three days or less. And the Sun should be free and cleansed [of the bad ones], and in the Midheaven, strong.

And by how much more the Moon were impeded, it will be that much worse for those whom they intend to hinder: for the Moon signifies the common people and underofficials.

Chapter II.13.3: On searching for a fugitive[577]

This pertains to those things which we set forth before about enemies. If it were a search for the purpose of killing the fugitive, let it be with the twelfth and its lord, also with the Moon, just as we said before in terms of fall and weakness. But if it were not for the purpose of killing, one must choose just as we will state in what follows.

---

[573] Reading the last part of this title with the 1551 al-Rijāl. Cf. al-Rijāl VII.99.

[574] Al-'Imrānī probably means it is better to have a malefic make her unfortunate, such as in *Carmen* V.36.16-18.

[575] Cf. al-Rijāl VII.99.

[576] Cf. the discussion of this in al-'Imrānī I.2.8.

[577] Cf. al-Rijāl VII.61.

Al-Khayyāt said,[578] let the Moon be joined to an infortune, nor should we put the Moon nor the planet to which the Moon is being joined, in the fourth.

And Māshā'allāh said,[579] it is necessary that the lord of the Ascendant and the lord of the seventh be conjoined. And he said, if the Moon were conjoined to a planet which is in the twelfth, he will lose the fugitive.

Chapter II.13.4: On making a robber or watchman[580] reveal what we are seeking[581]

Abu Ma'shar said, let the Moon and the planet to which she is being joined be in a rational sign formed in the image of a man. And this opinion is to be praised.

ꟸ ꟸ ꟸ

And everything which we said in this second book must be done after making the electional roots fit, and those things which follow [from] them. And one must beware of all the things which we said before must be avoided and watched out for.

And already it is good, since we have conceded that the twelfth house signifies animals, that the twelfth house and its lord be made fit in the election of their purchase.[582] But I have not made mention as to why I have found no one among the ancients who has testified about this.[583]

ꟸ ꟸ ꟸ

The book on the elections of praiseworthy hours by 'Ali bin Ahmad al-'Imrānī is completed, being translated from Arabic into Latin in the city of Barcelona by Abraham, a Spanish Jew who is called Salvacorda (he being the interpreter). His translation was com-

578 Cf. *On Elect.* §142.
579 Source unknown at this time.
580 *Excubatore.*
581 Cf. al-Rijāl VII.62.
582 *In electione emptionis eorum.*
583 Sahl bin Bishr associates the twelfth with buying animals in *On Elect.* §135 (see al-Rijāl VII.52.1), but he does not actually have us make the twelfth house fit.

pleted on Monday, the 7th of the kalends of October, on the 24th day of the Lunar month which is called Dhū al-Qa'dah,[584] *in the 3rd hour [after noon], with Aquarius ascending, in the year of our Lord 1133, the year of Alexander 1444, the year of the Arabs 527. With the Sun in Libra 9° 10', the Moon in the seventh degree of Leo, Saturn in Sagittarius, the fifth degree and fifty-five minutes, Jupiter in Aries, the seventeenth degree and twenty-four minutes, retrograde; Mars in Virgo, the tenth degree and twenty minutes; Venus in Virgo, the twenty-third degree and fifteen minutes; Mercury in Libra, the eleventh degree, retrograde; the Head of the Dragon in Aquarius, the nineteenth degree and seventeen minutes, therefore the Tail (its nadir) in a like degree and minute, if God wills.*[585]

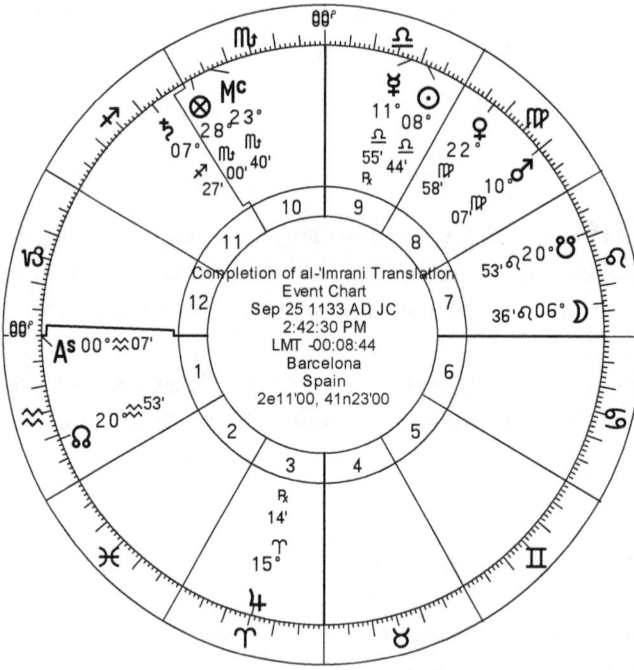

Figure 16: Approximate chart for the completion of the al-'Imrānī translation

[584] Lat. *Ducheida.* See al-Bīrūnī's *Chronology* pp. 332, 322, the eleventh month in the Arabic calendar.

[585] I have adapted this final paragraph a bit, following David Juste's comments to his forthcoming, updated edition of Carmody's classic work on Arabic astrological material in Latin. The manuscript descriptions of the date, time, and chart differ wildly, but Juste plausibly suggests that this is the proper reading of the date and time (see chart).

The Book of the Skilled VII: *On Elections*

Al-Rijāl

Prologue to the book:

'Ali bin Abī al-Rijāl said: "May God be praised and thanked again, Who is the Lord of good bestowals, [forms of] wisdom, and the sciences; He is the maker and creator of all things, and they are held in His hand through His will and governance; He is the beginning of all things, and the transformer of times: through His power He has raised the heavens up straight and established them, He has pressed down the earth and fixed it in place;[1] He has created all creatures, and knows all secrets; He has created things and given them an end, and after He has created them, He should be praised and blessed, just as befits His great nobility and loftiness."

Prologue of the author[2]

In this book I have gathered together all elections of the stars and the beginnings of matters, and I have applied them and established them firmly as well as I was able to and my understanding [could] manage it.

Know that the ancient sages were in disagreement in the method of elections, because there are those of them who affirm them and their profit, and [another] portion of them who deny and condemn them and their profit, and [their] judgments.[3] And I have already divided up and laid out these disagreements (and others), at the beginning of this book (in the first part, [concerning] questions) [4]—and in that, I spoke better than I knew.[5] And in this place I wish to say what I believe about their statements, and what is truthful and sound. And here I begin, with the aid of God.

---

[1] Reading *fixit* for what seems to be *figiavit* (a non-existent verb).

[2] Now al-Rijāl introduces Book VII itself, after the general prayer which preceded.

[3] Al-'Imrānī alludes to such people in his I.1.4.

[4] Probably referring to the early chapters on different opinions about victors, thought-interpretation, and so on: see Appendix A in *Search*.

[5] *Cui prima parte quaestionum; et in hoc locutus fui melius quam scivi.* This seems to be an attempt at modesty.

I am speaking of elections. Some are profitable (with the aid of God), without any doubt, and [their] success and good is manifest. And there are others which do not appear, nor do their significations receive success. For example, were some man to have manifest, truthful and firm significations in his nativity that he will not have a child (or if he did have one, [that] it would not live nor be raised), because he had the house and significators of children being harmed, or in the nativity he had the house and significators of marriage-union harmed (such as if Venus and the other significators were burnt up or in their own falls, or in bad places, remote from the aspects of the significator of the native),[6] or that infortunes would rule in the house of travel in the root of the nativity, and the significators of that house harming the significator of the native—and thus if any of these were harmed in the root of the nativity (namely, [the significator] of children, marriage-union, or travel)—if you wanted to look for an election for making a child, or at the hour for making a marriage-union or a journey, success will not appear in this election, because an election is not of so much power that it is capable of drawing away or removing what [such] planets signified in the root of the nativity. And understand the contrary about this, with respect to good and fortune.

However, elections do appear, and someone helps himself with respect to those having significators in the nativity such that a child could be had, or that the significators would be jointly[7] middling or good. Because if the election were good, and the significators of the root middling (or not very harmed), the election goes forward and draws this toward the good. And if the significators were good and the election good, it affirms the good, and it grows, and it sets him up to a great degree, because the goodness of the election helps the significators of the root—since if the significators were good and powerful in the root, they signify good. Likewise, if an election were powerful, good and fortunate, the matter grows: it is made powerful and affirmed, and fortune and every good appears in it as much as it can. And one path in elections is according to this road and opinion—and this view[8] is affirmed through the statement of Ptolemy, which he stated in the sixth say-

---

[6] Al-Rijāl might be describing aversion in this last condition.

[7] Reading *communiter* for what seems to be *communerales*. 1551 reads, *communes*.

[8] *Verbum*.

ing of [his] *Book of 100 Sayings*:[9] "Then an election of days and hours advances, when the time is well established from the birth. But if it is to the contrary,[10] it will in no way be successful, however much it may look towards a good outcome." And this is what I hold to be truthful, and with which I agree, and according to which I operate.

[Elections with unknown nativities, from Sahl]

But[11] I chastise you lest you make an election for one whose nativity you did not know: because when you will have made an election for him whose nativity and revolution of the year you *did* know, it will be good and outstanding for him (by the good will of God). And if you made an election for one whose nativity you did *not* know (and the revolution of his year, or at least you did not have the Ascendant of his question)—if you did not have a known nativity, there could be danger from this, because perhaps you will quickly take an Ascendant that is inimical and contrary to the root of the nativity: indeed so that you will give him as the Ascendant the twelfth, eighth, or sixth [house] of his root, and his enemies will be strengthened, and perhaps they will destroy or kill him, or perhaps you will move harm [towards] him, and the fortunes which you have collected for him would not be able to draw the evil back; or perhaps the fortunes will be inimical and contrary to his root, or they will be the lords of harming, bad places; or that infortune which you made cadent and weakened in your election, will perhaps be the significator and ruler in the root, with you not knowing it.[12] (Likewise, beware lest you make an election for evil people and enemies, unless you knew their nativity.)

You[13] see well with respect to those who make a journey by sea or land, when all of them depart, or they go out one day and advance toward an estate to which they go at one hour, that some of them quickly turn back with

[9] That is, Aphorism 6 of pseudo-Ptolemy's *Centiloquy*. Its original author is unknown. I have used 1551's translation, which is closer to the Greek (which suggests that the editor of 1551 did not approve of 1485's rendition).
[10] That is, if the client does not have a reliable birth time.
[11] For this paragraph, cf. the discussion in *On Elect.* §§1-5c.
[12] That is, a malefic is not always bad: if the malefic plays a key role in the success of the nativity, it would be wrong to unwittingly harm the election by taking it simply as a malefic and trying to marginalize its role. See al-'Imrānī's discussion in his I.1.4.
[13] Cf. *On Elect.* §§6a-b.

profit and good, and in a good state and fortune; and some will slow down, and some will turn back, infirm; and some who will profit nothing and will have no usefulness in that journey; and others will lose what they had, and some lose and destroy themselves on the journey. Likewise with respect to those who board a ship at one hour: of which some will perhaps be killed, others will leave, and perhaps all will advance to the place to which they are going at one hour—and some of them will turn back to the estate and their own place, with profit and good, and some who will return without profit, and some who will lose in such a way that they will never return to their own place: and this does not happen except through the discordance of their nativities, nor does the departure which they made at some day and hour profit them.[14]

Likewise,[15] some man will undertake a journey on an unfortunate and bad day, and he will be freed and make profit; and someone who will go out on a chosen day [that is] fortunate and good, will be hindered and lose: and this does not happen except through the discordances of their nativities.[16] And there are some for whom the fortunes make good and usefulness, and the infortunes evil and loss, and others for whom the infortunes make good and usefulness, and the fortunes evil and loss: and all of this happens through the will and power of the High God, and He should be blessed.

Know[17] that God, Whose names should be praised, has created all creatures, and He has made them all from the four natures, and He has attached the whole that is in the earth and the world of generation and corruption (the rational and the mute, the movable and fixed) to the heavens; and He posited for them causes and subtle proportions which the sages of this science understand and know; and the other prudent nobles of the natures and of philosophy know the cause and subtle proportion which He has posited between the magnet and iron, and between a father and child, and between one loving and the one loved—whence you should understand [this] and put your mind to this. And you should know that matters are tempered and driven forward through the concordance and agreement which exists between two properties (which are the high and the low), and matters are harmed and

---

[14] That is, an election which might be good for some nativities, might be bad for others.
[15] Cf. *On Elect.* §§7-8.
[16] That is, the discordance of their respective nativities with the time they have chosen to act.
[17] Cf. *On Elect.* §§10a-11a.

destroyed through the discordance and disagreement between these two properties.

Know[18] that the fortunes are of tempered natures and good complexions, but the infortunes are of the distorted and treacherous complexions: and even though [the infortunes] may receive,[19] they do not guarantee [success], because of their bad properties and treacherous natures: because they are just like robbers and bad men.

[A discussion of sources]

Know that the books of elections are many, but of them the ancient books belong to Dorotheus and Valens, and others whom we have already named when we spoke about the disagreements of the sages in the first part of this book.[20] And each of the sages of the Moors followed and appreciated one path of the ancients, and abhorred the other one, according to his intellect and thought, in what appeared truthful and right to him, and he passed over the other. And I am one of those who has done such, because I have proceeded by the path which seemed to me to be truthful and sound, and have passed over the others: because I have looked into the elections of all, and of their statements I have taken what seemed to me to be truthful and right, and what I saw could be verified through reason or experience. Those who have taken it upon themselves to fashion books of elections are: Māshā'allāh, *Abimegest*,[21] Theophilus the son of Thomas, al-Khayyāt, and al-Kindī. For these were the greater ones of them, and who spoke better and distinguished the matters better. And Abū al-Shaibānī[22] and Sahl bin Bishr, Abū Ma'shar, 'Ali bin Ahmad al-'Imrānī[23] and al-Hasan bin Sahl,[24] did not

---

[18] Cf. *On Elect.* §§11a-b.

[19] This probably refers to either receiving an application, or else one of the forms of reception (such as pushing nature or classical reception, *ITA* III.15, III.25). The point is that whenever the responsibility for the chart's dynamics depends on malefic planets, the success is questionable.

[20] This evidently refers to the many differing opinions described in *Skilled* I-III, on questions.

[21] Unknown, but this might actually be an honorific of Māshā'allāh (note the similarity to the word *Almagest*, the Arabic title for Ptolemy's *Suntaxis*, and meaning "the greatest").

[22] Lat. *Abuezaben.*

[23] *Haly filius Hamet Benbrany.* It is surprising that al-Rijāl would put Sahl and al-'Imrānī in second place, since so much of Book VII is copied directly from them.

speak as well as the others did. However, I have taken the better methods of each of them, and I have adjoined to them what seemed to me to be truthful and right. And I ask God that He should direct me in the path of truth.

Chapter VII.1: On the rules and roots which are necessary in this method, and which cannot be avoided

Utuluxius said,[25] If you were not able to avoid an election, and the Moon were unfortunate, make that infortune be the lord of the Ascendant.

If you could not make all of the significators of the election fit, always adapt and deploy the lord of the Ascendant.

If[26] there were a fortune in an angle (especially in the Midheaven), you should not care about another.

The usefulness which can come out of an election, is modest when the revolution of the year appears bad (and contrariwise [for a good one]).

Mars[27] does not make harm for journeys by water, just as Saturn does not [make] much for journeys by land.

On journeys,[28] the fixed signs are ill-omened, just as the movable ones are esteemed.

One[29] cannot draw back the harm of an infortune, when it is remote from an angle and peregrine, and in a sign divergent from and pernicious to its nature, unless [it is by] God.

Very powerful are Venus and the Moon in the southern quarter, and very weak in the eastern quarter.[30]

---

[24] *Alohaç filius Zaet.* My attribution of this Latin transliteration with al-Hasan bin Sahl is still a little speculative, since elsewhere the Latin reads more plausibly *Alhasen filius zahel* or *Alhaçen filius zahel.*

[25] According to VII.2.5 below, this is al-Khayyāt. See also al-'Imrānī I.2.11. See my Introduction for a discussion of this passage.

[26] Cf. *Carmen* V.5.11.

[27] That is, Mars *does* cause trouble for journeys by land, and Saturn does so by water (although this is not so for hunting and fishing). See *On Elect.* §116. The same is true for al-'Imrānī II.1.8.

[28] Cf. al-Rijāl VII.71.

[29] Cf. *Fifty Judgments* #21, 26, 37.

[30] Al-Rijāl might really be referring to their relation to the Sun: if rising before the Sun (and therefore being in the eastern quarter at dawn), they are weak by being in an eastern or diurnal position and moving towards the Sun; but if setting after the Sun (and therefore being in the southern quarter towards the west in the evening), they are strong by being in a western or nocturnal position and moving away from the Sun.

When[31] an infortune receives a fortune, it does not do much harm to it, especially if it were freed of an aspect of enmity.

The[32] misfortune of the planets grows much when they are in estranged places.[33]

It is not appropriate to do battle against an estate if the significator were the lord of the Ascendant of the revolution of the year of the world.

In every beginning, it is appropriate to make the heavens agree with the natures of the significators, and [to make] the significators agree with those which are being commingled with it.

An election is better and more fortunate and successful, where the diurnal planets are eastern from the Sun and in masculine signs, and the nocturnal ones are western from the Moon and in feminine signs.[34]

Applications of the Moon to Mars from the houses of Venus are to be abhorred, and to Jupiter from the houses of Mercury, and to the Sun from the houses of Saturn.[35]

There could be great fortune for him who has the lord of the eleventh from his Ascendant, and the lord of the eleventh from his Moon, and the lord of the eleventh from the Lot of Fortune, in their own domain,[36] or were the fortunes powerful.

If it happened that the lord of the bound of the conjunction or prevention which was before the beginning were made fortunate, that beginning will be fortunate and complete.

If the lord of the bound of the conjunction or prevention which was [before] the beginning were in good places and in a good status, and in its own houses, and its natures were in agreement with the natures of the matter, the matter will be lasting and fixed, and will last for a long time.

---

31 Cf. *Fifty Judgments* #2.

32 Cf. *Fifty Judgments* #26, 28, 29, 41.

33 That is, "peregrine" (Lat. *extraneus*).

34 This is a kind of combination of domain (*ITA* III.2) and the core concept of bodyguarding (*ITA* III.28), both of which draw on sect. By being eastern of the Sun, al-Rijāl means being in an earlier zodiacal degree (so as to rise before him); by being western of the Moon, he means being in a later zodiacal degree (so as to set after her, and she is advancing toward it in the zodiac). Probably he also prefers that the diurnal planets be so configured in a diurnal election, and the nocturnal ones so in a nocturnal election.

35 Or rather, to Saturn from the house of the Sun. These situations could be considered examples of the "opening of the doors," a traditional indicator of rain: see *Judges* §§Z.4-6.

36 Also known as *ḥayyiz* or *haiz*: *ITA* III.2 (Lat. *haiç*).

Chapter VII.2.0: On the principles of deeds

[Chapter VII.2.1: al-Kindī][37]

In the beginnings of deeds, it is appropriate to adapt the Ascendant and its lord, in [likeness and][38] good fortune.

And likeness[39] is that the Ascendant be of a nature like and appropriate to the matter, in quality and reason.[40] The "quality" is just like when we choose[41] what we want for journeys: that they be completed quickly[42] and have easy movements,[43] or fiery signs when we seek a judgment[44] or honor from the king. "Reason" is just like when we choose the signs of Mars in disputes.

[Furthermore], it is necessary that you adapt the place of the house, and the lord of the matter, and the lord of the lord of the matter: for the place of the matter signifies what will be in the beginning of the matter, and the lord of the matter signifies the middle, and the lord of the lord of the matter signifies the end of the matter. Likewise, the Ascendant signifies the beginning of him whose matter it is, and the lord of the Ascendant the middle, and the lord of the lord of the Ascendant signifies the end of him whose matter it is. Likewise, you should inspect the Lot of Fortune and its lord, and the lord of its lord: because if you could improve all of them and make them fortunate, that is the completion [of the whole matter].

And you should make them fortunate[45] by putting fortunes in them by aspect or application,[46] and through the agreement of natures, and you should throw the infortunes out of these places. You should beware lest the

---

37 Almost all of this subchapter is based on *Forty Chapters* Ch. 4. But Hugo and Robert read the division of categories (like "good fortune" and "likeness) differently: see Appendix C below for their version.

38 Adding based on Hugo's and Robert's al-Kindī §142, else the organization of the topics below would not make sense.

39 Reading for "good fortune" (*fortuna*).

40 Hugo and Robert have "manner" (*modus*).

41 Reading *cum eligimus* with 1551 for *excollegimus*.

42 This probably means the crooked signs, which have short ascensional times.

43 This probably refers to inferior planets, which move more quickly.

44 *Rationem*.

45 This is the category of "good fortune" mentioned in the first paragraph above. The next few paragraphs continue this theme of what makes the significators fortunate or unfortunate.

46 Note the distinction between an aspect by sign, and an application by degrees (*ITA* III.6-7).

lord of the Ascendant be retrograde, because its retrogradation signifies hindrance, prohibition, and slowness. And even should all the significators be good and signify the effecting of the matter, provided that the lord of the Ascendant is retrograde there will first be mistrust in the matter, and slowness, and it will not be completed except through labor.

You should beware lest the Tail be with any of the luminaries (when they are in the conjunction or the opposition), or that the luminaries should not be in [its] conjunction or the opposition.[47] And beware lest the Tail be in the Ascendant, nor in the place of the matter, nor with the Lot of the matter: because it harms matters through cheapness and mismanagement[48] and labor.

And attend to putting a fortune in the Ascendant, or in the place of the matter, or in the angles. Know that the primary fortune[49] is powerful in all matters, and in matters which we want to improve; and the lesser fortune[50] is powerful in all affairs of games, joys, vices, affectations,[51] friendship, and what is like this.

Beware in all matters lest you put the Moon in the Ascendant, because she is inimical to the Ascendant; but the Sun is not contrary to the Ascendant, but he discloses matters and unfolds them, and he loosens a matter which is bound up.

You should beware, as much as you can, lest the infortunes be in the Ascendant, nor in any of the angles—and especially if it were a lord of the bad places: because if the infortune were the lord of the eighth house, it signifies condemnation through deaths and through the allies of adversaries, and through great incarcerations. And if it were the lord of the sixth house, it signifies harm from the direction of enemies, slaves, infirmities, the removal of limbs, and short incarcerations, and four-footed animals. And if it were the lord of the twelfth, it signifies harm from the direction of labors, mistrust, enemies, and middling incarcerations. And if it were the lord of the

47 Al-Kindī seems to mean that an election should not happen right after an eclipse (when the conjunction or opposition would be on the Nodes), and that at the time of the election itself they should not be on the Nodes—particularly with the Tail.

48 *Miscurationem.*

49 That is, Jupiter.

50 That is, Venus.

51 *Affectamentorum.* Based on Hugo's al-Kindī, this seems to mean fancy clothing and jewels.

second, it signifies a situation happening[52] because of assets or allies, or eating and drinking. Therefore, you should beware as much as you can.

Attend[53] so that in the day, the Ascendant is of the diurnal signs, and in the night of the nocturnal ones; and that it be of the signs ascending directly, not of the crooked ones; and if you could, that the luminaries be in like signs, and that the lords of the aforesaid places be powerful, just as we have said before.

And[54] power is divided into two parts: one natural, and the other accidental. Natural, is that a planet be appearing eastern outside the rays, and in its own house or exaltation, bound, triplicity, or its own face, and that it is northern in its motion or latitude, and that it is direct or moving itself forward. And accidental is that it is made fortunate by a fortune, strengthened through a conjunction or by a trine or by a square or by an opposition, or by a sextile aspect, and that it is safe and cleared of the infortunes by all aspects.

[Chapter VII.2.2: Abū Ma'shar on the significators of the end][55]

And one portion of the sages[56] said that for making the end of the matter fortunate, five things must be inspected: one is the lord of the fourth house; second, the lord of the house of the Moon; third, the last[57] planet to which the Moon is going in the sign in which she is; fourth, the lord of the house of the Lot of Fortune; fifth, the fourth sign and the sign in which the Moon is.[58]

---

[52] *Occasionem.*

[53] Cf. also *Carmen* V.4.5.

[54] Cf. *Forty Chapters* §63. But al-Kindī is not extremely clear on exactly what kinds of planetary conditions and placements belong in each of the categories here. Either al-Rijāl has made his own decision, or his version of al-Kindī was more explicit.

[55] Cf. al-'Imrānī I.2.2.

[56] That is, Abū Ma'shar, quoted in al-'Imrānī Ch. I.2.2.

[57] *Postremus.* Normally one would observe only the *next* planet to which the Moon applies.

[58] But al-'Imrānī reads, "the fourth from the sign in which the Moon is." We should follow al-'Imrānī, because then he appends the view of someone else, who advocates using the fourth from the Lot of Fortune: in context, pairing these two together makes sense. If Abū Ma'shar had meant the fourth and the sign of the Moon (as the Latin al-Rijāl has here), we would expect it to be higher up in the list.

[Chapter VII.2.3: The Moon in the Ascendant][59]

Māshā'allāh and his associates say that the Moon in the Ascendant is bad and is to be abhorred,[60] and al-Kindī[61] says likewise. And they say that it is because she is cold and moist (even though she is a fortune),[62] while the Ascendant is hot—and [therefore their qualities] disagree.

But Abū Ma'shar does not abhor the Moon in the Ascendant,[63] and it seems that he adheres to the statement of Ptolemy that she is *hot* and moist:[64] and on account of this he does not hold her to be contrary to the Ascendant.

I however, say that she is bad and to be abhorred there, nor do I agree with the statement of Abū Ma'shar—because he himself disagrees in his own

---

[59] This subchapter must be read along with al-'Imrānī I.2.8. At first the passage seems disorganized, but al-'Imrānī's discussion (and al-Rijāl's response) can be boiled down to six points. (1) Māshā'allāh and al-Kindī (and 'Umar: see al-'Imrānī II.13.2) agree that the Moon should not be in the Ascendant, and especially for travel, because the Moon's qualities are contrary to the Ascendant's (which is hot). Al-Kindī also adds that the Sun is not a problem in the Ascendant. (2) Now, Abū Ma'shar disagrees with this prohibition about travel, but his opinion is inconsistent. Because on the one hand, when discussing travel in one of his books, he seems to approve of the Moon being in the Ascendant, and agrees with the well-known view of Ptolemy (from *Tet.* I.4) that the Moon is warming: this means that her qualities are *not* contrary to the Ascendant, so she is not prohibited from being there. The problem is that in other places (such as the quotes in *ITA* V.7), he says that the Moon is *cold*, not warm. (3) Not only that (adds al-Rijāl), but when talking about natal longevity procedures, he says that the Moon is one of the "cutting" planets which takes life away (probably when the Ascendant is directed to her): again, this suggests contrary qualities. So Abū Ma'shar's views are again inconsistent. (4) Because of this inconsistency, al-Rijāl agrees with the others that she should be prohibited. (5) But al-'Imrānī and al-Rijāl may be making different conclusions from all of this, or at least al-Rijāl's conclusions are a garbled version of al-'Imrānī's. (5a) Al-'Imrānī concludes that since she has a signification for every beginning and that she makes the Ascendant fortunate, she may be put there—which he says is an "appropriate place." (5b) But al-Rijāl, with very similar language, begins by saying the Moon signifies "few" journeys (perhaps he meant "short" journeys), *no matter* what she might otherwise mean for beginnings, and specifically says that the "appropriate place" for her is one in which she aspects the Ascendant. (6) Finally, both al-'Imrānī and al-Rijāl simply point out that there is disagreement about the role of the Sun in the Ascendant (which was mentioned by al-Kindī), but they do not discuss it further.

[60] *On Elect.* §23a gives the general prohibition, but because he is drawing on al-'Imrānī I.2.8, al-Rijāl means the prohibition related to travel(*On Elect.* §107).

[61] *Forty Chapters* §147.

[62] In *Tet.* I.4-5, Ptolemy explains benefic and malefic qualities in terms of the presence of (temperate) warmth and moisture. So, al-Rijāl is pointing out something of an inconstancy with Māshā'allāh (and perhaps al-Kindī), in that they consider the Moon to be a benefic even though they have made her be cold or cooling.

[63] Source unknown at this time.

[64] Ptolemy says that the Moon is somewhat heating but largely moistening, in *Tet.* I.4.

statement: because when he speaks about the directing of the releaser[65] and the cutters,[66] he says that the Moon cuts in the Ascendant, and takes life away, while [in his previous statement] he does not abhor her. Whence this is a conflict in sense, and a loss and weakness in reasoning.

And in addition to all of this she is bad on journeys, because she is of few journeys,[67] no matter what her significations are in other beginnings. And on account of this, it is appropriate for you to put her in a place befitting her, since she makes the Ascendant fortunate by aspect.

Those who abhor the Sun in the Ascendant[68] or in the house of the matter, say that the Sun is an infortune in the conjunction and opposition, and all do not agree in this.

[VII.2.4: The conjunction and opposition of the lights preceding the election][69]

You[70] should know that a thing which very much increases the fortune of beginnings, and improves them[71] with a great improvement and great fortune, and likewise in a nativity and all elections, is that the place of the conjunction at the hour of the conjunction (if the beginning were conjunctional), or the place of the opposition at the hour of the opposition (if the beginning were oppositional)[72] were safe from the infortunes and harms, and made fortunate; and likewise the lord of the sign of the conjunction or the lord of the sign of the opposition. (And you should know that the sign of the opposition is the sign of the luminary which was above the earth. And if one

---

[65] *Atazir hylech*, Ar. *al-tasyīr al-hīlāj*. That is, the primary direction of the longevity releaser (usually called the *hyleg* in Latin).

[66] The "cutters" are various planets and aspects and points which indicate death or other crises when the longevity releaser is directed to them.

[67] I am not sure what al-Rijāl means by this.

[68] Below, al-Rijāl himself does not approve of the Sun in the Ascendant, except in Leo and Aries (VII.2.7).

[69] For this whole subchapter, cf. al-'Imrānī I.2.10. Al-Rijāl does not simply copy all of the material, but seems to be a little choosy about his use of it (especially with the al-Kindī material).

[70] From here until the quote from Abū Ma'shar, al-Rijāl is presenting his more abbreviated version of al-'Imrānī, whose own text seems to be based on *Forty Chapters* §§478-79, 483, 488-89, 494-95a, and 536.

[71] Reading *fortunam...ea* for *fortuna...eam*.

[72] Al-Rijāl is referring to whether the time of the election comes after the most recent New Moon (conjunctional) or Full Moon (oppositional, sometimes called "preventional").

luminary were in the angle of the east and the other in the angle of the west, it will be the place of the one which was in the east.)[73]

When[74] the Moon is being separated from the conjunction or opposition [of the Sun], and goes towards an infortune, you should beware in all undertakings because all beginnings which come to be in this manner are bad and are to be abhorred: for if the place of the conjunction or opposition were made unfortunate, it signifies that the *beginning* of the matter will be bad; when the Moon is being separated from the conjunction or opposition of the Sun and she goes toward an infortune, it signifies that the *end* of that beginning will be bad and is to be abhorred.[75]

[And let the place of the conjunction or prevention be in one of the angles, and the Moon should be going to a conjunction of the fortunes: for this is a signification of exaltation and the perfected fortune of things, and their end will be praised.][76]

Next, if the place of the conjunction or opposition were good and fortunate, and in separating herself from it the Moon applies to infortunes, it signifies that the beginning of that matter will be good, and its end bad.

And if the place of the conjunction and opposition were unfortunate, and the Moon (in separating herself from thence) applied to fortunes, it signifies that the beginning of the matter will be bad, and the end good.

And if the place of the conjunction or prevention were fortunate, and the Moon (in separating herself) applied to a fortune, it signifies that the beginning and end will both be fortunate.

And if there were an infortune in the place of the conjunction or prevention, and the Moon (in separating herself from thence) applied to an infortune, it signifies that the beginning and end of the matter will be bad and to be abhorred.

---

[73] Ptolemy holds this view about the light above the earth (*Tet.* III.3), but not about the prevention being on the horizon.

[74] For the following paragraphs, cf. *Forty Chapters* §§483 and 495a. For al-Kindī, these statements have to do with elections for digging canals and constructing ships, but he probably would have agreed with observing the fitness of the conjunction or prevention in many different elections.

[75] This paragraph is ambiguous because a "beginning" here refers both to the action itself, and the first experiences or developments of the election. Al-Rijāl is saying that the place of the conjunction or opposition prior to the election indicates its first steps, while the planet to which the Moon applies next indicates the later development—just as the separation and application of the Moon at the time of the event do.

[76] I have supplied a missing paragraph which was in al-'Imrānī I.2.10.

And if the conjunction or prevention (or its lord) were in a succeedent, it signifies that the good and improvement which will appear in that matter, will be at the end and at its completion. And if the conjunction or opposition were cadent from the angle of the Ascendant (this is a statement about the Ascendant of the beginning of the matter or the election or nativity), it signifies that the matter will be condemned and will have no good: and this is the statement of al-Kindī, and I confirm it.

And you should attend, in all beginnings, to improving the place of the conjunction or prevention which is before the beginning, and likewise the lord of the house of that conjunction or prevention.

You[77] should know that the lord of the house of the conjunction or prevention is more individualized[78] than the lord of the quarters of the year are, and the lord of the quarter of the year is more individualized than the lord of the year. And if you could improve all of these, it will be better and more firm.

Abu Ma'shar said that if the lord of the election[79] were the lord of the sign of the Moon[80] at the revolution of the year of the world, or [it were] the lord of that year, or the lord of its Ascendant, and it were made fortunate at the revolution and in the election, it signifies loftiness and nobility in the matter undertaken, and in all of his deeds. And he said that if the lord of the Ascendant of the year of the world had no testimonies in the beginnings [of matters], or in the place of the luminaries, nor in the Midheaven, the matter will be low-quality and despised.

Al-Tabarī said[81] that if the place of the conjunction or prevention (and its lord) were in good bounds and in good places, the matter will be firm and lasting—and likewise he who will then be born, and he who (in such a constellation) had entered into some dignity at the hour of the undertaking, or that this would be according to the Ascendant of the nativity of that man.

Al-Kindī said that if the lord of the house of the conjunction or prevention which was before the beginning [of the action] were eastern at the hour of the beginning, and it were in its own house, or aspecting its own [house]

---

[77] See my notes to the version in al-'Imrānī I.2.10.

[78] *Proprior*, lit. "closer," in the sense that it is more particularized to the time and nature of the election.

[79] Probably the lord of the Ascendant of the election.

[80] Reading with al-'Imrānī, for "luminaries."

[81] Source unknown at this time.

from a trine or a sextile, it signifies improvement and good fortune in that matter; and if it did not aspect, it signifies no good.

[Chapter VII.2.5: Other considerations][82]

And you should make effort to improve beginnings [using] the lords of the triplicity of the Moon at the hour of the conjunction or prevention, because they have power in nativities and beginnings; wherefore, if they were received and made fortunate at the hour of the beginning, they signify good. And if at the hour of the beginning they were in a different status, they signify bad.

And that which helps in the good and in good fortune, is that the Ascendant of the election be a sign in which there was a fortune in the revolution of the year, and that there are fortunes in the angles (and especially in the Ascendant or Midheaven), or in the succeedents, and in the place of the matter.

Alaçmin[83] said that if the luminaries would aspect each other with a good aspect, they signify good and improvement in every matter undertaken, and especially if the Moon were "at the beginning of her own joy"—this is a statement that she be in the sign in which the Head was.[84]

Māshā'allāh said[85] [that] planets strengthen themselves when they are western from the Moon, just as they strengthen themselves when they are eastern from the Sun;[86] the rulership of the Moon is thus by night, just as the rulership of the Sun is by day.

Al-Tabarī said,[87] if in undertakings and elections you could not improve the Ascendant and the Moon both, [then] if the election were by day, first you should improve the Ascendant (and especially, if the Moon were under the earth, you should not care about her); and if the election were by night,

---

[82] For this subchapter, cf. al-'Imrānī I.2.11.

[83] Unknown at this time, but the Latinized name suggests 'Uthman. Al-'Imrānī has "al-Kindī" both for this and the other statements by "Alaçmin" below, but I cannot find the source of his quote in *Forty Chapters*.

[84] This may have been an idiosyncratic phrase of al-Kindī/Alaçmin or his sources. Being in that sign would indicate that the Moon is or is about to be in degrees of northern ecliptical latitude.

[85] Source unknown at this time.

[86] This is related to ancient definitions of bodyguarding (*ITA* II.28). Māshā'allāh means that the planets' bodies should be in an earlier degree of the zodiac relative to the Sun (so that they rise before him by diurnal motion), but they should be in later ones relative to the Moon (so that she moves towards them by planetary or zodiacal motion).

[87] These first two sentences derive from *Carmen* V.5.32-33.

first you should improve the Moon (and especially, if she were above the earth, you should not care about the other). And if you had space in the election,[88] you should make effort to improve both (namely the Ascendant and the Moon) in all ways. If the Moon were below the earth by day, and above the earth by night, the power and good of the Ascendant grows. And[89] if you had a hastened election, nor did you have space to improve the Moon, put Jupiter or Venus in the Ascendant or Midheaven: because in a matter they make for great improvement.

The ancient sages say that this[90] could be so in matters [such that] that they are not [intended to be] lasting and remaining for a long time. However, in matters which they do want to last and remain for a long time (such as a marriage-union or building, and what is like these), it is necessary to improve the Moon. And if she were harmed, you should attend to putting her in a place cadent from an angle, and a succeedent one; and if you could not [do this] at least from the angles,[91] [make it] in particular [so] that the Moon would not aspect the Ascendant nor its lord,[92] nor the lord of the house of the matter, nor her own lord, nor a planet signifying the matter by nature and its proper quality.[93] And if you could not draw her back from all of these places, draw her back from all of them which you could.

Alaçmin said,[94] it is better to improve the significators than to improve the Moon in her Head.[95]

[But] al-Tabarī says it is better to improve the lord of the house [of the matter] than the Moon or the Ascendant or another place—and I do not concede this, nor does al-'Imrānī[96] (who was before [me])[97] concede it: and

---

[88] *Spatium habueris in electione.* That is, if you had the freedom to pick from a broad range of times.

[89] Cf. *Carmen* V.5.11.

[90] Probably referring to the previous view by al-Tabarī.

[91] Comparing with al-'Imrānī, this means "and if you could not remove her from the angles."

[92] This probably means a degree-based aspect, since if she is in the angles she will of course be aspecting the rising sign itself.

[93] For example, Jupiter if it were for making money, or Venus if it were for a marriage.

[94] See my footnote to the other quote by "Alaçmin" above. The corresponding paragraph in al-'Imrānī read rather differently.

[95] See above, where he recommended putting the Moon in the sign of the Head.

[96] *Alambrim.*

[97] Reading *me* for *ego* ("I").

without a doubt [al-'Imrānī] would rather guard the spirit and the body [of the person] than perfect the matter, because the matter follows upon life.[98]

If[99] the Moon were in a slow motion like the motion of Saturn (and this is when she is moved less than 12° in one day and night), it then signifies slowness, complication, and hindrance in matters.

Al-Khayyāt says,[100] if you had a hastened election, and the Moon went towards a planet [that is an] infortune, make that infortune be the lord of the Ascendant; and if [the infortune is] clear and in a good status, it will be better; and if it received [her] from the Ascendant, it will likewise be better.

[VII.2.6: Things to beware of][101]

You[102] should beware lest the significators be applying to infortunes from the opposition or square; however, if the application were from the trine or sextile, it is not bad, especially if it were with reception.[103] [For] Māshā'allāh says that the aspects of the infortunes from the trine or sextile are good and fortunate—in which I do not agree with him.[104] On the contrary, I say that such aspects do not make [something] fortunate, nor do they make [something] unfortunate, nor do they prohibit evil and its harm.

And it is appropriate that you should beware of the conjunction of the Sun, because it is very bad and worthy of condemning.[105] And I do not agree with those who say that being in the heart[106] is good: on the contrary, I say it is worse and of greater harm. Likewise, you should beware of his square and opposition; and if there were reception in this, he will be of less evil and harm.

---

[98] In other words, personal and mental safety is more important than accomplishing some risky (though profitable) deed.

[99] Cf. *Carmen* V.5.6-7, and Sahl's list of impediments (*On Elect.* §22f).

[100] Al-Rijāl has taken this from al-'Imrānī I.2.11, but it has undergone changes. See my Introduction for a discussion of this passage.

[101] Al-Rijāl has taken parts of this chapter from al-'Imrānī I.2.12, and added some other material.

[102] For this paragraph, cf. *Fifty Judgments* #2, 5, and 31, and the footnote below.

[103] Cf. *Fifty Judgments* #2, 5, 31; and *Carmen* V.5.13.

[104] Here al-Rijāl is disagreeing with al-'Imrānī, who endorses Māshā'allāh's view.

[105] Or possibly, "liable to harm" (*damnabilis*).

[106] *Tasim*, referring to so-called "cazimi," being in the same degree as the Sun (and especially within only a few minutes of longitude). In *ITA* II.9, I provide a quote from ibn Ezra approving of being in the heart.

And you should beware lest the Ascendant be a sign in which there was an infortune, or that it was made unfortunate, in the revolution of the year.

Likewise, he[107] abhors it that the angles should be cadent—for example, that the tenth sign from the Ascendant should come by computation to be in the ninth[108] through the equation of the houses: and he calls such [houses] "retrograde." However, if they were remote while going forward,[109] it is good [and] complete—such as when the tenth house, by computation, comes into the eleventh through the equation of houses: and one calls this *anafamentum.*[110]

And you should beware lest the lord of the Ascendant or a planet to which the Moon is being joined, should be western by setting after the Sun: because such a planet is like one who is likened to being half-weary.[111]

Hermes says in the *Book of Longitudes*[112] that the Ascendant and the Midheaven (and those which were in them) are like a youth; the seventh is like one approaching being an old man, and the fourth is like an old man. And he says there that a planet gives, and that which grows in that house[113] he holds in the hand.

[Chapter VII.2.7: Planets in the Ascendant with the lights]

One must abhor the Sun in the Ascendant, unless he is in Leo or in Aries; and in the Ascendant with Saturn, he harms matters and does not permit them to be fulfilled, unless with great hardship and labor; and in journeys on the sea, they are certainly to be abhorred in the Ascendant. Saturn with the Moon in the Ascendant signifies thoughts,[114] great infirmity, death, and loss

---

[107] Al-Rijāl seems to be referring to al-'Imrānī here; see my footnote to al-'Imrānī's paragraph.
[108] Reading *nonam* for *undecimam* ("eleventh") along with al-'Imrānī and Sahl (*On Quest.* §1.7 or *Judges* §1.1). Al-Rijāl or the translator seems to have gotten this backwards: al-'Imrānī means that the tenth quadrant-based house (marked by the Midheaven) should not be in the ninth sign.
[109] *In antea.* The Latin al-'Imrānī understands this as "ascending" or "ascension."
[110] Or, *anasamantum.* This is probably from an Arabic transliteration of the Gr. *anaphora*, which refers to bringing or carrying up, a word applied to the succeedent places (in this case, the eleventh).
[111] *Semifesso.*
[112] Unknown at this time. But cf. *ITA* I.11, *BA* II.13, and Paul of Alexandria Ch. 7.
[113] Reading *domo* for *dono* ("gift"). Nevertheless, I do not understand what al-Rijāl means by this.
[114] *Cogitatus.* This might mean something more like "troubled thoughts," or thinking about things too much rather than feeling more carefree.

coming forth from the direction of the king, and the loss of assets, and the destruction of blood-relatives and of a partnership, and it signifies a journey [that is] not long.

If Jupiter were in the Ascendant with the Sun, it signifies sorrows, thoughts,[115] a modicum of good, and changing over from one place to another. And if he were in the Ascendant with the Moon, it signifies many waters, and youths, and concubines, a marriage-union, and honor.

If Mars were in the Ascendant with the Sun, it signifies sorrow, anxiety, and pains from the direction of enemies, and little advancement[116] from the direction of friends, and loss, and sudden death through iron or fire. And if he were in the Ascendant with the Moon, it signifies the contrariety of blood-relatives, while[117] he signifies victory and power through fraud and loss.

If Venus were in the Ascendant with the Sun, it signifies laziness, weariness, and seeking vain types of trust,[118] the accusations of friends and blood-relatives, and it signifies foul things in matters, and what women pursue.[119] And if she were in the Ascendant with the Moon, it signifies the good health of the body, and improvement, and usefulness from the direction of women, except that there will be filthy and suspicious deeds in this.

If Mercury were in the Ascendant with the Sun, it signifies sorrows and pains. And if he were in the Ascendant with the Moon, it signifies many works for the good, except that it signifies mismanagement between blood-relatives and friends.

If the Moon were in the Ascendant with the Sun, it signifies hardships, mistrust, spending and destroying, and pain in the eyes.

[Chapter VII.2.8: The quadruplicities and ascensions][120]

You should beware of the movable signs in every matter which you want to be firm and lasting. Likewise, you should beware of the fixed signs in matters which you want to be easy and which you want to pass by quickly.

---

[115] See footnote above.

[116] Reading *profectionem* for *perfectionem*.

[117] The Latin reads, "since" (*quare*), but this does not make sense to me.

[118] *Fiducias vanas*.

[119] *Causam mulierum*.

[120] For this subchapter, cf. al-'Imrānī I.2.7.

Likewise, you should beware of signs of straight ascensions in matters which you do not want to be lasting, and which should pass by quickly. Likewise you should beware of the crooked signs in matters which you want to conclude directly and evenly—because these signs are hard in all deeds and in all questions.

Chapter VII.3.0: On the signs and their significations[121]

[Chapter VII.3.1: Signs by quadruplicity][122]

Know that the movable signs signify the changing of things in an easy way, and their significations are not strengthened, nor do they last, in any manner. They are good for sowing, buying, selling, and for making betrothals. If someone will be taken ill in them, he will be freed (or die)[123] quickly; and [legal] cases in them are not prolonged; and one who flees, quickly turns back; and it is good to make a journey in them; and a promise made in them will not be completed; and dreams and fears in them will be lies. And beware lest you plant any plant in them, nor should you build in some work, because it is bad. And everything which you undertook in them which you wanted to last, will not be very lasting; however, do everything in these which you wanted to do within [a given] day, because it is good. But the lighter ones of the movable signs are Aries and Cancer, and they are more crooked and are changed more quickly; but Libra and Capricorn are more strengthened and more balanced.[124]

The fixed signs are appropriate and good for all matters which we want to last and remain for a long time. It is good to build in them, to establish marriages (after engagements are made in the movable ones);[125] And if some woman were rejected by her husband in them, she will never return to him; and journeys in them, and disputes and beginnings,[126] cannot be good unless they have many testimonies of the fortunes. And if someone were captured

---

[121] This chapter is taken verbatim by al-Rijāl from Sahl's *On Elect.*, §§12a-22a.
[122] Cf. *On Elect.* §§12a-18.
[123] Sahl himself does not mention dying.
[124] *Temperata.* For the use of these signs, see the corresponding section in *On Elect.*
[125] That is, get engaged under movable signs for a quick engagement, but married under the fixed signs for a lasting marriage.
[126] Sahl's *On Elect.* §14b has judgments (questions), not journeys and disputes. But al-Rijāl's reading does make sense.

in them, his incarceration will be prolonged; and should someone be subject to someone's anger in them, he will not be subject to his love;[127] and pacts which come to be in them will be good; foundations and buildings will be good in them. But Scorpio is the lightest of the fixed signs, and Leo is more fixed, and Aquarius is worst, and Taurus more balanced.

The common signs are good for partnership and friendships and brotherhoods, and matters which come to be in them often recur; purchases and marriages which come to be in them do not last long, and there will be deception in them. And one who was accused of some matter in them (through which [a punishment] is imposed on him), will be liberated from it (unless particularly in Pisces, because it has [only] a small appearance).[128] And one who was taken out of prisons in them, will be led back to prison again. And if some fleeing thing will be captured,[129] it will flee again. And he who will present an argument before an advocate or judge in them, will not have a firm judgment. And you should not board a ship in them, because if you boarded you will change from that ship[130] to another. And for one to whom something is promised in them, that promise will not be fulfilled. Receive gifts in them, and present them [in turn].[131] If someone will grow infirm in them, he will be healed and afterwards suffer a relapse. And whatever happened to a man in them (with respect to the good or bad), that matter will return to him again. And if someone will die in them, another will die after him by a few days in that same place. But it is good to change from one place to another in them; it is good to wash the head in them, to purify gold and silver, and sending boys to [learn to] read or to another teaching is good in them, and likewise [to loan] capital.[132]

Whence, when you wanted to undertake some matter (of the things which we have told you about before), you should put the Moon and the Ascend-

---

127 Sahl's version suggests that anger cannot be controlled (or, in the Arabic, that someone with whom one is angry, cannot be controlled).

128 What al-Rijāl (and perhaps Sahl, though this does not appear in Croft's Arabic) means is that Pisces has the shortest ascensional time of all the common signs (in the northern hemisphere), so that it passes across the horizon very quickly.

129 Sahl reads this as a fugitive person, but the Latin al-Rijāl evidently wants to include animals.

130 Reading "ship" for "thing," with Sahl.

131 Sahl does not have this, but it makes sense.

132 Sahl does not have this part about loans, but it makes sense.

ant[133] in signs agreeing with the matter which you are seeking, and make the Moon apply to fortunes with reception in those signs; and diurnal signs are better in deeds of the day, and nocturnal ones in deeds of the night. Afterwards, you should put the Moon and the Ascendant in them.

[Chapter VII.3.2: Other classifications of signs][134]

The flying signs are good for those who hunt on land and sea.

The royal signs[135] are good for kings.

The voiced signs are good for horn-players and singers and sounders of instruments.

The fiery signs are good and appropriate for [what is done with fire].[136]

[The equinoctial signs[137] are good for] truths, laws, and justice, [and those who work with scales].

The divergent signs[138]—and they are those by which night and day begin to be distinguished—are good in matters which are changed from one house[139] to another.

[Chapter VII.3.3: Instructions according to the nature of the election][140]

Afterwards, inspect to see of what nature the matter is (which you want to undertake), and which one of the signs of heaven agrees with that nature, and make the Moon and the lord of the Ascendant attach to that nature—and you should improve that nature, and fortify it, as much as you can, at the hour of the undertaking.

And when you wanted some matter from the king or a powerful person, or the master of a city, or from a powerful man whom[141] peoples revere, you should adhere to the Sun. And if you wanted it from some noble person, you should adhere to Jupiter. And if you wanted it from laborers or low-class

---

[133] Reading *et ascendens* for *in ascendente* ("in the Ascendant"), following Sahl (see also the similar statement immediately below).

[134] Cf. *On Elect.* §§19a-b.

[135] That is, the fiery signs.

[136] The Latin al-Rijāl combined this sentence with the next, but I have broken it up and added the appropriate statements from *On Elect.* §19b.

[137] Aries and Libra.

[138] Capricorn and Cancer, the solsticial signs (confirmed by the Arabic of *On Elect.* §19b).

[139] Or, changing from some "thing" (Sahl) to another.

[140] Cf. *On Elect.* §§20-21c.

[141] Reading *quem* for *quibus*.

men, you should adhere to Saturn. And if you wanted it from judges or soldiers, or men of arms, you should adhere to Mars. And if you wanted it from women, you should adhere to Venus.[142] And if you wanted it from writers and merchants, or for selling and buying, or for [legal] cases, you should adhere to Mercury. And if you wanted it from women who have rulership, you should adhere to the Moon.

Chapter VII.3.4: On the impediments of the Moon[143]

Afterwards, if you wanted to undertake some work, you should improve the Ascendant and its lord, and the Moon and the lord of her house—while watching out for the bad states of the Moon, just as Dorotheus and other sages said, for all undertakings and in all deeds. And there are ten [bad] states:

> The first is when she is burned up in front of the Sun, by 12°, and so many after [him]; but when she is after the Sun, she is of less evil.
>
> Second, when she is in the degree of her own fall.
>
> Third, when she is in the opposition of the Sun.
>
> Fourth, when she is joined bodily to the infortunes, or from the square or opposition.
>
> The fifth is when she is with the Head or Tail, within 12° (which is the boundary of an eclipse).
>
> Sixth, when she is in the last degrees of the signs, which are the bounds of the infortunes.
>
> Seventh is when she is cadent from the angles, or when she is in the burnt path (which is the end of Libra and the beginning of Scorpio)—

---

[142] The Latin al-Rijāl connected buying and selling and legal cases with Venus, but *On Elect.* is clear that these pertain to Mercury. I have switched the relevant clauses.

[143] Except for the last sentence, this subchapter is taken virtually verbatim by al-Rijāl from *On Elect.*, §§22a-f.

and this is worse than all of the misfortunes of the Moon, and especially in marriage-unions and all things pursued by women, and in buying and selling, and on journeys.

Eighth, when the twelfth-part[144] of the Moon is with the infortunes,[145] or when she is contrary to her own house,[146] or that she does not aspect her own house by some aspect.[147]

Ninth is when she has slow motion (and it is what the sages name [as being similar to][148] the motion of Saturn): and it is when she is moved by 12° or less in one day and night.

Tenth is what Māshā'allāh (and others after him)[149] has said: and it is when she is void in course.

[Chapter VII.3.5: Additional instructions][150]

Afterwards, attend as much as you can to improving the Moon, and you should never put her in the Ascendant,[151] because she is bad there, and signifies pains falling[152] in the body—unless the Moon were made very fortunate by a strengthened fortune, removed from the infortunes: because then she is not bad in the Ascendant, for buying and selling. And make the Moon and the lord of the Ascendant be aspecting the Ascendant: because when a planet does not aspect its own house, it is like a man when he is in a place where he cannot accomplish [something] useful, nor remove harm from [his home].

---

144 *Duodenaria.*

145 Sahl's Arabic has "in a twelfth-part with a malefic." But that suggests a bodily conjunction by sign or degree, which was already described above. Here, al-Rijāl suggests that the sign represented by the Moon's twelfth-part has a malefic on it, which is precisely the sort of thing described by Paul of Alexandria (Ch. 22, and the Olympiodorus commentary with examples). Then, *Carmen* V.5.5 has the Moon being in the sign indicated by a malefic's twelfth-part, also the type of thing described by Paul. I suggest that we should use the twelfth-part interpretation or Paul or al-Rijāl, not the "twelfth sign" of the Latin.

146 That is, she is in detriment (in Capricorn).

147 That is, she is in aversion to Cancer.

148 Adding this clarifying remark along with Sahl.

149 This phrase is based on Sahl, who credits Māshā'allāh and unnamed "sages of our time."

150 Cf. *On Elect.* §§23a-28, for all but the last sentence of this subchapter.

151 Sahl says one should not put her *waxing* in the Ascendant.

152 Reading *occidentes* for *occasiones.*

And when a planet does aspect its own house, it is just like a man being in his own house and guarding it, and those who would steal from the home fear him, and those who are outside likewise have fear of entering it.

And if the lord of the Ascendant were an infortune, make it be aspecting the Ascendant from a trine or sextile. And beware lest you put the lord of the Ascendant nor the lord of the house of the Moon (when they were infortunes) to be aspecting the Moon from an angle, nor should you likewise put them in any of the angles, however much they would aspect her.

Nor should you make the Lot of Fortune be cadent in some beginning or deed, nor removed from the aspects nor from the conjunction of the Moon;[153] and you should not care about the lord of the Lot, nor about its aspects to the Moon. And you should make an effort to put the lord of the Ascendant with the Lot, because it is a great improvement in matters, and multiplies [the matter's] usefulness. And you should never put the Moon in the second, sixth, eighth, or twelfth house from the Lot, because this constellation is to be abhorred.[154]

And always, in every beginning, put the Ascendant in a sign of straight ascension, because signs of straight ascensions in the Ascendant signify prosperity in matters.

And the fourth house from the Ascendant, and its lord, signify the end of the matter undertaken.

Afterwards, consider the fortunes and infortunes, and how they stand in power and weakness.

Dorotheus says,[155] if you saw the Moon to be harmed, and you had some hastened matter which you were not able to delay, you should not give the Moon any role in the Ascendant, but make her be cadent from it and its angles, and put a fortune in the Ascendant; and strengthen the Ascendant and its lord as much as you could.

And you should not forget the lord of the hour in any election, because in elections it has manifest power and signification.

---

153 In other words, do not let the Lot of Fortune be in aversion to the Moon.

154 Both the Moon and the Lot signify a flow of influences and events, so we want to coordinate them.

155 Cf. *Carmen* V.5.10-11. This is Māshā'allāh's version of it, as reflected in *On Elect.* §28. See my Introduction for a discussion of this passage.

THE FIRST HOUSE

Chapter VII.4: On the first house and its elections

The elections which I have put in this house are for entering a bath, and cutting the hair on the head, and letting oneself be bled, and doing cupping, and cutting the nails.

Chapter VII.5: On entering a bath[156]

The majority[157] of the sages of the astrologers say that an election for this is that the Moon be [in] one of the houses of Mars, not applying to Saturn nor Venus.

And if she were not in the houses of Mars, let her be in the houses of Jupiter or in the house of the Sun, or in her own house—and that she should not be in one of the houses of Venus nor Mercury.

However, I say that a better election which there could be for entering a bath, is that the Moon be in watery signs. And if she were in Cancer, let her be applied to Jupiter; and if in Scorpio, let her be applied to Venus.

And one who wanted to stay a long time in a bath, should put her in Cancer, applying to Jupiter from a trine or sextile, or to Venus—because an application to Venus signifies beauty for him who enters the bath, and clearness or an increase of a good appearance. And for one who wanted to leave it quickly, put the Moon in the movable signs.

And you should not want to enter a bath with the Moon appearing in hot and dry signs, unless you did this for healing [someone] of moistures or paralysis:[158] and then it is useful that she would be applying to the Sun or Mars from a trine or sextile. And if you wanted a bath for smoothing the body,[159] you should take the signs contrary to these, and planets contrary to these.

However, if you wanted to do it for oiling your body with some good-smelling things, a good election is that the Moon be under the rays (while

---

[156] Some of these instructions would seem to apply to modern spa treatments. Cf. al-'Imrānī II.2.5 (and maybe *On Elect.* §70a).

[157] For this paragraph, cf. al-'Imrānī II.2.5.

[158] Probably in cases of using hot and dry air, such as in a sauna.

[159] This suggests moisturizing the skin for suppleness.

separating herself from the Sun), and applying to some fortune. And if she were in one of the houses of Jupiter or Mars or the Sun, or in her own [house], it will be good.

Chapter VII.6: On cutting the hair on the head

The better election for this is that the Moon be in Libra or in Sagittarius, or in Aquarius or Pisces, applying to Jupiter or Venus. And in this matter, Venus is better, because she signifies a greater perfection of [the hair's] arrangement, and it will grow more slowly.

And[160] if [the Moon] applied to Mars or Saturn, it is not good. And you should beware lest [the barber] apply iron to your head when Mars was in the Ascendant, and likewise the Moon, nor when she applied to Saturn or Mars—and especially from the angles: because her application to Saturn signifies that until the hair grows [back], he will have some [troubled] thoughts and sorrows; and to Mars it signifies some accident of iron or an error in cutting it.

Chapter VII.7.0: On bloodletting and cupping[161]

[Chapter VII.7.1: Advice from al-Kindī][162]

The best that it could be in this, is that the [lord of][163] the Ascendant and the Moon be in airy or fiery signs, both made fortunate and received,[164] while appearing in their own lights (and likewise their lords).[165]

And you should beware lest you touch the limb with iron (or put [iron on it]), with the Moon appearing in the sign signifying that limb, nor when the lord of the Ascendant was in such a sign.

---

160 For this paragraph, cf. al-'Imrānī II.2.4.

161 In some cupping methods, the skin was scratched or cut so that the cup would draw blood and fluids through the scratch: thus al-Rijāl and others understand bloodletting and cupping to be closely related.

162 This section is excerpted (but with certain paragraphs out of sequence) from *Forty Chapters* Ch. 32.

163 Adding with al-Kindī.

164 Al-Kindī has them angular or succeedent, without mentioning reception.

165 In this context, being in "their own lights" means not being under the rays of the Sun.

And if the complexion of him whose [veins] you want to be let were declining towards sanguinity, the earthy signs will be better for him; and if he were choleric, watery ones will be better for him; and if he were phlegmatic, fiery ones; and if melancholic, airy ones.

And beware lest the lord of the eighth house be mixed with the Moon or with the lord of the Ascendant, nor with any of their lords, nor that it be in one of the angles. And attend so that the lord of the Midheaven is a fortune, and that it would aspect the Moon or the lord of the Ascendant. And beware lest the Moon be in the fourth house (nor [that] the lord of the Ascendant [be there]).

However, the difference between cupping and the letting of blood through a vein is that when you wished to extract blood with cupping, it is good that it be after the opposition [of the Sun and Moon], in the last part of the [Lunar] month. And if you extracted from a vein, it is better that it come to be in the first half of the month, while looking in both [cases] in addition at the constellations[166] and fortunes which we have stated.

[Chapter VII.7.2: Additional advice]

And I say that they should not be let if the Moon were in common signs, because it signifies that the bloodlettor will stab him more than one stabbing, or that it will be necessary for him to be let again, a short time later.[167]

And likewise, bloodletting is not good with the Moon going toward Mars from the opposition or from any square (and the opposition is worse), because it might signify that the vein will be maimed, or blood will go out more than it should, so that they would not be able to hold it [back]. But applications from the trine or sextile are not bad. And an application of the Moon to Saturn by body (or from the square or the opposition) is likewise to be abhorred, because it signifies that perhaps the blood will not go out, or perhaps it will be congealed or the vein will be contracted,[168] or the phlebotomist[169] will have melancholy and bad thoughts.

And if the Moon were in Aries or Libra, applying to Venus or Jupiter (or both), it signifies that he who is being let will not have fear nor [troubled]

---

166 That is, the various configurations.

167 Al-Rijāl is disagreeing with a view reported in al-'Imrānī II.2.8.

168 Or, "drawn in" (*attrahetur*). This probably refers to veins which are hard to reach and seem to disappear inside the flesh.

169 One would expect this to be the patient, not the bloodlettor.

thoughts about the bloodletting, and he will feel easy about it, and it will be advantageous for him, and[170] he will fill up what blood was taken from him, [though] it will last for a long time, and it will not do evil to him that it goes slowly after the letting. And the bad blood will go out of his body, and he will recover good [blood].

And likewise, if the Moon applied to Mars or to the lord of the Ascendant, it signifies that after the letting, choler will be moved.[171] And if she applied to Saturn, melancholy will be moved. And if the Moon were void in course, phlegm will be moved.

And beware, in letting by a vein, lest the Moon be in the Ascendant and the Ascendant be Gemini; and in letting with cupping, lest she be in the Ascendant and the Ascendant be Taurus.

Chapter VII.8: On cutting the nails[172]

The best in this is that the Moon would be increased in light and number, and received, and that she not be in Gemini or Pisces,[173] nor that any one of these signs be ascending.

And remove the Moon and the lord of the Ascendant from the aspects of the lords of these signs (which are Jupiter and Mercury), because these are the worst there could be for cutting nails, since they signify that while the nails will grow back, he who made them be cut will be in [troubled] thoughts and sorrows.[174]

And you will put the Moon in one of the houses of Venus or Mars, or in Cancer or Leo, since these are appropriate for the cutting of nails.

---

[170] In the rest of the sentence, reading tentatively for: *supplebit quid sibi ablatum est de sanguine longo tempore duraturum, et non faciet sibi malum quod post minutionem se tardet.* I should think that a better result would be that the body would replenish the blood *quickly*.

[171] I believe this means that the bloodletting will get rid of the choleric blood signified by Mars, so that choleric tendencies would be removed (and likewise for Saturn and black bile).

[172] Cf. al-'Imrānī II.2.3, which is shorter and differs in certain details.

[173] Al-'Imrānī reads, "Sagittarius."

[174] I believe this refers to the "patient," not the barber or nail-cutter.

THE SECOND HOUSE

Chapter VII.9: On the second house and its elections[175]

The elections which are in this house are: entrusting assets [to someone], seeking assets and debts, buying and selling, selling produce, giving capital, accepting capital, changing from one house to another, working alchemy.

[General significators in financial matters]

I say that it is appropriate for you to know that in all cases of assets, generally and as a whole, because it belongs to one's power of doing trade, and purchases and sales, it is right to make the second house and its lord fit, and Jupiter, and the Lot of Fortune (because [the Lot] is a great and strengthened signification).

However, in that which a man wants to retain for himself,[176] it is necessary that the Ascendant and the other angles be fixed signs, and that they not be of the remote angles (as we said before),[177] but that, it being a straight figure, every house is its own sign. And in matters which a man wants for buying and selling,[178] and for merchant dealings, you should inspect the contrary of all of this, while improving the roots of elections,[179] and in making them fortunate with Jupiter, according to what we said before.

Chapter VII.10: On managing[180] assets and seeking them, and taking on debts[181]

In this it is appropriate, as we have said before, that you make the second house fortunate, and its lord, and the Moon and her lord, Jupiter and the Lot of Fortune, and the Lot of assets; and remove Mars from all of these by put-

---

[175] For this chapter, cf. al-'Imrānī II.3.1.
[176] *Separatim.* See al-'Imrānī.
[177] Probably referring to VII.2.6 above. See also my Introduction.
[178] That is, if it is for items to be resold and not kept for oneself.
[179] Reading *electionum* for *electionem.*
[180] *Gubernando.*
[181] For this chapter, cf. al-'Imrānī II.3.1. I believe this election has to do with both paying back loans, and being paid back by someone else who has borrowed.

ting him in places which are cadent from these significators of assets which we stated: because Mars's losses[182] in matters of assets is very great, and likewise the loss of the Tail; however, the loss of Saturn in assets is less. And you should put the significators in signs which take and give,[183] because they are good in this house.

However, if you wanted to manage edible things, put the Moon in the Ascendant and in signs of much eating (which are Aries, Taurus, Leo, and the last half of Sagittarius, and Capricorn, and Pisces), and do not let the Moon nor the Ascendant be in the places[184] of Saturn.

Chapter VII.11.0: On buying and selling

[Chapter VII.11.1: Buying and selling, according to Sahl]

Know[185] that the Ascendant and its lord, and the planet to which the Moon is applying, are the significators of the buyer; and the seventh and its lord, and the planet from which the Moon is being separated, are the significators of the seller. And the tenth and its lord are the significators of the price, and the fourth and its lord are the significators of the thing which is sold. And the Moon is even a significator of the price. Whence, that one of these which you improved in the selling and buying, the matter will be improved [by it]. And that one which you harmed, the matter will be harmed [by it].

And[186] if you wanted to buy some thing, make the Lot of Fortune fit and put it in a house of Jupiter, and applying to[187] the fortunes: because in this it will be better for buying than for selling. And[188] if the Moon were in signs of straight ascension, and increased in light and number while applying to for-

---

182 I have read *damnum* as "loss" instead of "harm" (my usual word), because *damnum* has the specific meaning of losing assets due to fines or other things.
183 According to al-'Imrānī, these are the airy signs.
184 This should probably read, "conjunction," with al-'Imrānī.
185 For this paragraph, cf. *On Elect.* §§34-5 (and *Carmen* V.9.5-7, which is closer). In al-'Imrānī's II.8.3, al-Tabarī assumes that the client is selling, while the seventh house is the buyer.
186 For this paragraph, cf. *On Elect.* §§39a-d. Again, Sahl is assuming that the client (the Ascendant) wants to buy.
187 The Lot of Fortune cannot apply to anything; Sahl reads, "joined to."
188 Note the similarity of this sentence to al-Tabarī's in al-'Imrānī II.3.2.

tunes, the owner [of the election] will lose in the thing which is bought in that hour, and it will be better for the seller than for the one buying.[189] And it is necessary that Mars be cadent from Mercury and from the place of the Moon, because in purchases and sales and in debts, Mars signifies that there will be fear and a quarrel and contentions[190] there—and likewise with the Tail. Whence, it is necessary that you remove [the Tail] from the Moon especially; however, [the Tail] conveys less evil than Mars does in this.

And[191] if you wanted to sell, put the Moon in her own exaltation or triplicity, while separating herself from the fortunes and aspecting the infortunes ([but] not, however, applying to them).[192]

Nufil said,[193] if you wished to buy some thing, put the Lot of Fortune in one of the houses of Jupiter, while applying [to the fortunes], because the buyer will have good in this. And if you wanted to sell, put the Moon in her own exaltation or triplicity, being cadent from the infortunes and not aspecting them, and remote from the fortunes: because with this the sale will be completed according to your will.

[Chapter VII.11.2: The quarters of the Moon][194]

And if you wished to buy some thing for a fair price,[195] you should buy it when the Moon was in the second square of the Sun and in a diminished sign,[196] and she herself is diminished in light and number, conjoined to Mercury, and both [were] safe from the infortunes. And if she were not conjoined to Mercury, let Mercury be safe from the infortunes.

---

[189] This implies that the price will be high (due to the increasing Moon), and the negotiations dragged out (due to the straight signs).

[190] *Placita.*

[191] For this paragraph, cf. *On Elect.* §40.

[192] That is, she should be in a whole-sign aspect, but not an applying connection by degree.

[193] Author unknown, but note that it is practically identical to the view of Sahl above. But there is an important difference: for sales, Sahl makes the Moon be separating from benefics and aspecting (but not connected to) malefics; but Nufil almost seems to have the Moon being in aversion to malefics and either in aversion to benefics or else separating from them. It seems odd to me that al-Rijāl would include this redundant and obviously confused version of the same material.

[194] Cf. also al-'Imrānī II.3.2 and II.3.3.

[195] *Bono foro.*

[196] The signs from the beginning to Cancer to the end of Sagittarius, when the Moon will be moving southwards in declination: see *Carmen* V.43.1-3 and the figure below.

And if the Moon were in the first square of the Sun, the things which are bought at that time will be bought at their just price (what they are worth), and every deed which will be undertaken in it, there will be truth and justice in it. And if Jupiter aspected the Moon (with the Moon appearing in this place), he will have good fortune and rectitude in things which are sold.

And when she will have crossed over this square, and she were going to the opposite, then it is better for the seller and for one who seeks a contention or [legal] case, with he being the one undertaking the petition [for it].[197]

And when she is separated from the opposition and goes toward the second square of the Sun, then it is better for the buyer.

And when she is being separated from this quarter and is going toward the conjunction, then it is good for one who wanted to buy some thing, [especially][198] in secret, or a concealed thing which he does not want to be known by anyone—and especially if she were spotted[199] by a fortune.

And if she were in the two western quarters (which are from the tenth to the seventh, and from the fourth house to the Ascendant), and the lord of the Ascendant were diminished in its own motion, and the lord of the Midheaven safe from the infortunes, this is the best that it could be for the one buying the thing for a fair price.

---

[197] That is, it is better for an accuser (see *ITA* V.7, the view of al-Qabīsī).

[198] I have added this because al-Rijāl is combining two things which are kept separate by people like al-'Imrānī II.3.2, *Carmen* V.43.4-8, and al-Qabīsī (*ITA* V.7). When she is in the last quarter, it is generally good for everyone (including buyers) because the price will be fair; but when she approaches and enters under the Sun's rays, *then* it is good for hidden actions.

[199] *Prospecta*. This may simply indicate any aspect in general.

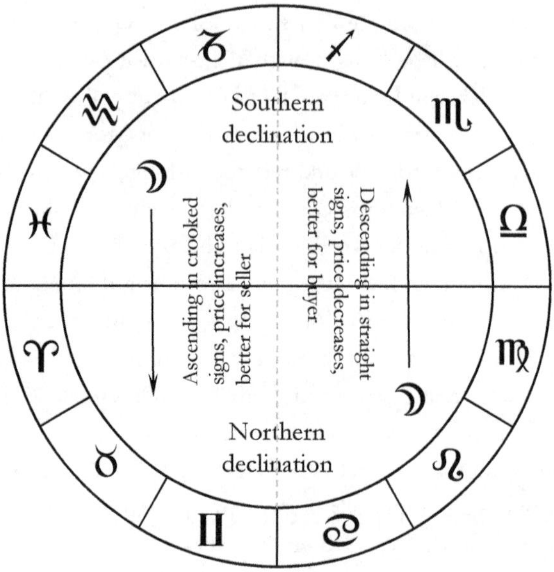

Figure 17: The Moon and prices, by declination (from *Carmen* V.43.1-4)

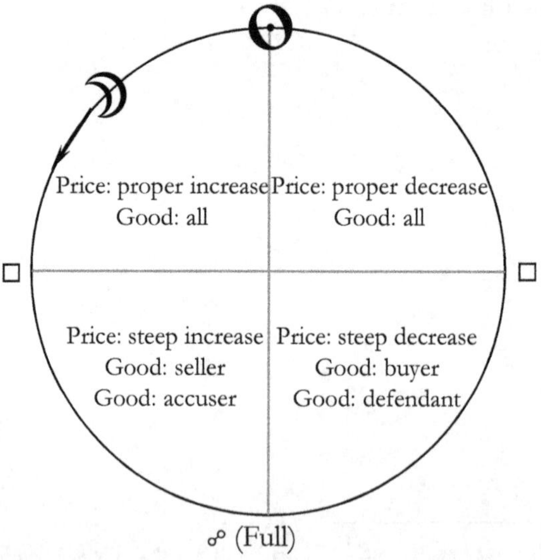

Figure 18: The Moon and prices, by lunar phase (from *Carmen* V.43.5-8)

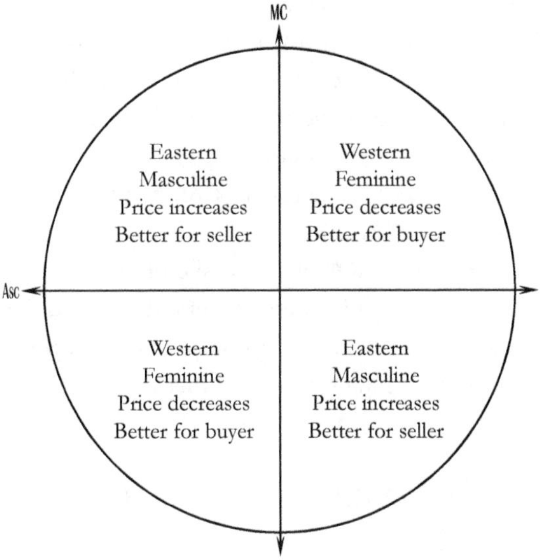

Figure 19: The Moon and prices, by quadrant (al-Rijāl VII.11.2, al-'Imrānī II.3.2-3)

[Chapter VII.11.3: Investments]

And[200] if you wanted to channel[201] [your] treasure in order to make profit from it, make the Moon and Mercury fit, or the lord of the house of assets,[202] and the degree of the house of trust,[203] and look to see in what place the lord of one of them is, and give Mercury a role in it; and fortify him, and give some commingling with one of the fortunes to the Moon, and remove Mars from them as much as you can, and let Mercury be direct and in his own house or exaltation or joy, having escaped from under the rays of the Sun, while he does not have any commingling with Mars nor Saturn; nor let him be in his own fall nor in the bounds of the infortunes (which are the ends of the signs).

And if you were hastened in channeling the riches or assets, and Mercury were retrograde, and you could not wait for when he would be direct, make

200 This paragraph and the next are based on *On Elect.* §§36-38.
201 *Mittere*, following the Arabic and Latin from *On Elect.*
202 The second.
203 The eleventh.

him safe from Mars in particular, and you should join him bodily with Jupiter or Venus, and you will apply him to them.[204] And make the Moon fit, because you would not be able to overlook her while Mercury is appearing retrograde; and make it so that the lord of the bound of the degree of the house of trust, or the lord of the house of trust, would be a fortune, aspecting Mercury, and do not let him be cadent from[205] [that fortune], nor should the fortunes be cadent from him.

And Valens and *Cadoros* said,[206] if you wished to channel money for making profit, you will adapt Mercury and make him direct, and the degree of the Lot of Fortune, and the degree of the house of trust, and you should beware lest Mars have any commingling with any of them.

Chapter VII.12: On selling produce[207]

You will do this in the second quarter of the [Lunar] month, and let the Moon be increasing in motion, and in increasing signs (and they would be the crooked ones),[208] and let her be in one of the two ascending quarters in the figure (which are the masculine ones),[209] and so that the lord of the Ascendant is in one of these places; and the Midheaven and its lord are safe; and the Moon safe, with Mercury, and light in motion.

Chapter VII.13: On giving capital[210]

You should know that the Ascendant and its lord are significators of the owner of the assets, who gives the capital, and the seventh and its lord sig-

---

204 *Et eum applices illis.* This seems redundant and does not appear in Sahl; but it is similar to *Carmen* V.5.20, which says that one may borrow money when Jupiter, Venus, and Mercury all aspect the Ascendant.
205 That is, "in aversion to."
206 Source unknown at this time.
207 *Proventus.* This refers to any concrete result or output: produce, yield, harvest. Cf. VII.11.2 above, al-'Imrānī II.3.2-3, and the source material in *Carmen* V.43.
208 Again, these are the ascending signs from *Carmen* V.43: the crooked ones, because they ascend from being southern in declination to northern.
209 The so-called eastern or masculine quarters: from the Ascendant to the Midheaven, and from the Descendant to the IC.
210 Cf. al-'Imrānī II.3.4, *On Elect.* §§29b-31, and *Carmen* V.20.

nificators of those accepting it. And the Moon and Mercury [are] significators of the capital.

And if there were an agreement[211] between the lord of the Ascendant and the lord of the seventh, and the Moon and Mercury were in the Ascendant or with its lord, made fortunate, the matter will be completed easily and well.

And if the Moon were under the rays of the Sun, the assets are harmed, because the Sun (who is [now] the significator of the capital) burns up the Moon.[212] And[213] if the Moon were in the burnt path, or she were toward the southern direction in latitude, or she were in the first degrees of Leo or Gemini or Sagittarius, or ascending in these degrees[214]—in all of these, it is not good for the giver, but it is good for the one accepting it.

One portion of the sages[215] said that it is not good to give capital in the hour of Saturn, nor that of the Sun.

And you should know that the Sun is the significator of the one giving the capital, and the Moon that of the one accepting it: because the Moon always receives [her light] from the Sun.

Chapter VII.14: On accepting capital[216]

Know[217] that this is the contrary of those things which we said before: because he who wants to accept capital should look to see that the Moon be in Leo, Virgo, Scorpio, or Sagittarius, or Aquarius, and that she be diminished in light while aspecting Venus or Jupiter or Mercury; and that the Ascendant be one of the signs which we stated before, and that the lord of the Ascendant and the lord of the seventh be safe from the infortunes, and that they have an agreement—namely of one with the other.

---

211 For example, a harmonious aspect such as a trine, or a difficult aspect (like a square) with reception, or a transfer of light, etc.

212 Or rather (as *Carmen* suggests), the assets may be harmed for someone who wants the matter to be public; but it might be good for someone who wants it to be kept secret.

213 Cf. *On Elect.* §§30c-31, and *Carmen* V.20.6.

214 Al-'Imrānī reads as though these degrees are ascending.

215 Certainly Abū Ma'shar: see al-Rijāl VII.100, in Part II of this book.

216 Cf. al-'Imrānī II.3.5.

217 For this paragraph, cf. *On Elect.* §§29a-b, and *Carmen* V.20.7.

And a portion of the sages[218] abhorred the hour of Mars in this, and likewise the hour of the Sun.

Chapter VII.15: On changing from one house to another

What[219] is necessary for looking at changing from one house to another: the same thing is necessary as for looking for a traveler in [his] entrance into cities.[220]

And it is more necessary in moving that one put Taurus or Leo in the fourth house, because this signifies the cleanliness[221] of the house and the goodness of the place, and that it is clear of creeping things. However, if Scorpio were there, it signifies that many creeping things are there, and of the poisonous ones, and especially if Saturn or Mars aspected there. And you should beware lest you put an infortune in the fourth, nor that one aspect there with a hostile aspect. And in this it is better that Venus be in the fourth.

But the root of the election for changing from one house to another, and from one habitation to another, is in making the Ascendant and the seventh house safe from the infortunes, and likewise the Moon, and that the Moon be applying to a fortune, and that that fortune be ascending northern, and increasing, and the Moon increasing in light and in number, and the lord of the eighth house and the lord of the second house be safe from the infortunes, and that the lord of the second be in the Ascendant or the fourth, or in the house of trust: because this is the best that it could be in this matter, with God's help.

---

[218] See Abū Ma'shar in al-Rijāl VII.100, but there al-Rijāl does not like the hour of Mars for anything.

[219] For the first three paragraphs, cf. al-'Imrānī II.3.6.

[220] See for example al-'Imrānī II.1.10, on making the second house fit. But note that the rest of the election focuses on the fourth house, since we are not just interested in what happens next (second house), but in choosing the character of the new home itself (fourth).

[221] *Limpiditatem*, which normally refers to brightness and clearness: but in this context it seems to indicate that the house is bright and clean.

Chapter VII.16: On the work of alchemy[222]

If you wished to get involved in the work of alchemy or with some other matter which works with fire, or with an affair which you wished to repeat many times, look in this so that the Moon is in common signs, safe from the infortunes, and likewise the Ascendant, and it is the best in this (if the work had to do with gold) that you adapt the Sun as much as you could, and likewise the planets of the other metals.[223]

---

[222] Cf. *On Elect.* §41. This topic is probably put in the second house because Sahl associates it with trying to make money by producing precious metals.

[223] For example, al-Bīrūnī's *Book of Instruction* (§§409-11) lists such things as lead for Saturn, tin for Jupiter, iron for Mars, jewels and pearls for Venus, quicksilver for Mercury, and silver for the Moon.

THE THIRD HOUSE

Chapter VII.17: On the third house and its elections

The elections of his house are: making friendship with brothers [and] blood-relatives, and teaching the sciences of the law.

[Friendship between relatives][224]

For brothers, it is appropriate to make the third house and its lord fit, while looking beforehand at the roots of elections, and that the lord of this house should be applying to the lord of the Ascendant from a trine or sextile, with reception; and that it aspect the Ascendant with a good aspect. And in this it is good that the lord of the Ascendant be in the tenth or eleventh house, and that the Moon would aspect them.

And if the matter were with older brothers, it is good to make Saturn fit, and that he should aspect there with a good aspect and with reception. And if it were with middle brothers, you will look at Mars in the manner of Saturn; and if it were with younger brothers, [look at] Mercury in the manner of Saturn; and if it were with sisters, make Venus fit according to this way which we have said before.

And you should look at an election for the friendships of parents[225] according to this, by doing with the fourth house what we have said about the third; and likewise for children, by doing with the eleventh[226] house what we do with the third.

Chapter VII.18: On beginning to demonstrate the sciences of the law[227]

In this it is appropriate to make the third house and its lord fit, Jupiter, and the luminaries (and if they were in one of the houses of Jupiter, it will be

---

[224] For this election, cf. al-'Imrānī II.4.1.

[225] This is a general word applying to parents and other relatives of their own or older generations.

[226] One would normally expect the fifth house here; al-'Imrānī says we should do the same with "the house of children," which seems more appropriate.

[227] Cf. al-'Imrānī II.4.2, which relates this to devotion to God—that is, religious law.

better). And if in addition you wanted to learn subtleties and principles,[228] adapt Mercury likewise, and make the significators which we stated be aspecting one to the other with a good aspect. Likewise, let it be that one aspects the house of the other from good aspects—and you should look at as many of these as you can.

[228] *Decreta.*

THE FOURTH HOUSE

Chapter VII.19: On the fourth house and its elections

The elections of this house are: undertaking the foundations of cities and forts and houses, and in drawing waters [from wells], and in the course of rivers, and in digging land, and in buying real estate, and settling [lands], and in making mills, and in sowing and planting trees, and in taking lands to be worked for payment, and taking houses for payment,[229] and on expelling and ejecting the devil from a house.

Chapter VII.20.0: On making the foundations of estates and homes

[Chapter VII.20.1: Building cities]

Know that only kings and high men make cities and great houses:[230] whence, if you wanted to make a good election for such a thing, look to see in what place they wanted to make it, and see in what clime it is, and what planet is the master of that clime, and in what division of that sign that place falls in, and what is the lord of that sign, and if it is a fortune or infortune, and if it has some partner with it or not, and of what kind are the lords of the triplicity of that sign, and what is the place of its division.[231]

---

[229] The Latin has taking lands for payment, and houses being worked for payment. I have switched the terms so as to make more sense of VII.26-7 below.

[230] Thus al-'Imrānī II.1.3 groups his version of this election with other elections for kings or powerful people.

[231] Al-Rijāl means that because the cities and houses of eminent people play a political role in the whole region, we should adapt the planets and signs which have mundane significations over that area. For more on the assignments of planets and signs to geographical regions, see *Tet.* II, *ITA* I, the mundane works in *WSM*, *BOA* Tr. 8, and my forthcoming mundane series, *Astrology of the World.*

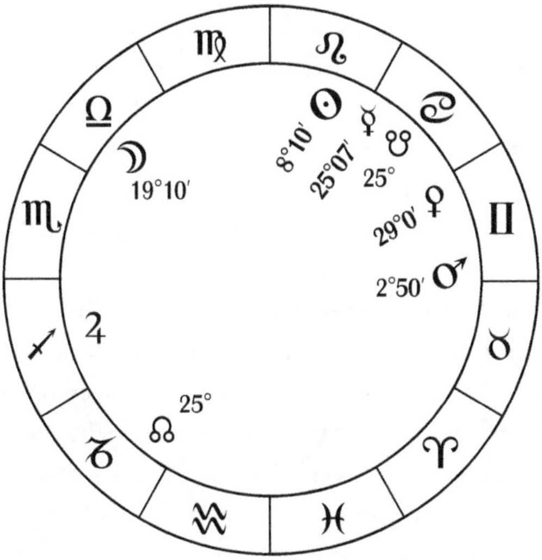

Figure 20: Foundation chart for Baghdad, from al-Bīrūnī[232]

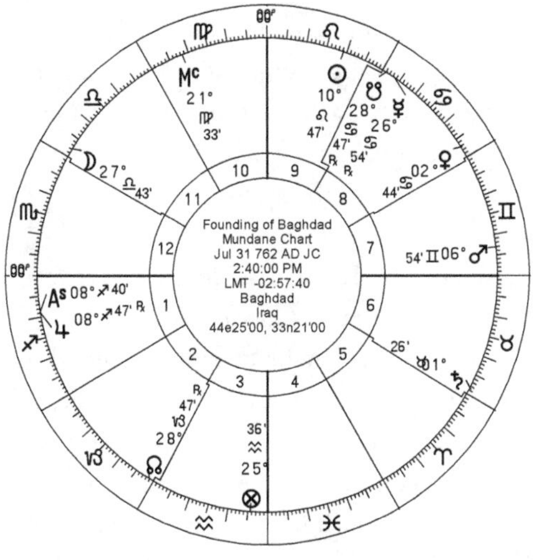

Figure 21: Approximate chart for founding of Baghdad (modern calculations)

---

232 The date in the Arabic calendar corresponds to July 31, 762 AD JC (see Holden 2003). Jupiter is in the Ascendant, though the exact rising degree is not known. According to al-Bīrūnī (*Chronology*, p. 262), Nawbakht the Persian was responsible for the timing of this chart. Other members of the team hired by Caliph al-Mansūr for this purpose included Māshā'allāh and 'Umar al-Tabarī. Holden points out that the astrologers used "a fixed zodiac that differed by about 4 degrees from the tropical zodiac."

Afterwards, if it happened that the lord of that place is Saturn, you should not be afraid of him: and make Jupiter be joined bodily to him at the beginning of the work, or put him in any of [Saturn's] angles. And put the Moon with Jupiter, increasing in light, or with Venus, or in the middle of them, and separating herself from Saturn; and make Saturn have a supported role[233] in the Midheaven and in the Ascendant at the beginning of the foundation of the city.

And if you could, let the Ascendant be one of the houses of Jupiter. And if it is not, still [let it] be safe from Mars.[234] And let Mars be cadent, and remote from the Moon and from the Ascendant, and from the lord of the hour of the beginning, and from the lord of the bound of the Ascendant; and that this lord of the bound of the Ascendant should be a fortune and direct in its motion, and increasing. And you should beware lest it be retrograde, and that the lord of the Ascendant should be in its exaltation or joy, and that the Sun be in a light sign and one of straight ascension.

And make it so that the Lot of Fortune and its lord are in the houses of a fortune, and that the Lot would aspect the Moon: because from the status of the Lot and its lord, and from the status of the Moon and her aspect with the Lot, will be known the fertility of the city, and the goodness of its lord and of its people, and the riches and good which will be had in it, and the profits and success which will come to the city from the markets. And remove Mars from the Lot of Fortune.

And make Saturn fit, as much as you could: because if Saturn were the lord of the division of the house (just as we said), and we improve him through the conjunction of Jupiter or through his good aspects just as we said, it signifies the durability of the city for a long time, and that there will be many peoples in it, and many settlers, and that they will have peace and agreement among them, and it will not be depopulated.

And the fertility of the city will be according to the power of Jupiter and the Moon and the Sun: because Saturn does not harm Jupiter in this place, after Jupiter was supported and the luminaries [were] improved; but he does signify that the city will last and that the people will inherit it, one from the other.

And you should beware of Mars as much as you can in building cities, because all of the sages say that if he had some partnership with the lord of the

---

233 Reading *partem* for *partitionem*.

234 Reading for *Et si non sit aliud* [*aliquid?*], *tamen salvum a Marte.*

place of the city, or that he would have a role in the rulership of the place, and that he would have a commingling with Jupiter and the lights at the hour of the undertaking of the work of the city, it signifies that there will be many hindrances in the city, and that it and its peoples will always be bound and besieged. And if Mars applied to the Lot of Fortune and its lord, and there were some aspect or some commingling between [them], it signifies a dearth and diminution of fertility, and that the lord [of the city] who was there will always be bad to his people.

And *Bericos*[235] (and other ancient sages with him) said that they found one city[236] which had been started for laboring, in which Mars was conjoined bodily to Jupiter and Venus, and they were in the succeedent of the Ascendant of that estate: whence, through this placement Mars harmed the king of that city and made him bad, irritating, and a doer of evil, and making many extortions upon the people of that city.

You should attend, therefore, as much as you could, in the beginning of cities, to make him cadent; and if you could not [do that], weaken him in that place of his, and strengthen Jupiter over him, and likewise strengthen the luminaries and the Lot of Fortune: because if he were weakened in his own place, and Jupiter is strengthened over him, and even the luminaries and the Lot of Fortune fortified, the city will not suffer great harm. Nevertheless, quarrels and labors will happen in the city.

And you should strive as much as you could, so that the dignity of the twelfth-part of the Moon would fall in the bound of a fortune,[237] or in a good place of heaven, or joined to a fortune: because this is a very good signification of the beginning of cities.

And al-Fadl bin Sahl said that the better way that an election for beginning the foundations of cities (or another work) could be, is that the Moon be safe from the infortunes, and far from the conjunction or opposition [of the Sun] and being burned up, and the burnt path, and that she not be void in course, nor should she be descending southern in latitude, nor at the end of a sign, nor in the first degrees of some sign, nor should she be in her own

---

235 Unknown at this time.

236 Based on the description here, this "city" must have been a small community of people devoted to laboring at some industry, and ruled by a petty autocrat, not exactly a "king."

237 I am not quite sure what this could mean. Perhaps the Latin al-Rijāl has conflated being in the bound of a fortune, and having a fortune in the sign indicated by the Moon's twelfth-part?

fall, nor in a welled degree, nor should the lord of her house not be aspecting her,[238] nor should the Moon be in the sixth house, nor in the twelfth, nor in one of the two Nodes (in which there is no latitude). But let her be increasing in light and motion,[239] and ascending toward the north in latitude, and that she should be in her own exaltation or in the exaltation of Jupiter, and let Jupiter or Venus be direct with her, and one of the angles of the Ascendant of the beginning (and especially in the Ascendant or in the tenth house), being in their own dignities, in their own domain.[240] And it is good in this that the Ascendant and the Moon be in earthy signs, especially in Taurus and Virgo.

Likewise, if the Head were with Jupiter in the Ascendant, and the luminary of the time in the Midheaven, it signifies that the city will last for a long time, and the peoples will advance in it and will have a good end in it.

And if the Ascendant were a common sign, it signifies that there will be many peoples there, of many customs, and especially if many planets aspected the Ascendant and the Moon.

And if it happened that Mercury is conjoined to the Tail at the beginning of some city, it signifies that there will be many lies there, frauds, and contentions within it. And if Jupiter were with the Tail, there will be harm in the nobles of the city. And if the Sun were with the Tail, there will be harm in the rulership of the city. And if Venus were with the Tail, it will be in women. And if Saturn[241] were with the Tail, there will be harm in old men and slaves. And if Mars were with it, there will be harm in all those who bear arms. And if the Moon were with the Tail, there will be harm in the common people of the city.

And if, at the beginning of a city, it happened that one of these planets is supported, in a good place and in a good state, it signifies good fortune and success in that part which pertains to it, according to the division which we have stated.[242]

---

[238] In other words, the lord of her own house *should* be aspecting her.

[239] For this sentence, cf. *On Elect.* §43a.

[240] See *ITA* III.2.

[241] Reading for *Mercurius*.

[242] That is, in the previous paragraph: Venus for women, etc.

[Chapter VII.20.2: Mundane significations of the houses]

And you should know that the Ascendant of cities is the significator of the life of its people: and its second house is the significator of assets, assistance,[243] and its means of subsistence;[244] and the third, the law; and the fourth the significator of what the end of the work will be, and what its situation[245] will result in, and the concealed places which are in the city (such as treasures, and the like); and the fifth house signifies the children which the people of the city will have; and the sixth, the slaves which will be there, and the infirmities which will happen to the people of the city; and the seventh signifies their marriage-unions and [legal] cases; and the eighth, their greater houses and their helpers; and the ninth house signifies their customary morals and travels; and the tenth signifies professions, works, and their masters; and the eleventh, friends and allies; and the twelfth house signifies beasts, armies, and their enemies.

Whence, in the house where there was an infortune, or its lord were made unfortunate, judge evil and harm in its signification; and in that one of them in which there was a fortune or its lord made fortunate (at the beginning of the city), judge good and power in its signification. And if Saturn were in one of the angles of the city, separated [from other planets] by himself,[246] it signifies delay in the work, and in the deeds of that city. And if Mars were there, it signifies evil deeds, robbery,[247] and losses, and the burning of the air. And if Saturn and Jupiter were eastern at the beginning of cities, with one aspecting the other from a good aspect, and they were in good places and supported, this is a good signification that the city will be firm and fruitful, for a long time.

[Chapter VII.20.3: Other authorities]

And Hurrazād said,[248] a better election which could be had for beginning buildings is that the Ascendant and its lord and the Moon be in earthy signs

---

243 *Valimenti.* This word can also refer to monetary value.

244 *Victui.*

245 *Causa.* Unfortunately, this Latin word is so general it is hard to know what al-Rijāl means.

246 *Per se separatus.*

247 Or, pillaging or the taking of booty (*raubariam*).

248 *Harzet.* Cf. al-'Imrānī II.1.3, who does not name the source.

or watery ones, and the Moon increasing in light (from seven days up to fourteen), and increasing in motion and number, and likewise ascending northern in her latitude and in her declination, even while going from her own fall toward her own exaltation, while applying to a planet [which is] a fortune [and] appearing in its own exaltation or in the exaltation of the Moon, [while it is also] eastern and free from the infortunes; and let the Moon be above the earth by night and under the earth by day,[249] applying to a planet [which is] a fortune, on the right of the Ascendant; and that she[250] should be in signs of long ascensions (which are from Cancer up to the end of Sagittarius):[251] whence, if you could have all of these states fulfilled, it is best; otherwise, you should have as many of them as you can.

And[252] you should beware lest the Moon be up to 90° from the Tail, because then she is in the worst status she can be in, because then she is descending southern in her latitude;[253] and this is the lowest when she would be in this condition in Virgo up to Libra, because she is likewise descending in declination.[254] And if in addition she were diminished in light and motion, it is even worse: whence, when all of these states of the Moon are gathered together, they harm her much.

Likewise, you should beware lest the infortunes be in the Ascendant, nor in the fourth house: because if they were there, it signifies that the building will be harmed through waters and rains and the coursing of water[255] after it was completed; and it signifies delay and labors at the beginning of the work—and this is if Saturn were the harmer. But if the harmer were Mars, it signifies that it will be burned up or torn down or destroyed by enemies.

---

[249] That is, in her *ḥalb*: see *ITA* III.2.

[250] Or perhaps, "it," the planet to which she applies.

[251] The signs of direct ascension, in northern latitudes. In southern latitudes (such as in Australia), these signs are crooked, and the long or direct or straight signs are from the beginning of Capricorn to the end of Gemini.

[252] I believe this paragraph and the next are continuing the view of Hurrazād, since at the end of the last paragraph al-Rijāl connects a statement to these and attributes it to Hurrazād.

[253] What al-Rijāl means is that the Moon is in her southern "bending," which is 90° later than the degree of the Tail. Since the Tail marks the point where the Moon crosses the ecliptic while moving southward in latitude, the southern bending marks her lowest point before finally moving northwards again.

[254] The transition from Virgo to Libra is the transition from signs in northern declination, to those of southern declination. Thus, when the Moon is southern in both latitude and declination, al-Rijāl is suggesting it is even worse.

[255] Or literally, "aqueducts" (*aqueductus*).

And *Nufil* said,[256] according to the statement of the other sages preceding him: if you wanted to build a house which was for yourself and your progeny, adapt the Moon and the Ascendant and its lord, and the Lot of Fortune (because these are more necessary significators for having riches, completion, and durability in the home), and likewise adapt Mercury. And you should make effort as much as you can to remove Mars from all of these significators. And if you could not, make it so that Venus is in a good place of the figure, and you should strengthen her up above Mars from his trine or sextile; or that she should be in an angle, raised up over him.[257] And remove Saturn from her as much as you could, because Mars with Venus harms [only] a moderate amount, since he always has joy and cheerfulness with her, and with the Moon when he aspects her with a good aspect. However, when Saturn has a commingling with Venus, he increases in his harm, or when he aspects from a strong place and from places in which he has a dignity. And make it so that the Moon is increasing in light and motion, and that Jupiter and Venus are joined bodily with her, either in the trine or sextile or her square, and remove Saturn and Mars from her: because Saturn is a significator of applying oneself to[258] a work, and its good order and durability, and end, and it signifies that his deed will be delayed, and that he will grow fatigued in it. And Mars signifies that it will be ripped down or burned up or harmed by robbers or bad men. And in these statements and this election, he agrees with Hurrazād [above].[259]

Chapter VII.21: On extracting waters by digging and making streams or brooks[260] flow off[261]

This election[262] is good if the Moon is under[263] the earth, in a fixed sign and in the third house from the Ascendant, or in the fifth, and that the As-

---

256 Cf. *On Elect.* §§43-45d. Sahl may be one of the "other sages" mentioned here.

257 That is, she should be overcoming him from a superior sextile, trine, or from a superior square.

258 *Appositurae.*

259 *Hazet.* But again, cf. Sahl in *On Elect.* §§45b-d.

260 *Zequias* (1485), *zequiis* (1551), for the Ar. *sāqīyyah.* This word can refer to many types of waterways, natural or artificial.

261 Cf. al-'Imrānī II.1.6.

262 For this paragraph, cf. *On Elect.* §§50a-d.

263 Reading with al-'Imrānī and Sahl for "above."

cendant and its lord are safe from the infortunes, and made fortunate, and Saturn is eastern. And if the Moon were above the earth, let her be in the eleventh house. And if Saturn were in the eleventh house, it will be good, but not if he is joined to the Moon by body. And make Jupiter fit, nor should there be an infortune in the Midheaven.

If[264] the Moon were in the first square of the Sun, it will be good; and attend as much as you can so that the Moon is made fortunate and received in an angle, nor should the angles be remote by the number of the figure (as we have said before),[265] and that the lord of the Ascendant is eastern and in one of its own dignities, and in an angle or going toward an angle; and the Ascendant is in a watery sign, and made fortunate by an strengthened fortune. Likewise, the Moon and the Lot of Fortune should have that characteristic. And adapt the place of the conjunction and opposition which was before the beginning of the work.

Chapter VII.22: On buying real estate[266]

In all of these matters, it is good that the house of real estate (which is the fourth from the Ascendant) be made fit, by adapting beforehand the things which we said before.[267]

[Chapter VII.22.1: Buying land for purposes of construction]

And[268] if the real estate were a habitation (such as a house and the like), let the Moon be in her house or exaltation, or in the Midheaven, while aspecting the lord of the Ascendant, and remove Mars from her aspects. And[269] let the fourth house be a fixed sign; and let the lords of the angles be eastern, increasing in their motion, and ascending toward the north.[270]

---

264 Al-Rijāl has taken this from al-'Imrānī, but it is originally from *Forty Chapters* §§482-83.
265 See my Introduction.
266 For this whole chapter, cf. al-'Imrānī II.5.1.
267 Al-'Imrānī II.5.1 clarifies that this is the material on buying: see II.3.2-3, and al-Rijāl VII.11.1-2.
268 Cf. *On Elect.* §49c.
269 Cf. *Forty Chapters* §475.
270 Probably ascending in northern ecliptical latitudes.

[Chapter VII.22.2: Buying land for purposes of cultivation][271]

And[272] in buying every manner of real estate, make it so that the fortunes have dignities in the angles, and especially in the Ascendant and the fourth, and that the luminaries aspect the Ascendant and the fourth house from a good aspect. Nor should there be a retrograde planet in the angles, nor should their lords be retrograde.

Al-Kindī said,[273] the fourth house should not be a fiery sign, nor [should there be one] in the ninth, nor in the fifth, nor in the eleventh, nor a fiery planet in [the fourth], and especially if the infortunes were strengthened in that house.[274] And do not let Saturn aspect the fourth house, if it were a watery sign. And if the Midheaven were made unfortunate, it will be bad.

And[275] you should know that the Ascendant and its lord signify the matter and likewise the buyer and the profit which there was in it, and the habitations; and the Midheaven and its lord signify the things which were rooted there above the face of the earth (such as trees and the like). And the seventh[276] and its lord signify the real estate and the inhabitants, and those who serve the owner of the real estate. (And it is said [by certain people] that they signify its herbs and vegetables.)[277] And the fourth[278] and its lord signify the good of the earth and the sowings which are there. Whence, that one of these significators which was harmed, signifies harm in that matter; and that one of them which was improved, signifies improvement in its signification.

['Umar] al-Tabarī said: Jupiter and the planet from which the Moon is being separated, are the significators of the one who buys the real estate; and

---

271 Most of this election is based on *Forty Chapters* Ch. 14.1.

272 This paragraph is from al-Kindī, *Forty Chapters* Ch. 14, §469.

273 This paragraph corresponds to *Forty Chapters* Ch. 14, §§472-473. But Hugo's version of the first sentence reads more reasonably to me, especially because he includes some explanations. Hugo's al-Kindī warns us of having an *infortune* in the ninth, eleventh or fifth, and to avoid having a fiery sign or planet in the fourth, when it is also in aversion to the fortunes.

274 According to al-Kindī, it is especially if they were in aversion to the fortunes.

275 This paragraph corresponds to *Forty Chapters* Ch. 14, §470. See the figures in al-'Imrānī II.5.1, which show the differences between al-Kindī and the Māshā'allāh group/*Carmen*.

276 Reading with al-Kindī and al-'Imrānī, for "fourth."

277 This is an insertion by al-'Imrānī: he is pointing out that the Māshā'allāh group (Sahl, al-Khayyāt, and "Dorotheus" in *Judges* 4.5, 4.8, and 4.9) make this attribution in questions about purchasing fields.

278 Reading with al-'Imrānī and al-Kindī, for "seventh."

the planet to which the Moon applies, is the significator of the end, and what there will be with respect to the real estate and the sale.

Chapter VII.23: On settling land[279]

In this, it is appropriate that the Moon be received by a fortune, and that fortune likewise be in an angle or succeedent, and that the lord of the Ascendant and the lord of the house of the Moon be in good states. And attend so that some fortune is in the house of assets, and that it is safe from the infortunes, and that the lord of the Lot of Fortune is there. Al-Kindī said that the lord of the Lot of assets should be there, and make it so that the place of the conjunction or prevention is in an angle.

And, that the Moon (when she separated herself from the conjunction or prevention) is applying to a fortune that is strengthened, in an angle or going towards an angle, and that the lord of the conjunction or prevention should be a fortune; and likewise the [lord of] the house of the Moon and the lord of the fourth house.

Chapter VII.24: On making a mill[280]

In this, look to see that the Ascendant and the Moon are in Aries or Libra, or at the end of Virgo; and beware lest the Moon be in Cancer or Capricorn (because they are signs in which days and nights are made [the most] divergent).[281] And if the Moon and the lord of the Ascendant were in the aforesaid signs, safe from the aspects of the infortunes, it will be a good election for this.

And if the election were for another type of mill,[282] you will take this same election.

---

279 For this chapter, cf. al-'Imrānī II.5.2, though it is based on *Forty Chapters* Ch. 16.4. Hugo's version of al-Kindī differs in a few details.

280 For this chapter, cf. al-'Imrānī II.5.3.

281 The idea is that the mill's weight has to be very evenly distributed, so we need the equinoctial signs rather than the solsticial signs.

282 Al-'Imrānī specifies that he means mills suspended from ships: see his further explanation there.

Chapter VII.25: On sowing, and planting trees[283]

If your election were for sowing things which are supposed to bear fruit in that year (such as garden vegetables, wheat, and the like), whichever one of them is appropriate in that season, make it so that the Moon is in movable signs. And if she were in Capricorn or in Cancer or Virgo, it will be good; and let the Moon be increased in number; and likewise it is good in Pisces.

However, if your election were for planting trees, make it so that the Moon is in fixed signs, and particularly in Taurus or Aquarius; and that Saturn is in a good status, or in a succeedent, or in some one of his own dignities, and that he has some testimony in the Ascendant; and that the Ascendant is one of the signs which we said before; and that Jupiter is aspecting Saturn in a good aspect, and from a place in which he has some dignity. And in all of this you should beware of Mars. And the lord of the exaltation has greater power in planting trees, than does the lord of the house.

And al-Khayyāt said,[284] let the lord of the house of the Moon be aspecting the Moon in a watery sign. And if the Ascendant were not fixed, let it be common, and its lord be eastern, ascending in its latitude.

Chapter VII.26: On leasing lands[285]

In this, it is appropriate that you make the Ascendant and its lord fortunate, and that the lord of the Ascendant be going towards an angle, in an earthy sign (and likewise the Moon), or that it is in the angle of the earth; and let the planet from which the Moon is being separated be a fortune, free of the infortunes, because it is the significator of the owner whose land it is; and that the lord of the seventh should be a fortune, and it should have some agreement which you could [arrange] with [the lord] of the Ascendant. And likewise, the planet to which the Moon applies should have some agreement with the planet from which she is being separated.

---

283 For this chapter, cf. al-'Imrānī II.5.4.

284 This is virtually identical to Sahl's *On Elect.* §§51-52a, but Sahl (and al-'Imrānī's version in II.5.4) differ in certain respects.

285 Cf. al-'Imrānī II.5.5. This election seems to assume that the client (Ascendant) is the owner of land, and wants to pay someone else (the contract worker, the seventh), to work it.

And you will take this election for leasing out brooks and for settling[286] lands.

And you should know that the Ascendant and its lord, and the planet from which the Moon is being separated, are significators of the owner whose land it is, and the fourth house and its lord the significators of the land itself; and the seventh and its lord, and the planet to whom the Moon goes, [are] significators of the one who is taking the land for payment. Whence, attend to adapting that one of these places which you want to improve more.

Chapter VII.27: On leasing out homes and produce for payment[287]

You should know that the Ascendant is the significator of the owner of the houses, and the seventh the significator of the one who is staying on [the land], and the Midheaven the significator of the price,[288] and the fourth house the end of the matter. Whence, adapt that one whose signification you wanted to improve.

> [*Dykes's proposed correct version:*] You should know that the Ascendant is the significator of the one who is staying on [the land], and the seventh the significator of the owner of the houses, and the Midheaven the significator of the price, and the fourth house the end of the matter. Whence, adapt that one whose signification you wanted to improve.

---

[286] Reading *populandis* more in accordance with al-'Imrānī, for *postulandis*.

[287] Cf. al-'Imrānī II.5.6. In my own view, this election is backwards. For one thing, both this chapter and the previous one have the Ascendant signifying the owner of the land, and the seventh as the contract worker—which makes the house assignments redundant. Next, the second paragraph clearly links this election with *Carmen* V.8 (and its descendants in Sahl and al-Khayyāt, in *Judges* §§4.11-12), which has it the other way around: the Ascendant is the contract worker seeking to rent the rights to the land, and the seventh is the owner. (In fact, many of the elections and questions that have to do with leasing and business arrangements can be confusing as to who is doing what role.) So, I propose that this election is the reverse of the previous one: the client is the contract worker seeking to work someone's land for a fee (in order to gain profit), and the seventh is the owner of the property. In indented paragraphs below I have provided what I believe is the correct reading of the election, based on *Carmen* and the Māshā'allāh group.

[288] Reading with al-'Imrānī and *Carmen* for *loci* ("place").

Now, if the Ascendant were made unfortunate, it signifies that the owner of the house will commit a betrayal. And if the seventh house were made unfortunate, it signifies that the one who holds [the lands] for payment will commit the betrayal.

> [*Dykes's proposed correct version:*] Now, if the Ascendant were made unfortunate, it signifies that the one who holds [the lands] for payment will commit a betrayal. And if the seventh house were made unfortunate, it signifies that the owner of the house will commit the betrayal.

And the planet to which the Moon applies is the significator of the [person who is][289] the lodger. And the planet from which she is being separated, the significator of the one who receives the lodger.[290] And the lord of the Moon [is] the significator of the end of the matter.

> [*Dykes's proposed correct version:*] And the planet to which the Moon applies is the significator of the one who receives the lodger. And the planet from which she is being separated, the significator of the [person who is] the lodger. And the lord of the Moon [is] the significator of the end of the matter.

['Umar] al-Tabarī said,[291] in this it is appropriate to adapt Jupiter and Saturn, and that the one should aspect the other with a good aspect.

Chapter VII.28: On removing phantasms from the home[292]

If there were something in some home or other place, which men were panicked about, or some omen[293] which scares them from the home or is annoying to those staying in it, and you wanted to remove it from the home

---

289 *Domini.* Typically, medieval Latin texts refer to the people indicated by houses as the "owners" or "masters" of the topic, so that the client is sometimes called the "owner of the question."

290 Namely, the client wanting the election, who is assumed to be renting out his property and receiving lodgers.

291 Cf. also *On Elect.* §§48-49b.

292 Cf. *On Elect.* §§60a-b.

293 *Signale.*

(or [that it would] flee the [place]) through incantations or some other means, or through some spiritual power[294] which you wanted to practice there, you should beware lest the Moon be in the Ascendant, nor should the Ascendant be Leo nor Cancer, nor Scorpio nor Aquarius; nor should the Moon be in any of these signs, but let her be in the other signs, while separating herself from an infortune [and] applying to a fortune.

---

[294] *Magisterium* (following Niermeyer).

THE FIFTH HOUSE

Chapter VII.29: On the fifth house and its elections

The elections which are in this house are: laying with women for having a child, giving an infant to be nourished, removing it from [the breast], baptizing, circumcising, and putting on new clothing, concerning gifts, on sending couriers, on writing papers for the sake of sending them, on food and drinks, on good-smelling things, on sending pigeons to attract others, on taking a dead [fetus][295] from the belly of the mother.

Chapter VII.30: On lying with a woman so that one may have a son[296]

The election which is appropriate in this is that you should make the Ascendant a masculine sign and one of straight ascensions, and [make] the angles fixed signs,[297] and [put] the lord of the Ascendant in the Ascendant or in the Midheaven or in the eleventh; and that the first planet which crossed over the degree of the Ascendant on the horizon[298] should be a fortune. And adapt the luminaries as much as you could in this election (and especially the luminary of the time),[299] and there should not be an infortune in any of the angles—however let there be a fortune here, safe and strong.

And in this,[300] it is appropriate to look at the lord of the Ascendant and to guard it, lest it be made unfortunate in the ninth month from the time of conception: because that will be the time of birth. And if you were able to guard it so that it would not be made unfortunate from the seventh month, nor in the tenth month from the conception, it will be better: because the

---

[295] *Creaturam.*

[296] Cf. al-'Imrānī II.6.1.

[297] If this rule were strictly followed, then only Leo could be on the Ascendant: it is the only masculine, straight, fixed sign. But al-'Imrānī reads this "fixed" quality as the angles not being remote—that is, that the Midheaven be on the tenth sign and not the ninth (but perhaps on the eleventh sign).

[298] Al-'Imrānī specifies that this must be through "its own motion," i.e., motion in the zodiac and not by diurnal rotation or directions.

[299] That is, the sect light.

[300] For this discussion of months, cf. Abū Bakr I.2 and I.5, in *PN2*.

birth could be in these three aforesaid times, whence it is necessary that it be fortunate at these times, and powerful, and likewise the luminaries.

And you should beware of the lord of the sixth[301] or eighth house: if they were unfortunate, they should not have any commingling with the aforesaid significators. And even beware of the infortunes and the Tail.

And al-Khayyāt said, the best that there could be in this is that the Moon should be in the Ascendant, in the trine of the Sun. And he said you should beware of the burnt path, and make Venus fit: because if Venus is harmed, there will be harm upon the mother. And if the Moon would be harmed, there will be harm upon the body of the [fetus] created. And make the fifth house and its lord fit.

And it is appropriate that this should happen in unequal hours of the day and night (such as the first, third, fifth, and the like).

And if it happened that the Ascendant is Libra, with it being safe, and likewise with its lord being free, it will be good because it is a rational sign; wherefore the Midheaven will be Cancer, which is a sign of many children. And let the [other] significators be[302] in masculine signs, because this signifies that the conception will be of males.

And it is necessary that in this matter you should avail yourself of natural facts which come to be by physic, and to gather together the good from that which is appropriate to this matter: because the heavenly deeds are fulfilled and appear according to what natural materials receive.[303]

And[304] you should know that eastern planets are reputed to be masculine, and when they are western, feminine; and those which were in the two masculine quarters we consider them to be masculine, and those in the feminine quarters, feminine.

Chapter VII.31: On giving the native to be nourished[305]

In this, you should look to see that the Moon is conjoined to Venus by body, and both are safe. And if Venus were descending in her latitude, it will be better.

---

[301] Reading with al-'Imrānī for "seventh."

[302] Reading *sint* with al-'Imrānī for *sunt.*

[303] See al-'Imrānī and my footnote to this paragraph there.

[304] See for instance *ITA* I.11 and *BA* II.15.

[305] Cf. al-'Imrānī II.2.1.

And in the whole of what we have said, it is appropriate to adapt the original roots of elections just as we have said before, and to make the Moon fit and guard her from an infortune, and burning, and to apply her to the fortunes.

Chapter VII.32: On taking the native from the breast[306]

In this, you should look to see that the Moon, being far from the Sun, is applying to the lord of her own house, and that the Ascendant is the house of a fortune. And in this, one portion of the sages abhors the houses of Venus.

And other sages say that when the breast is taken away from the infant, and the Moon were in the mansion which is called *al-Ṣarfah,*[307] the infant will not feel pain on account of the breast, nor will it seek it.

Others say that when the lord of the Ascendant and the Moon were in signs signifying vegetables which sprout,[308] the native will aspire towards things which sprout, and it will not care about the breast.

Chapter VII.33: On circumcising and baptizing[309]

In this it is better that the Moon be elevated over Venus,[310] and Venus applying to Jupiter. And you should guard the Ascendant and its lord, and Venus, and the Moon, from all aspects of Saturn, and especially[311] the Moon and the Ascendant: because Saturn signifies that it will be good for him to be cut another time, and that there will be much poison there. And make it so that the lord of the Ascendant is ascending in latitude, and the Moon and its

---

306 Cf. al-'Imrānī II.2.2.

307 "The diversion" (Dykes) or "The change" (Burnett 2000, Table II), Lat. *Azarfa.* "Change" would be *ṣarrafa.* This mansion seems to be centered around stars in or near Leo's tail. See al-Rijāl VII.101, in Part I of this book.

308 Al-'Imrānī calls these signs of seeds, and identifies them as the earthy signs.

309 Cf. al-'Imrānī II.2.9.

310 This probably means overcoming her by a superior square, in the tenth sign from Venus.

311 Reading *specialiter* (following al-'Imrānī) for *separatim.*

lord [are] in northern signs and in the succeedents. And you should beware lest Mars be in an angle nor in the Ascendant, nor the Moon in Scorpio.[312]

Chapter VII.34: On cutting and putting on new clothes[313]

In this it is better that the Moon be in movable signs, made fortunate; and if she were in common ones, it is not bad.

You should beware lest the Moon be in the conjunction of the Sun, nor his opposition, nor that the Sun should be in the Ascendant nor its opposite.

And[314] you should beware likewise of the fixed signs at the beginning of the incision, unless it were garments for bearing arms: because in that, the fixed ones are not bad.

And put the Sun in the Midheaven, and let the Moon be waxing in light.

And adapt the house[315] and its lord at the hour of buying and cutting the fabrics, and even when putting them on.

And you will put them on in a movable sign. And among all the fixed signs, the worst is Leo.

Chapter VII.35: On handing over gifts[316]

In this it is appropriate that you should adapt the fifth house and its lord and the hour in which you want to send the gifts. And you will do the same in receiving them.

And in sending gifts, you should look at the elections which we stated in the chapter on giving capital.[317]

And in receiving gifts, [we should consider all of the things which we put forth before at the beginning of that treatment].[318]

---

312 Al-'Imrānī reads as though Mars should not be in any angle, and that neither the Moon nor the Ascendant should be in Scorpio.

313 Cf. al-'Imrānī II.2.13, which is organized differently.

314 Here, al-'Imrānī warns us against *Leo* (as al-Rijāl tacks on at the end), not all fixed signs.

315 Al-'Imrānī reads this as being the second house.

316 Cf. al-'Imrānī II.6.2.

317 See Ch. VII.13 above.

318 Adding with al-'Imrānī. See VII.9-10, corresponding to al-'Imrānī II.3.1.

[Also], it is good to make the lord of the Ascendant be elevated over[319] the lord of the seventh house.

Chapter VII.36: On sending couriers[320]

In this you should look to see that the Moon is applying to a planet which was the significator of the one to whom you are sending the messenger: so that if it were a king, to the Sun; if a judge or merchant, to Jupiter—and according to this path with the others. And do not let the Moon nor that planet be cadent from the angles, and they should be free of the infortunes.

Chapter VII.37: On writing papers[321]

When you wanted to write a paper, make it so that the Moon is applying to Mercury, she being safe from the infortunes; and that Mercury is powerful, not made unfortunate nor retrograde nor harmed; and that the Ascendant and its lord are safe from the infortunes and their rays.

Chapter VII.38: On foods

This chapter and the other two which follow it pertain more to kings and high men, and the wealthy, and men of leisure,[322] for other people, who supply their sustenance through daily labor, are not in need of rules of this kind.

> Therefore, those who are weighed down by excessive and inordinate eating, observe that if the Moon were in Taurus, applying to Venus, cow meat is not harmful for eating.[323]

---

319 Probably overcoming it from a superior square.

320 Cf. al-'Imrānī II.4.3.

321 Cf. *On Elect.* §143.

322 *Quiescentes* (1485), *otiosorum* (1551). For the rest of this paragraph and the beginning of the next, I have followed 1551 as being a bit clearer.

323 In the list below, Cancer, Scorpio, and Sagittarius are missing. The logic seems to be that it is appropriate to eat whatever foods match the sign she is in—provided that she is in a good condition, etc.

And if she were in Pisces, applying to Jupiter, it is not harmful to eat fresh and salted fish.

And if she were in Libra or Aquarius, received, milk and whatever comes to be from it is not harmful.

And if she were in Virgo, made unfortunate by Mars, it is harmful to eat cooked and raw cabbages.

And[324] if she were applying to Mars from the trine, or the Sun from a trine, it is not harmful to eat of diverse banquet foods. And if she applied to Saturn, you should beware of the consumption of old meats and salted ones. And if she applied to Venus, it is not harmful to eat types of fruits.

And if she were in Aries or Capricorn, applying to Jupiter, it is not harmful to eat types of castrated [animals], [and] small and large goats. And if she were in the square of Saturn and this opposition and his conjunction, it is not good to eat any carrion meats.

And likewise, if she were in Leo, it is not good[325] to eat any hunted meats.

And likewise if she were in Virgo, while applying to Mars, it is not harmful to eat any manner of cabbages.[326]

And if she were in Gemini and its triplicity, applying to Mercury, it is bad[327] to eat the meats of birds with a hot complexion.

And if she were in Leo, and applied to Saturn, it is bad to eat every cold food. And if she applied to Mars, it is harmful to eat every hot food.

---

324 I am not sure if this continues the material on Virgo, or is a separate statement.
325 One would expect this to read that "it is not harmful" to eat them.
326 Presumably this is only in a good aspect to him, unlike the statement above.
327 Again, one would expect this to read, "it is not harmful."

Chapter VII.39: On drinks[328]

When you wanted to make wine from grapes or raisins, see that the Moon is in Pisces or in Taurus, applying to Venus: because this signifies that the wine will be good and will be drunk with delight, joy, and good fortune. And you should beware lest the infortunes should aspect the Moon: because if Saturn aspected her, it signifies that it will be harmed and will become vinegary,[329] and when it will be drunk, there will not be a [proper] taste to it, or it will be drunk in sorrow, [troubled] thoughts, or pain. And if Mars aspected her, it signifies that vapors will come to be in the wine, and that the vessel in which it was, will be broken, and when it is drunk, quarrels and labors will happen. And the aspect of Jupiter and Mercury are good in this, and likewise the aspect of the Sun (if it were from a trine or sextile).

Chapter VII.40: On getting involved in things with a good smell

In this,[330] look to see that the Moon is in Aries or in Leo or Sagittarius, or that the Ascendant is one of these signs, and that Venus is in the Ascendant, and the Moon in the tenth, applying to Venus: because this signifies that the confection will be of a good odor, and that the one who made it, will be happy with it.

However,[331] when you wanted to make fumigations in particular,[332] it is good that the Moon be received by Mars or by the Sun, because it is a matter which comes to be through fire.

And if you made some good-smelling confection, and the Moon were in Gemini while applying to Mercury, it signifies that the matter will be well completed.

---

328 *Potationibus*, which is really about drinking parties, not brewing or fermenting drinks. But it is also possible that this election could work for preparing drinks before a party, since many ancient wines were spiced and watered down beforehand. Cf. *On Quest.* §13.17.

329 *Acetosum*.

330 This part of the election pertains to actually mixing perfumes and oils, or perhaps even incense.

331 I am not sure if this has to do with preparing incenses, or actually burning them.

332 Reading *specialiter* for *separatim*.

Chapter VII.41: On sending pigeons so that they would lead others

When you wanted to send pigeons so that they would attract others and would return to their nests, look to see that the Moon applies to a planet which is not burned up quickly: because this signifies that they will go safe and will return. And beware lest the Moon apply to Mercury, because he has many settings, and often burning and retrogradation happen to him: and when something of this happens to [the client], the pigeons will not be safe nor secure from capture.

And when you sent birds, it is good that the Moon be in a watery sign and applying to Venus, and Venus should be in a sign of straight ascensions: because this signifies that they will not go astray on their path, nor will water run out for them. And if you sent them with the Moon applying to Mars, they will get tired and return, especially if the sign were airy. And if the Moon applied to Saturn, they will go astray on their path and will be dispersed on account of thirst or because of what is like that.

And certain sages said that in this they have experienced that birds return to their own nests on the day in which the Moon returns to that sign, or on that day when she will apply to that planet another time.

Chapter VII.42: On taking a created [fetus] from the mother's belly[333]

When you wanted to do this, look to see that the Moon is diminished in light, descending southern in latitude and declination (or one of them), and that the Moon is in the Ascendant, and the lord of the Ascendant in the aspect of Jupiter and Venus. And the better signs for this matter are the feminine ones, and those of straight ascensions.

[333] Cf. *On Elect.* §§58a-b and *Carmen* V.18.

THE SIXTH HOUSE

Chapter VII.43: On the sixth house and its elections

In this house are these elections: healing infirmities, working with a syringe, healing the eyes, taking laxative medicine, taking binding medicines, [taking medicine] through the nose, doing gargles, producing vomiting, buying captives and slaves, giving a decree or the law to slaves and captives, domesticating horses, buying large and small beasts.

Chapter VII.44: On healing the infirm

When[334] you wished to heal an old infirmity, put the Moon in Taurus and its triplicity (however, Taurus is better, because it signifies earthy infirmities).[335] And let the Moon be safe from the infortunes, and be in one of the angles of the Ascendant,[336] because on account of this the Moon will be more powerful, and will have greater security so that the infirmity will not cause a relapse after the infirm person is healed. And you should beware of the applications of the Moon to Saturn, because it always signifies long [times] in matters, and delays.

And Māshā'allāh said,[337] look to see in what place of the body the infirmity is: if it were in the parts of the head or throat or in the chest, you will begin to work when the Moon was in Aries, Taurus, or Gemini: because they are of the upper part of the body. And if the infirmity were in the parts of the belly up to the hanging bits,[338] begin to work when the Moon is in Cancer, Leo, or Virgo, because these are of the middle part of the body. And if the infirmity were in the lower part of the body, work on it when the Moon is in Libra or Scorpio or Sagittarius. [But if it is an infirmity from the knees

---

334 Cf. *On Elect.* §§64a-b.

335 Crofts herself corrected the Arabic to read, "the Moon is in her triplicity, Taurus is better because…". There are two questions here: (1) can she be in either the watery triplicity or the earthy one, but the earthy one (which is led by Taurus) is better? Or (2) must she be in the earthy triplicity, and of the three signs Taurus is the better one?

336 But the Arabic and Latin Sahl read that the *fortunes* should be in the angles of the *Moon* while she is in Taurus.

337 Cf. *On Elect.* §§65a-c.

338 *Pendile.* That is, the genitals.

downwards, let her be in] Capricorn or Aquarius or Pisces.[339] And[340] in all of these places, let her be applying to fortunes and increased in light and number.

And he[341] even said: every infirmity and pain which is from the head up to the hanging bits[342] will be healed with the Moon appearing from the angle of the earth, going up to the angle of the tenth house according to the ascension of heaven, and [this] part is called the "ascending" part. And if the infirmity were from the hanging bits up to the feet, it will be healed when the Moon is from the Midheaven, descending to the angle of the earth, and this part is called the "pressed-down" part. And it is appropriate that there be a fortune in the Ascendant, because it signifies good and improvement.

And[343] if you wanted to heal an enchanted[344] or bewitched person, make it so that Mercury is in his own bound. And you would do the same if you wanted to heal a demon-possessed person.

Chapter VII.45: On healing with a syringe[345]

If you wanted to work with a syringe, you should put the Moon in Libra or Scorpio, and it will be better; and the lord of the Ascendant should not have any aspect with the lord of the sixth house, and the Moon should be applying to Venus. This constellation signifies that it will be useful and will have a good end.

---

339 In Sahl's own Arabic as well as the Latin al-Rijāl, the middle part of the body included Capricorn, Aquarius, and Pisces, and the lower legs were completely omitted except in the Latin Sahl. This is contrary to the zodiacal order and obviously wrong, and I have followed Crofts in correcting this paragraph.

340 Sahl does not have this sentence.

341 Apparently, Māshā'allāh: cf. *On Elect.* §§6a-c, based on *Carmen* V.27.26.

342 In Sahl, the navel.

343 Source currently unknown.

344 Reading with 1551 for what seems to be *faturatum*, which sounds like someone in a trance state or other altered state of consciousness.

345 This resembles *On Elect.* §61a, and *Forty Chapters* §635.

Chapter VII.46: On healing the eyes[346]

When you wished to heal the eye from infirmities which happen in the eyes (such as a diminishment of vision, or whiteness in the eye, or surface flesh which it is necessary to be cut with iron, or other infirmities), look to see that the Moon is increasing in light and number, free from the infortunes, and especially from Mars (because he is malign and of great harm in infirmities of the eyes), especially during the Moon's increase; but if Saturn aspected her while she were increased in light and number, at the beginning of the month, it will not do harm to her.

And when she will be separated from the opposition [of the Sun], and Mars aspected her from the trine, and with her applying to a fortune, then Mars will not do great harm to her. [And do not strengthen Mars][347] in infirmities: because all of the sages are agreed that Mars is a great harmer of all organs of the head.

And likewise, they say that for every working of iron which would be necessary for the improvement of the body, one must look at the sign signifying that limb, and not to touch that limb with iron [when either the Moon][348] or the Ascendant are put in it. And likewise, you should beware lest you touch some place of the body with iron, with the Moon appearing in a common or movable sign.

Chapter VII.47: On taking laxative medicine[349]

In taking laxative medicine, the sages are discordant:

[1] However, Ptolemy says[350] that this is a good election if the Moon were in the moist triplicity (which is Cancer, Scorpio, and Pisces). And Hermes, who was before him, says that same thing.

[2] But Valens, *Feytimus*,[351] and al-Tabarī (of the moderns),[352] agree with them in saying that in this Taurus and Virgo, Scorpio, and Pisces are good.[353]

---

[346] Cf. al-'Imrānī II.2.7 (which is a jumble of statements by al-Khayyāt largely mirroring *On Elect.*), and *On Elect.* §§69a-d, and *Carmen* V.39-40.

[347] Adding with *On Elect.* §69c.

[348] Adding with *On Elect.* §69d.

[349] As one will see below, this includes any purgative medicine.

[350] Cf. *Cent.* #21, which only mentions Scorpio and Pisces.

And Māshā'allāh[354] and al-Khayyāt and *Minegeth*[355] and many others of the modern astrologers agree with this opinion.

However, al-Kindī[356] has the opinion which I affirm, even though all of the others whom we have named did speak well and did not go astray: because those who identified[357] the watery signs speak well for guarding the body and for purging it from superfluous humors, without pain and infirmity. And those who change away from these signs say this for drawing out infirmity and hindrances from the body, and for relieving the superfluous humor separately.[358]

However,[359] the opinion of al-Kindī (with whom I agree) is that the Moon should be in the latter half of Libra or the first half of Scorpio, and that the lord of [her] house should be powerful, fortunate, eastern, and in an angle; and there should be a planet making it fortunate, likewise in an angle and eastern; and that the lord of the Ascendant should be of such a condition. And likewise, remove the infortunes from the Moon first, and from the Ascendant and from the angles. (And[360] make it so that the application of the Moon is to Venus, because Venus is better in this matter, and more conducive to success than Jupiter is, and she signifies greater laxative effect, and he who drinks it will be happy—because Jupiter strengthens the spirit and prohibits it so that it is not so laxative.)[361] and make it so that the Moon is received by a fortune; and if her lord were an infortune, make it so that it receives her from the trine or sextile.

---

351 This might not actually be an individual, but some honorific or descriptive term pertaining to Valens.

352 Source unknown at this time.

353 For Scorpio and Pisces, cf. *Cent.* #21; Taurus and Virgo might both be considered cud-chewing signs (see below).

354 Source unknown at this time.

355 Unknown, but probably identical to *Nimagest* in VII.73.

356 See below.

357 *Excollegerunt.*

358 That is, the opinion of the first group (pseudo-Ptolemy and Hermes) is valid for removing excess humors through routine maintenance, like modern people who take regular colonics. But the opinion of the second group (Valens *et al.*) is valid for medical intervention, a side effect of which is removing excess humors.

359 The rest of this chapter is taken from *Forty Chapters* Ch. 34, except for some parenthetical remarks by al-Rijāl. Cf. also al-'Imrānī II.2.10.

360 This remark seems to be al-Rijāl's own.

361 Again, *Cent.* #19.

And if you wanted to purge some limb of the body separately,[362] you should guard these things which we have said before, and beyond that put the fortunes in the sign signifying the limb, and you will strengthen the sign as much as you can. And likewise, adapt the lord of the fourth house.

And if what you have done were for chilling or heating, or for moistening or drying,[363] put the Moon and the lord of the Ascendant in one of those signs which are of that nature which you wanted to create,[364] always making it fortunate.

And[365] you should beware lest one of the significators or the Ascendant be in one of the cud-chewing signs, because this signifies that the receiver of the medicine will vomit it up before it does its work.

(And I say[366] that if you gave medicine for purging melancholy, it is good that the Moon be applying to Jupiter; and if for purging choler, let her apply to Venus; and if for purging phlegm, let the Moon apply to the Sun. And you should beware lest the planet to which the Moon or the lord of the Ascendant applies, be retrograde, because likewise it signifies that the medicine will be vomited up. And if the medicine were a potion, Scorpio is better in this; and if it were for an electuary, Cancer is better; and if it were a pill, Pisces is better. And if the Moon were in the Ascendant when taking the medicine, it signifies an abscess. And you should beware lest the Moon and the lord of the Ascendant be in the fourth house, because it signifies destruction—and likewise in the eighth. And in this constellation [of significators], you should beware when letting blood from a vein.)

And if you wanted that he should be purged from below and from above,[367] put the significators in cud-chewing signs, always making the sign and significators fortunate, just as we have said.

And you should beware, as much as you could, lest the significators be cadent, nor unfortunate, nor should it be a strengthened infortune: because this signifies great evil. And likewise, you should beware as much as you could lest the lord of the house of death be in one of the angles, nor should it have a commingling with any of the significators, nor should it have great

---

362 That is, as opposed to a general laxative effect throughout the body.

363 *Desiccando*, which can also to refer to "draining" the moisture out of something.

364 For example, if you want more of a drying effect, put them in dry signs.

365 Cf. al-'Imrānī II.2.11.

366 This paragraph is now al-Rijāl talking, not al-Kindī.

367 That is, if one wanted vomiting—perhaps in addition to the laxative effect.

power there; and when you will have maintained all of this, you will have what you wanted from the medicine.

Chapter VII.48: On giving binding medicine

In this, it is good that the Moon be in the degrees of her exaltation, joined to Jupiter by body[368] or applying to him; and it is good in this that the Moon and the planet to which she applies, be of slow motion (without [actual] retrogradation).

And if the Moon and the planet to which she applies, and the lord of the Ascendant, were ascending to the north,[369] it is better and more excellent for this. And beware of Mars and Venus in this.

Chapter VII.49: On giving medicine through the nose and for vomiting and gargling[370]

A good election in this is that the Ascendant and the Moon and the significators be in cud-chewing signs, by attending to the constellations[371] and elections which we have stated for drinking medicines.[372]

And al-Tabarī said that it is good that the Moon be diminished in light, and in Taurus, and descending in latitude.[373]

And al-Khayyāt said[374] that it is good that the Moon and the lord of the Ascendant be in Cancer or Leo or Virgo, and that the Moon be applying to the fortunes; nor should she apply to a harmed planet.

And others said[375] that it is good that the Moon be in Aries or Taurus, diminished in light, and applying to fortunes. And you should wholly beware of the aspect of Jupiter,[376] especially in Aries: because he harms on account of the hotness of the Sun.

---

368 Cf. *Cent.* #19.

369 Probably in ecliptical latitude, but perhaps in declination.

370 For the first three paragraphs, cf. al-'Imrānī II.2.12.

371 That is, the planetary configurations.

372 Cf. VII.47 above.

373 Al-'Imrānī's version has her ascending in the circle of her apogee.

374 Cf. *On Elect.* §62b.

375 Cf. *On Elect.* §62a.

376 But Sahl reads this as the square or opposite aspect of the Sun, which is probably correct.

Chapter VII.50.0: On buying slaves[377]

[Chapter VII.50.1: The opinion of al-Kindī][378]

If the slave which you want to buy were for performing a service, you will look at the face[379] appropriate to that service, and you should make it fortunate and put it in the Ascendant or in the place of the Moon, with both appearing fortunate. And if he were a laborer, make them be in low-class signs, at the end of Sagittarius or in Gemini, with them being fortunate; and Aquarius is likewise good, except that it signifies that perhaps he will be a deceiver, and wise about ways of life.[380]

And if the slave were male, put the places of the significators and the signs in masculine places; and if she were a woman, put them in feminine ones. And if you wanted a female slave for lying with her or for having a child from her, you should put Virgo in particular [in such places] for this, and remove the infortunes and their lights from them, and strengthen them with fortunes and their lights.

And if in this you wanted to improve[381] some limb, put the Moon in the sign of that limb, made fortunate by the lights of the fortunes.

And[382] others said: In buying slaves it is appropriate that the Ascendant and the Moon be in fixed signs, and those of straight ascensions, and domesticated shapes—and likewise the lord of the Ascendant. And make the sixth[383] house and its lord fit, and let it being applying to the lord of the Ascendant from a good aspect, with reception; and likewise make the Moon and her lord fit, and the lord of the house of slaves.

---

377 The first part of this chapter is equivalent to *Forty Chapters* Ch. 25, §§579-81. Then al-Rijāl gives a version of *Forty Chapters* Ch. 19 (§§512-14) which is very abbreviated and different from Hugo's, and finally reviews others' opinions.

378 For this subchapter, cf. *Forty Chapters* §§579-81, and 512-14.

379 *Faciem.* Hugo renders this as "celestial shape."

380 Hugo's al-Kindī simply says that Aquarius is better for the sciences: perhaps al-Rijāl means that the slave will be more clever than he should be, and thinks about how to take advantage of his master.

381 But Hugo's al-Kindī understands this as branding, not "improving."

382 Now al-Rijāl turns to al-'Imrānī II.7.1, which is based on *Forty Chapters* Ch. 19 (§§512, 514, 516).

383 Reading with al-Kindī and al-'Imrānī, for "fourth."

And beware lest the Ascendant nor the Moon nor the lord of the sixth house be in Leo. And the better ones of these are Taurus and the end of Sagittarius.

[Chapter VII.50.2: The opinion of others]

And others[384] said that the Moon and the lord of the Ascendant should be in human signs and in other signs which appear fortunate—except for Aries, Scorpio, and Capricorn; and that the sixth house and its lord should be agreeing with the Ascendant and its lord.

And others said[385] that the slave will be according to the nature of the sign, and of the animal from which it is named: just like Pisces, which signifies power;[386] and in this way with the others; and this is a good conclusion.

And they say[387] that when the infortunes were below the earth, the slave will be false.

And Sagittarius particularly signifies that the slave will be good and lawful.

Chapter VII.51.0: On giving the law[388] to slaves and captives, and domesticating horses[389]

[Chapter VII.51.1: An opinion from Carmen][390]

A good election in this is that you make the Ascendant and its lord fit (because the Ascendant is the significator of the master); and the seventh belongs to the one to whom he gives the decree or law; and the Midheaven [is] the significator of the occasion for which he gives him the decree or law; and the fourth [is] the significator of the end of the [new] legal status, and what kind of status he will have in that. Whence, if the Moon were made

---

384 Abū Ma'shar, according to al-'Imrānī II.7.1. But Abū Ma'shar has probably gotten this from *Forty Chapters* Ch. 19, and it derived originally from *Carmen*.
385 According to the Paris 16204 manuscript of al-'Imrānī, this is Abū Ma'shar again. But see *Carmen* V.11, and *On Elect.* §§71a-72.
386 But see al-'Imrānī II.7.1, and *Forty Chapters* §515.
387 *On Elect.* §§71a-b; cf. al-'Imrānī II.7.1.
388 From the context of *Carmen* and Sahl below, this chapter is really about freeing slaves.
389 Cf. al-'Imrānī II.7.2, who (like in *On Elect.* §§75a*ff*) understands this as manumitting slaves, not "giving the law."
390 Cf. *Carmen* V.13.5-8.

unfortunate, and the seventh house, it signifies that perhaps he will be reduced to servitude just as he was before.

[Chapter VII.51.2: An opinion from Sahl][391]

And Sahl bin Bishr said, in this it is appropriate that the Moon be clear of every harm, and increasing in light and number, and applying to fortunes, and that that fortune be eastern, [and] likewise increasing: because if the fortune were increasing and western, it signifies that he will have good, but pains and infirmities could happen to him [which are] never separable from him until he would die. And the increase of the Moon's light signifies the good health of the body, and the increase of number signifies that he will profit in a prosperous way.[392]

And in this it is good that the Sun and the sign of the Midheaven be safe from the infortunes. And if these were made unfortunate, they signify that some entanglement of the nature of that sign will happen to the master.

And it is good that at the hour of giving the degree or law to the slave, that the luminaries be aspecting each other from a trine or sextile, because this signifies that there will be love between the slave and his master, and that he will have good from him; however, an aspect of the square in this is in the middle, and the aspect of opposition signifies that the slave will have contentions or [legal] complaints with his master.

And for any slave or captive to which the free legal status[393] would be given, if the Moon were made unfortunate, slavery will be better for him. And it is good in this to put the Moon in fixed signs.

---

[391] For this subsection, cf. *On Elect.* §§75a-77b.

[392] Reading *prospere* with 1551 for an illegible word in 1485.

[393] *Ordinamentum.*

Chapter VII.52.0: On buying beasts, large and small

[Chapter VII.52.1: The opinion of Sahl][394]

When you wanted to buy animals, large and small, you should make the Moon be applying to fortunes, with that fortune appearing direct, eastern, and ascending in latitude. And you should beware of the applications of the infortunes, because they signify the loss of the beast.

And if the beast which you wished to buy were domesticated so that it is already ridden, you should buy it with the Ascendant being in a common sign, and the Moon in a fixed sign (with the exception of Aquarius and Scorpio). And if the planet to which the Moon applies were direct, ascending in latitude, it signifies that the beast [will increase in price and body; but if it were retrograde ascending, it][395] has some wound in its body: however, on the whole he will profit from it.[396] And if it were direct and descending, it signifies that its body is complete and sound, but you will not have the price from it which is enumerated to you.

And if the beast which you want to buy were small,[397] so that it is never ridden, make it so that the Ascendant is a [common sign but the Moon in a][398] movable sign, applying to a fortune. And you will guard the roots of the elections which we told you in the first chapter.[399]

[Chapter VII.52.2: The opinion of al-Kindī][400]

And others said:[401] in this it is appropriate that the Ascendant and the Moon be in a sign similar to that animal which you wanted to buy, whether it be an animal for riding, or a cow or flock-animal or pig, or something else you want; or in a sign which is more near to that thing in its nature; and that it be made fortunate by the lord of that sign, or by another (if she were not

---

394 Cf. *On Elect.* §§135-37. To my mind there is ambiguity in this election, because it recommends that the planet to which the Moon applies be ascending (probably in its epicycle or apogee), which increases the price. But the increase in price should benefit the seller, not the buyer.
395 Adding based on Sahl.
396 Or rather, the seller will profit, because the ascension means the price is still increased.
397 Sahl reads that it is untamed, that is, not ridden *yet.*
398 Adding with Sahl.
399 This probably means the criteria of being direct and ascending, etc., just above.
400 Cf. al-'Imrānī II.7.3.
401 *Forty Chapters* §578.

received); and if the lord of that sign were not a fortune, it does not make evil when aspecting from an aspect of friendship and with reception.

And[402] if the beast were masculine, put the significators in masculine signs and degrees; and if it were female, in female ones.

And make the sixth house and its lord fit.

And it is good that the Ascendant and the significators be in Leo or at the end of Sagittarius. And if it were a cow, you should improve Taurus. And if flock-animals, Aries; and if goats, Capricorn; and thus with the other animals of the zodiac.

And for any house, adapt its likeness and make it fortunate with the fortunes, and remove the infortunes.

[Chapter VII.52.3: Another opinion]

And you should know that when the Moon is being separated from a fortune and applies to an infortune, and that infortune were in a sign of a fortune,[403] that beast will be bad and will bite and strike. And if the infortune were in a human sign, the beast will be liable to panic or it will not permit itself to be harnessed. And if the Moon applied to infortunes, things will happen to him after the purchase, in accordance with this.

---

402 Cf. *Forty Chapters* §§580, 582-83, and *Carmen* V.12.4.

403 This should probably read, "infortune."

THE SEVENTH HOUSE

Chapter VII.53: On the seventh house and its elections

In this house there are, of elections: marriage-unions, disputes, buying arms and clever devices for conflicts,[404] confronting one with another, making peace with enemies, tearing down forts and estates, making an instrument for conflicts, partnerships and every matter which there is between two people, searching for a fugitive, making a robber confess the truth, hunting by land and by sea, playing at chess and board games, [lying down with women],[405] and the like.

Chapter VII.54: On marriage-unions[406]

You[407] should know that the Ascendant and its lord and the Sun are significators of the man; and the seventh and its lord and Venus, significators of the woman; and the Midheaven and its lord, the significators of what happens between them in terms of good or evil; and the fourth house and its lord, the significator of the end. And the planet from which the Moon is being separated, belongs to the man, and the planet to which she applies, to the woman.

And[408] the Moon herself signifies the good and evil which each one of them will have, due to their good status or through their condemnations.[409]

And Mercury signifies a child which they will have with each other, [if it is with or aspecting the fortunes].[410]

---

[404] This originally appeared later in the list, but I have put it here so as to match the order of chapters.

[405] Adding based on the chapter sequence below.

[406] This whole chapter corresponds closely to *Carmen* V.16.

[407] *Carmen* V.16.1.

[408] Cf. *Carmen* V.16.4.

[409] That is, the Moon's condition at the election will indicate the joint good and bad for the marriage itself. *Carmen* only mentions that if the Moon is harmed at the election, it will be bad for both.

[410] Adding with *Carmen* V.16.5.

And[411] when the Moon and Venus were in movable signs, they signify that their joy will not be lasting. And if the woman were a widow, it signifies that she has made a fraud against the other husband which she had.

The[412] signs which are good [when the Moon is in it] and which are contrary in this matter, according to the agreement of the majority of the sages:

All of Aries is bad.

Taurus is good from the first degree up to the twentieth, and the rest bad.[413]

In Gemini, the first half is good and the other half bad.[414]

[Avoid marriage when the Moon is in Cancer.][415]

Leo is good except that it signifies that one will deceive the other with respect to assets.

Virgo is good for [a man] contracting [a marriage-union] with a widow, but it is not good for a man [in the case of a woman electing the marriage], because it signifies that she will quickly lose her first husband.

Libra is good for being betrothed, and bad for getting married.

The first half of Scorpio is good for making a marriage-union with a virgin,[416] because it signifies that she will be obedient to her man, and good and just; and its last half is bad, because it signifies that they will

[411] *Carmen* V.16.6.
[412] Cf. V.16.8-20, on which this passage was originally based. *On Elect.* §§80a-c also uses this material from its own Dorothean source.
[413] *Carmen* has the beginning and end of Taurus bad, but the middle good.
[414] In *Carmen* it reads just the opposite.
[415] Adding with *Carmen* V.16.12.
[416] Or perhaps, "young woman."

not last in love, and perhaps that the woman will fornicate with her slave.

The Moon in Sagittarius is good for a marriage-union, except that the woman will be wise about the ways of life.[417]

The Moon in Capricorn is bad at its beginning, good in the middle and end: and it signifies that the woman will be obedient to her husband; and it is better for a widow than for a virgin, except that it signifies few children.

The Moon in Aquarius is not good for a marriage-union, because it signifies that the woman will have the will and appetite of a man.

The Moon with Pisces is good, because it signifies that the woman will be good and just, except that it signifies that she will have empty[418] words, because of which the husband will hate her.

All of what we have said is understood to be when the Moon was in the Ascendant, in one of these signs at the hour of the marriage-union.

You[419] should know that Venus has the greatest power in marriage-unions, nor could it be a good marriage-union with Venus being conjoined to the infortunes or aspecting them, or that she would be in her own fall, or cadent from an angle, or retrograde or burned up.

And in this it is better that the Moon be in the house of a fortune and in the bound of a fortune, and that Jupiter be aspecting Venus and the Moon.

And the best time there could be for a marriage-union is that Jupiter be elevated over Venus from a right square (in the tenth house of Venus herself),[420] and Venus at that hour would even be ascending above the Moon, in

---

417 *Carmen* says Sagittarius is good for a lot of things, but that in general it is better to postpone the marriage.

418 *Vanis.* This can range from speech that is meaningless and pointless, to being lying, conceited, or vain.

419 Cf. generally *Carmen* V.16.20-29, and *On Elect.* §§81a-c.

420 That is, overcoming her.

the tenth house of that Moon (and according to this, the Moon will be in the opposition of Jupiter). And when this happens, it will be a very good election, because it signifies many children and much good, by the good will of God.

Likewise, a good time for a marriage-union is when Jupiter, Venus, and the Moon would be aspecting, one to the other, from a trine: and the signs of many children are likewise good in this.

And[421] when it happened in a marriage-union that Venus is in a masculine sign and Jupiter in a feminine sign, it signifies that the marriage will be better for the man than for the woman; and if they were contrary to this, it signifies the contrary. And in this it is good that the Moon be increasing in light and number.

And it is appropriate, in a marriage-union, that you look at the nativities of the man and woman, if you were able to have them. And if you found fortunes in the Midheaven in their nativities, it signifies that they will have offspring in the first year of the marriage-union. And if the lord of the Midheaven were after the Midheaven, it signifies that she will not be impregnated in the first month of the marriage-union. And if you found a fortune in the same place in both nativities (in the nativity of the woman and of the man), it signifies that both will esteem each other. And you will judge the same thing in the nativity of men, [if a fortune is in the same sign].[422]

And[423] if you wanted to know which of them will be strengthened over the other, you will look to see if you found in the twelfth[424] house of one of them, the Moon of the other person: and judge that the one whose Moon was [in that house of the other], will be strengthened over the other.[425]

---

421 This paragraph is taken from a bit later in *Carmen*: V.16.34-36.

422 Adding based in *Carmen* V.16.29. That is, this synastry method also works for friendship.

423 *Carmen* V.16.30-32.

424 Pingree's *Carmen* has "the house of misery," which Pingree identifies as the sixth. But al-Rijāl could be correct here.

425 Suppose that the man's twelfth house (or if following Pingree's interpretation, the sixth) were Gemini, and the woman's natal Moon were in Gemini: then the woman will subjugate the man.

And[426] a good constellation for a marriage-union is that a fortune be in the Ascendant, or aspecting it. And it is not good to make a marriage-union with an infortune appearing in the Ascendant, nor that it should aspect it. And it is good to make a marriage-union with the Moon increasing in number.

In a marriage-union in which the Moon were conjoined with an infortune in the Ascendant, it signifies that the man and that woman will always be in quarrels and contrariety and suspicion, one toward the other. And likewise if such a constellation were in their nativity: that one of them which had this, will be conquered and will be supported by the other.[427]

And if the place of the Moon [in] their nativities at the hour of the marriage-union were above the earth, they will come together and make peace after the quarrels [which] they likewise have.[428]

Chapter VII.55: On elections for a dispute

[According to Sahl][429]

In this it is appropriate that you make the Ascendant some house of the three higher planets, and more supported in this are the houses of Mars; and that Mars should be in the sextile of the Ascendant or its trine; and that the lord of the Ascendant be in the Ascendant or in the eleventh or tenth. And beware lest it be in the fourth, nor in the seventh nor eighth. And likewise you should beware lest it be burned up, nor cadent from an angle, nor applying to a planet cadent from an angle, nor that it should receive it;[430] and make the lord of the seventh house to be applying to the lord of the Ascendant, or be in the Ascendant or in the second house from the Ascendant.

---

426 This section corresponds to *Carmen* V.16.33 and 37-40.

427 *Carmen* puts this a bit differently, namely that if their natal Moons are opposed to each other, they will have discord.

428 Reading more with *Carmen* than the Latin *convenire se habent et pacificare postquam rixam similiter habuerint.*

429 For this section, cf. *On Elect.* §§85-90b.

430 Sahl reads this as though it should not be applying to a cadent planet which *does not* receive it. This is echoed by "ibn Hebeteth" below.

And if you wanted that they should confront each other or join themselves [in conflict] and that there should be war between them, put Mars in the angles, and you should apply him to a fortune which has dignity in the Ascendant, and one which is of the nature of the Ascendant. And you should never go to a dispute unless Mars would have rulership in the dispute, and that he would be the lord of the Ascendant, and that he should be powerful, in a good place, not harmed nor mistrusted[431] nor burned up, and that he should be in a sign of straight ascension. And you should never put him [anywhere] except on the side[432] of the Ascendant, because then his aid will be on the side of the one who goes to the dispute, and be of his association and army, and they will be saved and conquered, with the aid of God.

And you should make the second house and its lord fortunate, for the army of the one who goes to the dispute, and the eighth and its lord for the army of the enemy; and you should not put the lord of the second in the seventh or eighth, but put the lord of the eighth in the second house from the Ascendant; and put the Lot of Fortune and its lord in the Ascendant or in the second, and remove them from the seventh or eighth. And you should beware lest the Moon nor the lord of her house be harmed before the business is begun.

And likewise, you should guard the dignity of the twelfth-part of the Moon. And it is necessary in the causes of wars that you make the planets of war fit (which are Mars, Mercury, and the Moon, and the lord of the house in which the Moon is): whence you should consider and them and make them fit, and you should not forget any of those things which are the roots of wars.

And you should know that, [for] any of the two armies which moved or went out in that constellation or election which we stated, and they will confront each other in order to engage in conflict, that one of them will conquer who was born by night or who had, in his nativity, Mars in a better place: because Mars is the significator and the lord of war; and perhaps they will come together likewise and have peace between them, and this on account of the good constellation which both had in the departure to the dispute.

All of this is the statement of Sahl bin Bishr, who spoke well, and was right in all of this.

---

431 *Suspectus.*

432 *In parte.* But see Sahl, who renders this as being in the "domain" of the Ascendant.

And *ibn Hebeteth* said,[433] when you wanted to make an election for a dispute, you should direct the Ascendant and make the Lot of dispute, which is taken from Mars to the Moon, and is projected from the Sun.[434] And you should beware lest this Lot nor the lord of its house fall in the fourth house nor the seventh: because if this Lot fell in any of these two places, it signifies that the enemy will conquer, because the fourth house signifies being pressed down, and the seventh signifies hindrance. You should even beware lest it be in the eighth, because there it signifies weakness and delay.

Likewise, make the Lot of victory, which is taken from the Sun to Mars, and is projected from Ascendant.[435] And you should beware lest it nor its lord fall from[436] any of the stated places.

And you should beware lest you go into a dispute with an enemy when the Moon was in Taurus [while] commingling herself with Mars, because this is a bad signification and a bad constellation for the one undertaking it. However, when the Moon would be in Gemini or Cancer, put her in the trine of Mars, and so that both fortunes would aspect her, and you should start to have the conflict with the one you wanted to, or begin the legal case with the one you wanted to, because the one beginning it will conquer in this constellation.

And likewise you should beware lest Saturn be with the Moon in any of the stated signs.

And when you wanted an election for some man who wants to attack his enemy or do evil to him, or take his power for himself, you should look in this so that the Moon would be safe from the infortunes, and let a fortune aspect: because this signifies that the one undertaking [the action] will conquer the other, and will take his power from him, and the one undertaking it will last and be strengthened.

And[437] when you wanted to go into a dispute, make the Ascendant be the house of a high planet, and [put] its lord in the Ascendant or in the tenth or in the eleventh, and beware lest it be in the seventh or eighth, nor burned up,

---

433 Probably ibn Hibinta (see Introduction). I am not sure how much of this little section comes from him.

434 I have not seen this Lot before.

435 I have not seen this Lot before.

436 *Ab.* But this probably should read "in."

437 Again, this is from *On Elect.* as above in the first paragraph.

nor applying to a planet cadent from the angle which [does not] receive it, nor to a planet who is entering into burning. And[438] make it so that one of the two luminaries (or both) would apply to the lord of the Ascendant, because it signifies that the owner of this election will conquer.

༄ ༄ ༄

Al-Fadl bin Sahl said,[439] it is good that you send the one who is going into the dispute, on the day of Jupiter and in his hour, or on the day of Venus and her hour, or on the day of the Sun and his hour. And you should make the Ascendant be the house of a fortune, and that that fortune should be eastern, in the Ascendant or in the Midheaven or in the eleventh, and the lord of the hour with it or [with] the other fortune.

And if there were a fortune in the Ascendant, it signifies that there will be safety of the body and profit for the one who goes; and if the fortune were joined bodily with the Moon, it signifies joy. And if a fortune were applying to her and she were increased in light, it signifies nimbleness on the journey, and good fortune in that business, especially if the Ascendant and the Moon were in signs of straight ascensions—and these are the signs which Dorotheus and all the sages of Babylonia identified, who said that the signs of crooked ascensions signify labors, and particularly the movable ones among them, which confirm labors and destroy every matter which men want to move forward.[440]

And if the Sun were in the Ascendant in such an election as we have said before, it signifies boldness, great power, and the completion of the business, except that it is bad for profiting and having advantage [from] the affair, because perhaps he will return penniless and empty, especially if he happened to be in a feminine sign or in his own fall, or he were aspected by some infortune. And if the Moon were in the Ascendant or in the Midheaven, and it were a nocturnal election, and she were applying to a fortune, and were free from the infortunes, it signifies elevation and great power, and particularly if

---

[438] For this sentence, cf. *On Quest.* §7.8 (*Judges* §7.48).

[439] I am not sure exactly how much of this part of the chapter belongs to al-Fadl bin Sahl.

[440] This probably depends on the context. *Carmen* V.2 says the opposite: that the straight signs are difficult, presumably because they indicate more time (and thus more effort), while the crooked signs are faster-moving and so normally indicate ease.

she were in her own exaltation, or the lord of her exaltation [were] free of burning and retrogradation.

ꕤ ꕤ ꕤ

And I say[441] that it is good to make the Ascendant one of the fixed signs, and especially that it would be of straight ascension, and that the lord of the Ascendant be in the Ascendant or in the tenth or eleventh, nor should the ascending sign be of the common ones, unless you had great haste in choosing: because if [a common sign] were there, it signifies that the one undertaking [the action] will regret the dispute. Nor should it be of the movable ones, because it signifies that the one undertaking [the action] will not complete what he wants.

And you should put the Lot of Fortune in the power of the one undertaking [the action]—which is the Ascendant, the second, tenth, and eleventh; and you should beware lest it be in the power of the enemy (and that is the seventh, eighth, fourth, and fifth). And you should do the same with the lord of the Lot of Fortune, because that one in whose power it is, will be the victor. And I say that it is useful that you should beware of the movable signs in all disputes, and especially Aries and Libra.[442]

And you should know that when the lord of the seventh will be weakened, and you have made it unfortunate, you will be weakening your enemies and their soldiers, and you will be destroying their travels.[443] And if you strengthened these places, you will be strengthening your enemies and their assistants. And the lesser harm of the two infortunes is that of Mars, and especially if Venus were in the Ascendant, applying to him, and giving him her own power.[444]

And if the Ascendant were Cancer, it is very bad for the one undertaking [the action], because it is movable, and the lord of the Ascendant will be the Moon, who is lower than all [the other planets], and the lord of the seventh will be Saturn, who is higher than all [the other planets]; and that the Moon is

---

441 The rest of this chapter is probably al-Rijāl's own opinion, which must be based in part on other, unknown sources.

442 Perhaps because, as equinoctial signs in which the length of day and night are the same, it suggests an equality of force on each side (which tends to prolong conflicts).

443 Reading *itinera* for *itineratores*. This probably means that they will not be as mobile or advance as well as they want to.

444 Also known as "pushing power" (*ITA* III.16), which would require Venus to be in her own domicile or exaltation while applying to him.

of many changes and differences, and many impediments. And Capricorn is better as the Ascendant than all [the other] movable [signs], especially if you put the Moon in the second (which is Aquarius). And if you could not put her there, put her in Sagittarius, made unfortunate, and giving her own power to Saturn.[445]

I even say that if the lord of the seventh house were an infortune, it is not good that it should be in the Ascendant, since it would not signify security unless it were in its own fall[446] or combustion or in one of them.

If,[447] at the hour when your enemy went out to attack you, you found the lord of the Ascendant in an angle and strengthened, and it seemed that he would conquer, give your election to the one who wanted to go out against him; [make] the Ascendant a movable sign, and the lord of the Ascendant in a fixed sign or a common one, and received, and make the lord of the seventh and the planet to which the Moon applies, cadent from an angle.

And if the lord of the seventh house were an infortune, and direct in its motion, or eastern, or it had a power or dignity in its place, make it so that the Moon is separating herself from it. And beware lest the lord of the Ascendant be in the seventh.

Chapter VII.56: On buying arms for war[448]

In this it is appropriate that the Moon be in her own house or exaltation or triplicity, conjoined to Mars at the end of the [Lunar] month: because all the sages say that the Moon with Mars at the beginning of the month is bad, and likewise with Saturn at the end of the month; and that one should beware of her in these states.

---

445 In this case, it would be impossible for the Moon to push power to Saturn, because she is not in her own domicile or exaltation in Sagittarius. Perhaps the source of this statement used phrases like this very loosely, and al-Rijāl really means she will push her "management" to him (i.e., applying to him).

446 This sentence does not really make sense. No malefic planet is in its own fall when in the opposite of its own sign. Al-Rijāl is probably trying to say that we should be careful when putting planets into houses (such as the lord of the seventh into the first), because malefic planets might backfire and harm the one putting them there, unless they are strongly weakened.

447 In this paragraph, al-Rijāl is imagining that an enemy has already advanced against the client, and the astrologer must choose a time for his client to respond effectively to the attack.

448 Cf. *On Elect.* §91, which differs in certain respects.

Chapter VII.57.0: On confronting [others] in wars and making peace

[Chapter VII.57.1: Making war, according to al-Kindī][449]

The adjustments[450] which come with respect to confrontations for conflicts[451] or wars, for him who is made a rebel, and for one who is against the one who is its owner.[452]

Al-Kindī said, it is appropriate for the king (or him against whom someone is made a rebel) that he should not squabble with that rebel until the Moon is made fortunate: because the Moon and the lord of the Ascendant always belong to the one who is made the rebel, and it is always appropriate for the rebel that he should beware of squabbling when the Moon is made unfortunate, and he seeks war when she was made fortunate (and especially if the lord of the Ascendant were likewise made fortunate and in the Ascendant). And you should beware of squabbling when the lord of the Ascendant or the Ascendant were made unfortunate.

And if the one who was made a rebel were going toward the direction of the east, it is appropriate for him to engage the war with the Moon appearing in the parts of the west; and if it were towards the west, he should put the Moon in the east; and if it were towards the south, he should put her in the north; and if it were towards the north, he should put her in the south.[453]

And it is appropriate for him who wants to attack the one who was made a rebel, that he should begin to attack when Mars was in the parts of the eastern heaven (and they are from the tenth degree of Taurus up to the tenth degree of Leo, and from the tenth degree of Scorpio up to the tenth degree of Aquarius): you will do this if the one who was made a rebel were [attacking] from the direction of the east. However, if it were from the direction of the west, begin to attack him when Mars was in the parts of the western

---

[449] This subchapter is drawn from *Forty Chapters* §§406b-08.

[450] *Correctiones.*

[451] *Litium*, which in Latin can also refer to lawsuits; but al-Kindī's context is war.

[452] This odd sentence is due to the fact that al-Rijāl has not explained al-Kindī's context. First of all, al-Kindī is talking about cases of rebellion, and gives the Ascendant and the Moon to the initiator of the conflict: i.e., the rebel. In this election, al-Kindī is warning that initiating conflict under a fortunate Moon is good for the initiator, and bad for the responder (because the attack will be forceful); but initiating under an unfortunate Moon is bad for the initiator and good for the responder (because the attack will be weaker). Al-Rijāl himself wants to expand this to cases beyond kings and rebels.

[453] In other words, he should fight with the Moon at his back. This is the opposite of Māshā'allāh's view on gaming in VII.64 below.

heaven (which are from 10° of Leo up to the tenth degree of Scorpio, and from 10° of Aquarius up to the tenth degree of Taurus).

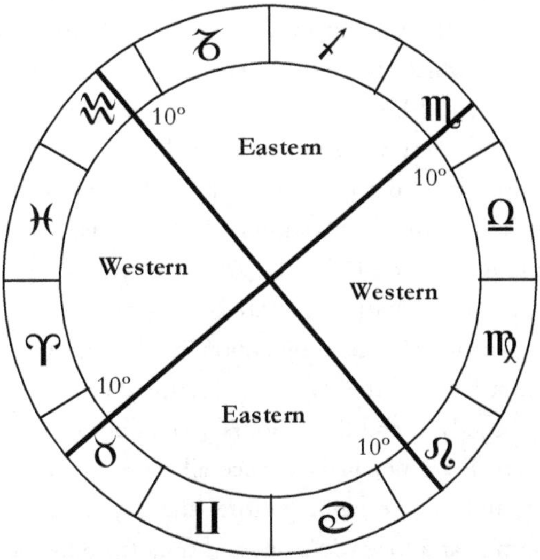

Figure 22: Al-Kindī's cardinal directions for fighting

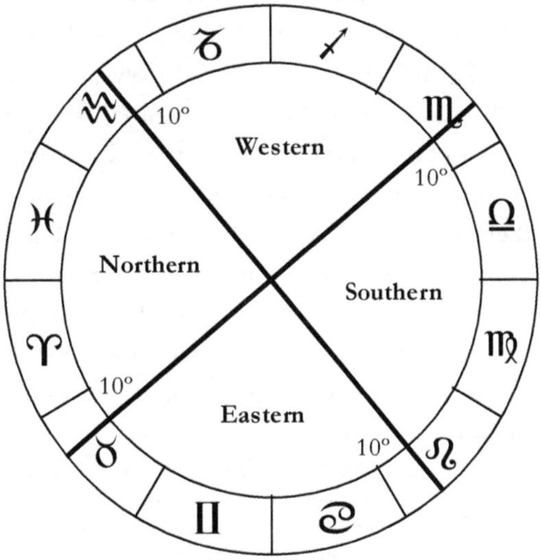

Figure 23: Al-Rijāl's proposed correction to al-Kindī[454]

[454] Al-Rijāl (II.2) points out that al-Kindī's division of the zodiac would only allow the armies to advance from the east or west, rather than from all directions. So, he proposes a different division, apparently based on the four royal stars and the seasons: the Sun is in

[Chapter VII.57.2: The burnt or scorched hours, according to al-Kindī][455]

And for whichever one of the directions [it was], it is appropriate that one should beware of undertaking business in the bad, "burnt" hours: and they are from the hour in which the Moon is conjoined to the Sun in one minute, until she crosses over 12 hours: because these hours are to be abhorred in every high deed and every noble thing. And likewise, the 12 hours which begin after 84 hours,[456] up to 12 hours [more], are likewise those called "burning"; and likewise from 192, another 12 hours, [and yet another group between 84 and] 96 from those first 12. And thus you will go, by doing that until all the hours of the [lunar] month are completed.

For example, put it that the conjunction of the Sun and Moon was on Sunday, at the first hour of the day, with the middle of the Sun's body appearing on the Ascendant: and these hours should be computed through the seasonal hours which are unequal: whence all the hours of the day of Sunday[457] are burnt; and on the night [before] the day of the Moon, they are separately "unburnt"; and they will be good hours from the beginning of that night, and the whole day of Monday and its night, and Tuesday and all of the following night, and all day Wednesday. And afterwards, the burnt hours begin at the first hour of the night which follows the day of Wednesday,[458] and up to the morning of Thursday[459] which follows, and after that the day and night of Friday, and the day and night of Saturday, and likewise the burnt hours begin in the morning of the day of Sunday, and they will fill up the whole day up to the beginning of the night. And likewise, you will begin from the night [before] Monday, and you will do it just like you did before, and you will go thus by doing that until the whole month is filled up, and another conjunction begins. And you will begin from the hour of the conjunction (at whatever hour it is), and you will draw out the burnt hours according to this method and numbering which we have said before. And if

---

Taurus at the middle of spring, which is associated with the east, etc., and the constellation Taurus (with which the tropical sign Taurus used to correspond) contains the royal star Aldebaran; likewise for the other seasons and royal stars: summer and Regulus (Leo), autumn and Antares (Scorpio), and winter and Fomalhaut (really in Piscis Australis, but close to Aquarius).

455 This subchapter is drawn from *Forty Chapters* §§409-13.

456 Reading for "96." The second group lasts from 84 hours *until* 96 hours. See figure below.

457 That is, from sunrise on Sunday morning until sunset.

458 That is, at sunset on Wednesday evening.

459 Reading with Hugo's al-Kindī, for *veneris*.

some squabble were begun in these hours, it signifies that the initiator of the squabble will be destroyed, or an impediment will happen to him in his body, betrayal among his allies and associations, and his matters, so that if he would begin in the [first] four hours of the first twelve, he will be destroyed; and if in the following four [hours], he will have impediment in his body; and if he undertook it in the last four, there will be loss in his associations and allies.

Day	Hours	Scorched/Burnt
1 – Sunday	Diurnal 0-12	**Scorched**
	Nocturnal 12-24	Unscorched
2 – Monday	Diurnal 24-36	Unscorched
	Nocturnal 36-48	Unscorched
3 – Tuesday	Diurnal 48-60	Unscorched
	Nocturnal 60-72	Unscorched
4 – Wednesday	Diurnal 72-84	Unscorched
	Nocturnal 84-96	**Scorched**
5 – Thursday	Diurnal 96-108	Unscorched
	Nocturnal 108-120	Unscorched
6 – Friday	Diurnal 120-132	Unscorched
	Nocturnal 132-144	Unscorched
7 – Saturday	Diurnal 144-156	Unscorched
	Nocturnal 156-168	Unscorched
8 – Sunday	Diurnal 168-180	**Scorched**
	Nocturnal 180-192	Unscorched

Figure 24: Time-based scorched period, from New Moon on Sunday morning

Comment by Dykes. This time-based approach to the scorched (or burnt or "combust") period is very close to the method of determining the crisis hours in decumbiture charts, and may in fact be related to them.

In this method, the scorched hours are computed according to seasonal hours (the same as are used for computing "planetary" hours). Instead of counting an hour as being a standardized 60 minutes, the period between sunrise and sunset is divided evenly by 12, as is the period between sunset and the following sunrise. Since the actual length of daylight varies throughout the year, the 12 "hours" or daylight divisions in summer will each last for a long time, and those of the night will be shorter; but in winter, the 12 daylight divisions will be shorter, and the nighttime ones longer—not to mention that the actual lengths will also vary and become more extreme depending on one's latitude.

For example, suppose that the New Moon al-Kindī describes, took place late in winter in the northern hemisphere, when days are very short and the nights long: in that case, the 12 scorched hours from sunrise to sunset on Sunday, would last for a much shorter time than the 12 scorched hours from sunset on Sunday to sunrise on Monday. Accordingly, the actual distance traveled by the Moon would be shorter in the former, and longer in the latter. Likewise, if the New Moon took place at some time during daylight hours, the scorched hours would be composed of some shorter hours and some longer ones, since they would be a mixture of some daylight hours and then however many nighttime ones it took to yield 12.

But if we used an idealized 60-minute hour and the Moon's average daily speed (13° 10' 36"), she will end up being in her idealized quarters and semi-quarters at some of these times, because she will have traveled approximately 45° between the beginning of each period of scorched hours. For example, if the scorched hours began on Sunday at dawn, they would end at sunset after the Moon had traveled 6° 35' 18" (while she is still burnt up, under the rays of the Sun). The next period would begin on Thursday at dawn, when the Moon has traveled about 45° from her original position; the next period of scorched hours would take place at about 90° from her original position (i.e., an idealized first quarter Moon); and so on. *However*, since seasonal hours are uneven, and because the Sun also moves, these scorched hours will not always coincide strictly with the true quarters and semi-quarters: for by the time the Moon reaches, say, 270° from her original position (an idealized third quarter), the Sun will already have moved about 21°, and so the Moon's position will fall short of the true third quarter. This means that calculating the actual time of the scorched hours a bit complicated, since one cannot simply look at the Moon to tell just when they begin and end: one really needs tables of sunrises and sunsets, or an astrology program which lists the times of the planetary hours.

A distance-based version of the scorched hours is given in Māshā'allāh's *Book of Aristotle* II.4 (in *PN1*).[460] There, the scorched period is defined as 12°

[460] In Appendix D is yet a third version, attributed to the Indians.

of *distance* traveled by the Moon (close to her average every day), instead of 12 seasonal *hours*. This version makes a bit more sense, if we remember that the Moon is often taken to come out of the Sun's rays at a distance of 12°. If we treated the non-scorched period as one defined by 84° of distance traveled instead of 84 hours of time, then the Moon's position at the beginning of the scorched hours will coincide almost exactly with her quarters: the next scorched period will happen at about 96° from her original position—but since the Sun will have moved about 7° in the meantime, they will be almost exactly 90° apart, i.e., the true first quarter. The next period will put her at 192° from her original position, but since the Sun will have moved about 14° in the meantime, this also puts her at almost exactly 180° from him: the Full Moon. And so on with the rest.

And so, the time-based scorched period is an idealized division of the zodiac into 8, using the quarters and semi-quarters, and is more complicated to reckon. The distance-based scorched period uses only the actual quarters, and is relatively easy to reckon (in many cases one may do this from sight alone).

Chapter VII.57.3: On making peace with enemies, [according to al-Kindī][461]

Al-Kindī said: look to see if you found the lord of the Ascendant and the lord of the seventh in one sign, and if there were some planet [that is a] fortune between them: it signifies that some man will get involved for peace between them. And if that same planet were in one of its own dignities, it signifies that the man is known, a native of that city.

And his status will be according to the status of that planet in that place, with respect to easternness or westernness, or retrogradation or direct motion:[462] and judge according to this for the status of that man and his power. And if the planet were a foreigner in that place,[463] it signifies that the man will be a stranger to that land (and the foreignness of the planet is from the house or exaltation, not more).[464] And if it had the triplicity, bound and face,

---

461 This subchapter is drawn from *Forty Chapters* Ch. 11.8.
462 Hugo's al-Kindī adds that one should note its angularity.
463 That is, "peregrine" (*peregrinus*).
464 That is, even being in a minor dignity will still count as being peregrine, for the purposes of this rule.

it signifies that the man will be born in that land, but he will not be naturally from there.

And if you wanted to know which of the two sides the man esteems more, you would look to see in what sign that planet has more dignities (in the ascending sign or in the sign of the seventh): and that one of them in which it had dignity, judge that he draws himself more towards that side, and will esteem it more.

And if you wanted to know the office of the man, look at the nature of that fortune which was between the two significators. And if it were Jupiter, you should say that he is a man of law, justice, and intellect. And if it were Venus, it will be a man of vices, honored and clean.[465] And commingle with it the nature of another planet which will be commingled with that fortune, just as we have stated about this in many places of this book. So that if it were Saturn, he will be of the old men or what is like these; and if it were Jupiter, he will be of the men of the law, a judge or advocate or an honored man, or what is like these; and if it were Mars, he will be a warlike man; and if it were the Sun he will be of the nature of kings and high men; and if it were Venus, he will be of the nature of prophets, and a clean man; and if it were Mercury, he will be of the merchants or writers; and if it were the Moon, he will be of the verbose men, and those telling stories.[466]

Afterwards, you should look to see what sign of [its] houses of heavens it has a greater and better aspect [with], and judge according to the nature of that house: so that if it aspected the house of the Ascendant and had dignities in the sign of the Ascendant, the man will be a blood-relative [or] one close to the one who has begun the squabble, or the man whom it is believed has [begun it]. And if [the dignity and aspect] were in the second, it will be one of his own allies; and if in the third it will be one of his own blood-relatives or friends; and if in the fourth, of the manner of parents or grandparents or what is like these; and if in the fifth, of the children or those of the likeness of his children; and if in the sixth, of men inferior to him, or of his own slaves and what is like these; and if in the seventh, from his own adversaries; and if in the eighth, of the allies of his own enemies and of his critics; and if in the ninth, of the men of the law and who have already made jour-

---

[465] *Limpidus*, which can also mean "clear." Hugo uses *mundus*, which can mean "clean, polite."

[466] Al-Kindī has it that he is a messenger or underofficial of some legation, which makes more sense. Perhaps al-Rijāl means that he will be more of a common man, who enjoys talking.

neys with him; and if in the tenth, of the nature of the king; and if in the eleventh, of the allies of the king and his friends; and if in the twelfth, it will be of his own enemies.

And likewise, you should look to see if that planet which was the mediator in the sign between the lord of the Ascendant and the lord of the seventh, were an infortune: it signifies that the man who will intervene between the one who was made a rebel and the other one will mismanage, flip-flop, and cause harm. And if it were Saturn, he will be an old man or deceiver, [and] of deep thoughts. And if it were Mars, he will be an angry man, a killer and one of great betrayals, and according to the nature of Mars. And commingle with them the nature of the planet which it aspects from its own house, with a better aspect.

Chapter VII.58: On tearing down the forts and estates of enemies[467]

You should begin an election for tearing down the forts of enemies by the contrary of the beginning of buildings, which we stated [before],[468] neither more nor less. And you should make the Ascendant be an airy sign or a fiery one, and the Moon and the lord of the Ascendant should be in such signs.

And al-Tabarī said,[469] the Ascendant should be a sign of straight ascensions, and the lord of the Ascendant should be western;[470] ascending after the Ascendant,[471] diminished in motion, and applying to such a planet, while [itself] going toward its [own] fall, and [it should be] remote from the angle (but it should not be retrograde).

And, however, it is good that the Moon should be eastern and diminished in motion and light, and remote from an angle, and applying to a planet which is likewise remote and even going toward its fall or toward the fall of the Moon.

And if the Moon were above the earth, make it so that she would apply to a planet which is below the earth, nor should the lord of the Ascendant be

---

467 Cf. al-'Imrānī II.1.5.

468 Cf. VII.20.3 above, and al-'Imrānī's own II.1.3-4.

469 I am not currently sure how much of the following really belongs to al-Tabarī.

470 This probably means that it should be about to "sink" under the rays of the Sun. Being "western" and "sinking" is the same word in Latin and Arabic.

471 Reading with al-'Imrānī for "and the first planet which has the Ascendant after [its] ascending."

retrograde. And it is good that this should happen in the last quarter of the [Lunar] month, and the Moon should not aspect the lord of her own house, nor the Sun.

And this election is for the fort of an enemy, and with such an election you will be strengthened with respect to the fort and you will destroy it. But if it were another destruction, or by other means, an easier election could come to be by looking at and improving the root of the elections just as we have stated in all matters.[472]

Chapter VII.59: On making arms and clever devices for subduing enemies—namely galleys and other vessels of the sea[473]

In this it is appropriate that the Ascendant be a fixed sign; and if all four angles were fixed signs and of straight ascensions, it will be better. And it is good that the Moon and the lord of the Ascendant be in the angles, and that there be a powerful and eastern fortune in the Midheaven, and in its own dignities, and with a quick motion; and that the Moon be in her own greater motion.

And make Mars fit, as much as you can.

And likewise make the lord of the conjunction or prevention which was before the deed, fit; and that the first application which the Moon made after her separation from the said conjunction or prevention, should be to a fortune.

And if the lord of the Ascendant were entering an angle, it will be good. And it is good that it should aspect the fourth house, because the fourth house is the place of the ship and what is likened to that; afterwards, it is good to improve the fourth house and to put a fixed[474] sign there.

And other sages[475] say that it is good in this that the Moon should be in Taurus or Gemini, because the shape and form of a brook is in these signs.[476] And in this you should beware of the aspects of Mars.

And it is good that the Moon should be above the earth.[477]

---

472 What al-Rijāl might be getting at is al-'Imrānī's comment, that all of this is important for *permanently* destroying a fort. But if one did not want to go through all of this trouble with a difficult election, one should choose an easier election that follows general rules.

473 Cf. al-'Imrānī II.1.7, though most all of this is based on *Forty Chapters* Ch. 17.

474 Al-'Imrānī reads, "watery."

475 Cf. *Carmen* V.23.3-4.

476 The constellation Eridanus.

And when you wanted to put these ships in the water, look at the other such election, to see how it is.[478]

Chapter VII.60: On a partnership, and every matter which comes to be between two people

A[479] general statement in every matter which there is between two people, is that the Ascendant is the significator of the one initiating the matter, and the seventh house the significator of the other; and the tenth belongs to what passes between the two (and if it were a squabble, it will likewise be the significator of victory); and the fourth house the end of the matter. Likewise, the Moon is the significator of what passes between them, and the planet from which the Moon is being separated, is the significator of the one who initiates, and the planet to which the Moon applies [is] the significator of the other one. And the lord of the fourth house [is] the significator of the end. And you should look to see which one (namely, [which] house) the lord of the Midheaven aspects more and with a better aspect: that of the Ascendant, or of the seventh, and in which one of those two houses it has greater dignities, and judge that that one will be more supported in the matter.

However,[480] in a partnership or association, it is good that the Ascendant be a common sign, and the Moon in a common sign. And Leo is good in this matter, because the Sun and his house are good in an association, since the Sun gives a portion from his own light to the Moon and the other planets.

And it is not good in this that the Moon be in the Ascendant in movable signs, unless in Capricorn alone (because it is good in this), nor in the fixed signs (unless in Leo alone, because it is good in this).

And the application of [an infortune][481] to the Moon or the lord of the Ascendant will be abhorred, and especially if it were Mars.

---

477 This resembles *Forty Chapters* Ch. 17, §490, except that the phrase used in Hugo's version typically means being in one's own apogee.

478 This is probably Ch. VII.76 below. See also *Carmen* V.25.

479 Cf. al-'Imrānī II.8.1, and *On Elect.* §34.

480 Cf. al-'Imrānī II.8.2, and *Carmen* V.19.1-16.

481 Adding and slightly changing the reading based on *Carmen* V.19.15-16: the al-Rijāl text originally read, "the application of the Moon to the lord of the Ascendant."

Chapter VII.61: On searching for a fugitive[482]

An election for searching for a fugitive should be looked at for the most part just as it is looked at in an election for enemies. Whence, if [the fugitive] were of the manner of one who has been made a rebel, you should take the election just as we have stated [before]: from the seventh house and its lord and from the Moon, by weakening and making them be cadent, according to the constellations which we have said before.[483] However, if the fugitive were of the other [kinds of] enemies,[484] you should take an election in this from the twelfth house and its lord. And if the fugitive were not of these two types, you should look in this just as we have said before.

Al-Khayyāt said,[485] the Moon should be applying to the infortunes, nor should you put her, nor the planet to which she applies, in the fourth house.

Māshā'allāh[486] agrees that the lord of the Ascendant and the lord of the seventh should be applying, one to the other; and he says that if the Moon were applying to some planet in the twelfth or sixth house, it signifies that the fugitive will be destroyed and lost.

Chapter VII.62: On making a robber reveal [what we are seeking][487]

Abu Ma'shar said that it is good in this that the Moon and the planet to which the Moon applies, be in rational signs, of human forms; and in this he spoke well and had a good opinion.

And I say that likewise it is good in this that these and the Ascendant be in signs of straight ascensions, so that they would confess the truth and not something else.

---

482 Cf. al-'Imrānī II.13.3.

483 See Ch. VII.57a. In this case, al-Rijāl imagines that the client is initiating a search for the rebel, so the client gets the Ascendant (whereas in cases of rebellions, the rebel initiated the conflict and so got the Ascendant).

484 Al-'Imrānī says, "for the purpose of killing the fugitive." That is, for people who are not opponents in direct conflict, but someone you want to hunt down.

485 Cf. *On Elect.* §142, and see al-'Imrānī II.13.3.

486 Source unknown at this time.

487 Cf. al-'Imrānī II.13.4.

Chapter VII.63: On hunting by land and by water[488]

When you wanted to have an election for this, you should put the Moon in Taurus or its triplicity.

[Hunting land animals]

And the sages said that it is appropriate for one who wanted to hunt over land, that he should put the Moon in Aries, Leo, or Sagittarius, applying to Mars from a trine or sextile with reception: because this signifies that he will have whatever he wanted from the hunt; and that the dogs and other beasts with which he hunts (in whatever kind of hunt it was) will be strengthened.

And when you wished to hunt [by land], it is appropriate that you apply the Moon to fortunes, and you put a fortune[489] in the Ascendant, [but] an infortune in the seventh, and that the infortune should be Mars because he signifies blood; however, if that infortune were Saturn, it signifies that they will see the prey but will not capture it.

But in hunting by water, you should attend so that the Moon is in the Midheaven, applying to Venus in the seventh house: because this signifies that they will capture whatever they wanted.

However, if you wanted to hunt beasts having claws like foxes, wolves,[490] and what is like these, do it in this so that the Moon is received by Mars, and one of them is in the Midheaven.

However, if it were your intention to get little beasts like hares, boars, and what is like this, you should beware as much as you can lest Mars be in one of the angles, because if he were there the hunter will not be safe, but the stated little beast will do evil to him.

And likewise it is the worst in this that the Ascendant should be of the four-footed signs (which are Aries, Leo, Sagittarius), because this signifies that the little beast will kill a rider belonging to the hunter. And if the Moon were made unfortunate by Mars in the Ascendant, it signifies the same (and I have experienced it many times). Nor have I ever seen a hunter who left on a hunt with Taurus or Gemini or Scorpio ascending who caught anything, even

---

488 Al-'Imrānī II.1.11 has material on hunting, but it is rather different and much shorter.

489 Or perhaps, "the" fortune to which the Moon is applying?

490 I have switched *lepores* ("hares") here with *lupi* ("wolves") below, because wolves are more like foxes than hares are, and wolves are not little beasts.

though he had good dogs and the like, and he was a good hunter. And everyone whom I have seen leave on a hunt with Taurus ascending, I have never seen it but that he entered *latorinas*[491] or rough places and high ones, of a type that he was not able to have the prey. And everyone I have seen leave on a hunt with Capricorn ascending, I have seen that the prey was concealed from them in *sarcialibus*[492] or rough places, so that they were not able to have it.

[Hunting birds]

All of this which we have said up to now, is for hunting wild beasts, especially four-footed ones. However, if it were your intention to hunt birds, a good election in this is that the Moon be in one of the airy signs (which are Gemini, Libra, and Aquarius), and she should be applying to Mercury, and Mercury strong, receiving the Moon: because this signifies that he will capture whatever of the birds he wanted.

However, for quail and large partridges, it is particularly appropriate that you apply the Moon to Mercury and Venus both. However, for other birds an application of the Moon to one of them suffices (namely, to Mercury or to Venus), with the Moon appearing in airy signs just as we said before. When the Moon was in these signs, and she were applying to Saturn, he will not catch the prey which he wants, but rather he will perhaps capture some owl or bad bird in which there is no usefulness. However, when hunting *aygrovuum*[493] or *astardam*,[494] it is the best it could be that Mercury be with Mars.

However, for hunting ducks and other aquatic birds, it is appropriate that the Moon be in an airy sign, applying to a planet appearing in a watery sign, because there is a good election in this which signifies that you will catch whatever you wanted.

However, in hunting with a hawk, it is more true in this that the Moon should be in Gemini. And in hunting with sparrowhawks or *siverilis*,[495] it is

---

491 Unknown, but perhaps a misread for *lapicidinas*, "stone quarry" (which would make sense as Taurus is an earthy sign).

492 Unknown. But it is probably related to *sario*, a medieval verb having to do with clearing uncultivated land that has many thickets or underbrush.

493 Unknown, but note the similarity to *gruem*, "crane." This and the next word might refer to hunting birds that live on the edge of the water.

494 Unknown, but note the similarity to *astur*, "hawk." It might also be *astariam*, referring to hunting on a flat plain adjacent to a sea.

495 Unknown at this time.

more true in this that the Moon be in Aquarius, applying to Mars from the trine or sextile.

[Fishing]

However, what is better in hunting by sea is that the Moon be in Cancer, going towards Jupiter, with Jupiter appearing in Pisces: for this is the best election which could be had in hunting by sea, since it signifies that he will catch much. And if Jupiter were eastern, he will catch tiny fish; and if western, thick fish. And in every hunt by water, look at the applications of the Moon to Venus, because there is likewise much good in this.

[Training animals to hunt]

And if you wanted to teach dogs to hunt, you should look in this so that the Moon is in Aries, conjoined to Mars: because this signifies that they will learn well how to hunt, and they will kill well; but if Jupiter did not aspect, it signifies that the dogs will harm the prey, and if Jupiter did aspect, they will save them.

And if you wanted to teach leopards, consider in this that the Moon should be in Leo, applying to a Mars which is appearing in Aries: because this election is the best that could be had, for it signifies that they will be powerful in hunting and in saving the prey. And if in this the Moon were in Leo, while applying to Mars, and Mars in Scorpio, it signifies that the leopards will catch the prey with much pain and labor, and they will not save it.

And if you wanted to teach hawks or sparrowhawks or falcons, you should look in this to see that the Moon be in Aquarius, applying to Mars, and Mars in Scorpio: because that is a better and stronger election in this.

[Other advice]

And if, on a hunt, the Moon applied to a retrograde planet, it signifies that he will catch nothing, and will have pain and labor on the hunt. And if the Moon were in the Ascendant, it signifies great nimbleness in hunting. And when Mars was in the Midheaven, it signifies that the birds and beasts with which one hunts will [be lost].[496] And if the Moon were in the Midheaven, made unfortunate by Mars, it signifies that the hunter will lose the hawk and will go to seek him.

It is appropriate for him who wanted to hunt with an eagle in particular, that the Moon be in Aries, applying to a Mars which is appearing in Capricorn, because the Moon signifies that he will hunt through the land and air as much as he wanted.

And generally on every hunt, a good election is that the Ascendant be a movable sign, and the Moon in the Midheaven, made fortunate by Jupiter, and Jupiter in the Ascendant, and Mars in the seventh house, and Saturn cadent (or he should not aspect the Ascendant); and Venus in the Ascendant or Midheaven, and with the Moon applying to her: because [for] the one who rode out to hunt with such a constellation, his riders will be strengthened, and the animals with which he hunts will be happy, and he will capture whatever he wanted, nor will it annoy him, nor will he nor his riders be tired out, nor his associates, and he will return sound and cheerful, without being worn out and [any] other irritation.

Chapter VII.64: On playing at board games, chess, dice, and what is like that

If you wanted, at the beginning of a game, that the game would be broken up quickly,[497] you will make the Ascendant a movable sign, and [put] the Moon likewise in a movable sign. And if you wanted the game to last, make the Ascendant a fixed sign, and likewise [put] the Moon in a fixed sign.

And if the Moon applied to fortunes, the one who first plays will make a profit; and if it applied to a fortune and afterwards to an infortune, it signifies that the one who first plays at the beginning will make a profit, and afterwards he will lose. And if she applied to infortunes, the one who plays first will lose, and if she applied to infortunes and after that to fortunes, he will lose at the beginning and afterwards make a profit.

And for playing chess in particular, it is good that the Moon apply to Mercury, and afterwards to Mars (who is of a different form in chess),[498] and

[496] Reading a version of *perdo* ("to lose") in the context of the next sentence, for *expergetur* ("will be woken up").

[497] *Cito separetur.*

[498] I am not sure what this means.

that both should receive the Moon. And if the Ascendant were a common sign, it signifies that neither one will make profit, nor the other.

And in playing at dice, it is good that the Moon should apply to Venus or Mercury.

And if there were a fortune in the Ascendant, the one beginning the game will make a profit; and if in addition there were an infortune in the seventh, the other will lose much.

And if the lord of the Ascendant were in the Midheaven, the one who begins will make profit; and if the lord of the Ascendant aspected the lord of the seventh from the opposition, it signifies that one will steal from the other. And if the Moon will be separated from Mercury and applied to the lord of the Ascendant, it will happen to the one beginning the game that it is revealed to him; and if the Moon will be separated from Mercury and applied to the lord of the seventh, it will happen to the other that it is revealed to him.

And if the lord of the Ascendant were retrograde, it signifies that the one beginning will play with fraud. And if the lord of the Ascendant and the lord of the seventh were both strengthened in the Midheaven, it signifies that they will leave the game equally.[499]

And if Mercury were in the Ascendant and the Moon with him, it signifies that they will have many words and discussions about the game. And if Mars were in the Ascendant, it signifies that in that game many lies will be spoken. And if Saturn were in the Ascendant, one will not make profit from the other, and they will separate from the game, being bored. And if Jupiter were in the Ascendant, they will separate themselves with anger.[500] And if Venus were in the Ascendant, they will separate themselves, being cheerful and of good will. And if the Moon were in the Ascendant, it signifies that the one who ought to profit will make [his] profit quickly. And if you played with the Moon in the Ascendant, you should beware lest you begin the game, because they will quickly profit from you.

And if the Ascendant were a common sign, and the lord of the Ascendant in a common sign, it signifies that other people, after that game, will play in the same game after them.[501]

---

499 I take this to mean they will each lose and win to roughly an equal degree.

500 *Cum ira.* But this would probably read, "without anger."

501 Note how this follows from the description of common signs in VII.3.1, based on *On Elect.* §16a*ff.*

And Māshā'allāh said,[502] when you wanted to play a game, look to see in what direction the Moon is, whether in the east or west or in the south or north, and you should place yourself to sit so that your face is opposite[503] the face of the Moon, and you will make profit. And you should know that the east aids the north, and the west [aids] the south. And likewise, if you saw two people playing, and you wanted to know which of them will profit, look to see which one of them held his face opposite the face of the Moon: because he will profit.

However,[504] in games of "shingles,"[505] or everything which is cast forth, you should look in this so that the Moon is in movable signs, and you should beware of Taurus or the common signs. And it is good that the Moon applies to fortunes. And if she applied to Mars from some place in which he had a triplicity,[506] it is likewise good. And you should beware in this lest Saturn have some commingling [with her].

And when you wanted to win, do for yourself what I told you about dice, and draw your face toward the direction in which the Moon was. And when you go out of your home in order to go to the game, in this way make the lord of the Ascendant be applying to the fortunes, and that it is in the Midheaven or in the eleventh house, and in addition to all of this you should put it above the earth, free from the infortunes and from burning: because when you will have done this, you will profit.

Chapter VII.65: On lying down with women

When you wanted to lie down with women, you should look into those signs which have delight in that business, which are: Aries, Capricorn, Leo, and Libra, because these signify great power in this, and because they[507] will not cease.

And if in addition the Moon applied to Venus and Mars, it will be better, because Venus signifies the joy which they will have with one another, and

---

[502] Source unknown at this time. But compare this with VII.57.1 above, in the context of rebellions.

[503] *Contra.* That is, you should sit opposite the Moon, facing her.

[504] For this paragraph, cf. al-'Imrānī II.1.13.

[505] *Scindulae.* This probably refers to games like dominoes, in which tiles are played onto the table.

[506] Al-'Imrānī has her aspecting him from a trine.

[507] I believe this means the women involved will not want to stop having sex.

delightful ways,[508] and Mars signifies much sperm. And you should beware lest the Moon apply to Saturn, because he signifies coldness, tedium, and an abhorrence of the deed. And if the Moon applied to the Sun with reception, it signifies great delight and the appropriateness of both [partners] in this matter. And you should beware lest the Moon be in Pisces, because it signifies that infirmities will happen there. And if the Moon were in Gemini, Libra, [or] Aquarius (which are the human signs), it is good in this because it signifies delight and joy. And if the Moon applied to Jupiter, it signifies that the woman will defend herself from the business by reason of the law.

And if you wanted to lie down with a woman so that she would not conceive, put the Moon in Gemini, Leo, or Virgo,[509] and so that she would apply to Venus, and not have an aspect towards Jupiter. And beware, when you wanted to lie down with a woman so that she would not conceive, lest the Moon be in Cancer, Scorpio, or Pisces (and these are the signs of many children). And if the Moon aspected Mars, the generation [of children] will be prohibited.

And if Venus were in the Ascendant, in Libra or Pisces, he will have much joy and delight. And if Saturn were in the seventh, it will happen that it will make them discordant.

---

508 *Rationes.*

509 These are the so-called "sterile" or "barren" signs.

THE EIGHTH HOUSE

Chapter VII.66: On the eighth house and its elections

The elections which are in this house are: the testaments of death,[510] and inspecting the situation of inheritances.

Chapter VII.67: On a testament of death[511]

For one who wants to make his [last] testament, it is appropriate that he not do it when the Ascendant and the Moon were in movable signs,[512] because this signifies that the testament will not be observed.

However, in this it is good that the Moon be deficient in number and increasing in light, and that she does not apply to a planet appearing under the rays: because it signifies that he will quickly die.

And [it is] especially [bad] if the Moon were conjoined to Mars (nor should she be in his square nor opposition). Nor should Mars be in the Ascendant, nor should he aspect it by a bad aspect: because it signifies that the man will not[513] change the testament, and that he will die from that infirmity, nor will testament be observed, or it will be lost or stolen. However, if Saturn had the constellations with the Ascendant and the Moon which we have said about Mars, it signifies that the man lives so far,[514] and that the testament will be guarded and observed in his life and even after his death.[515]

---

510 That is, one's last will and testament.

511 Cf. *On Elect.* §§97a-100, and *Carmen* V.42 (on which this is directly based).

512 There seems to be a difference in the concept of the election, between *Carmen* and al-Rijāl. *Carmen* seems to imagine someone on his deathbed, so one worries as to whether a sick person will be able to finish the will. Therefore, V.42.1 says one *should* use movable signs, because it shows that the will is quickly changed according to his wishes. But al-Rijāl seems to imagine a healthier person, since he is more worried about someone changing or challenging the will much later on—therefore he counsels *against* movable signs, in favor of fixed signs that will make the will last. It is also possible that al-Rijāl is indirectly drawing on Māshā'allāh's version of Dorotheus, and not 'Umar's.

513 Based on *Carmen* V.42.4, this seems to mean that the man will never *finish* changing it, before he dies.

514 That is, he will live longer and not succumb to whatever illness has led him to make the will.

515 Again, a difference between *Carmen* V.42.6 and al-Rijāl. *Carmen* is worried that Saturn will create a delay so that the partial changes are not considered valid after he dies, whereas al-Rijāl believes Saturn will make the changes last.

And if Jupiter or Venus were with the Moon and with the lord of the Ascendant in such constellations, it signifies that he who makes the testament should live thus far, and that afterwards he will make another testament.

And in making it so that the testament is firm, it is good that the Ascendant and its lord and the Moon are in firm, fixed signs, because it signifies the firmness of the testament.

Chapter VII.68: On the situation of what is left by the dead[516]

In this, it is appropriate that you put one of the houses of Venus or Jupiter in the eighth house, and that the house and its lord are safe from the infortunes, and that that same lord of the eighth is in a succeedent. And if it were in the second house it will be better, while the eighth and its lord are appearing safe as we have said before.

And it will be good that the degree of the eighth house is the bound of Jupiter or Venus, if you could [do that], and that [the Moon][517] should aspect the lord of the eighth house from a good aspect.

[516] Cf. al-'Imrānī II.9. I am not exactly sure what kind of election this is.
[517] Adding based on al-'Imrānī.

THE NINTH HOUSE

Chapter VII.69: On the ninth house and its elections

The elections which are in this house are: on the election of journeys and for journeys of transporting [goods], on journeys from which a man wants to return quickly, on journeys which a man wants to make in secret, on journeys by water, on buying a ship and boarding it, and on making it be moved, on putting a ship in the water, on teaching the sciences and masteries, on teaching singing and types of jokes, [and] on the entrance to a city for one who has come from a journey.

Chapter VII.70.0: On an election for travel

[Chapter VII.70.1: Travel according to Sahl][518]

It is appropriate for any man that he should not initiate a journey unless it is according to his nativity and according to the revolution of his year, or according to the Ascendant of the figure of his question (if he did not have his nativity).[519] And according to this, make the Moon and the Ascendant of the nativity fit, or the Ascendant of the revolution or of his question, and adapt the house in which is the matter for which he goes.

And you should beware lest his Ascendant be cadent according to the Ascendant of his departure. And if his journey were to the king, make the tenth of his nativity the Ascendant of the departure. And if it were for merchant dealings, make the eleventh of his nativity the Ascendant of the departure. And thus for the others, according to this method. And you should make the house in which his question was,[520] the ascending sign of his departure.

---

518 For this subchapter, cf. *On Elect.* §101*ff.* But some of the statements below are in parallel to *Carmen*, suggesting that perhaps this passage is from al-Khayyāt.

519 Another clear reference to the doctrine of the "root" in elections, suggesting that elections must be based on a root such as a nativity (and its revolution) or a valid horary chart that shows success.

520 That is, based on what kind of question it is: such as getting something from the king, which would make the house of the question the tenth (as he just stated).

And[521] it is good that the Moon be in the tenth or fifth,[522] aspecting the lord of her own house. And you should beware lest she be made unfortunate, nor should she be aspected by the infortunes, and you should make her fortunate by fortunes that are strengthened.

And[523] let her be increasing in number, and [let] Mercury have escaped from the rays, and be safe from the infortunes. And you should beware lest the Moon be in the sixth or twelfth, because it signifies harm and delay on the journey. And if the Moon were increasing in light, it signifies that he will quickly apply to the place to which he wants to go, safe and calm. And if the Moon or Saturn or both were in the Ascendant or in the seventh, or one of them in the Ascendant and the other in the seventh, infirmities (especially quarrels, killings, and losses) will happen [to him] on the journey or in the place to which he goes.

[Chapter VII.70.2: The Ascendant of the departure, according to the Indians][524]

And the sages of India say that for him who departs on a journey, and the Ascendant was Aries, robbers will oppose [him], but if he attacks them he will conquer. And if the departure were for going to besiege a fort or city, he will capture it.

And if the Ascendant were Taurus at the hour of the departure, he will gain cattle, goats, pigs, deer and what is like that, and precious stones.

And he who went out with the Ascendant being Gemini, will gain arms or slaves knowing [various] masteries.

And with Cancer ascending, he will be safe and sound and well fortunate in matters, and in all of his deeds.

And with Leo ascending, he will conquer and profit, and evil will come to another instead of[525] him.

---

[521] For this paragraph and the next, cf. the opinion of al-Hasan bin Sahl below.
[522] Al-Rijāl is excerpting a little bit here, since Sahl says both that the Moon should be angular, and that the fourth house is bad (and so one should prefer the fifth).
[523] For this paragraph, cf. *Carmen* V.12.2-7.
[524] Source unknown at this time, but the listing of signs like this sounds like Dorotheus.
[525] *Pro.* This might also include people working for him, or other people in his presence.

And with Virgo ascending, he will be lively and will gain slaves.

And with Libra ascending, he will be middling in good and evil.

And with Scorpio ascending, he will labor and will not have what he seeks, and sorrows will happen to him; afterwards, he will gain a little bit of profit.

And with Sagittarius ascending, he will apply himself to what he wanted, and will gain horses and arms, and will do things from which he will have great income.

And with Capricorn ascending, he will be weary and will be irritated, nor will he have what he wants, and he will gain mistakes[526] and will receive irritation from enemies.

[*Aquarius missing*]

And with Pisces ascending, he will gain precious stones and will have what he wants, and will be sound in his body.

[Chapter VII.70.3: Further advice]

Zaradusht said, the Ascendant of the one who makes the journey is at the point when he exits his own home, and the Ascendant of the entrance of one traveling is at the point when his vision falls upon or sees, his own house.

Al-Hasan bin Sahl said,[527] a better election for undertaking a journey is that the Moon should be increasing in light and number, free from the infortunes, and she should not be in the second house, nor the eighth, nor the sixth, nor the twelfth; and she should be aspected by fortunes, and Mercury should have escaped from burning and be free from the infortunes; and the lord of the Ascendant should not be burned up, nor made unfortunate, and let it be in a good place of the figure; and there should be a fortune in the Ascendant or in one of the angles: because such an election signifies the sal-

[526] Or, "offenses" (*peccata*).

[527] For this paragraph, cf. *Carmen* V.21.2-5 and 8.

vation of the body, nimbleness, or joy on the journey, good trust, and applying himself to what he wants.

And if you were not able to have all of this, you should make the Moon be aspecting the Ascendant, and likewise the lord of the Ascendant, and they should both be safe from the infortunes. And if the Moon were conjoined to Jupiter or Venus by body, or in their aspects by trine or sextile, it is the best that it could be.

And Ptolemy said,[528] when the Moon is being separated from the degree of the conjunction of the Sun, and suddenly she aspects with Saturn from a trine or sextile, and after him she aspected with some fortune, it signifies that matters which will be undertaken in that time, will be completed, and they will be lasting, and its owner will rejoice in them, and they will last for as long as are the lesser years of the Moon,[529] in terms of the number of years or months or days. And if this [period] passed by,[530] they will last for as long as are the lesser years of Saturn[531] (likewise in the number of years, months, or days): and this, because the Moon would be applying to Saturn at the beginning of the month.[532]

[Chapter VII.70.4: Additional material from Sahl][533]

And[534] you should know that the Ascendant is the significator of the estate from which he who makes the journey, has separated himself. And the seventh is the significator of the land to which he goes. And the tenth [is] the significator of the path or journey while withdrawing from his own home. And the fourth house [is] the significator of the journey on his return to his own home. Whence, that one of these places which was improved, signifies goodness in its signification; and that one of them which was harmed, signifies harm in its signification.

---

528 A pseudo-Ptolemy, perhaps inspired by *Cent.* #93. But it does not sound like a paragraph that belongs here.

529 That is, 25.

530 That is, if the relevant period passed by and the successful situation were still in effect.

531 That is, 30.

532 Because if the Moon had applied to Saturn while waning (after the opposition of the Sun at the Full Moon), Saturn would create problems because he would add to the signification of cold and decay which the waning Moon already signifies.

533 Cf. generally al-'Imrānī II.1.8.

534 For this paragraph, cf. *On Quest.* §9.1 (*Judges* §9.1), and *Carmen* V.21.1.

And[535] you should beware lest the Moon be conjoined with infortunes by body, nor in their square or opposite aspect: because the aspects of the infortunes to the Ascendant introduces less evil than those to the Moon do: and this is particularly [so] in journeys, because the aspect of the Moon to Mars at the beginning of the [Lunar] month signifies robbers and harm on the part of a king.

And beware lest you ever put the Moon in the fourth house, because there she is the worse; but you should put her in the fifth, because it signifies great fortune, and that he will quickly return from his travel and will have what he wanted; and good successes, and many profits, and good health and safety of the body, and nimbleness in his deeds. Likewise, the Moon is liable to be abhorred in the Ascendant, both in the entrance and in the departure: because it signifies infirmity and great labor on the journey.

And[536] if you wanted to go to the king, you should apply the Moon to the Sun, [with him being] in a good place of the figure (in the Ascendant, tenth, or eleventh): because if he were cadent, [the client] will have no good. And likewise, if he were in the seventh or fifth, it signifies labor and a modicum of good. And if he were in the west or fourth, it signifies a modicum of good, and great and long labor. And if you wanted to go to noble men or advocates or judges or men of the law, you should apply the Moon to Jupiter, with Jupiter being in the angles or in a good place of the figure, just as we said about the Sun. And if you wanted to go to men who are put in charge, or men of arms or squabbles, you would apply the Moon to Mars from a trine or sextile: however, you should beware of his conjunction, nor should you put him in an angle, but put him in a succeedent.[537] And if you wanted to go to old men or men of low stock, apply the Moon to Saturn from the trine or sextile, nor should you put him in an angle, but in a succeedent. And if your departure were to women, you would apply the Moon to a Venus who is appearing in a masculine sign; and if you could, put the Moon in the places we said about Jupiter. And if your departure were to writers and merchants or sages, you would apply the Moon to Mercury, and see that Mercury is not under the rays nor retrograde, nor aspecting the infortunes: because when the planet to which the Moon applies, or who aspects the Ascendant, or the lord of the

---

535 For the rest of this subchapter, cf. *On Elect.* §§105a-13b (as well as *On Quest.* §9.1 or *Judges* §9.11).

536 Al-'Imrānī II.1.8 attributes this material to al-Khayyāt.

537 This could be the whole-sign angles and succeedents of the *Moon*, not the houses themselves.

seventh, were slow in motion or retrograde or made unfortunate, it signifies hardship and regret on the journey.

Chapter VII.71: On journeys for reasons of touring around[538]

For one wanting to make a journey on the occasion of walking around, it is appropriate that you should make the Moon be separated from a fortune and applying to a fortune: because this is good, and signifies that he will be happy with those whom he will encounter, nor will he have sorrows from those whom he will leave behind him.

And if it happened that the Moon is in the Midheaven, he will be honored on his tour, and be glad, and he will rejoice in the places in which he enters, and in the places through which he will pass.

And if the Moon were void in course at the hour in which he moved himself to go touring, and after her departure from that sign and entrance to the next she applied to Venus by aspect or conjunction, it signifies that he moves himself by touring or having fun, but he does not have great delight in that tour or entertainment, and after he entered into it and had associates and joking people, he will be cheerful in his own entertainment.

And if, in his departure to the special and noted place, the Moon and the Ascendant were in common signs, and the Moon applied to a fortune, and there were a fortune in the Ascendant,[539] it signifies that he will rejoice in the place to which he goes, and that he will be change from that place to another in which he will be happy and will tour around more so than in the first [place].

And he who moved himself by going touring with the Moon appearing in an earthy sign and applying to Venus, and the Ascendant is likewise an earthy sign, and the Moon and Venus both aspecting the Ascendant, he will have many comforts, and many places, and good sights. And if the Ascendant were a fixed sign, he will tour around in beautiful labors and the works of palaces, and his entertainment will have a good end.

---

538 *Spaciandi*, which really means to promenade and walk around, but also suggests spreading out and getting more space. This chapter seems to be about going on vacations and adventures for fun.

539 Or perhaps, "and *the* fortune were in the Ascendant," namely the one to which the Moon is applying.

And he who went out touring with the Moon being conjoined with Mars by body, or applying to him from a bad aspect, will stumble or fall on the journey, and he will go through heights and valleys.

And in this, the worst which it could be in moving for touring around, is that the Moon would be aspecting Saturn in any manner, because it signifies that he will be solitary and sad. And in this, it is even bad that the Moon would be separating herself from a fortune and applying to an infortune, because this signifies that he will have greater fun in the place from which he has separated, than in the place to which he goes.

However, for one who wants to go touring by water, it is appropriate that you put the Ascendant in a watery sign upon his entrance into the water, and that Venus would be in the Ascendant or in the Midheaven. And if you wanted to remain on the water very much and to go by it for a long time, you should make the Ascendant a fixed sign, and the Moon in the Midheaven, because this signifies that you will last long on the water and will have good going and good winds. And if Venus were applied with the Moon from a common sign, men who will join themselves with them on his journey, will rejoice with them. And if you wanted it that the journey would not be prolonged, nor that it would last long upon the water, you should make the Ascendant a movable sign, and some fortune in it, and you should beware lest an infortune be in it: for if a fortune were there, it signifies that they will go out from thence, sound and happy; and if there were an infortune there, perhaps they will go out from thence while fleeing with fear. And if it were Mars in the Ascendant, it signifies that anger will happen, and they will not have pure wills, one to the other.

And for him who wanted to go touring by land, you should make the Ascendant an earthy sign, and let there be a fortune in it. And if you wanted that the journey should last, make the Ascendant a movable sign, because it is better for moving; however, if you wanted to stay and rest there, you should especially make the Ascendant a fixed sign: and that is good for lasting and for having wideness and breadth in touring around.

And if he wanted it to last enough in his travels,[540] and to be sound, safe, and secure, you should put Jupiter in the Ascendant or Midheaven, because he is a weighty planet and signifies staying, being safe, good, and fortune.

---

[540] *Deporto*, here and below. I am not wholly confident about this translation, since *deporto* and *deportum*, normally have to do with burdens, but also carrying something away: perhaps we are to think of someone traveling with many bags.

And for one who wanted to have many joys on his travels, nor that he should have sorrow on it, nor weariness, you should put Venus in the Ascendant or Midheaven.

And he who went out for touring around, and the Ascendant was a watery sign, and the Moon in the Ascendant and Venus in the Midheaven, it could not be but that he would have hindrances by reason of rains and waters. And the best thing which there could be in going touring, is that the Moon would be separated from Venus, [and] void in course, nor that she would have an application unless it is in the next sign, and that application is then likewise to Venus: because if it were so, it signifies that the travels will be prolonged, in good, joy, and vices. And when he will separate herself from that trip and enter into another, [he will have] comfort and joy with women, or with what is like that, with respect to which he will enjoy himself, by the will of God.

Chapter VII.72: For one who wanted to return quickly from his journey[541]

When you wanted this, put Jupiter in the square of the Sun and Venus in its sextile or joined with her,[542] and you should put the Moon between the fortunes, separating herself from one and applying to the other, and that she should be increased in light and number: because this signifies that he will return quickly, safe and with profit.

Chapter VII.73: On journeys which a man wants to make in secret

Ptolemy said,[543] in such a matter you should put the Moon so that she is under the rays of the Sun, separated from the Sun and applying to a fortune, and free of the infortunes—and especially so that they are not in her angles: because they harm her much.

541 Cf. the end of al-'Imrānī II.1.8, who attributes this to al-Tabarī; it is loosely based on *Carmen* V.22.

542 Al-Rijāl has Venus and Jupiter in the square of both of the luminaries; I am not sure which planet al-Rijāl means by "its" here.

543 Source unknown at this time, but cf. *On Elect.* §120b and 141a. For this topic, cf. *Carmen* V.5.4 and V.35. This election essentially tries to recreate the situation of a thief who successfully steals and is not caught.

And *Nimagest* said,[544] when you wanted to make some business of yours private, and so that it would never be uncovered nor appear, you should begin it when the Moon is in Scorpio and under the earth.

And others said,[545] it is good in this that the Moon should be under the rays of the Sun; however, if she were separated just as Ptolemy said, [let her be] applying to fortunes, and free from the infortunes.

And al-Hasan bin Sahl said,[546] when you wanted to do some thing in secret and concealed, you should put the Moon or the lord of the Ascendant under the rays of the Sun, not burned up, but remote from the body of the Sun, and made fortunate and safe from the infortunes, nor should the Moon nor the Sun aspect the Ascendant, nor should one aspect the other from any aspect.

And if you wanted safety in that matter, make the lord of the Ascendant fortunate, and the Moon, with them being under the rays, and so that one of them is aspected by the fortunes. And if the business you wanted was for doing harm, you should make them unfortunate.

And always, if the Moon and the significator of the matter were in the angle of the earth or under the earth, they signify hidden things.

Chapter VII.74: On journeys by water[547]

You should know that for entering upon the water and journeys by water, and in the care of ships, it is necessary to have much consideration and to follow the roots of elections, and to consider the principles of this matter. Because [this] matter is one which cannot be hidden from the sages of this science, since the greater root which is in journeys by sea is [1] the Ascendant in which the [construction of the][548] ship was begun (because it signifies for how much time the ship must last, and what kind of safety that ship will have, and who will go in it.

And I have heard from men whom I believed, and I have seen ships which went by sea for ten years and more, to whom an incident has never

---

544 Unknown at this time, but probably identical to *Minegeth* in VII.47.

545 Cf. *On Elect.* §120b and 141a.

546 Again, cf. *On Elect.* §141a.

547 This chapter seems to reflect al-Rijāl's own experiences and thoughts. But he is also ranking the elections of the following chapters here.

548 Adding based on al-Rijāl's comments below.

happened (nor to those traveling on them), nor any danger. And I have seen other ships to which incidents always happen, through the contrariety of the winds or through encountering enemies, or through some other manner of incident which happens on the sea. And [I have seen] other ships which are destroyed and are lost, as well as everyone who went on them. Whence, what we have said about [1] the start of making the ship, is one root.[549] And the second root is [2] the hour at which the ship is bought.[550] The third root is [3] the hour at which it is put in the water (and this is a strong root).[551] The fourth root is [4] the hour at which the man boards the ship.[552] And the fifth root is [5] the hour at which the ship is moved.[553] And all of these roots must be observed.

And I saw men who boarded a ship with the Moon appearing more fortunate than she could [ever] be, being conjoined to Jupiter by body in Pisces (which is a watery sign), and Venus was aspecting them from a good aspect, and the infortunes were cadent from them: however, it did not happen to them that the ship was moved, because they did not have wind, but after some days they had wind, and they moved on Wednesday, in the third hour of the day,[554] with the Moon[555] appearing in Scorpio, and the Ascendant [in it], and the places of the planets were according to what you see in the figure [below].[556]

And I had seen, in the second part of the *Book of Natures*[557] (which talks about the judgments of hours), that he who goes by sea in the hour of Saturn will die or be lost, or the sea will project him onto land or faraway islands, and by God this happened to that ship just like the book described. Whence,

---

549 See above, Ch. VII.59; also VII.75.2 below.

550 See VII.75 below.

551 See VII.76 below.

552 See below, VII.76.5 (which does not have special instructions).

553 That is, when it leaves the dock and begins the journey. See VII.76.5 below, which does not have special instructions.

554 That is, a couple of hours after sunrise, in the planetary hour of Saturn.

555 This should probably be, "Venus."

556 Unfortunately, 1485 has a blank chart, and 1551 has no chart at all (nor does the Castilian version). Based on the information given, it would have been between September 23 and October 10 in AD 1002 or 1014. But in all but one of these cases, both malefics aspect the Moon-Jupiter combination in Pisces by sign. So until we can get a better manuscript source in Latin or Arabic, even the year will remain unknown.

557 This is the book which al-Rijāl attributes to Abū Ma'shar in VII.100 (probably the *Kitāb al-Tabā'i'*), drawing on its description of planetary house. I have translated VII.100 separately and put it with the material on planetary hours in Part II of this book.

it is appropriate for every astrologer wanting to make an election for going by sea, that he should first look at the election for making the ship, and afterwards when it was bought, and after that when they put it in the water, and after that when they boarded it, and after that when it moves. And if you could not have these elections, one should not get involved in making an election for that ship, because great errors could happen there: because where I saw that ship in the hour of Saturn just as we said, I said to my associate (who understood something of this science), "these men are lost": and once a little bit of time had passed, all lost [their lives].[558]

Chapter VII.75.0: On buying the ship, and boarding it, and moving it

We have already described, in Chapter 59,[559] the election for making a ship; [now] we just want to show the elections for buying a ship and boarding it, and for moving it. And all of these are similar and conjoined, namely one to the other.

[Chapter VII.75.1: Buying or building a ship][560]

Dorotheus said, when you wanted to buy a ship or make it, begin this with Jupiter and Venus appearing in the angle of the earth, in a watery sign or in a sign of the nature of Jupiter or Venus. And good signs for the Moon in this matter are Taurus or Gemini or the beginning of Cancer, or Virgo or Sagittarius or the last degrees of Capricorn (because the beginning of Capricorn is earthy, and its end watery). And if the Moon or the Ascendant were in Pisces, it is best. However, in this the best of all the signs is Taurus, and after that Pisces, and after that Gemini, and after that the last degrees of Capricorn.

---

[558] Note al-Rijāl's shrugging indifference to the deaths of many men. If he had known the electional chart and even knew within an hour when they were setting sail, why didn't he or his friend try to stop them? The charitable thing would be to assume that he came too late to the docks, by which time he could no longer warn them.
[559] That is, VII.59 above.
[560] Cf. *Carmen* V.23.

[Chapter VII.75.2: Building a ship][561]

And after that, it is appropriate that the Sun be in the trine of the fortunes, and the Moon increased in number, motion, and light, and latitude, and aspected by one of the fortunes.

And you should beware lest Mars be aspecting the Ascendant or the Moon, because when Mars harmed one of these, it signifies that the ship will have a bad end on the occasion of fire, or piracy, and what is like these.

And if the ship would be started and the Moon was in Aquarius, and Mars and the Sun were conjoined with her by body or aspecting her from the square or opposite, it signifies that the ship will throw into the water what there is of its cargo in order to liberate the men from death, or it will be burned up in the day, or great harm or great fear will happen to it.

However, if the Moon were not in Aquarius, and she were in a watery sign and in the aspects of the Sun and Mars which we stated before, it signifies that the ship will be lost, and everyone who boarded it, and they will be drowned and will go to the bottom of the earth.

And if the Moon were not in a watery sign, and she were in a dry sign and in the aspects of the Sun and Mars which we said before, it signifies that the ship will be broken [while] on the sea, by striking some rocky cliff, or something likened to that, and it will be lost,[562] and the majority of the things which were on it will be lost.

And if the Moon were not in a dry sign, and she were in a human one and in the aforestated aspects of Mars and the Sun, it signifies that the ship will encounter robbers and enemies who will kill those who are on the ship, so that it is lost and the ship is sunk on that occasion.

---

561 This section is based on *Carmen* V.24.

562 *Expergetur*, but reading as deriving from *perdo*.

Chapter VII.76.0: On putting the ship in the water

[Chapter VII.76.1: Electing by the Moon's sign][563]

If, the hour at which the ship is projected into the water, the Moon were in Aries or the beginning of Aries, and the fortunes aspected her and not the infortunes, it signifies that it will go well and without labor.

And if the Moon were in Taurus just as we said, it signifies that they will have many waves on the sea; and if an infortune aspected her, it signifies that it will be lost.

And if the Moon were in Gemini, with 8° having been passed,[564] it will be good, because it signifies usefulness and a good journey, except that it signifies that they will make a long journey, and will return slowly.

And if the Moon were in Cancer, it signifies that they will have few waves, and that they will go well and will be successful and will profit on that journey.

And if she were in Leo, it signifies that loss will happen to them on the sea; and if the infortunes aspected her there, it signifies losses of diverse kinds.

And if she were in Virgo, it signifies that they will return slowly.

And if they were in Virgo, with 10° having been passed, it signifies that it is not good, because it has a bad signification for journeys on the sea and land.

And if she were in Scorpio, it signifies that they will have a good journey, but some fear will befall them.

And if she were in Sagittarius, it signifies that they will have harm through waves.

And if she were in Capricorn with 9° of it having been passed, it will be good, and it signifies good, but they will have some labor.

And if she were in Aquarius, it signifies that they will delay and will have labor on the journey, but the end will be good.

And if the Moon were in Pisces, it signifies harms and anxieties.

And these aforesaid significations are when the Moon was in signs, not having any aspect of a fortune or infortune.[565]

---

563 Cf. *Carmen* V.25.1-13, and *On Elect.* §§122a-e.

564 These degrees (here and below) may refer to the positions of fixed stars, probably in the Lunar mansions.

[Chapter VII.76.2: Saturn and the Moon, in relation to the horizon][566]

And if the Moon were under the earth with infortunes or fortunes, it is bad: because when she is under the earth, and Saturn (who is weighty) were with her, it signifies that great harms and labors will befall the men who are on that ship, and they will have bad winds and strong waves, and water will enter the ship, and they will die and be lost on account of that. And if the Moon were under the earth and Saturn were stationary, aspecting her from a trine, it signifies that the majority of the things which are carried in the ship will be tossed into the sea in the hope of escaping [the dangers],[567] and after many pains and labors they will be freed. And if the Moon were under the earth, and Saturn aspected her from the trine just as we said, and he were not stationary, it likewise signifies that they will escape after many labors, anxieties, and dangers—however this is less than the other [situation], because when Saturn will be stationary, his aspect is worse. However, if the constellation were just as we said, and Mercury were with Saturn, the harm is diminished and weakened. Likewise, if the fortunes aspected Saturn, his evil and harm is diminished, and especially if the fortunes were in good places, and supported, and aspecting Saturn.

And you should know that when a ship is put in the water, if Saturn were not in the aforesaid constellations [while] harming the Moon as we said before, but it happened that he is in the sign in which he was in the nativity of that man (or in the square or opposite or trine of that same sign), it likewise signifies evil and harm.

And if Mars were just as we said with respect to Saturn, and he were below the earth and the Moon above the earth, and he harming her, it signifies that anxieties will befall the ship, [and] evil and dangers on the occasion of waves and winds, just as we said about Saturn—and more [than that], because quarrels, killings, and malevolence will happen among those who are on the ship, and their enemies will strike at them; and it signifies that they will draw their blood with iron, and what is like that.

---

565 In other words, the fortunes and infortunes which do aspect her will modify these general statements.

566 This section is drawn from *Carmen* V.25.14-27.

567 Reading *evadendi pericula* for *evadendi personas*. But it might also be read as *salvandi personas*, "saving the people [on board]," which amounts to the same thing.

And these significations are worse and associated with it more[568] if Mercury were with Saturn, and Saturn and Mercury both aspected the Moon, and the Moon were below the earth: because such a constellation signifies harm from which no one can escape. And Mars signifies the same when he is with Mercury. And if, [for] Saturn and Mars, one of them aspected the Sun and the other the Moon, it likewise signifies labors and great dangers; and worse if the aspects were from the opposition.

[Chapter VII.76.3: The luminaries and the benefics][569]

Or, if the Sun and Moon were safe from the infortunes, and Jupiter in the square of the Moon, and the ship were put in the sea at that hour, it will be good because it signifies good nimbleness, trust, success, and profits. And if the Sun likewise aspected Jupiter or the Moon or Venus, with Jupiter aspecting the Moon just as we said, it will be better and always more conducive to success. And in all cases, when the Moon was with a planet or aspected it (whether that planet was a fortune or infortune), Mercury will strengthen it in what it was.

And if the Moon were above the earth and Venus alone aspected her,[570] it signifies safety and good, profits and successes, and good fortune which will happen on that journey; however, labors and pains will happen on the occasion of waves and winds, because the aspect of Venus on her own is not like what it is when Venus and Jupiter both aspect (because Venus is weak by herself). And if the Moon and Jupiter were both above the earth, and Venus under the rays, it signifies that neither waves nor labors will befall them on the journey, and that the ship will go safe and with the good which he wants. And if Venus and Jupiter aspected the Sun and the Moon, and Mercury were with one of them, this will be the best constellation which could be had for putting a ship in the water, nor could a better one be found.

---

568 Reading *afflictae* for *affixae*.
569 This section is drawn from *Carmen* V.25.28-33.
570 That is, without Jupiter (see below).

[Chapter VII.76.4: More on the Moon, benefics, and malefics][571]

And if there were an infortune in the Ascendant and a fortune were with the Moon, or a fortune were in the Ascendant and an infortune with the Moon, it signifies that dangers and labors will happen on the sea, but they will escape from them. And if the Moon were not aspected by a fortune nor by an infortune, and she were in an angle and in the good signs which we stated at the beginning of this chapter, it will be good for putting the ship into the water. And likewise, if the Ascendant were empty of fortunes and infortunes, and it were one of the aforesaid signs in which it is good that the Moon is [in it], it will be good.

[Chapter VII.76.5: The hour of the election][572]

And the hour at which we must inspect for putting the ship in the water, is the hour when men release themselves from it.[573]

And a man should reckon his journey as being at the point at which he puts his foot on the ship.

And[574] the beginning of the motion [away from shore] should be reckoned when the ship is full [and] complete, and laden with all of its necessary things, and begins to move itself and set sail: he should reckon his journey from that hour.

[Chapter VII.76.6: Elections for land versus sea travel][575]

And when you wanted to go by sea and land: if it were by land, and the Moon were not in a dry sign, and the infortunes were in fixed signs or were harming the dry signs, you should draw yourself back from that journey—it is not good. If you wanted to go by water, and the Moon were not in a wa-

---

571 This section is drawn from *Carmen* V.25.34-36.

572 This section is drawn from *Carmen* V.25.37-38.

573 That is (according to *Carmen*), when the ship is first released and pushed away into the water.

574 This sentence is not in *Carmen*, and may represent something preserved in Māshā'allāh's version.

575 This section is drawn from *Carmen* V.25.39-42. Cf. *On Elect.* §§116-17b, and al-'Imrānī II.1.8.

tery sign nor in one like water, and the infortunes were in watery signs, that journey will not be good, because it signifies labors and harms.

And if the Moon aspected the infortunes and were in a moist or dry sign which the fortunes are aspecting, it does not signify harms on that journey, because if that man will not die yet due to the completion of his days,[576] he will return to his own home.

And the worst that it is for the infortunes in this, is that they be stationary: and Mars [for travel] on land is malign, and Saturn [is so] on the water. And the worse significations which they would have, is when Jupiter does not aspect them. [The worst is that the Moon is in a bound or figure of the fortunes, with an infortune aspecting her from opposition or square, with Jupiter and Venus (either separately or together) not aspecting her.][577]

Chapter VII.77: On learning sciences and teachings[578]

In this it is appropriate that the Ascendant be a human sign, and the Moon in a human sign, and the lord of the Ascendant in the Midheaven or entering the Midheaven; and that the lord of the Midheaven have an agreement[579] with the lord of the Ascendant, and that the Moon is conjoined with Mercury or applying to him from a good aspect.

And Mercury should be in a good status, made fortunate and strong. And it is good in this that Mercury aspect the lord of the Ascendant, and that the Moon is not diminished in light nor descending in latitude.[580]

And make the ninth house fit, as much as you can—however, for learning how to write, what we have said must be inspected, and more: because the tenth must [also] be made fit, since it is the significator of masteries, and in writing there is knowledge and the work of a mastery, and on account of that it should not be put off in the sciences and masteries.

---

576 That is, unless he dies due to old age or other reasons unrelated to the journey.

577 I have added this last sentence based on *Carmen* V.25.43.

578 Cf. al-'Imrānī II.10.1, and *On Elect.* §§59a-c.

579 *Convenientiam.* That is, some kind of aspect or relationship conducive to success (such as a trine with reception).

580 Al-'Imrānī has this as the apogee, not ecliptical latitude.

Chapter VII.78: On learning singing and other entertaining things[581]

In this it is appropriate to adapt the Moon, Venus, and Mercury, because these are the roots of this matter; and that Venus be in one of her own dignities, and likewise Mercury would be applying to her. And likewise, the Moon should be in one of her own dignities or in Pisces, or separating herself from Mercury and applying to Venus.

And the Ascendant should be a sign agreeing with this matter, and Venus should have a dignity in it. And if Venus and Mercury both had dignity in the degree of the Ascendant (such as that it would be the house of one and the bound of the other), it will be best; nor should Venus nor the Moon, nor Mercury, be remote from the angles, unless the Moon would be in the ninth house (because it is the house of knowledge) and she were made fortunate and strong there—it does not signify evil nor harm in this matter, but rather it signifies the completion of the matter, with the other significators appearing fortunate and strengthened just as we said before.

And likewise, if the lord of the Ascendant were in the ninth, made fortunate and strong, it will be the best.

And some sages say that for learning the *oud*[582] and what is like that, it is good that the Moon should be in Capricorn. And for learning the tambourine[583] and what is like that, it is good that the Moon be at the end of Leo. And for learning the trumpet and every other instrument which is played with the mouth, it is good that she be in signs not having a voice, or which are mute. And for learning to sing notes,[584] or reading [aloud], it is good that she be in signs having a voice, and particularly in Gemini and Virgo.

And with all of this, adapt the ninth house and its lord. And for those of them whom you see are reaching for a mastery,[585] likewise adapt the tenth house and its lord, because it is good for every beginning in masteries.

---

581 See al-'Imrānī II.10.2.

582 *Illud* ("that"), which cannot be right because the Latin al-'Imrānī specifically says "playing the lyre." Perhaps the Castilian manuscript read *aloud* (from *al-oud*, "the *oud*") , which was later mis-corrected in the Latin to *illud*.

583 *Tamburum*.

584 *Notatos*. I believe this must mean reading written musical notes: this would involve the Mercurial art of reading and writing.

585 *Intendere…ad maneriem magisteriorum*.

Chapter VII.79: For the entrance into a city, by the one who comes from a journey[586]

You should note that the path for following this matter [lies] in making the second house and its lord fit, in this manner: you should put a fortune in it, and its lord above the earth, and the Moon in the third or fifth or eleventh, applying to a planet receiving her (be it a fortune or infortune).

And it is very abhorrent that the Moon should be in the angle of the earth or the eighth or sixth or twelfth. And if you could put the Moon in the second in this, being received and made fortunate, it is not bad.

And if the one who enters wanted to stay long in that place, put the lord of the second and the Moon in the angles. And if the Moon had some reception with Saturn from a good aspect, it is good in this. And if the one entering wanted to depart quickly from the city, put the Moon in the third or fourth, received: because this signifies that he will depart quickly from thence, with what he wants. And if you put the lord of the second in the Ascendant, it is good there. And the lord of the Ascendant in the second is likewise good. And if the one entering wanted to obtain something from the king, it is appropriate that you should make the Midheaven fit. And if he wanted to procure or obtain something for lawful trade, make the lord of the eleventh fit, and the second.

Generally, I say about all those entering (of whatever sort they are): you should look at the second house and its lord, so that they are safe from the infortunes, the rays [of the Sun], and [their] falls. And if the lord of the second were burned up, it signifies that the one entering in that city will die in that entrance. And it is likewise the worse if the lord of the second were in the seventh, and more strongly than that if it were an infortune: because it signifies harm in the body and his assets for the one entering, and that he will have many contrarieties and many who bring [legal] cases against him, and quarrels, and a bad status with respect to his assets and associations.

And if the Moon were in the angle of the earth, it signifies that the one entering will die in that city before he goes out from thence.

And the best election which would be found for an entrance, is that Jupiter be the lord of the second, and that he be in the eleventh or the second,

---

[586] For this chapter, see broadly *Carmen* V.21-22, *On Quest.* §9.2 (*Judges* §9.12), and *On Elect.* §§103b, 118, 121.

having an application with the Moon: because this is the best election which could come about for an entrance.

And you should not forget the Lot of Fortune, but you should put it in the angles or in the eleventh or fifth, because it is the best signification for the good health of the body, and for the cause of assets and for the one entering, so that he would have his petitions [made] easy. And likewise it is good that this Lot should apply to the lord of the house of the Moon, and this likewise is a good signification on account of the end [of the matter].

THE TENTH HOUSE

Chapter VII.80: On the tenth house and its elections

These are the elections of this house: entering a dignity and leaving from it;[587] receiving a magistracy,[588] on making magistrates or judges, on receiving tax revenues[589] or on making [someone] an overseer,[590] and for going with the king, for going in to the king, for presenting one's case or reasoning to the king, on learning masteries, on learning to hold arms, on learning to swim in the waters.

Chapter VII.81.0: For entering into a dignity

[Chapter VII.81.1: General advice]

Al-Khayyāt said:[591] you should be careful, in this, of the luminaries, and clear them of the infortunes, and make them be received, in their own places; and you should put the fortunes in the Ascendant and its angles, with them being direct (and the better one of them is Jupiter), and that the Sun be in his own house, free of the infortunes. And if the infortunes were stronger than the fortunes, and were safe from retrogradation, and the fortunes were harmed, operate through the infortunes, because there will not be evil in this.

And[592] you should not make some dignity which pertains to reason and is in the manner of arms, without making Mars a partner: and he should be supported and in a good status, or that he should be the lord of the Ascendant, not harmed. And you should beware lest the aid of Mars be in any place [other] than the Ascendant, nor that you should give him a role in another place.

---

587 Al-Rijāl may have meant to include the election for removing someone from a dignity, but it does not appear here. Al-'Imrānī describes it in his II.1.2.

588 *Alcaydiam*. I believe that the Latin is a bit mixed up in this sentence, as some items seem to be out of order or do not well match the chapter titles below.

589 That is, being in charge of levying and collecting taxes.

590 *Almuxerif*, undoubtedly from the Ar. *al-mushrif*.

591 Source unknown at this time.

592 Cf. al-'Imrānī II.1.1.

And al-Hasan bin Sahl said: when you wanted to make a dignity fit, adapt the Moon and the lord of her house, and you should put her in a good place from the Ascendant, and the lord of the Ascendant in a good place of the figure, and in one of the houses of Mars or Jupiter; and let Jupiter aspect the Ascendant from the trine or sextile, because it will be better; and put a fixed sign in the Ascendant, and let the lord of the seventh be safe from retrogradation and burning, and from the infortunes: because such an election signifies that he who receives the dignity will be powerful, lawful, and truth-telling in his deeds and matters.

Al-Fadl bin Sahl said:[593] good elections for receiving crowns and kingdoms and great rulerships are that the Moon should be clear, safe, and should not be in the signs of the houses of the infortunes: because if she were there, it signifies that he will be strong, and will do unjust things and do evil. And likewise, she should not be in Cancer, because even it signifies harms and injustices; and worse than this is if the lord of the Ascendant were in Cancer or in one of the houses of the infortunes.

And[594] if the Ascendant were a fixed sign and the Moon in a good place of the figure, in an angle or succeedent, [and] she were fortunate, it signifies that that kingdom or rulership will last for a long time—especially if she were in Leo or in its triplicity.

[Planets in the Ascendant]

And if there were a fortune in the Ascendant, it signifies the goodness of that king, and good customs and good deeds. And if there were an infortune there, judge evil: because Mars signifies crookedness and holding onto long anger, and deceptions; and Saturn there signifies what is low-class, and insignificant things, and slowness in deeds.

And if the Sun were in the Ascendant, it signifies many armies, and many allies, and high and great fame, and he will be appointed for a long time, and great rulership, and a high kingdom.

---

593 Because I do not have access to al-Hasan bin Sahl in Arabic, I cannot be sure how far his opinion reaches across the paragraphs which follow this one. But for this paragraph, cf. *On Elect.* §§128b-c.

594 Cf. al-'Imrānī II.1.1.

And if Jupiter were in the Ascendant, it signifies that he will be upright and of upright morals, and just journeys and judgments, and a lover of the good and the law, and victorious, and he will have many friends.

And if Mercury were there, it signifies that he will stand to the side[595] because he does not want comfort, and he will be wise and have good morals, and he will know how to do his deeds through morals and the masteries of good thoughts and of the great value in himself.[596]

And if Venus were there, it signifies that he will have much pride and many delights, hilarities, and joys, and he will be happy and nimble.

And if the Moon were there, it signifies boldness and a good name. And if the Head were there, it signifies a high status and rulership and victory over his enemies, and especially if it were with the Fortunes.

[Chapter VII.81.2: The three superiors]

And the best signification which there could be for conquering and for great power, is that Jupiter be elevated above the Sun (that is, in the tenth from the Sun) or above the Moon, or above the Ascendant, from a royal sign, and that the Sun would be in a royal sign. And better for having a name and good reputation is that Jupiter be in this constellation which we said, in a movable sign: because the movable signs are the exaltations of planets, and they signify being renowned.[597] And if he were in common ones, it signifies changing and recurrence in his causes and deeds. And if he were in fixed signs, it signifies lastingness and fixity, and a long time. And if Jupiter were cadent from the Sun, and the Moon [cadent] from the Ascendant, and it[598] did not aspect one of them at the beginning of [his] rule, it signifies evil.

And if at the beginning of the rule Mars were in a good place of the figure, or in a house of Jupiter, received by him, it signifies that he will be bold and of vain glory, and he will want it that his commands be advanced, and a victor in his own wars and squabbles, and a guardian of causes and of his own matters, and especially if the beginning were by day and the Sun aspected him from any angle or from a strong place.

---

595 This is my best rendering of *stabit ad partem*, but I believe there might be a problem with the Latin. If it is correct, it may mean that he will prefer intellectual and moral virtues over fame and power.

596 *Et in se magni precii.*

597 So, according to this opinion it would be very good for Jupiter to be in Aries (which is both royal and movable), overcoming the Moon in Cancer, and with the Sun in Leo.

598 I believe this refers to the Moon not aspecting either the Sun or Jupiter.

And if Saturn were in such a constellation just as we said about Mars, and in such states, it signifies that the king will populate cities and will be bold and powerful. And if he were in such improvements[599] and receptions just as we said before, and he were in the eleventh, and the Lot of Fortune with them, or the Lot of boldness,[600] it will be much better; and more strongly than that if Mars were [arranged] in this manner, because it signifies great honor, power, and usefulness.

[Chapter VII.81.3: Planets elevated in various ways]

And if it happened that a fortune would be in the tenth from the Ascendant or in the tenth from the luminary of the time,[601] and the lords of these two places were in good places of the figure, and in their own domains[602] and dignities, and in their own exaltations, or eastern, supported, it signifies power, goodness, fortune, and advancement,[603] and a long time. And if they had some dignity in the conjunction or opposition which was before the beginning of the rulership, or they were elevated in their own angles, and ascending in their latitudes towards the north, and increasing in their motions, and the planets aspecting them [and] in agreement with them would likewise not be diminished nor in the welled degrees nor the dark ones,[604] it signifies the greatest power and greatest good which there would be in this matter.

[Chapter VII.81.4: Dignities by natural significations of the planets]

And you should look to see which of the planets was the significator of that dignity according to the natures and proper qualities of the planets and dignities:[605] because if it were a kingdom, it will be the Sun, and if it were the dignity of a magistrate or judge, it will be Jupiter; and if it were the dignity of the leader of an army[606] or holding the frontier, it will be Mars; and if it were

599 That is, improved planetary conditions.
600 *Audaciae*. This could be the Hermetic Lot of Courage (*ITA* VI.1.6), or perhaps the Lot of heroism and bravery (*ITA* VI.3.2).
601 That is, the sect light.
602 *Haiç*. See *ITA* III.2.
603 Reading *profectionem* for *perfectionem* ("completion").
604 See *ITA* VII.9.1 and VII.7 for the welled and dark degrees.
605 Al-Rijāl provides more information about these below.
606 Reading *alcaidiae militiae* for *alcaidiae vel militiae*.

a dignity over lands or the law, Saturn; and if it were the dignity of the chancery or a clerkship, it will be Mercury; and if it were a dignity of the ranks of the people, it will be the Moon.

[Chapter VII.81.5: Comparison with the nativity]

You should even look to see of what kind of rulership or power that planet[607] has in the nativity of the one who has the dignity, and in the hour in which he receives the dignity: because if it happened that the planet, at the hour of the dignity, is at the summit of its apogee, or ascending towards it, and ascending in its epicycle and ascending to the north in latitude, and increasing in motion, it signifies great power for the one who receives the dignity, and especially honor and praise, and that he will conquer all of his enemies, and could hardly ever by conquered nor contradicted in his speech or orders, because all of the planets will obey and give their own virtues to a planet which was in such a state as we have said before—be it of the high [planets] or the inferiors.

And if it were eastern, it signifies that he will have a good dignity and a firm one, without regret.[608] And if it were burned up, it signifies many labors and terrors. And if it were a fortune or made fortunate, it signifies that the one who receives the dignity will hold onto justice, and the people will have good with him. And if it were an infortune or made unfortunate, it signifies that he will be crooked and an evildoer, and the people will be full of troubles with him.

And if you knew his nativity, and you found that that planet had rulership in the nativity, or in his tenth house, or it had rulership over the estate or in the clime in which he is supposed to have power, these significations will be more fixed and more strengthened.

And if in the Midheaven there were a fortune which is in the exaltation of the Sun or Moon or Jupiter, it signifies much power for good, and honor, height, and praise. And if both luminaries (or one of them) were in the bright degrees and the infortunes were in the tenth house, and Jupiter and Venus and Mercury and the Head (or any of them) were there, and the others aspected there, and the sign were the house of a very good fortune, it signifies power and fortune, and that the dignity will be fixed and lasting for him and

---

607 The planets in VII.81.4.

608 Or perhaps, without "pain" (*pena*).

his children and nephews, and especially if the sign were the house of Jupiter or Mercury, and they aspected there (because these signify children and nephews).

And if the affair were diurnal, and Saturn were in the eleventh, in his own exaltation, and Jupiter had a commingling with him by aspect or conjunction, it signifies lastingness in that good, and that he will populate cities and lands, and will be powerful in his rulership; however, he will be weak, with an infirm body. And if the affair were nocturnal, and Mars were in the eleventh, in his own exaltation, and he had a commingling with Jupiter by conjunction or aspect, it signifies great power, victory and extensive fame, and he will be wise and fortunate, holding armies in his hand, and squabbles, and a kingdom and rulership. And if the Lot of Fortune were with him, it signifies greater power, and greater boldness in killings, and he will have greater delight in arms and horses and soldiers, and in making journeys.

Likewise, you should look to the Lot of Fortune, and to the Lot of nobility (which is taken in the day from the degree of the Sun to the degree of his exaltation, and in the night from the degree of the Moon to the degree of her exaltation, and it is projected from the Ascendant).[609] You should even look at the Lot of a kingdom and victory, which is taken in the day and night from the degree of the Sun to the degree of the Moon, and it is projected from the degree of the Midheaven.[610] Afterwards, if these Lots came into good and fortunate places, and with the fortunes, it signifies great nobility and honor for that lord.

After that, you should look at each of the twelve houses: and in the one where you found a fortune, judge good and fortune in the signification of that house and its nature, such as assets, brothers, children, slaves, and what is like these. And according to this manner, you will likewise judge about an infortune in accordance as you found it. However, the seventh house signifies his adversaries and litigants, and a planet which was there signifies the same thing. And the fourth house and a planet which were in it, signifies parents and grandfathers, and from what nature he comes, and the land and the estate from which he is, and the places which are taken on in that rulership. And if an infortune were cadent and especially under the earth, it signifies the weakness of enemies, and their being pressed down and being

---

609 Sometimes called the Lot of exaltation: see *ITA* VI.2.37.

610 I have not seen this Lot before, and it is probably incorrect.

despised; and the better one of these is that the lord of the Ascendant and the lord of the tenth are in angles.

And you should not put off inspecting his releaser and likewise the planet with which it agrees, the house-master;[611] and if you found it in an angle[612] or in the tenth, or eleventh or fifth, it signifies that he will last in that rulership for as long as are the lesser years of that planet. And if it were not in one of these places, but it were in a succeedent, it signifies months according to that number. And if it were cadent but [still] aspecting the Ascendant,[613] it likewise signifies months. And if it were cadent from the Ascendant and from the angles and their aspects, it signifies [that] number of days. And likewise, look at the planets aspecting it—namely, those who add a number and who subtract [a number], and do in this just as you did in the lives of nativities.[614] And make a direction[615] of the degree of the releaser to the bodies of the fortunes and infortunes, and to their rays. And you will do likewise [with] the degree of the Midheaven, and you should know what kinds of rays will fall there, and with respect to this you will judge at what time good and evil will befall him.

And other sages say,[616] when you wanted to adapt a dignity for a master of soldiers, put the Moon in one of the houses of Mars, and let Mars be aspecting her from a trine or sextile, and likewise let the fortunes aspect her, and put a fixed sign in the Ascendant.

And if it were a dignity for exalting the king, put the Moon in one of the houses of Jupiter, or made fortunate in [the house of] the Sun; and you should make the Ascendant likewise, and you should beware lest the lord of the Ascendant nor the lord of the house of the Moon be retrograde: because this retrogradation subtracts from his power and reputation.

---

[611] *Alcochoden.* That is, the *kadukhudhāh*, one of the lords of the longevity releaser (preferably the bound lord).

[612] *Angulo.* This should probably read, "Ascendant."

[613] Such as from the third or ninth.

[614] For some simple instructions on the longevity releaser and the house-master, cf. *Forty Chapters* Ch. 3.3, and *ITA* VIII.1.3.

[615] *Ataçir.*

[616] Cf. *On Elect.* §128a.

Chapter VII.82: On an election for a dignity of the land, or for tax revenues or the law

For this,[617] put the Moon in one of the houses of Saturn, applying to Saturn from a trine or sextile, and let it be in the beginning of the [Lunar] month, and let the fortunes aspect her: because this signifies the fortune of the matter, and that it will last long.

And you will know his lastingness from the bounds in which these planets were: which if both were in the bounds of fortunes, and both planets were made fortunate, it signifies their lesser years (of the number of [their] years).

And if the sign of the Midheaven at this hour were a fixed sign, it signifies that the dignity which he had (or that office) will be good so long as he lasted in it. And if that sign were common, made fortunate,[618] and the fortunes aspected it just as we said, it signifies that he will have two offices, or he will change from one office into another. And if it were a movable sign, grief and labors will befall him many times. And they will not hinder him nor harm him, with the Midheaven appearing strengthened and fortunate through the existence of the fortunes in it, or through their aspects (just as we said).

Chapter VII.83: On adapting the dignity of magistrates[619]

For a dignity of magistrates or judges, it is appropriate that the Moon be in one of the houses of Jupiter, [with him] aspecting her from a trine or sextile, with Venus making both fortunate.

---

617 For this paragraph, cf. *On Elect.* §127, which is much briefer.

618 *Fortunatum*. But it might be *fortunarum*, "belonging to the fortunes," just as al-Rijāl recommended the bounds of the fortunes in the previous paragraph.

619 Cf. al-'Imrānī II.1.1, which is a bit different.

Chapter VII.84: On adapting the dignity of a chancery-clerk or clerkship, or those who bear books of computations

In this matter[620] it is useful that you should put the Moon in one of the houses of Mercury, and he should be aspecting her from a trine or sextile, and both fortunes should aspect them (and likewise the degree of the Midheaven) from fixed signs, and the Midheaven should likewise be a fixed sign.

And when it happened at the beginning of some affair, that Venus would be at the end of her latitude in the north, or in her own greater motion, or in her own greater power, any planet which would then aspect her (be it of the superiors or inferiors) will be obedient to him;[621] and for the one to whom it happened in this manner, fortune[622] in his own dignity will be signified, [and] great honor and great power and the greatest obedience from the people, and especially if that man were from the direction of the west (because Venus is a significatrix of the west and its kings). And any planet to which it happened that it would be at the summit of [its] apogee or in the degree of its exaltation, in whatever adaptation of anyone's dignity, it signifies that that planet will be more famous and more supported than the others. And if that same application were by night, and the Moon applied to this planet, the planets will obey it ([that is], the other nocturnal planets). And if the application were by day, and the Sun applied to the stated planet, the planets will obey it ([that is], the diurnal planets).

And in this place, concerning the obedience of "the planets," he wants to say that "the people which were of the nature of those planets," and "those in which that planet had virtue," will be more obedient to that master.

And if that planet (which was in such a status at the hour of the dignity) had testimony and power in the nativity of that lord, the matter will be more firm and lasting. And if it had testimony in the revolution of the year of the world, the significations of this will be multiplied, and [its] power and significance is affirmed.

---

620 For this paragraph, cf. al-'Imrānī II.1.1.

621 For an explanation of this phrase, see below. Al-Rijāl (or his source) seems to mean that if the planet signifying the office or dignity were in an excellent condition, then people signified by any *aspecting* planets will be obedient to the person put into that office or dignity.

622 Reading *fortuna* for *fortunam*.

Chapter VII.85.0: On choosing from among equal men, which of them they will make a lord and a greater [person][623]

This chapter is very necessary for all men, and especially for kings, when they look at their faithful [followers], and at those they have put in charge, and their seneschals, and want to know which of them will be more faithful and lawful, and more truth-telling in that matter which he holds onto (or in his office).

[Chapter VII.85.1: Triplicity lords of the Ascendant][624]

When it is asked of you about one [particular] association of men (whom the king wants to send for the sake of a squabble or for another matter), as to which one of that association is greater and more lawful and more true, look at the Ascendant and the lords of its triplicity: and give each of them to each of those men, according to the order in which the inquirer has named them to you: namely, the first [triplicity lord] to the first one, the second to the second, and the third to the third. And look to see which of them had greater power and greater dignity in the place in which it was, and if it were a fortune or infortune. And if it were an infortune and it was Mars, and the Moon were made unfortunate and void of [the aspects of] the fortunes,[625] and the other two lords of the triplicity were weakened in their own places, judge that the one whose significator was Mars will be more powerful and more lawful and better in what [the client] wants; however, it signifies that the [matter] for which they chose him could not be successful, nor [would he be able] to apply [himself] to what they bid him [to do].[626] And if that infortune were Saturn, it signifies a long time and delay in the matter for which he

---

623 Cf. *Judges* §7.183, which attributes all of this material (and more) to al-Ṭabarī, although al-Ṭabarī himself recognizes Māshā'allāh as being one of his sources. Of course, these questions are more appropriate to questions than elections. For Sahl's version of some of this (which would seem to confirm the relation to Māshā'allāh), see *On Quest.* §§13.13-14. Note that al-Rijāl or his source is taking the notion of "choice" very strongly here: for although this is really a *question about* whom to choose, the fact *that* a choice is involved, makes him connect it with elections. This further suggests a long-lasting overlap between elections and questions.

624 This is the second method described in *Judges* §7.183.

625 The Moon is included here as a significator of how the *matter* will turn out, rather than indicating the intrinsic qualities of the man being chosen.

626 Hence the Moon being in a poor condition. Surely if she were in a good condition, he would be successful.

was chosen. Afterwards, you should consider if the fortunes aspected that infortune which was the master of the one role in that triplicity, and what kind of power that infortune has in its own place, and in what bound it is (if it is in the bound of a fortune or infortune), and [look at] the fortune aspecting it, to see what kind of power or dignity it has in its own bound: and through this path, judge according to what you found.

And if the three lords of the triplicity were equal in the power and goodness of their own places and in the fortunes which they had, and none of them were of a better status than the other, judge that the first one is better than the second, and the second [better than] the third. And if the planet which was the more powerful of the two lords of the triplicity were a fortune, and it was not made unfortunate, it signifies that he will be successful in that conflict for which he goes, or that for which he was sent, and he will be lawful and of good obedience, and pure will toward him who has sent him. And if it were an infortune, and it had [a better] improvement [than] its associates, it signifies that the man will go beyond the command of his master, and he will do things which will not be according to the will of his master. And if the fortunes aspected [such an infortune] from strong, good, and appropriate places, it signifies that he will conquer and will complete [his mission], but through violence and evil deeds. And if the planet were a fortune, and the infortunes cadent from it,[627] and it [were] in a good and strong place, it signifies that he will conquer and easily fulfill [his mission], and through good means, and he will be obedient to his master, and will complete what he wills.

And you should know that if Mars aspected the lord of the triplicity in this matter, and [that triplicity lord] was the one who went by reason of conflicts and killings,[628] and the aspect were from the trine or sextile, it does not harm. Likewise, if the Moon aspected there from such an aspect.

And if the first and second lord of the triplicity were both infortunes and strengthened, and the fortunes aspected them from the angles, judge the goodness of those whose significators they are, and especially in the significations of conflicts, and the stronger one in that is Mars.

---

627 That is, in aversion to it.

628 That is, if Mars aspected the triplicity lord representing the one whom we choose as being best.

[Chapter VII.85.2: Choosing among many possibilities][629]

And if the men which they said that you should choose were more than three, you should know the Ascendant as we said before, and first you should take the planet which had greater dignity in the Ascendant, and afterwards the next one which follows it in dignities, and thus until you have completed these planets which had dignity in the Ascendant, in order; and you will group them together with the three which were the lords of the triplicity, and you should consider the virtue of each of them in its own situation, and judge according to what you found with respect to their power, [good] fortune, and misfortune, and judge through that one according to the path which we told you before with the lords of the triplicities.

[Chapter VII.85.3: Choosing by the applications of the Moon][630]

Likewise, you should look at the applications of the Moon in this matter: because if she were applying to a cadent planet, and[631] one harmed, judge that that one which was first in the search is not good. And if after that she applied to a planet which is remote from an angle of the Ascendant,[632] judge that the second one in the question is not bad, but he will be weak in power and of little fame. And if she applied to a planet appearing in an angle, it signifies that the one whose significator it was [in] that application, will be good and supported, and he will complete that for which he was chosen.

---

629 This is the fifth method described in *Judges* §7.183.

630 This is the third method described in *Judges* §7.183, and it also appears in *On Quest.* §13.14. In John's Latin, this has to do with answering more than one question at a time, not choosing among multiple candidates for the same question. However, the instructions in his second paragraph do make more sense if we look at it in al-Rijāl's and 'Umar's way.

631 Reading *et* for *aut* ("or"), which makes more sense when comparing it with the next planet. But the point is that the better the condition and angularity of the planet, the better it is as a candidate.

632 Reading *remotus ab angulo ascendentis*, for *remotus ab angulo aspicientis tamen ascendens.* The original would read, "remote from an angle of the one aspecting, but ascending."

Chapter VII.86: For one who wanted to go with the king or another lord[633]

When you wanted to go with the king or with another lord through his land, put Jupiter in the Ascendant or in the seventh, because this signifies good for the one going on that journey, and that he will have pleased him. And beware lest you put Jupiter in the fourth, because it is abhorrent in this matter. And the Moon should be aspecting him from one of the angles, and likewise [so should] Venus.

And you should beware lest Saturn and Mars (or any of them) be in the Ascendant, nor in any of the angles, nor be with Venus, nor should the Moon be under the rays, nor with the Tail, nor with the infortunes: because it is a bad constellation, and the one who makes the journey in that [constellation] will not return; and he who will grow infirm in it, will die; and he who went to squabble will be killed or conquered.

Chapter VII.87: On putting the king in the house of his rulership[634]

When you wished to put the king in his own house of rulership, you should make the Ascendant a fixed sign, and likewise the house of the end[635] a fixed sign, and [put] the lord of the Midheaven in a place clear of the infortunes, and the lord of the Ascendant in a good place, and received; and the lord of the tenth should not aspect the eleventh with an inimical aspect, and the Moon should aspect the lord of her own house in a friendly way, and the lord of the fourth house should aspect the fortunes. And if you could not observe all of this, let the Moon be received, and the lord of the fourth house be in a good place, aspecting the fortunes—and if it were not this, you should remove it[636] from the Ascendant and its aspects, and make it so the fortunes would aspect the sign[637] of the end and the Midheaven. And this suffices, with the will of God.

---

633 Cf. *On Elect.* §§123a-c.

634 That is, for taking power or the accession to the throne. Cf. *On Elect.* §§125a-26c.

635 The fourth. That is, make sure the IC is in the fourth sign.

636 This seems to mean the lord of the fourth.

637 Reading with Sahl for "lord."

Chapter VII.88: For one who wanted to give his argument in the presence of the king[638]

In this, you should put Leo as the Ascendant, and the Sun in the Midheaven, and the Moon in the Ascendant, applying to the fortunes and to the lord of the Midheaven.

Chapter VII.89: On seeking the defense of the king[639]

If you were one who wanted to frustrate[640] someone else with the king,[641] make the Moon be increased in light and let her and the Ascendant be safe from the infortunes, and the lord of the Ascendant in a good place, and in a good status from the Ascendant, and in one of its own dignities, and direct, and safe from the infortunes (be it a fortune or infortune). And you should put the lord of the seventh in a bad place from the Ascendant, and the fortunes should not aspect it, nor should any of the luminaries.

And if another wanted to frustrate you with the king,[642] and you wanted to reckon[643] the matter in front of the king so as to show your reasoning, you should make the Moon diminished in light, and the Ascendant and its lord and the Moon unfortunate,[644] and you should make the lord of the seventh fortunate, in a good place from the Ascendant, and supported: because with this your reasoning will be better and stronger.

---

638 Cf. *On Elect.* §124, which is really about attaining a dignity.

639 Cf. *On Elect.* §§129a-30. Sahl conceives of these differently. But the basic idea of the election is the same: the person who initiates the trouble should do it with a waxing Moon and the lord of the Ascendant strong, with the lord of the seventh weak.

640 *Disturbare.*

641 Al-Rijāl is reading this as though the client wants to make a complaint against someone else so as to get the king's help against him. But Sahl understands this as though the client himself wants to be the enemy of the king.

642 Again, al-Rijāl treats this as though someone else is trying to ruin the client's reputation with the king, but Sahl understands it as the client responding to a *king* who is already angry with him.

643 *Computare,* lit. "to count, compute, reckon."

644 The idea is that the Ascendant signifies the person initiating the matter. Therefore, if your enemy is making his case against you to the king, then he is the Ascendant and should be weakened, while you are the seventh and should be strengthened.

Chapter VII.90: On learning masteries[645]

When you wanted an election for learning any mastery, make the tenth house (which is the significator of masteries) and its lord fit, and the Moon; and you should put the planet which was the significator of that mastery through its own nature and proper quality, in one of its own dignities and supported: such as Mars, who is a significator of craftsmen and guardians of the frontiers,[646] and such as the Sun, who is the significator of every mastery with which gold and silver is purified, and what is like that; and thus according to this [approach] for all the others.

And for all, give a role and application to Mercury, because he is a principal significator of mastery as a whole, and especially of subtle works, such as making an astrolabe, drilling holes in pearls, and painting: whence it is necessary that he be in a good state and that the Moon would be in some dignity of hers, and that she would apply to the planet which was the significator of that work, from a good aspect and with reception. And if it happened that she would be in the house of the planet signifying that mastery, it will be better. And in addition it will be better if she were in a house signifying that mastery, according to the signification of the houses.

And you should put the Ascendant in a sign agreeing with that mastery. And if that mastery were of earthy matters, put the Moon in earthy signs; and if it were of watery matters,[647] you should put her in watery signs; and according to this for the rest.

Chapter VII.91: On learning to bear arms[648]

In this, it is appropriate that the Ascendant and the Moon be in the triplicity of Aries, and Mars should be made fit in his own place and status, and the Moon should be in her own fall, especially in learning to bear arms while riding. And if the Moon were in her own exaltation in this, it will be much better. And likewise, it is best that the lord of the Ascendant be in its own

---

[645] Cf. al-'Imrānī II.11.3.

[646] Reading *curatorum* (or perhaps *comitum*) *limitaneorum* for *curatorum linteaminum*. Al-'Imrānī reads "butchers" (Lat. *carnificum*), which could be the true reading for *curatorum*, but would leave *linteaminum* unexplained.

[647] Reading *rebus* with the previous sentence, for *signis*.

[648] Cf. al-'Imrānī II.11.2.

exaltation. And if you could not have it there, put it in the Midheaven or entering into it.

And some sages say that in learning to wrestle, it is particularly good that the Moon be in Gemini.[649]

Chapter VII.92: On learning to swim in waters[650]

In this, it is good that the Moon be in watery signs, and that the lord of the Ascendant be in the Midheaven or entering into it, and made fortunate; and that the Moon be ascending in the north,[651] and in one of her own dignities (and the better sign in this is Cancer).

---

649 Omitting *separatim* as being a likely redundant and incorrect repetition of *specialiter* earlier in the sentence.

650 Cf. al-'Imrānī II.11.1.

651 I am not sure if this is by ecliptical latitude or declination.

THE ELEVENTH HOUSE

Chapter VII.93: On the eleventh house and its elections

These are the elections of this house: beginning matters which a man does for having a good name and a good reputation; demanding some petition; fulfilling promises; and seeking love and friendship.

Chapter VII.94: On matters which happen for the sake of acquiring a good name and reputation[652]

It is appropriate in the beginning[653] that you make the eleventh house and its lord fit, and you should make the Ascendant be one of the signs of Jupiter. And it will be better if you could put Jupiter in the eleventh house or in the Ascendant, or aspecting them from a good aspect. And it is even appropriate that Jupiter should be strengthened and safe from the infortunes. And if the lord of the eleventh were in the Ascendant, or the lord of the Ascendant in the eleventh, it is likewise good.

And it is good that the Sun be safe from the infortunes and in the tenth, and the Moon applying to him from a trine or sextile. And if in addition the Moon were separating herself from the lord of the eleventh or from Jupiter, it will be better, because it signifies that the matter will be renowned, manifest, and complete.

And it even agrees with all [of this] that the significators be aspecting one to the other from good aspects, and particularly [aspecting] the luminaries and the Ascendant and the eleventh,[654] and that they should be received. And if you could not make all of them fit, adapt whichever of them you could, always by guarding the roots of the elections.

---

652 Cf. al-'Imrānī II.12.1.

653 Reading with al-'Imrānī, rather than "that you make the beginning of the eleventh house fit…".

654 Reading *undecimam* with al-'Imrānī, for *decimam* ("tenth").

Chapter VII.95: On fulfilling promises and demanding petitions[655]

In this,[656] it is appropriate that you make the eleventh house and its lord fit, and the Lot of Fortune and its lord, and both (or one of them) should aspect the Ascendant. And the lord of the Ascendant and the Moon should be received by the lord of the eleventh and by the planet [which is] the significator of the matter sought.

Now, the Ascendant and its lord are the significators of the one seeking, and the seventh and its lord belong to the one from whom it is sought: whence it is appropriate that the seventh house be safe, otherwise the petition will be lost. And the Moon is the significator of the thing sought.

Afterwards,[657] if the petition were from old men or any of those which are of the nature of Saturn, you should make the degree of the eleventh house a dignity of Saturn. And if the petition were from a scribe or from [someone of] the significations of Mercury, you should make the eleventh house a dignity of Mercury (namely [his] exaltation, house or bound). And adapt the planetary significator of the one from whom it is sought: so that if it were an old man, adapt Saturn, and you will work with all of the planets according to this reasoning.

Al-Tabarī said:[658] in this, it is appropriate that Mercury be applying to Jupiter and Venus, and that the lord of the Midheaven be agreeing with the lord of the Ascendant.

And if the question were for the sake of assets, make the second and the lord of the Ascendant fit, [so] that there should be a friendly application between the lord of the second house and the lord of the Ascendant, and no infortune would cut off [the light] between them,[659] and the lord of the eleventh and the lord of the Lot of Fortune should likewise be aspecting it[660] from good aspects.

And if it were for a matter of women or a marriage-union, do with the seventh house and its lord what we said about the second house and its lord. And you should work with the other houses in this manner.

---

655 Cf. al-'Imrānī II.12.2.

656 For this paragraph, cf. *On Elect.* §132a.

657 For this paragraph, cf. *Carmen* V.14.6-7.

658 According to al-'Imrānī II.12.2, this is al-Khayyāt.

659 See *ITA* III.23 for different forms of "cutting."

660 I am not sure who or what is meant by "it" here.

Chapter VII.96: On seeking love and friendship[661]

For seeking love and friendship, it is appropriate that the Moon be made fit, and likewise the eleventh house and its lord, and that both be received by Venus from a trine. And if the reception were from the house or exaltation, it will be better. And if it were not such, the aspect should be from a trine, and the Moon should be received by Jupiter or by the lord of her house. And if the Moon were not thus nor in any of the dignities of Venus, let her be safe.

And if the friendship were for reasons of earning assets, let the Lot of Fortune be in the Ascendant; if it is real estate, let it be in the fourth house; and you should work with all of the other houses according to this.

---

[661] This chapter is based on *Forty Chapters*, Ch. 22 (§§546-49), but al-Rijāl has probably gotten it from al-'Imrānī II.12.3.

THE TWELFTH HOUSE

Chapter VII.97: On the twelfth house and its elections

The elections of this house are: racing horses so that one would conquer the other, [and] at the hour in which a king or another would catch his enemy who is less powerful than he is.

Chapter VII.98: On the racing of horses[662]

One sage[663] said that one who wanted to win when racing horses, should put the lord of the hour in the Ascendant when he begins to go from his own home [to the race].

Al-Kindī said[664] that, in addition, he will always win by observing the roots of the elections. And if the lord of the hour were in the tenth, [the horse] will run in the middle of the first [horses] and the last ones; and if it were in the seventh, [the horse] will run with the last ones. And if it were in the angle of the earth, [the horse] will be last and will remain behind. And you should beware lest the lord of the hour be in its fall, because it signifies that the beast will fall.

And al-Kindī said[665] that it is good in this matter that the Moon be in Sagittarius or in the middle of Libra.

---

662 For this chapter, cf. al-'Imrānī II.1.12.

663 Al-'Imrānī II.1.2 attributes this to al-Kindī, but see my footnote there.

664 This is not actually al-Kindī, but a version of Sahl (and probably ultimately from Māshā'allāh), *On Quest.* §12.1 (*Judges* §12.1). Al-'Imrānī's own Arabic must have been a little ambiguous in addition to incorrectly mentioning al-Kindī, because al-Rijāl believes that everything from here to the end is al-Kindī: my reading of the Latin al-'Imrānī suggests that he was identifying sentence above with both an unnamed person and al-Kindī, but al-Rijāl mistook this to be a reference to everything in the present paragraph.

665 This is not from *Forty Chapters*, but some other unknown person, maybe the "sage" mentioned above, who is identical to al-'Imrānī's "certain person" in his II.1.12.

Chapter VII.99: On the hour at which a king would catch his enemy or a less powerful person[666]

If you wanted to elect so that the king would catch his enemy, make it so that the twelfth house is made unfortunate, and likewise its lord made unfortunate and weak. And if its misfortune were [coming] from the lord of the Ascendant, it will be better. And if it were not this [at the] beginning of the journey,[667] make it so that the Moon is made unfortunate by the Sun, and that the Sun is in a good place. And if she were made unfortunate by some other [planet] and not the Sun, it will be better.[668]

Al-Tabarī said, when the king or another wanted to catch an enemy who is of lesser power than him, let the Moon be in the conjunction or opposition or in the burnt path, or with the Head or with the Tail, or she should be in the Ascendant (and this for the reason that the Ascendant is inimical to her according to her opposition [to its nature]),[669] or that she should be in the aspect of the infortunes or before her eclipse by three days, and that the Sun should be safe and clear of the infortunes, and that the fortunes should be in the Midheaven.

And if the Moon were made more unfortunate, there will be worse and greater harm for that enemy: because the Moon is the significator of the people and a lesser type, and slaves.

Here the elections taken according to the twelfth houses, are fulfilled; and let God be praised and very much thanked for it.

---

666 Cf. al-'Imrānī II.13.1-2. I have read the last part of this title with the 1551 al-Rijāl, as it is clearer.

667 Reading with al-'Imrānī for *principium intrandi iter.*

668 This probably means it is better to have a malefic make her unfortunate, such as in *Carmen* V.36.16-18.

669 See the discussion in al-Rijāl VII.2.3.

Chapter VII.100: On the significations of the hours[670]

Chapter VII.101: On elections according to the Moon's motion through the mansions[671]

Chapter VII.102.0: On the times in which hope is had that [one's] petitions would be fulfilled[672]

You should know that in determining the times of matters, there are differences according to the differences going forth from judgments—so that there would be matters and fortunes there which would not be able to pass beyond tomorrow, and there are other matters and fortunes there which can pass beyond days and not more, and others which can pass beyond months. And the greater category which there is in this, is when matters pass beyond years.

And in knowing and determining the times, it is necessary to have great understanding and subtlety in one's regard for astrology, because it is good for one to know the natures and fortunes of the planets, and the organization of questions and their natures, and it is good for one to distribute and adapt the natures, and judge according to one's intention and subtlety. And I will speak in this according to how my own understanding and sense was able to engage it.[673]

[Chapter VII.102.1: Lengths of time from Sahl's On Times §3 and "Dorotheus/Ptolemy"]

Dorotheus said,[674] the times are taken in seven ways:

First, from what [distance] there is between one significator and another.

---

670 I have translated this chapter for Part II of this book.

671 I have translated this chapter for Part I of this book.

672 Most of these timing techniques really have to do with questions (i.e., "horary"), not elections. But al-Rijāl has included them here because al-'Imrānī discusses some of them in his I.5 above.

673 Or rather, al-Rijāl will copy what material from other authors he believes makes sense.

674 Perhaps from Māshā'allāh's version of Dorotheus (since it matches so much of Sahl's *On Times* §3), but cf. also pseudo-Ptolemy's *Cent.* #81.

Second, from the assemblies [by transit][675] which there would be between the two significators.

Third, from the directing[676] of one of them, to the place of the other.

Fourth, from what [distance] there is from one significator up to the place of the matter asked about.

Fifth, from matters which preserve the gift of a planet, and which add and subtract.[677]

Sixth, from the assembly[678] of a significator with the place of the matter asked about.

Seventh is the direction[679] of a planet to the place agreeing with the matter by nature.

However, others (with the exception of Ptolemy)[680] say that these matters are determined in five ways, and there are others[681] who say [it is] in four ways—and this [is] according to the diversities of their understandings, senses, and opinions.

[Chapter VII.102.2: Al-Rijāl's view, based on Vettius Valens][682]

And here I want to state the opinions which seem to be better to me, according to my own understanding (and may God direct me in this). I say that the time in which a matter ought to appear, and the significations which the planets signify in the nativity (with respect to good and evil), is when [1] that same planet had rulership in a distribution,[683] or [2] conveying it by some number of its own years (the lesser or middle or greater ones), or [3] by the ascensions of the sign in which it is, by giving one year to every degree ac-

---

675 *Convenientiis.* That is, the real-time transit of one, to the body of the other. I have added the point about transits in accordance with the other lists of ways (see my Introduction).
676 *Athaçir* (Ar. *tasyīr*). That is, directing by ascensions.
677 That is, the number of its planetary years (whether greater or lesser), put into the correct time-units based on the issue at hand (days, months, etc.).
678 *Convenientia.* Or perhaps, "arrival." That is, the real-time ingress of the planet into the place of the matter.
679 Again, a primary direction. This is just like #6, but using directions instead of transits.
680 That is, in *Cent.* #81.
681 Such as al-Hasan bin Sahl, described below.
682 This subchapter shows that al-Rijāl had access to at least the basic approach to timing from Valens *Anth.* VII.2-3 and 6, just as the next subchapter reveals the survival of *Anth.* III.12-13.
683 *Divisione,* which in this instance probably means profections in particular (see the last half of this paragraph), but it should refers to any kind of time-lord scheme, including distributions proper (the direction of something through the bounds).

cording to the ascensions which it had in that place where it was in the heavens.[684]

Afterwards, if it happened that the planet which signified good or evil in the root would be the lord of the application of the year,[685] and in that year it arrived to some category of the three categories of its own years, or to the number of the ascensions of the sign, then its signification which it had signified in the root (with respect to good and evil) will appear and be strengthened.

> And if two or three planets would be conjoined together in signifying some matter, with them appearing in one sign or in signs aspecting each other, and agreeing in one signification, all of their lesser years will be conjoined, and from this comes one time in which the fulfillment of that signification in which they agreed, should be expected.
>
> And join together the lesser years of two of them, [and] not more: it will likewise be a time of attending to the matter.
>
> And the lesser years of each of them separately will likewise be a time.
>
> And the lesser years of each of them separately, joined [together] with the ascensions, are likewise a time.
>
> And the ascensions of a sign, joined with the years of two or three planets, are likewise a time.
>
> (And all of these ways come to be through the lesser years of the planets, and not by the others.)[686]
>
> And if the years of two or three planets which signified a matter, were conjoined together, and one-half of them would be taken, it is likewise

---

684 See my table of ascensional times at www.bendykes.com; ascensional times are also calculated by the Delphic Oracle astrology program.

685 This sounds like a profection, but could easily be a distribution (in which the planet is the bound lord or distributor of some directed point). In other words, if some planet is the lord of the year during a period when one of its sets of planetary years or the ascensions of its sign is *also* fulfilled or due, the effect should be more dramatic at that time.

686 That is, not using the greater or middle years.

a time. And if the ascensions of a sign would be joined to this half, it is likewise a time.

And the ancient sages operated and judged through all of these ways: and according to the virtues and weaknesses which the planets had in their own places, [so] will their significations appear. And the ascensions of a sign are taken according to what agrees with the place of a planet through its appearance in an angle or in the other houses, just as we have said before in this our book.[687]

And it has been verified through habitual practice[688] that the signification belongs to the planet [which is] stronger in its own place, and according to its own proper quality in being a fortune and infortune; and after this, the planet which follows that one in power, and thus through the others according to this ranking.

Of the rest, when one of two planets which are of the nature of some *bebenie*[689] had rulership in a distribution of the nativity[690] or in the sign of the application[691] or in a *firdārīyyah*, then will be the time at which its signification will appear; and that one of these two planets which was stronger in its own place and in itself, its signification will be more powerful.

[Chapter VII.102.3: Endemadeyg of the Persians][692]

And in a book *Endemadeyg of the Persians*[693] it is said:[694] if the Lot of Fortune were spotted by the fortunes or infortunes in some nativity, and

[687] I am not currently sure where al-Rijāl has stated this, but he is referring to statements in Valens (II.28, VII.2), in which angular and succeedent planets mature when their full period has expired, but cadent ones will expire in less time, proportional to the amount of their sign they have traversed.

[688] Reading *exercitationem* for *existentiam* ("existence, emergence"). But this could be *existimationem* ("opinion, judgment"). Or, the Latin translator might have meant *existential* in terms of outcomes and what emerges, which is a valid but not obvious meaning.

[689] Meaning uncertain. This is a typical Latin transliteration for *biyābānīyah,* from the Pahlavi word for "fixed," referring to fixed stars; but I am not sure how it fits here. On the other hand, the paragraph seems simply to say that when two planets partner together (such as in distributions and *firdārīyyāt*), the stronger one will have the more powerful outcome.

[690] This must be distributions proper.

[691] A profection.

[692] Cf. Valens III.12-13.

[693] Source unknown at this time. Based on comments al-Rijāl makes below, *Endemadeyg* seems to be the title of the book and not the author's name; but I am not sure if "of the Persians" is part of its title, or simply indicates that it was handed down from the Persians.

through this it signified good or evil, and you wanted to know at what time that signification will appear, look at the planet aspecting it (through which it had the signification), to see from where it is aspecting it: and if it aspected [the Lot] from the opposition, judge that the signification will appear towards 7 years; and if it aspected it from the right trine, it will appear toward 9 years; and if from the left trine, towards 5 years; and if from the right square, toward 10 years; and if from the left square, toward 4 years; and if from the right sextile, toward 11 years; and if from the left sextile, toward 3 years.[695] And if a planet were in the twelfth from the Lot of Fortune, and both were in two degrees of equal days and equal ascensions, that signification will appear towards 12 years.[696] And if a planet were in the second from the Lot of Fortune,[697] and likewise they were in the aforesaid degrees, its signification will appear in the second year, since the significators which were in these degrees [are] of equal days and equal ascensions, as they say: they have an application, but not a natural one. For example, in the degrees of equal days, if one of the significators were in the twentieth degree of the sign of Gemini, and the other in the tenth of Cancer: because these two degrees (and the others which are corresponding to them) have equal days and equal ascensions.

Since these methods are from Valens (whose commented work was called the *Bizidāj* in Pahlavi), perhaps the *Endemadeyg* was a version of it.

694 This paragraph and the next are originally taken from *Anth.* III.12, but Valens uses this method to identify crisis times, namely when malefic planets are on or aspecting the Lot of Fortune by sign; he does not include benefic planets or just any planetary aspect.

695 In other words, the Lot of Fortune counts as its own first house, so the number of years will equal the number of derived signs or houses attributed to the location of the aspecting planet.

696 Both here and below, Valens does not confine these effects to signs which have similar days or ascensions. But one can see why a Persian commentator might have added it, because planets adjacent to a sign are normally in aversion to it; but some authors allowed the use of alternative sign relations, used to get around aversions. A Hellenistic description of this can be found in Schmidt 2009, pp. 275-78; for medieval descriptions, see *ITA* III.25 (my commentary). Thus at the end of the sentence, al-Rijāl quotes them as saying this is an "application" (or connection), but not a "natural" one.

697 This is indeed vague in Valens. Valens says it will be every 2 years if the malefic is "connected" to it (*sunaphē*), which implies being in the next sign (i.e., touching the sign of Fortune); but what about a malefic that is actually on the Lot itself, which Valens mentions in the first sentence (III.12.1)? One would expect that to be a "connection," but then it is mysterious why it would get two years, and then the adjacent sign nothing.

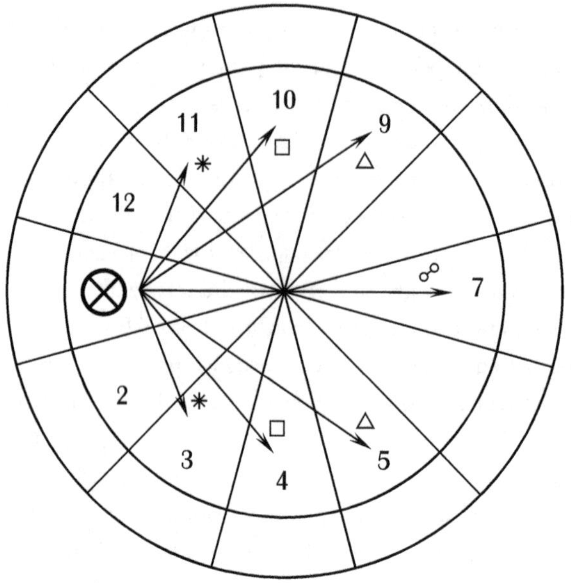

Figure 25: Years given to planets aspecting the Lot of Fortune (*Anth.* III.12)

They even say[698] that if the lord of the Lot of Fortune were in Aries in the root of the nativity (be it made fortunate or unfortunate), that signification of good or bad will appear towards 19 years; and if in Taurus, toward 25 years;[699] [and if in Gemini, toward 20 years; and if in Cancer, toward 25 years]; and if in Leo, toward 12 years; and if in Virgo, toward 8 years; if in Libra, toward 30 years; and if in Scorpio, toward 15 years; [and if in Sagittari-

[698] *Anth.* III.12. Again, Valens discusses this in the context of crisis years only. The rationale behind the assignment of years is based on sect, triplicities, exaltations, and the lesser years of the planets, though I do not understand it completely. For one thing, the years assigned to each sign are based on the triplicities: for example, Venus and the Moon are earthy triplicity lords, and their planetary years are assigned to all the earthy signs. But the reason why particular planets get a certain sign does not always make sense to me. Sometimes, it seems that the triplicity lord matching the sect of the signs gets one assignment, and the other one two signs (thus the Sun is the diurnal triplicity lord of fiery signs, and he gets the sign of his exaltation, while Jupiter gets the others; the Moon is the nocturnal lord of earthy signs, and she gets one of them while Venus gets two); but for air and water, this is reversed: the lord matching the sect of the signs gets two assignments, and the other one a single sign: thus Mars is the nocturnal lord of water, and he gets two signs—and the planet being assigned the third sign is the Moon, when it should be Venus. So, more thought has to be put into understanding why these assignments are being made.

[699] Reading with Valens for "15," and adding Gemini and Cancer from Valens.

us, toward 12 years]; and if in Capricorn, toward 50 years;[700] and if in Aquarius, toward 30 years; if in Pisces, toward 15 years.

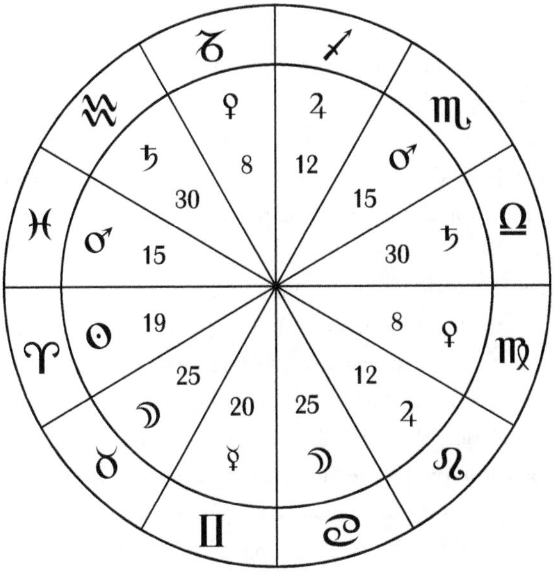

Figure 26: Years given to the signs (derived from the planets' lesser years) when the lord of Fortune is in them (*Anth.* III.12)

	Lesser	Middle	Greater	Greatest
♄	30	43 ½	57	265
♃	12	45 ½	79	427
♂	15	40 ½	66	284
☉	19	69 ½	120	1,461
♀	8	45	82	1,151
☿	20	48	76	480
☽	25	66 ½	108	520

Figure 27: Table of planetary years

700 This should be 8, per Valens. Below we will see that al-Rijāl tries to explain the value of 50.

And the manner of the signification and of the good or bad which happens, will be known from the nature of the sign, and of the significations of that house in which it was, according to [the order of] the houses.

And the sages of Iraq[701] say that the reason why they assigned these categories of the years to the signs, is that when the lord of a house were in any degree of some sign, on any day of some solar month, it will not return to that same degree nor on that same day of that month through its average course or through its direct motion, except in that many years which were ended in this place, and they are taken from them according to the lesser years of the sign.[702]

And the reason for the lesser[703] years of the planets is: if a planet is being joined with the Sun in one degree, it is not joined with him in the same degree, except toward as many years as there are lesser years of the planet. And the greater years are according to the number of degrees belonging to the bounds of that planet, through all the signs. And the middle years of the planet are the average of the greater [years] put together with the lesser years: and this is for the five planets exclusive of the luminaries.

And what he[704] said there (namely that if the lord of the Lot of Fortune were in Capricorn, that its signification would be 50 years), [is] because he gathered together both revolutions of Saturn (which [equals] 60 years), and

---

701 Reading *alyrac* or *alayrac*, for *layrac*.

702 This paragraph begins to explain the lesser years (which he continues in the next paragraph), not the reason why each sign gets a certain number of years in the Valens diagram. The lesser years generally have to do with the completion of cycles. According to Evans (pp. 304-05), the lesser years for the superior planets (Mars, Jupiter, Saturn) is gotten from the sum of (1) the number of tropical cycles elapsed (that is, the average amount of time it takes for a planet to make a complete revolution), and (2) the number of synodic cycles elapsed in that time (i.e., the period between retrogradations). So for example, between 1965 and 1980, where the opposition of Mars to the Sun occurred on roughly the same day, Mars had made 8 revolutions, and 7 synodic cycles: 8 + 7 = 15. The lesser years of the Sun and Moon are based on a relation between their cycles and positions relative to each other. The Sun's years are based on the metonic cycle, such that after 19 years (of 365.25-day calendar years) the Sun and Moon will return to the same positions on the ecliptic on the same day (Evans, p. 185). The lesser years of Mercury and Venus are based on the number of their tropical cycles or revolutions, such that after so many years they will return to the same degree on the same day, having completed so many revolutions. For the Moon, after 25 years (of idealized, 365-day Egyptian years) she has the same phase relationship with the Sun: on our calendar, that's about 6 days short of exactly 25 years.

703 Reading *minorum* for *malorum* (1485) and *maiorum* (1551).

704 Perhaps the author of the *Endemadeyg*.

subtracts from them the *firdārīyyah* of the Sun (which is 10 years), for the reason that the Sun is one root of the Lot of Fortune, and his exaltation and fall are in the squares of Capricorn.[705]

And I say that fortune and misfortune[706] befall the native when the ones making [the Lot] fortunate or the ones making [it] unfortunate, were in the aforesaid places from the Lot of Fortune. And if the lord of the Lot of Fortune were in the signs, made fortunate or unfortunate, its signification will appear according to the number of the aforesaid years through every sign, and it signifies according to the status which it had. This is what the one who wrote the book *Endemadeyg of the Persians*, said.

[Chapter VII.102.4: Eclipses, based on Ptolemy]

Now, the times in which the significations of eclipses appear, are in this manner: in a lunar eclipse, they will be so many months as there were hours [in the eclipse]; and in a solar eclipse, you will give one year for every hour [of the eclipse].[707]

And if the eclipse were in the Ascendant, its significations will begin immediately. And if in the Midheaven, they will begin in the middle of the determined time. And if in the west, they will appear at the end of these determined [times]. And if it appeared between the Ascendant and the tenth, count how many hours of the eclipse there were, and afterwards consider how far the place of the eclipse is, up to the degree of the Ascendant by equal degrees, and look to see what kind of proportion it is with respect to 180, and you would take a like proportion with respect to the hours of the eclipse. And if it were lunar, you will match the months, and if solar, years: and the signification of the eclipse will be in that time. And if it happened between the Midheaven and the west, you will make this same proportion, [and] you will adjoin it to the middle of the determined [time]: if months,

---

705 The Sun is exalted in Aries, and in fall in Libra. Of course, the value of 50 years is simply mistaken and should be 8 (the lesser years of Venus), as in Valens.

706 Reading *infortunium* for *infortuna*.

707 That is, for total eclipses (not partial, annular, etc.). Ptolemy (*Tet.* II.6) tells us to use equinoctial (or standard 60-minute) hours. The period of a solar eclipse begins at the first contact of the Sun and Moon, until they separate completely. The period of a lunar eclipse begins with the first umbric period and ceases at the end of the last one. For example, the total lunar eclipse of December 2011 lasted for 3h 32m 16s, which gives a period of about 3.5 months for the effect.

months; if years, years; and where the number reached (in whatever manner you wanted), the signification will be appearing and strong in that time.

[Chapter VII.102.5: 'Umar al-Tabarī on times in a nativity]

'Umar al-Tabarī said[708] that if an infortune [which was] a harmer were in some good nativity, in one of the angles (especially Mars in a diurnal one or Saturn in a nocturnal one), and it were in the Ascendant or tenth, it will hold back and delay the [good] fortune of that native, and he will be in a miserable life until the lesser years of that planet passed by, or the number of the ascensions of the sign in which it was, would pass by. And if these two passed by and the [good] fortune of the nativity did not appear, by adding the lesser years to the number of the ascensions of that sign will likewise be a time. And if in a bad nativity a fortune were in one of these two places, the native will have good and prosperity of the manner of [its] nature, for as long as are its lesser years, or as are the number of the ascensions of the sign in which it was, or of both joined together.

However, concerning the time and directing[709] of the [longevity] releaser in the nativity, and of the degrees by which the direction comes to be, we have already spoken in the first part of [the book about judging] a nativity, in the chapter on the releaser and the house-master.[710] And one of his[711] methods is when [the directed releaser] encounters the body of a fortune or its rays, or when it entered the bound of a fortune: because then it signifies good, from its own manner and proper quality; likewise, when it encounters the both of an infortune or its rays, or it enters the bound of an infortune: it signifies evil from its nature and proper quality. And when it encounters the cutters,[712] it likewise cuts off the life and time—in all of this, by giving one year to every degree of ascensions, and one month to every five minutes [of ascensions].[713]

---

708 Source unknown at the time, but note the similarity to Valens VII (described above).
709 *Athaçir.*
710 Usually known as the *hīlāj* (or *hyleg*) and *kadukhudhāh* (or *alcochoden*). See al-Rijāl IV.3-4.
711 Or perhaps, "its," referring to the concept of directing. Al-Rijāl is referring to *TBN* I.4.2, I.4.8, and II.2, in *PN2*.
712 That is, the planets which indicate crisis or death.
713 See a table of ascensions, with instructions, at my site: www.bendykes.com.

[Chapter VII.102.6: Al-Hasan bin Sahl on indicators of quickness or slowness]

Al-Hasan bin Sahl said[714] that the times exist in four ways: hours, days, months, and years; and likewise the signs are of four natures: fiery, airy, earthy, and watery. Of them, the lighter ones are the fiery ones, and after these the airy, and after that the watery, and after that the earthy.[715] And of them, the lighter ones are the movable ones, afterwards the common ones, and after that the fixed ones. Likewise, the lighter ones are masculine in their manners, and the weightier ones are feminine.

And[716] what is from the Ascendant to the Midheaven is light, of the nature of hours; and from the Midheaven to the west more weighty, of the nature of days; and from the west to the angle of the earth, more weighty, of the nature of months; and from the angle of the earth to the Ascendant much more weighty, of the nature of years.

And[717] the Moon, because she is light and quick, is of the nature of hours; Mercury and Venus, of the nature of days; the Sun and Mars, of the nature of months; Jupiter and Saturn, of the nature of years.

And[718] the greater quickness which the Moon and the other planets have, is when they are eastern; and the greater slowness and weightiness, when they are western.

[Chapter VII.102.7: Lengths of time from Sahl's On Times §3][719]

And all of the times in every judgment, are in five ways:

One, by looking at the degrees which there were between the planet which applies, and the other to which it applies (whether the application is by ray or by body), by putting them as years or months or days or hours, according to the places in which they were in the figure, and according to the

[714] Much of this section is close to al-'Imrānī I.5.0-1, and *On Times.*

[715] This is the normal Aristotelian ordering of the "natural places" of the elements.

[716] This paragraph is based on Sahl's *On Times* §3, and is more consistent in applying times to the quarters than John's version or Hermann's (in *Search* II.5.2).

[717] This is very close to Ptolemy *Tet.* IV.10 on transits, though Ptolemy gives days to the Moon, and months to Mercury, Venus, the Sun, and Mars.

[718] This paragraph is based on Sahl's *On Times* §3. But it also matches Ptolemy's natal interpretation of easternness and westernness in *Tet.* III.5.

[719] This subchapter is based on al-'Imrānī II.5.2. See my discussion of times in the Introduction.

signs in which they were, by the ranking which we stated with respect to lightness and weightiness.

The second way is by looking to see when a planet would be in such a degree and minute in which the planet to which it applies, is.[720]

The third is by looking to see how much there is between two planets by equal degrees (and not by ascensions),[721] and putting down that number as days.

The fourth is by looking to see when the applying planet is separated from the planet to which it applies, by degree and minute.[722]

The fifth way is by looking to see how great is the number of the lesser years belonging to the planet which is the ruler in the figure, and which had greater signification in it, by rendering them as days, months, or years, according to the ranking which we stated about lightness and weightiness.

And you will judge that the signification will be and will appear according to what you found with respect to the lightness and weightiness of the planets, and according to the lightness and weightiness of the signs, and according to the weightiness and lightness of the places of the figure; and you will commingle one with the other, and you will determine the hours, days, months or years according to what you found, and you will be made certain, by God.

And[723] if the giving planet and the receiving planet were both in the quarter of heaven which is from the Ascendant to the Midheaven, and both [were] eastern and there was reception between them, you will give an hour or day to each degree which was between them. And if they were between the Midheaven and the west, you will give a month or a year[724] to each degree.[725] And if they were from the fourth to the Ascendant, they will be years in all instances.[726]

---

720 This either means that we should note the time at which the applying planet perfects the aspect by transit, or when it reaches the degree in which the slower planet *had been* in the chart for the event (since even the slower planet keeps moving, and might have moved into a later degree before the aspect perfects.

721 That is, by using zodiacal degrees.

722 Or rather, to see when the aspect perfects, not when it separates (since it will separate immediately after perfecting.

723 For the following paragraphs, cf. *On Times* §3, and above in VII.102.6.

724 This should probably be "a day or a month."

725 Missing here is the statement about planets between the Descendant and the IC, which should at least be months but possibly years.

726 *Modis.*

And if the planets were eastern in themselves and western in the figure,[727] the degrees which were in the figure will be days or months.

And the signs in themselves have a role and power in these times, just as we have said; and you will determine years or months or days.[728] Likewise, if the signs were in the quarters of the figure according to that,[729] they signify weightiness and lightness, hours, days, months, or years.

And the sages say[730] that if you had some judgment of planets signifying days by [their] degrees, you should not want to transfer [the units of measurement] to months until [time] has passed through one revolution of the Moon (which is one [Lunar] month), because perhaps[731] one planet will be separated from the other, and the Moon will arrive at the place of the matter or to the lord of the Ascendant, or the lord of the Ascendant will apply to the Ascendant or to the place of the matter, and that matter and signification will be on that day, if God wills.

And others say:[732] take the termination of the time from the one which signified that the matter would be, because just as it signified the matter through its motion and its applications and separations, so will it signify the time when it applied to the places which signify power.[733]

---

727 For example, if they were rising before the Sun (eastern by solar phase) but in a "western" quadrant (such as between the Midheaven and the Descendant).

728 This is probably a reference to *On Times* §2, which says that the signs ruled by the lighter planets are themselves light, while those ruled by heavier planets are themselves heavier.

729 This seems to refer to the previous paragraph. Al-Rijāl seems to mean that if the sign of a heavy planet (such as Aquarius) were in a part of the chart were in a quadrant that suggested speed (such as between the Ascendant and the Midheaven), its units of time might be closer to days and months, rather than months to years.

730 Namely, Sahl in *On Times* §3, but Hermann in *Search* II.5.2 credits both Sahl and 'Umar with this view. Here, Sahl is reminding us of two things. First, within a Lunar month the Moon will have made every possible transit to every other planet and place: so before we give up on a measurement by days, we must be patient because she might provide the timing for up to a month, through her own transits. (Al-Rijāl reminds us explicitly of this below.) Second, even within the Lunar month there are other planets which might indicate the timing by their own transits.

731 That is, "perhaps *before* a full Lunar month has passed."

732 Source unknown at this time.

733 This probably means a transit to the degrees which were on the angles at the time of the chart.

[Chapter VII.102.8: Other opinions]

Al-Hasan bin Sahl said: We have looked and hoped for the times which the sages stated, and we have found another path in them which ought to be observed along with the others: and it is the natures of the planets. Because if you wanted a time because of kings or lords of revolutions of the world, or in the changing of weather, you will determine this from the Sun, because he is a significator of kings, and through him the seasons are changed, and in the seasons even the status of the planets.[734] And the Moon is the significator of travels and legations, changes, and every matter which is completely changed and removed, through her speediness and lightness, and the changing of her own status. Likewise, the other planets signify matters agreeing with their natures and proper qualities, and each of them draws to itself the part with their significations.[735] Whence, when you wanted to determine the time of some judgment, you should know the nature of that matter, and which one is the significator which signified it, and you will take the time from the planet which is of the nature of the matter all by itself,[736] and you will determine the time with respect to hours, days, months, or years, just as we said before about the natures of the places and signs and degrees.

And you should know that when the fortunes aspect the significator which signified good and fortune, they shorten the time and accelerate it; and if the infortunes aspected it, they prolong the time and slow it down. Likewise, when the infortunes aspect a significator which signifies evil and misfortune, they shorten the time and accelerate it; and if the fortunes aspected it, they prolong that misfortune and delay it.

A planet which is light through its nature and place, if it were retrograde, signifies slowness. A planet which is weighty through its nature and place, if it were retrograde, signifies shortness.

And[737] if it were asked of you about some matter which ought to be, as to when it will be and appear, take [the distance] from the lord of the hour up to the degree of the Midheaven, or up to the lord of the Ascendant, and look

---

734 *Et in temporibus status etiam planetarum.* Meaning somewhat uncertain.

735 Reading *trahit ad se* with 1551 for *trahit se ad*, though this seems redundant.

736 *Separatim.* But it might be *specialiter* ("especially").

737 This paragraph seems to be taken from al-Tabarī (*Judges* §4.19). There, 'Umar considers two Lot-like calculations. The first uses the distance from the lord of the hour to the lord of the Ascendant, which is then projected from the Midheaven—but it is only used to determine *if* something will come to be. The other calculation is taken from the lord of the hour to the Midheaven. But there are some differences between the two descriptions.

to see how many degrees there were between them: and give a day or month or year in this manner to every degree: if the lord of the hour and the lord of the Midheaven were in movable signs, they will be days; and if in common ones, they will be months; and if in fixed ones, years.

And[738] if it were asked of you about some matter, and you judged that the matter will be, and you wanted to know when, look to the planet signifying that the matter will be, and when the Moon applies to it, and if it[739] were in a fixed sign, and in an angle or a succeedent: you will give a year to every degree which was between them. And if it were in a common, succeedent [sign], give one year to every 10° which were between them.[740] And if it were in a common [sign that is] cadent from the angle, give one year to every 2° 30'. And if it were in a movable sign and in a succeedent, give one month to every 2° 30'. And if it were in a movable sign and cadent from the angle, give one day to every 2° 30'.

[Chapter VII.102.9: Times for rulerships and dignities]

And if it were asked of you for a king or for someone having a dignity, as to when he would lose that kingdom or be removed from that dignity, look at the significator. And if you found it in the Midheaven or in its exaltation, judge that he will last according to the quantity of the lesser years of the significator, and you should not add anything above the minor years for a king, but subtract from them according to what you saw from the place of the significator and its power and weakness in its own place and in itself: and perhaps you will have to put them as being months or days, according to what you found in the status of the aforesaid significator.

However,[741] if you wanted to know when the dignity would be taken away from the one having the dignity, you should make a direction[742] of the degree of the Midheaven, by degrees of ascensions. And when you found it applying to the body of an infortune or its rays, and it did not have a commingling with a fortune, and it happened that the lord of the Midheaven is made un-

---

[738] This paragraph is extremely close to Jirjis in *Judges* §4.22, but some of the attributions of months or years differ.

[739] I take this to be the significator, not the Moon.

[740] Jirjis gives a month for every degree, not a year for every 10°.

[741] This paragraph comes from 'Umar (see *Judges* §10.14), who attributes these views to Valens. 'Umar then repeats similar ideas in *TBN* II.3.

[742] *Athaçir.*

fortunate at that time, it cuts off [the dignity].[743] And when the Moon applied by her motion to that degree and to the place of the infortune or its rays ([that is, the one] applied [to] by the direction of the degree of the Midheaven), judge that the taking away [of the dignity] and [its] occasion, will happen on that day. And if Jupiter or Venus aspected that place by any aspect, they remove the incident and defer it until they are separated by that same aspect. And this is known in another manner: which is that you compute from the degree of the Midheaven up to an infortune by equal degrees,[744] and give one year, month, or day to each degree (according to the lightness or heaviness of the signs).

And I[745] have experienced many times that when the lord of the exaltation of the Ascendant, or the lord of the house of the Moon, or the lord of the Lot of Fortune, aspected the Ascendant or had rulership in the figure, it will signify the quantity of the time, and how much remains in the dignity according to its places and dignities. And the lord of the bound of the degree of the Midheaven does the same thing.[746]

And[747] a kingdom was never lost unless the Sun, in a revolution of that year, was in an angle and the Moon in the sixth or in the second house.

Likewise,[748] if the lord of the tenth applied to the lord of the fourth, the kingdom is lost. And if the lord of the tenth applied to the lord of the Ascendant, the king will last in his kingdom. And if the lord of the tenth or the lord of the Ascendant applied to the lord of its own fall, it signifies a dividing up of the kingdom.

Likewise,[749] look to see in what sign is the planet signifying the matter, and in which quarter, and according to the quantity of the ascensions of that sign give it days, months, or years, according to what agrees with the status of the planet and its place, and the sign, following the determinations which

---

743 I have read this last part as meaning that "the lord of the Midheaven is made unfortunate *by transit* at the time indicated by the direction."

744 Degrees of the zodiac. But in *Judges*, the text clearly demands degrees of ascensions, which makes more sense.

745 Al-Rijāl.

746 This sounds like a distribution of the Midheaven through the bounds, but al-Rijāl may be referring to the location of the lord and its transits, as with the others.

747 Source unknown at this time, nor does it make astrological sense to me: *Et nunquam regnum fuit amissum nisi fuerit in revolutione illius anni Sol in angulo et Luna in sexta vel in secunda domo.*

748 This paragraph is very similar to Sahl in *On Quest.* §10.7 (*Judges* §10.12).

749 The next two paragraphs are generic enough that they may have come from any number of sources.

we have said. And perhaps it will be days or months according to the number of its own lesser years, or greater ones or middle ones.

Likewise, matters and the time are determined by the form of the planetary significator: which if it were eastern, [the time is] when it becomes western; and if western, when it becomes eastern; and if retrograde, when it goes direct; and if direct, when it goes retrograde; and if burnt, when it will appear and becomes eastern. All of these are times in which the significations should be fulfilled.

[Chapter VII.102.10: 'Umar al-Tabarī on times]

'Umar al-Tabarī said[750] that if the significator would be burned, its signification will appear in that time.

And when the Moon entered the Ascendant, it is likewise a time; if she had some rulership in a house, it will likewise be the time of the appearance of that matter.

And if the two fortunes would be conjoined in one of the angles of the Ascendant, it is likewise a time.

And if the Sun had some dignity or some share in the matter, and he entered upon the Ascendant, the matter will be moved at that time, and it is one of the times—and if the fortunes were joined in the house of the matter, it is likewise a time.

And all of these times which you took through these applications, you will take by degrees of ascensions and by equal degrees,[751] by beginning first from that one of them which was less.[752] And if it went past it,[753] you will take another.

Likewise, when the Moon or the lord of the Ascendant applied to a planetary fortune having a likeness in the nature of the matter,[754] that application

[750] The next few paragraph are probably from a work of 'Umar's on times, which Sahl partially excerpts in his own *On Times* and are laid out rather clearly in *Search* II.5.2.
[751] That is, both by ascensional degrees and zodiacal ones.
[752] I am not sure whether this means zodiacal degrees versus ascensions, or shorter and longer time-units (such as days versus weeks).
[753] That is, if the event has not appeared by the lesser amount of time.
[754] Such as Jupiter in questions about wealth.

will be a time of the appearance of the matter. And the number of degrees which was between them in that same application, is likewise a time.[755]

And when the Moon had dignity and rulership in the matter, the greatest time which one ought to give her is one month, because the transits through all natures in so much [time], and through her house, and through the lord of her own house, and through the Ascendant and its lord, and through the fortunes and infortunes.

And when the lord of the house of the matter applied to a fortune, it is likewise a time. And when the Moon applied to a fortune it is likewise a time.

And[756] that which signifies that a matter will be [happening] shortly and quickly, is that the significator of the matter be in one of the light quarters, and eastern of the Sun, and of quick motion in itself, and received, and the one which receives it is likewise of quick motion and safe from the infortunes: because when all of these states are joined, they signify that the matter will be fulfilled quickly. And when [something] is subtracted from these, it is subtracted from the matter in terms of shortness, and it will be more delayed until the time reaches years.[757]

And[758] perhaps the time will be toward so many days as are the degrees from the significator up to the degree of the Ascendant, by making a day from every degree; or perhaps the time will be when the Sun, through his own motion, arrives at the Ascendant or the house of the matter.

And this[759] is made certain and verified for [both] a weighty and a light planet if it were the lord of the house of the Sun, with the Sun appearing in a succeedent. It is verified for kings and in matters which are fit for lasting a long time. However, if the planet were weighty, and it were the lord of [the Sun's] house, it cannot certify matters which are not fitted for lasting long (such as infirmities or a theft, and what is like these).

And Valens said:[760] if it were asked of you about the time of some matter, when it will be, look at the Sun at the hour of the question: and if you found him in an angle, say that the matter in which trust is had that it would be, will [happen] when he reaches the Midheaven. And if he were in a succeedent,

---

755 That is, the first sentence talked about a real-time transit, while this second sentence refers to symbolic times by degree.

756 *Search* II.5.1 attributes the views in this paragraph to 'Umar al-Tabarī.

757 That is, each missing indication of shortness will tend to make the time longer, until we are left with an event that will take years.

758 This paragraph continues some of the material from *On Times* §3 (see above).

759 This paragraph might be referring to the previous one, but it is not from *On Times*.

760 Source unknown at this time.

look at the lord of the house in which he was, and when [that planet] applied to the Midheaven, then the matter will be.

Here is ended the seventh part of the complete book of 'Ali bin al-Rijāl

APPENDIX A: RULERSHIPS

Sign	Domicile	Exaltation	Detriment	Fall
♈	♂	☉	♀	♄
♉	♀	☽	♂	
♊	☿		♃	
♋	☽	♃	♄	♂
♌	☉		♄	
♍	☿	☿	♃	♀
♎	♀	♄	♂	☉
♏	♂		♀	☽
♐	♃		☿	
♑	♄	♂	☽	♃
♒	♄		☉	
♓	♃	♀	☿	☿

Figure 28: Major dignities and counter-dignities

Triplicity	Diurnal	Nocturnal	Participating
Fire	☉	♃	♄
Air	♄	☿	♃
Water	♀	♂	☽
Earth	♀	☽	♂

Figure 29: Triplicity lords

♈	♃ 0°-5°59'	♀ 6°-11°59'	☿ 12°-19°59'	♂ 20°-24°59'	♄ 25°-29°59'
♉	♀ 0°-7°59'	☿ 8°-13°59'	♃ 14°-21°59'	♄ 22°-26°59'	♂ 27°-29°59'
♊	☿ 0°-5°59'	♃ 6°-11°59'	♀ 12°-16°59'	♂ 17°-23°59'	♄ 24°-29°59'
♋	♂ 0°-6°59'	♀ 7°-12°59'	☿ 13°-18°59'	♃ 19°-25°59'	♄ 26°-29°59'
♌	♃ 0°-5°59'	♀ 6°-10°59'	♄ 11°-17°59'	☿ 18°-23°59'	♂ 24°-29°59'
♍	☿ 0°-6°59'	♀ 7°-16°59'	♃ 17°-20°59'	♂ 21°-27°59'	♄ 28°-29°59'
♎	♄ 0°-5°59'	☿ 6°-13°59'	♃ 14°-20°59'	♀ 21°-27°59'	♂ 28°-29°59'
♏	♂ 0°-6°59'	♀ 7°-10°59'	☿ 11°-18°59'	♃ 19°-23°59'	♄ 24°-29°59'
♐	♃ 0°-11°59'	♀ 12°-16°59'	☿ 17°-20°59'	♄ 21°-25°59'	♂ 26°-29°59'
♑	☿ 0°-6°59'	♃ 7°-13°59'	♀ 14°-21°59'	♄ 22°-25°59'	♂ 26°-29°59'
♒	☿ 0°-6°59'	♀ 7°-12°59'	♃ 13°-19°59'	♂ 20°-24°59'	♄ 25°-29°59'
♓	♀ 0°-11°59'	♃ 12°-15°59'	☿ 16°-18°59'	♂ 19°-27°59'	♄ 28°-29°59'

Figure 30: Table of Egyptian bounds

Sign	**0° - 9°59'**	**10° - 19°59'**	**20° - 29°29'**
♈	♂	☉	♀
♉	☿	☽	♄
♊	♃	♂	☉
♋	♀	☿	☽
♌	♄	♃	♂
♍	☉	♀	☿
♎	☽	♄	♃
♏	♂	☉	♀
♐	☿	☽	♄
♑	♃	♂	☉
♒	♀	☿	☽
♓	♄	♃	♂

Figure 31: Table of "Chaldean" faces or decans

APPENDIX B: TYPES OF SIGNS

Following are a few special categorizations of the signs based on this book and other medieval authors. Some categories (such as those of many children) are universally agreed upon, while traditional authorities disagree on others. See the sources mentioned in the footnotes for other categorizations.

Fertility and growth:

- *Many children*: Cancer, Scorpio, Pisces
- *No children (sterile)*: Gemini, Leo, Virgo
- *Seeds/sprouting*:[1] Aries,[2] Taurus, Virgo, Capricorn

Reason and passion:

- *Rational*: Gemini, Libra, Aquarius
- *Human*:[3] Gemini, Virgo, Libra, first half of Sagittarius, Aquarius, sometimes Libra
- *Fully voiced*:[4] Gemini, Virgo, Libra,
- *Partly-voiced*:[5] Aries, Taurus, Leo, Sagittarius, Capricorn, Aquarius
- *Mute*:[6] Cancer, Scorpio, Pisces
- *Much eating*:[7] Aries, Taurus, Leo, last half of Sagittarius, Capricorn, Pisces
- *Licentious/indecent*:[8] Aries, Taurus, Capricorn, Libra "in part," Pisces
- *Lecherous*:[9] Aries, Taurus, Leo, Libra, Capricorn "in part," Pisces
- *Delighting in sex*:[10] Aries, Capricorn, Leo, Libra

---

[1] Al-'Imrānī II.2.2, al-Rijāl VII.32.

[2] According to Abū Ma'shar in *ITA* I.3 (probably because spring begins when the Sun is in it).

[3] Al-Bīrūnī's *Book of Instruction* §352.

[4] See *ITA* I.3.

[5] See *ITA* I.3.

[6] See *ITA* I.3.

[7] Al-'Imrānī II.3.1, al-Rijāl VII.10.

[8] Rhetorius Ch. 5.

[9] Rhetorius Ch. 76.

[10] Al-Rijāl VII.65.

Other:

- *Chewing the cud:*[11] Taurus, Capricorn (and others?)
- *Four-footed:*[12] Aries, Taurus, Leo, last half of Sagittarius, Capricorn
- *Royal:* Aries, Leo, Sagittarius

---

[11] Al-'Imrānī II.2.11.

[12] See Sahl's *Introduction* §1; cf. al-Rijāl VII.63, which must be only a partial list.

Appendix C: General Instructions on Elections, from al-Kindī

Following are short passages and sections from al-Kindī's *The Forty Chapters* (2011), which present general considerations for elections:

§81.[1] On the other hand, the conjunction of the planet with the Lot analogous to itself (or a regard to [the Lot]) increases its powers for that effect: such as if Jupiter would be united with the Lot of money,[2] or would regard it.[3]

§153. Therefore, the force of the Ascendant and the one from whom the Moon recedes (in the way it was described above with respect to strength),[4] provided that the Ascendant obtains some likeness with the nature of the quaesited matter,[5] and if it acquires the comfort of the fortunate ones (namely their presence or regard) or some shared bearing,[6] [and] even [if] the strength and prosperity of the Moon [is present],[7] they convey victory in the cause, and success to its agent—particularly if the weakness and misfortune of the seventh and the one with whom the Moon's application comes to be, is discovered.

§550.[8] But in all of these things, the Lot of Fortune and her lord should be in a strong place or blessed by the fortunes with reception. Furthermore, to the extent that opportunity permits it, let the star (through whose signifi-

---

[1] This section is only in Robert.

[2] The Lot of money (or assets or substance or resources) is taken by day and night from the lord of the second to the degree of the second, and projected from the Ascendant. For more information, see *ITA* VI.2.4.

[3] See also §141, which has similar information. My sense is that only an aspect by sign is needed, and not necessarily by degree; but surely an aspect by degree would be more helpful.

[4] See the end of §139, §§63-72, §§77-78, and *ITA* IV.2.

[5] See §142 above.

[6] See §144 above.

[7] See esp. *ITA* IV.5.

[8] Reading this paragraph with Robert. Hugo only has the first sentence: "Moreover, greatly desire the Lot of Fortune or its lord to be made fortunate, received from a strong place."

cation the decision is sought),[9] regard, assist, and receive the lord of the east and the Moon and the Lots of Fortune and of money.

§552. Therefore, whenever a question came out into the open about those things which pertain to the signification of some house, let the reception of its lord be sought, namely [let the lord receive][10] the Moon and the lord of the Ascendant and the Lot of Fortune and the Lot of money; also, you will place the lunar lord (no less even the lords of the Ascendant and of the fourth) cleansed of the infortunes, and strong. For the leadership and signification of these lays bare the end of the question.

Chapter 4: On beginning affairs[11]

§142. Before everything [else], the Ascendant and its lord must be established, with a certain [1] likeness[12] and [2] prosperity[13] being observed.

[1] Likeness is observed when the Ascendant itself preserves the nature of the quaesited matter, or a likeness of its nature, in quality and manner. But then [1a] the quality of the nature is noted when someone does not neglect to arrange the fiery signs if an inquirer is concerned about the quick and certain outcome of matters, or about some dignity or kingdom; again, the [1b] manner must be brought to bear, just as we look at the signs of Mars when asking about war.

§143. Besides that,[14] [3] the place of the question (or rather, of the quaesited matter) and its lord must be noted. For the place of the question suggests the beginning of the matter and the affair. Also, its lord regulates the middle. But the lord of its lord resolves the end of the whole matter. Likewise, the Ascendant too maintains the querent's affairs, in the aforesaid order. Even the Lot of the quaesited matter and its lord,[15] and the lord of its house, testify to the same thing and in the same order.

---

[9] This seems to mean the natural significator of the partner, as described in §551.

[10] See the footnote to §551.

[11] This chapter may be compared to al-Rijāl VII.2.1.

[12] *Similitudo*. Robert reads, "suitability of form."

[13] Robert reads, "good fortune" (*fortuna*).

[14] This section presents a third category to observe, besides [1] the likeness and [2] the prosperity: namely, [3] the appropriate arrangement and choosing of the places, Lots, and their lords.

[15] For example, the Lot of money for financial matters, or the Lot of children for children: see *ITA* VI for these formulas and instructions. Robert adds the Lot of Fortune as

§144. Once these things have been established in the order written above, [2] the prosperity or benevolence is increased by the stars' being situated in their own places or in their regard or friendly application, with the unfortunate ones being expelled from these same places. One will even have be beware lest the lord of the Ascendant or of the quaesited matter appear retrograde: for even though all things may be promised as being able to come about, the effecting of the matter will follow after very much labor and long desperation, with many adverse obstacles.

§145. I reckon one must even avoid having the Tail accompany the Sun or Moon (with them being in the assembly or opposition), or just one of them (with none of them being in an assembly or opposition),[16] and also lest [the sign] it possesses be in the Ascendant or the place of the matter or the Lot of the matter. For [the Tail] corrupts affairs with the causes of low-class people, namely it being wrested away by ignoble people.[17]

§146. On the other hand, one should rejoice if the fortunate ones should appear in the Ascendant or in the place of the question, or [in] the pivots. For the greater fortunate one[18] reinforces everything whose perfection you are inquiring about; also, the lesser fortune[19] establishes and stimulates jokes and women, appetite, even the ornamentation of clothing, gold and gems, even loves and what is like these.

§147. Moreover, we warn you to beware in every question lest the Moon ever occupy the Ascendant, because from that very place she always turns against affairs generally. But the Sun never does so from there: rather, he brings about the matter and removes delay.

§148. Again, it seems one should take the greatest care lest the infortunes hold onto the Ascendant and the pivots, particularly [those infortunes] ruling over the unlucky [places]: namely, the sixth and twelfth and eighth. For if an infortune rules over the eighth, the danger of death, the helpers of his enemies, and hard captivity threaten [him]. Also, the lord of the sixth encourages

---

well, which makes sense (but al-Rijāl has *only* the Lot of Fortune, and not the Lot of the matter). According to Robert, the Lot of Fortune pertains to the inceptor (or the one who undertakes the matter), and the Lot of the particular matter to the thing asked about.

16 Reading for the transliteration of the Arabic, *alestime vel izticbel.*

17 Although the Tail can indicate things and people of low status, Hugo is probably adding a bit too much into the delineation. Robert puts it more generally: "it makes the matter unfortunate, subtracts, weakens, impedes, and, drawing it out, aggravates it." Al-Rijāl agrees more with Robert.

18 That is, Jupiter.

19 That is, Venus.

that one will have to beware the same thing from enemies and slaves and a long-term illness, and from a brief captivity, and sometimes even from four-footed animals. Again, if the same [infortune] has rulership over the twelfth, it signifies punishments, being afflicted by loss of hope and labor, even enemies [and] a captivity of moderate length. Again, with it claiming the rulership of the second, he will undergo loss because of money and friends, even a marriage [or] drinking.[20]

§149. We[21] even order you to take diligent care that a diurnal Ascendant and straight sign be ascending in a diurnal [chart], but a nocturnal and straight one in the night.[22] Likewise the Sun and Moon as well.[23] Remember to make sure that the lords which we stated before, be strengthened in all things we wrote before. Also, none doubts but that the counsel of the stars and the benefit of the signs happens according to their status and the signification of [their] nature.

---

[20] This list of indications for the second house can be viewed in terms of its whole-sign angles: money (the second itself), friends (eleventh), and the financial aspects of a marriage (eighth, the second from the seventh), drinking or partying (fifth).

[21] Cf. *Carmen* V.4.5.

[22] Reading with Robert for Hugo's choppy sentence. This assumes one wants a long process or result, since signs of straight ascension make things last longer.

[23] This probably means that the sect light should be in a sign of the appropriate gender/sect, and in a sign of straight ascensions.

Appendix D: Three Versions of the *Bust*

The following excerpts from *ITA* VIII.4 and the *Book of Aristotle* II.4 present three versions of the *bust* or "scorched" or "burnt" or "combust" hours, to complement al-Rijāl's VII.57.2, which is itself taken from al-Kindī's *Forty Chapters* Ch. 11.7. (1) The first is a version attributed to the Indians, and attributes planetary rulers to sets of 12 hours after the Full Moon, in the order of the hierarch of the planets; it also divides the periods into three, attributing each 1/3 to the triplicity lords. (2) The second is the version described by al-Kindī and al-Rijāl, in which the unequal seasonal hours after the New Moon are divided into scorched/burnt and unscorched/unburnt hours (with some division of these periods into electionally-relevant periods). I have a lengthy comment on this method following al-Rijāl VII.57.2. (3) The third is described by Māshā'allāh in the *Book of Aristotle* II.4 (in *PN1*), which is based on distance instead of time. For a discussion of these methods, see my Introduction.

> [(1:) al-Qabīsī IV.23] And from this the *bust*,[1] which is a thing the Indians very much used to observe. For they counted 12 hours after the conjunction [of the Sun and Moon], and they apply them to the Sun, and they divide the 12 hours in the domain[2] of the Sun into three, and they judge, with respect to every 4 hours, according to the judgment of the lords of the triplicity of the Sun at the hour of the conjunction. Then they even give Venus 12 hours after the 12 hours of the Sun, and they divide them again into three, and they judge over every one-third division according to the lords of the triplicity of Venus at the hour of the conjunction. After this, they do likewise with Mercury and the rest of the planets through their successions, until the orb reverts back to the Sun after 84 hours, and they do not cease to do thus frequently until it comes to the following conjunction.

---

[1] A transliteration of the Sanskrit *bhukti*, the ecliptical distance traveled in a particular time. See al-Bīrūnī's *Book of Instruction*, §§197-98. In *BA* II.4 it is defined as 12°, roughly the average distance traveled by the Moon in one day. But here it is defined in terms of seasonal hours, such as the first 12 seasonal hours after the New Moon.

[2] *Ḥayyiz*, here being roughly synonymous with sect.

[(2:) al-Qabīsī IV.24] And certain people said that the *bust* is this: that after the conjunction there are 12 unequal hours[3] which are called "burnt," and it is not good to undertake some work in them; and after these 12 are 72 "unburnt" hours, in which the undertaking of works is useful; and after the 72 unburnt hours, 12 burnt ones,[4] up to the conjunction which comes after. After this, they divide these 12 hours into 3 divisions, and they said that one who undertakes to wage war in the first four hours will have to fear the loss of his own soul; and one who undertook it in the second 4 hours will have to fear the corruption of his own body without the loss of his soul; and he who undertook it in the last four hours will have to fear the corruption of his assets and companions.

[(3:) *Book of Aristotle* II.4] But the *buht*,[5] in a foreign language, is the Lunar progression by day and night. For example, it is the course of the Moon through the night and day whenever she crosses the boundary of the Sun all the way to 12°, the necessary main points of which Dorotheus indeed arranged candidly enough in [his] fifth book.[6]

[3] I.e., seasonal hours (sometimes called planetary hours): the period of daylight or night divided by 12, which gives hours of more or less than the standardized or equinoctial sixty minutes.

[4] These correspond to the hours belonging to the Sun and his triplicity Lords in the previous paragraph.

[5] Ar. *al-buht/bust* (Lat. *albust*), a transliteration of the Sanskrit *bhukti*, the ecliptical distance traveled in a particular time. In this case, the Moon will be separated from the Sun by about 12° in one day.

[6] Probably referring to *Carmen* V.41.15 (the chapter is attributed to a "Qitrinus the Sadwali"). Here, when determining critical days for illnesses, the Moon's motion in certain numbers of days is equated with her aspects to her beginning position.

APPENDIX E:
THE *ESSENTIAL MEDIEVAL ASTROLOGY* CYCLE

The *Essential Medieval Astrology* cycle is a projected series of books which will redefine the contours of traditional astrology. Comprised mainly of translations of works by Persian and Arabic-speaking medieval astrologers, it will cover all major areas of astrology, including philosophical treatments and magic. The cycle will be accompanied by compilations of introductory works and readings on the one hand, and independent monographs and encyclopedic works on the other (including late medieval and Renaissance works of the Latin West). In the future, this cycle will be supplemented by Hellenistic and Renaissance series.

I. Introductions

- *Traditional Astrology for Today: An Introduction* (2011)
- *Introductions to Astrology: Abū Ma'shar & al-Qabīsī* (2010)
- Abū Ma'shar, *Great Introduction to the Knowledge of the Judgments of the Stars* (2014)
- *Basic Readings in Traditional Astrology* (2013-14)

II. Nativities

- *Persian Nativities I*: Māshā'allāh's *The Book of Aristotle*, Abū 'Ali al-Khayyāt's *On the Judgments of Nativities* (2009)
- *Persian Nativities II*: 'Umar al-Tabarī's *Three Books on Nativities*, Abū Bakr's *On Nativities* (2010)
- *Persian Nativities III: On Solar Revolutions* (2010)

III. Questions (Horary)

- Hermann of Carinthia, *The Search of the Heart* (2011)
- Al-Kindī, *The Forty Chapters* (2011)
- Various, *The Book of the Nine Judges* (2011)

IV. Elections

- *Choices & Inceptions: Traditional Electional Astrology* (2012)

V. Mundane

- *Astrology of the World* (multiple volumes): Abū Ma'shar's *On the Revolutions of the Years of the World*, *Book of Religions and Dynasties*, and *Flowers*; Sahl bin Bishr's *Prophetic Sayings*; lesser works on revolutions, prices, and weather (2012-13)

VI. Other Works

- Bonatti, Guido, *The Book of Astronomy* (2007)
- *Works of Sahl & Māshā'allāh* (2008)
- Firmicus Maternus, *Mathesis* (TBA)
- Al-Rijāl, *The Book of the Skilled* (TBA)
- *Astrological Magic* (TBA)
- *The Latin Hermes* (TBA)
- *A Course in Traditional Astrology* (TBA)

GLOSSARY

This glossary is an expanded version of the one in my *Introductions to Traditional Astrology* (*ITA*), with the addition of other terms found in *Judges*. After most definitions is a reference to sections and Appendices of *ITA* (including my introduction to it) for further reading—*not* the Appendices of this book on elections.

- **Adding in course.** See **Course**.
- **Advancing**. When a planet is in an **angle** or succeedent. See III.3 and the Introduction §6.
- **Advantageous places**. One of two schemes of **houses** which indicate affairs/planets which are more busy or good in the context of the chart (III.4). The seven-place scheme according to Timaeus and reported in *Carmen* includes only certain signs which **aspect** the **Ascendant** by **whole-sign**, and suggests that these places are advantageous for the *native* because they aspect the Ascendant. The eight-place scheme according to Nechepso (III.4) lists all of the **angular** and **succeedent** places, suggesting places which are stimulating and advantageous for a planet *in itself.*
- **Ages of man**. Ptolemy's division of a typical human life span into periods ruled by planets as **time lords**. See VII.3.
- **Agreeing signs**. Groups of signs which share some kind of harmonious quality. See I.9.5-6.
- ***Alcochoden***. Latin transliteration for ***Kadukhudhāh***.
- **Alien** (Lat. *alienus*). See **Peregrine.**
- ***Almuten***. A Latin transliteration for ***mubtazz***: see **Victor**.
- **Angles, succeedents, cadents.** A division of houses into three groups which show how powerfully and directly a planet acts. The angles are the 1st, 10th, 7th and 4th houses; the succeedents are the 2nd, 11th, 8th and 5th; the cadents are the 12th, 9th, 6th and 3rd (but see **cadent** below). But the exact regions in question will depend upon whether and how one uses **whole-sign** and **quadrant houses**, especially since traditional texts refer to an angle or pivot (Gr. *kentron*, Ar. *watad*) as either (1) equivalent to the **whole-sign** angles from the **Ascendant**, or (2) the degrees of the **Ascendant-Midheaven** axes themselves, or (3) **quadrant houses** (and their associat-

ed strengths) as measured from the degrees of the axes. See I.12-13 and III.3-4, and the Introduction §6.

- **Antiscia** (sing. *antiscion*), "throwing shadows." Refers to a degree mirrored across an axis drawn from 0° Capricorn to 0° Cancer. For example, 10° Cancer has 20° Gemini as its antiscion. See I.9.2.
- **Apogee**. Typically, the furthest point a planet can be from the earth on the circle of the **deferent**. See II.0-1.
- **Applying, application**. When a planet is in a state of **connection**, moving so as to make the connection exact. Planets **assembled** together or in **aspect** by sign and not yet connected by the relevant degrees, are only "wanting" to be connected.
- **Arisings.** See **Ascensions**.
- **Ascendant**. Usually the entire rising sign, but often specified as the exact rising degree. In **quadrant houses**, a space following the exact rising degree up to the cusp of the 2nd house.
- **Ascensions.** Degrees on the celestial equator, measured in terms of how many degrees pass the meridian as an entire sign or **bound** (or other spans of zodiacal degrees) passes across the horizon. They are often used in the predictive technique of ascensional times, as an approximation for **directions**. See Appendix E.
- **Aspect/regard**. One planet aspects or regards another if they are in signs which are configured to each other by a **sextile**, **square**, **trine**, or **opposition**. See III.6 and **Whole signs**. A connection by degrees or orbs is a much more intense of an aspect.
- **Assembly**. When two or more planets are in the same sign, and more intensely if within 15°. See III.5.
- **Aversion.** Being in the second, sixth, eighth, or twelfth sign from a place. For instance, a planet in Gemini is in the twelfth from, and therefore in aversion to, Cancer. Such places are in aversion because they cannot **aspect** it by the classical scheme of aspects. See III.6.1.
- ***Azamene***. Equivalent to **Chronic illness.**
- **Bad ones.** See **Benefic/malefic.**
- **Barring**. See **Blocking**.
- **Bearing** (Lat. *habitude*). Hugo's term for any of the many possible planetary conditions and relationships. These may be found in III and IV.

- **Benefic/malefic**. A division of the planets into groups that cause or signify typically "good" things (Jupiter, Venus, usually the Sun and Moon) or "bad" things (Mars, Saturn). Mercury is considered variable. See V.9.
- **Benevolents.** See **Benefic/malefic.**
- **Besieging**. Equivalent to **Enclosure**.
- **Bicorporeal signs.** Equivalent to "common" signs. See **Quadruplicity.**
- **Blocking** (sometimes called "prohibition"). When a planet bars another planet from completing a **connection**, either through its own body or ray. See III.14.
- **Bodyguarding**. Planetary relationships in which some planet protects another, used in determining social eminence and prosperity. See III.28.
- **Bounds.** Unequal divisions of the zodiac in each sign, each bound being ruled by one of the five non-**luminaries**. Sometimes called "terms," they are one of the five classical **dignities.** See VII.4.
- **Bright, smoky, empty, dark degrees**. Certain degrees of the zodiac said to affect how conspicuous or obscure the significations of planets or the Ascendant are. See VII.7.
- **Burned up** (or "combust," Lat. *combustus*). Normally, when a planet is between about 1° and 7.5° away from the Sun. See II.9-10, and **In the heart.**
- **Burnt path** (Lat. *via combusta*). A span of degrees in Libra and Scorpio in which a planet (especially the Moon) is considered to be harmed or less able to effect its significations. Some astrologers identify it as between 15° Libra and 15° Scorpio; others between the exact degree of the **fall** of the Sun in 19° Libra and the exact degree of the fall of the Moon in 3° Scorpio. See IV.3.
- ***Bust***. Certain hours measured from the New Moon, in which it is considered favorable or unfavorable to undertake an action or perform an **election**. See VIII.4.
- **Busy places**. Equivalent to the **Advantageous places.**
- **Cadent** (Lat. *cadens*, "falling"). This is used in two ways: a planet or place may be cadent from the **angles** (being in the 3rd, 6th, 9th, or 12th), or else cadent from the **Ascendant** (namely, in **aversion** to it, being in the 12th, 8th, 6th, or 2nd). See I.12, III.4, and III.6.1.
- **Cardinal.** Equivalent to "movable" signs. See **Quadruplicity.**
- **Cazimi:** see **In the heart**.
- **Celestial equator**. The projection of earth's equator out into the universe, forming one of the three principal celestial coordinate systems.

- **Choleric**. See **Humor**.
- **Chronic illness (degrees of)**. Degrees which are especially said to indicate chronic illness, due to their association with certain fixed stars. See VII.10.
- **Cleansed**. Normally, when a planet is not in an **assembly** or **square** or **opposition** with a **malefic** planet, but possibly indicating being free of *any* **aspect** with a malefic.
- **Clothed**. Equivalent to one planet being in an **assembly** or **aspect/regard** with another, and therefore partaking in (being "clothed in") the other planet's characteristics.
- **Collection**. When two planets **aspecting** each other but not in an applying **connection**, each apply to a third planet. See III.12.
- **Combust.** See **Burned up.**
- **Commanding/obeying.** A division of the signs into those which command or obey each other (used sometimes in **synastry**). See I.9.
- **Common signs.** See **Quadruplicity.**
- **Confer**. See **Pushing**.
- **Configured.** To be in a whole-sign **aspect**, though not necessarily by degree.
- **Conjunction (of planets)**. See **Assembly** and **Connection**.
- **Conjunction/prevention.** The position of the New (conjunction) or Full (prevention) Moon most immediately prior to a **nativity** or other chart. For the prevention, some astrologers use the degree of the Moon, others the degree of the luminary which was above the earth at the time of the prevention. See VIII.1.2.
- **Connection**. When a planet applies to another planet (by body in the same sign, or by ray in **aspecting** signs), within a particular number of degrees up to exactness. See III.7.
- **Convertible**. Equivalent to the movable signs. See **Quadruplicity**. But sometimes planets (especially Mercury) are called convertible because their **gender** is affected by their placement in the chart.
- **Convey**. See **Pushing**.
- **Corruption**. Normally, the harming of a planet (see IV.3-4), such as being in a **square** with a **malefic** planet. But sometimes, equivalent to **Detriment**.
- **Counsel** (Lat. *consilium*). A term used by Hugo and other Latin translators of Arabic, for "management" (III.18). An **applying** planet **pushes** or gifts

or grants its counsel or management to another planet, and that other planet **receives** or gathers it.

- **Course, increasing/decreasing in**. For practical purposes, this means a planet is quicker than average in motion. But in geometric astronomy, it refers to what **sector** (or *nitaq*) of the **deferent** the center of a planet's **epicycle** is. (The planet's position within the four sectors of the epicycle itself will also affect its apparent speed.) In the two sectors that are closest to the planet's **perigee**, the planet will apparently be moving faster; in the two sectors closest to the **apogee**, it will apparently be moving slower. See II.0-1.
- **Crooked/straight.** A division of the signs into those which rise quickly and are more parallel to the horizon (crooked), and those which arise more slowly and closer to a right angle from the horizon (straight or direct). In the northern hemisphere, the signs from Capricorn to Gemini are crooked (but in the southern one, straight); those from Cancer to Sagittarius are straight (but in the southern one, crooked).
- **Crossing over**. When a planet begins to **separate** from an exact **connection**. See III.7-8.
- **Cutting of light**. Three ways in which a **connection** is prevented: either by **obstruction** from the following sign, **escape** within the same sign, or by **barring**. See III.23.
- ***Darījān***. An alternative **face** system attributed to the Indians. See VII.6.
- **Decan**. Equivalent to **face.**
- **Declination**. The equivalent on the celestial **equator**, of geographical latitude. The signs of northern declination (Aries through Virgo) stretch northward of the **ecliptic**, while those of southern declination (Libra through Pisces) stretch southward.
- **Deferent.** The circle on which a planet's **epicycle** travels. See II.0-1.
- **Descension**. Equivalent to **fall.**
- **Detriment** (or Ar. "corruption," "unhealthiness," "harm."). More broadly (as "corruption"), it refers to any way in which a planet is harmed or its operation thwarted (such as by being **burned up**). But it also (as "harm") refers specifically to the sign opposite a planet's **domicile**. Libra is the detriment of Mars. See I.6 and I.8.
- **Dexter**. "Right": see **Right/left.**
- **Diameter**. Equivalent to **Opposition.**

- **Dignity** (Lat. "worthiness"; Ar. *ḥaẓẓ*, "good fortune, allotment"). Any of five ways of assigning rulership or responsibility to a planet (or sometimes, to a **Node**) over some portion of the zodiac. They are often listed in the following order: **domicile**, **exaltation**, **triplicity**, **bound**, **face/decan**. Each dignity has its own meaning and effect and use, and two of them have opposites: the opposite of domicile is **detriment**, the opposite of exaltation is **fall**. See I.3, I.4, I.6-7, VII.4 for the assignments; I.8 for some descriptive analogies; VIII.2.1 and VIII.2.2*f* for some predictive uses of domiciles and bounds.
- **Directions**. A predictive technique which is more precise than using **ascensions**, and defined by Ptolemy in terms of proportional semi-arcs. There is some confusion in how directing works, because of the difference between the astronomical method of directions and how astrologers look at charts. Astronomically, a point in the chart (the significator) is considered as stationary, and other planets and their **aspects** by degree (or even the **bounds**) are sent forth (promittors) as though the heavens keep turning by **primary motion**, until they come to the significator. The degrees between the significator and promittor are converted into years of life. But when looking at the chart, it seems as though the significator is being **released** counterclockwise in the order of signs, so that it **distributes** through the bounds or comes to the bodies or aspects of promittors. Direction by **ascensions** takes the latter perspective, though the result is the same. Some later astrologers allow the distance between a significator/releaser and the promittor to be measured in either direction, yielding "converse" directions in addition to the classical "direct" directions. See VIII.2.2, Appendix E, and Gansten.
- **Disregard**. Equivalent to **Separation**.
- **Distribution**. The **direction** of a **releaser** (often the degree of the **Ascendant**) through the **bounds**. The bound **lord** of the distribution is the "distributor," and any body or ray which the **releaser** encounters is the "**partner**." See VIII.2.2*f*, and *PN3*.
- **Distributor**. The **bound lord** of a **directed releaser**. See **Distribution.**
- **Diurnal**. See **Sect.**
- **Domain**. A **sect** and **gender**-based planetary condition. See III.2.
- **Domicile.** One of the five **dignities**. A sign of the zodiac, insofar as it is owned or managed by one of the planets. For example, Aries is the domicile of Mars, and so Mars is its domicile **lord**. See I.6.

- **Doryphory** (Gr. *doruphoria*). Equivalent to **Bodyguarding**.
- **Double-bodied**. Equivalent to the common signs. See **Quadruplicity.**
- **Dragon:** see **Node**.
- **Drawn back** (Lat. *reductus*). Equivalent to being **cadent** from an **angle**.
- **Dodecametorion**. Equivalent to **Twelfth-part.**
- ***Duodecima***. Equivalent to **Twelfth-part.**
- ***Dustūrīyyah***. Equivalent to **Bodyguarding.**
- **East** (Lat. *oriens*). The Ascendant: normally the rising sign, but sometimes the degree of the Ascendant itself.
- **Eastern/western**. A position relative to the Sun, often called "oriental" or "occidental," respectively. These terms are used in two major ways: (1) when a planet is in a position to rise before the Sun by being in an early degree (eastern) or is in a position to set after the Sun by being in a later degree (western). But in ancient languages, these words also refer mean "arising" or "setting/sinking," on an analogy with the Sun rising and setting: so sometimes they refer to (2) a planet arising out of, or sinking under, the **Sun's rays**, no matter what side of the Sun it is on (in some of my translations I call this "pertaining to arising" and "pertaining to sinking"). Astrological authors do not always clarify what sense is meant, and different astronomers and astrologers have different definitions for exactly what positions count as being eastern or western. See II.10.
- **Ecliptic.** The path defined by the Sun's motion through the zodiac, defined as having 0° ecliptical latitude. In tropical astrology, the ecliptic (and therefore the zodiacal signs) begins at the intersection of the ecliptic and the celestial equator.
- **Election** (lit. "choice"). The deliberate choosing of an appropriate time to undertake an action, or determining when to avoid an action; but astrologers normally refer to the chart of the time itself as an election.
- **Element**. One of the four basic qualities. fire, air, water, earth) describing how matter and energy operate, and used to describe the significations and operations of planets and signs. They are usually described by pairs of four other basic qualities (hot, cold, wet, dry). For example, Aries is a fiery sign, and hot and dry; Mercury is typically treated as cold and dry (earthy). See I.3, I.7, and Book V.
- **Emptiness of the course.** Medievally, when a planet does not complete a **connection** for as long as it is in its current sign. In Hellenistic astrology,

when a planet does not complete a connection within the next 30°. See III.9.

- **Enclosure**. When a planet has the rays or bodies of the **malefics** (or alternatively, the **benefics**) on either side of it, by degree or sign. See IV.4.2.
- **Epicycle.** A circle on the **deferent**, on which a planet turns. See II.0-1.
- **Equant.** A circle used to measure the average position of a planet. See II.0-1.
- **Equator (celestial)**. The projection of the earth's equator into space, forming a great circle. Its equivalent of latitude is called **declination**, while its equivalent of longitude is called **right ascension** (and is measured from the beginning of Aries, from the intersection of it and the **ecliptic**).
- **Escape**. When a planet wants to **connect** with a second one, but the second one moves into the next sign before it is completed, and the first planet makes a **connection** with a different, unrelated one instead. See III.22.
- **Essential/accidental.** A common way of distinguishing a planet's conditions, usually according to **dignity** (essential, I.2) and some other condition such as its **aspects** (accidental). See IV.1-5 for many accidental conditions.
- **Exaltation.** One of the five **dignities**. A sign in which a planet (or sometimes, a **Node**) signifies its matter in a particularly authoritative and refined way. The exaltation is sometimes identified with a particular degree in that sign. See I.6.
- **Face**. One of the five **dignities**. The zodiac is divided into 36 faces of 10° each, starting with the beginning of Aries. See I.5.
- **Facing**. A relationship between a planet and a **luminary**, if their respective signs are configured at the same distance as their **domiciles** are. For example, Leo (ruled by the Sun) is two signs to the **right** of Libra (ruled by Venus). When Venus is **western** and two signs away from wherever the Sun is, she will be in the facing of the Sun. See II.11.
- **Fall**. The sign opposite a planet's **exaltation**. See I.6.
- **Familiar** (Lat. *familiaris*). A hard-to-define term which suggests a sense of belonging and close relationship. (1) Sometimes it is contrasted with being **peregrine**, suggesting that a familiar planet is one which is a **lord** over a degree or **place** (that is, it has a **dignity** in it): for a dignity suggests belonging. (2) At other times, it refers to a familiar **aspect** (and probably the

sextile or **trine** in particular): all of the family houses in a chart have a **whole-sign** aspect to the **Ascendant**.

- **Feminine**. See **Gender**.
- **Feral.** Equivalent to **Wildness.**
- **Figure**. One of several polygons implied by an **aspect**. For example, a planet in Aries and one in Capricorn do not actually form a **square**, but they imply one because Aries and Capricorn, together with Libra and Cancer, form a square amongst themselves. See III.8.
- ***Firdārīyyah*** (pl. *firdārīyyāt*). A **time lord** method in which planets rule different periods of life, with each period broken down into sub-periods. See VII.1.
- **Firm**. In terms of signs, the **fixed** signs: see **Quadruplicity.** For houses, equivalent to the **Angles**.
- **Fixed.** See **Quadruplicity.**
- **Foreign** (Lat. *extraneus*). Usually equivalent to **peregrine**.
- **Fortunate**. Normally, a planet whose condition is made better by one of the **bearings** described in IV.
- **Fortunes.** See **Benefic/malefic.**
- **Free**. Sometimes, being **cleansed** of the **malefics**; at other times, being out of the **Sun's rays**.
- **Gender**. The division of signs, degrees, planets and hours into masculine and feminine groups. See I.3, V.10, V.14, VII.8.
- **Generosity and benefits**. Favorable relationships between signs and planets, as defined in III.26.
- **Good ones.** See **Benefic/malefic.**
- **Good places**. Equivalent to **Advantageous places**.
- **Greater, middle, lesser years**. See **Planetary years.**
- ***Ḥalb***. Probably Pahlavi for "sect," but normally describes a rejoicing condition: see III.2.
- ***Ḥayyiz***. Arabic for "domain," normally a gender-intensified condition of ***ḥalb***. See III.2.
- **Hexagon**. Equivalent to **Sextile.**
- ***Hīlāj*** (From the Pahlavi for "releaser"). Equivalent to **Releaser**.
- **Hold onto**. Hugo's synonym for a planet being in or **transiting** a **sign**.
- **Horary astrology**. A late historical designation for **Questions**.
- **Hours (planetary)**. The assigning of rulership over hours of the day and night to planets. The hours of daylight (and night, respectively) are divided

by 12, and each period is ruled first by the planet ruling that day, then the rest in descending planetary order. For example, on Sunday the Sun rules the first planetary "hour" from daybreak, then Venus, then Mercury, the Moon, Saturn, and so on. See V.13.

- **House**. A twelve-fold spatial division of a chart, in which each house signifies one or more areas of life. Two basic schemes are (1) **whole-sign** houses, in which the **signs** are equivalent to the houses, and (2) **quadrant houses**. But in the context of dignities and rulerships, "house" is the equivalent of **domicile.**
- **House-master.** Often called the *alcochoden* in Latin, from ***kadukhudhāh*** (the Pahlavi for "house-master"). One of the lords of the longevity **releaser**, preferably the **bound lord**. See VIII.1.3. But the Greek equivalent of this word (*oikodespotēs*, "house-master") is used in various ways in Hellenistic Greek texts, sometimes indicating the **lord** of a **domicile**, at other times the same longevity planet just mentioned, and at other times a kind of **victor** over the whole **nativity**.
- **Humor.** Any one of four fluids in the body (according to traditional medicine), the balance between which determines one's health and **temperament** (outlook and energy level). Choler or yellow bile is associated with fire and the choleric temperament; blood is associated with air and the sanguine temperament; phlegm is associated with water and the phlegmatic temperament; black bile is associated with earth and the melancholic temperament. See I.3.
- **In the heart.** Often called *cazimi* in English texts, from the Ar. *kaṣmīmī*. A planet is in the heart of the Sun when it is either in the same degree as the Sun (according to Sahl bin Bishr and Rhetorius), or within 16' of longitude from him. See II.9.
- **Indicator**. A degree which is supposed to indicate the approximate position of the degree of the natal **Ascendant**, in cases where the time of birth is uncertain. See VIII.1.2.
- **Inferior**. The planets lower than the Sun: Venus, Mercury, Moon.
- **Infortunes.** See **Benefic/malefic.**
- ***'Ittiṣāl***. Equivalent to **Connection**.
- **Joys.** Places in which the planets are said to "rejoice" in acting or signifying their natures. Joys by house are found in I.16; by sign in I.10.7.
- ***Jārbakhtār*** (From the Pahlavi for "distributor of time"). Equivalent to **Distributor**; see **Distribution.**

- ***Kadukhudhāh*** (From the Pahlavi for "house-master"), often called the *alcochoden* in Latin transliteration. See **House-master.**
- ***Kaṣmīmī*:** see **In the heart**.
- **Kingdom**. Equivalent to **exaltation**.
- **Largesse and recompense**. A reciprocal relation in which one planet is rescued from being in its own **fall** or a **well**, and then returns the favor when the other planet is in its fall or well. See III.24.
- **Leader** (Lat. *dux*). Equivalent to a **significator** for some topic. The Arabic word for "significator" means to indicate something by pointing the way toward something: thus the significator for a topic or matter "leads" the astrologer to some answer. Used by some less popular Latin translators (such as Hugo of Santalla and Hermann of Carinthia).
- **Linger in** (Lat. *commoror*). Hugo's synonym for a planet being in or **transiting** through a **sign**.
- **Lodging-place** (Lat. *hospitium*). Hugo's synonym for a **house**, particularly the **sign** which occupies a house.
- **Lord of the Year.** The **domicile lord** of a **profection**. The Sun and Moon are not allowed to be primary lords of the Year, according to Persian doctrine. See VIII.2.1 and VIII.3.2, and Appendix F.
- **Lord.** A designation for the planet which has a particular **dignity**, but when used alone it usually means the **domicile** lord. For example, Mars is the lord of Aries.
- **Lord of the question**. In questions, the lord of the **house** of the **quaesited** matter. But sometimes, it refers to the client or **querent** whose question it is.
- **Lot**. Sometimes called "Parts." A place (often treated as equivalent to an entire sign) expressing a ratio derived from the position of three other parts of a chart. Normally, the distance between two places is measured in zodiacal order from one to the other, and this distance is projected forward from some other place (usually the Ascendant): where the counting stops, is the Lot. Lots are used both interpretively and predictively. See Book VI.
- **Lucky/unlucky**. See **Benefic/malefic.**
- **Luminary**. The Sun or Moon.
- **Malefic**. See **Benefic/malefic.**
- **Malevolents.** See **Benefic/malefic.**
- **Masculine**. See **Gender**.

- **Melancholic**. See **Humor**.
- **Midheaven**. Either the tenth sign from the **Ascendant**, or the zodiacal degree on which the celestial meridian falls.
- **Movable signs.** See **Quadruplicity.**
- ***Mubtazz***. See **Victor.**
- **Mutable signs**. Equivalent to "common" signs. See **Quadruplicity.**
- ***Namūdār***. Equivalent to **Indicator.**
- **Native.** The person whose birth chart it is.
- **Nativity**. Technically, a birth itself, but used by astrologers to describe the chart cast for the moment of a birth.
- **Ninth-parts**. Divisions of each sign into 9 equal parts of 3° 20' apiece, each ruled by a planet. Used predictively by some astrologers as part of the suite of **revolution** techniques. See VII.5.
- ***Nitaq***. See **Sector**.
- **Nobility.** Equivalent to **exaltation**.
- **Nocturnal**. See **Sect**.
- **Node.** The point on the ecliptic where a planet passes into northward latitude (its North Node or Head of the Dragon) or into southern latitude (its South Node or Tail of the Dragon). Normally only the Moon's Nodes are considered. See II.5 and V.8.
- **Northern/southern.** Either planets in northern or southern latitude in the zodiac (relative to the ecliptic), or in northern or southern declination relative to the celestial equator. See I.10.1.
- **Not-reception**. When an **applying** planet is in the **fall** of the planet being applied to.
- **Oblique ascensions**. The **ascensions** used in making predictions by ascensional times or primary **directions**.
- **Obstruction**. When one planet is moving towards a second (wanting to be **connected** to it), but a third one in a later degrees goes **retrograde**, connects with the second one, and then with the first one. See III.21.
- **Occidental**. See **Eastern/western**.
- **Opening of the portals/doors**. Times of likely weather changes and rain, determined by certain **transits**. See VIII.3.4.
- **Opposition**. An **aspect** either by **whole sign** or degree, in which the signs have a 180° relation to each other: for example, a planet in Aries is opposed to one in Libra.

- **Optimal place**. Also called "good" and "the best" places. These are probably a subset of the **advantageous places**, and probably only those houses which **aspect** the **Ascendant**. They definitely include the Ascendant, tenth, and eleventh houses, but may also include the ninth. They are probably also restricted only to houses above the horizon.
- **Orbs/bodies**. Called "orb" by the Latins, and "body" (*jirm*) by Arabic astrologers. A space of power or influence on each side of a planet's body or position, used to determine the intensity of interaction between different planets. See II.6.
- **Oriental.** See **Eastern/western**.
- **Overcoming**. When a planet is in the eleventh, tenth, or ninth sign from another planet (i.e., in a superior **sextile, square**, or **trine aspect**), though being in the tenth sign is considered a more dominant or even domineering position. See IV.4.1 and *PN3*'s Introduction, §15.
- **Own light**. This refers either to (1) a planet being a member of the **sect** of the chart (see V.9), or (2) a planet being out of the **Sun's rays** and not yet **connected** to another planet, so that it shines on its own without being **clothed** in another's influence (see II.9).
- **Part.** See **Lot**.
- **Partner**. The body or ray of any planet which a **directed releaser** encounters while being **distributed** through the **bounds.** But in some translations from Arabic, any of the **lords** of a place.
- **Peregrine**. When a planet is not in one of its five **dignities**. See I.9.
- **Perigee**. The position on a planet's **deferent** circle which is closest to the earth; it is opposite the **apogee**. See II.0-1.
- **Perverse** (Lat. *perversus*). Hugo's occasional term for (1) **malefic** planets, and (2) **places** in **aversion** to the **Ascendant** by **whole-sign**: definitely the twelfth and sixth, probably the eighth, and possibly the second.
- **Phlegmatic**. See **Humor**.
- **Pitted degrees**. Equivalent to **Welled degrees**.
- **Pivot.** Equivalent to **Angle.**
- **Place**. Equivalent to a **house**, and more often (and more anciently) a **whole-sign** house, namely a **sign**.
- **Planetary years**. Periods of years which the planets signify according to various conditions. See VII.2.
- **Possess**. Hugo's synonym for a planet being in or **transiting** a **sign**.
- **Prevention**. See **Conjunction/prevention.**

- **Primary directions**. See **Directions**.
- **Primary motion**. The clockwise or east-to-west motion of the heavens.
- **Profection** (Lat. *profectio*, "advancement, setting out"). A predictive technique in which some part of a chart (usually the **Ascendant**) is advanced either by an entire sign or in 30° increments for each year of life. See VIII.2.1 and VIII.3.2, and the sources in Appendix F.
- **Prohibition**. Equivalent to **Blocking**.
- **Promittor** (lit., something "sent forward"). A point which is **directed** to a **significator**, or to which a significator is **released** or directed (depending on how one views the mechanics of directions).
- **Pushing**. What a planet making an **applying connection** does to the one **receiving** it. See III.15-18.
- ***Qasim/qismah***: Arabic terms for **distributor** and **distribution**.
- **Quadrant houses.** A division of the heavens into twelve spaces which overlap the **whole signs**, and are assigned to topics of life and ways of measuring strength (such as Porphyry, Alchabitius Semi-Arc, or Regiomontanus houses). For example, if the Midheaven fell into the eleventh sign, the space between the Midheaven and the Ascendant would be divided into sections that overlap and are not coincident with the signs. See I.12 and the Introduction §6.
- **Quadruplicity.** A "fourfold" group of signs indicating certain shared patterns of behavior. The movable (or cardinal or convertible) signs are those through which new states of being are quickly formed (including the seasons): Aries, Cancer, Libra, Capricorn. The fixed (sometimes "firm") signs are those through which matters are fixed and lasting in their character: Taurus, Leo, Scorpio, Aquarius. The common (or mutable or bicorporeal) signs are those which make a transition and partake both of quick change and fixed qualities: Gemini, Virgo, Sagittarius, Pisces. See I.10.5.
- **Quaesited/quesited**. In **horary** astrology, the matter asked about.
- **Querent**. In **horary** astrology, the person asking the question (or the person on behalf of whom one asks).
- **Questions**. The branch of astrology dealing with inquiries about individual matters, for which a chart is cast.
- **Reception.** What one planet does when another planet **pushes** or **applies** to it, and especially when they are related by **dignity** or by a **trine** or **sextile** from an **agreeing** sign of various types. For example, if the Moon

applies to Mars, Mars will get or receive her application. See III.15-18 and III.25.

- **Reflection**. When two planets are in **aversion** to each other, but a third planet either **collects** or **transfers** their light. If it collects, it reflects the light elsewhere. See III.13.
- **Refrenation**. See **Revoking.**
- **Regard**. Equivalent to **Aspect.**
- **Releaser**. The point which is the focus of a **direction**. In determining longevity, it is the one among a standard set of possible points which has certain qualifications (see VIII.1.3). In annual predictions one either directs or **distributes** the longevity releaser, or any one of a number of points for particular topics, or else the degree of the **Ascendant** as a default releaser. Many astrologers direct the degree of the Ascendant of the **revolution** chart itself as a releaser.
- **Remote** (Lat. *remotus*). Equivalent to **cadent**: see **Angle**. But see also *Judges* §7.73, where 'Umar (or Hugo) distinguishes being **cadent** from being **remote.**
- **Render**. When a planet **pushes** to another planet or place.
- **Retreating**. When a planet is in a cadent place. See III.4 and the Introduction §6, and **Angle.**
- **Retrograde.** When a planet seems to move backwards or clockwise relative to the signs and fixed stars. See II.8 and II.10.
- **Return, Solar/Lunar**. Equivalent to **Revolution**.
- **Returning**. What a **burned up** or **retrograde** planet does when another planet **pushes** to it. See III.19.
- **Revoking**. When a planet making an applying **connection** stations and turns **retrograde**, not completing the connection. See III.20.
- **Revolution.** Sometimes called the "cycle" or "transfer" or "change-over" of a year. Technically, the **transiting** position of planets and the **Ascendant** at the moment the Sun returns to a particular place in the zodiac: in the case of nativities, when he returns to his exact natal position; in mundane astrology, usually when he makes his ingress into 0° Aries. But the revolution is also understood to involve an entire suite of predictive techniques, including **distribution, profections**, and ***firdārīyyāt***. See *PN3*.
- **Right ascensions**. Degrees on the celestial **equator** (its equivalent of geographical longitude), particularly those which move across the meridian when calculating arcs for **ascensions** and **directions**.

- **Right/left.** Right (or "dexter") degrees and **aspects** are those earlier in the zodiac relative to a planet or sign, up to the **opposition**; left (or "sinister") degrees and aspects are those later in the zodiac. For example, if a planet is in Capricorn, its right aspects will be towards Scorpio, Libra, and Virgo; its left aspects will be towards Pisces, Aries, and Taurus. See III.6.
- **Root**. A chart used as a basis for another chart; a root particularly describes something considered to have concrete being of its own. For example, a **nativity** acts as a root for an **election**, so that when planning an election one must make it harmonize with the nativity.
- **Safe**. When a planet is not being harmed, particularly by an **assembly** or **square** or **opposition** with the **malefics**. See **Cleansed**.
- ***Sālkhudhāy*** (from Pahlavi, "lord of the year"). Equivalent to the **lord of the year**.
- **Sanguine**. See **Humor**.
- **Scorched**. See **Burned up**.
- **Secondary motion**. The counter-clockwise motion of planets forward in the zodiac.
- **Sect.** A division of charts, planets, and signs into "diurnal/day" and "nocturnal/night." Charts are diurnal if the Sun is above the horizon, else they are nocturnal. Planets are divided into sects as shown in V.11. Masculine signs (Aries, Gemini, *etc.*) are diurnal, the feminine signs (Taurus, Cancer, *etc.*) are nocturnal.
- **Sector**. A division of the **deferent** circle or **epicycle** into four parts, used to determine the position, speed, visibility, and other features of a planet. See II.0-1.
- **Seeing, hearing, listening signs**. A way of associating signs similar to **commanding/obeying**. See Paul of Alexandria's version in the two figures attached to I.9.6.
- **Separation**. When planets have completed a **connection** by **assembly** or **aspect**, and move away from one another. See III.8.
- **Sextile**. An **aspect** either by **whole sign** or degree, in which the signs have a 60° relation to each other: for example, Aries and Gemini.
- **Shift** (Ar. *nawbah*). Equivalent to **Sect**, and refers not only to the alternation between day and night, but also to the period of night or day itself. The Sun is the lord of the diurnal shift or sect, and the Moon is the lord of the nocturnal shift or sect.

- **Sign**. One of the twelve 30° divisions of the **ecliptic**, named after the constellations which they used to be roughly congruent to. In tropical astrology, the signs start from the intersection of the ecliptic with the celestial equator (the position of the Sun at the equinoxes). In sidereal astrology, the signs begin from some other point identified according to other principles.
- **Significator**. Either (1) a planet or point in a chart which indicates or signifies something for a topic (either through its own character, or house position, or rulerships, *etc.*), or (2) the point which is **released** in primary **directions**.
- **Sinister**. "Left": see **Right/left.**
- **Slavery.** Equivalent to **fall**.
- **Sovereignty** (Lat. *regnum*). Equivalent to **Exaltation**.
- **Spearbearing**. Equivalent to **Bodyguarding.**
- **Square**. An **aspect** either by **whole sign** or degree, in which the signs have a 90° relation to each other: for example, Aries and Cancer.
- **Stake**. Equivalent to **Angle.**
- **Sublunar world.** The world of the four **elements** below the sphere of the Moon, in classical cosmology.
- **Succeedent**. See **Angle.**
- **Sun's rays** (or Sun's beams). In earlier astrology, equivalent to a regularized distance of 15° away from the Sun, so that a planet under the rays is not visible at dawn or dusk. But a later distinction was made between being **burned up** (about 1° - 7.5° away from the Sun) and merely being under the rays (about 7.5° - 15° away).
- **Superior**. The planets higher than the Sun: Saturn, Jupiter, Mars.
- **Supremacy** (Lat. *regnum*). Hugo's word for **Exaltation**, sometimes used in translations by Dykes instead of the slightly more accurate **Sovereignty**.
- **Synastry.** The comparison of two or more charts to determine compatibility, usually in romantic relationships or friendships. See *BA* Appendix C for a discussion and references for friendship, and *BA* III.7.11 and III.12.7.
- ***Tasyīr*** (Ar. "dispatching, sending out"). Equivalent to primary **directions**.
- **Temperament**. The particular mixture (sometimes, "complexion") of **elements** or **humors** which determines a person's or planet's typical behavior, outlook, and energy level.

- **Testimony**. From Arabic astrology onwards, a little-defined term which can mean (1) the planets which have **dignity** in a place or degree, or (2) the number of dignities a planet has in its own place (or as compared with other planets), or (3) a planet's **assembly** or **aspect** to a place of interest, or (4) generally *any* way in which planets may make themselves relevant to the inquiry at hand. For example, a planet which is the **exalted** lord of the **Ascendant** but also **aspects** it, maby be said to present two testimonies supporting its relevance to an inquiry about the Ascendant.
- **Tetragon**. Equivalent to **Square.**
- **Thought-interpretation**. The practice of identifying a theme or topic in a **querent's** mind, often using a **victor**, before answering the specific **question**. See *Search.*
- **Time lord**. A planet ruling over some period of time according to one of the classical predictive techniques. For example, the **lord of the year** is the time lord over a **profection**.
- **Transfer**. When one planet **separates** from one planet, and **connects** to another. See III.11.
- **Transit**. The passing of one planet across another planet or point (by body or **aspect** by exact degree), or through a particular sign (even in a **whole-sign** relation to some point of interest). In traditional astrology, not every transit is significant; for example, transits of **time lords** or of planets in the **whole-sign angles** of a **profection** might be preferred to others. See VIII.2.4 and *PN3.*
- **Translation**. Equivalent to **Transfer.**
- **Traverse** (Lat. *discurro*). Hugo's synonym for a planet being in or **transiting** through a **sign**.
- **Trigon**. Equivalent to **Trine**.
- **Trine**. An **aspect** either by **whole sign** or degree, in which the signs have a 120° relation to each other: for example, Aries and Leo.
- **Turn** (Ar. *dawr*). A predictive term in which responsibilities for being a **time lord** rotates between different planets. See VIII.2.3 for one use of the turn.
- **Turned away**. Equivalent to **Aversion**.
- **Turning signs**. For Hugo of Santalla, equivalent to the movable signs: see **Quadruplicity**. But *tropicus* more specifically refers to the tropical signs Cancer and Capricorn, in which the Sun turns back from its most extreme declinations.

- **Twelfth-parts.** Signs of the zodiac defined by 2.5° divisions of other signs. For example, the twelfth-part of 4° Gemini is Cancer. See IV.6.
- **Two-parted signs**. Equivalent to the double-bodied or common signs: see **Quadruplicity.**
- **Under rays.** When a planet is between approximately 7.5° and 15° from the Sun, and not visible either when rising before the Sun or setting after him. Some astrologers distinguish the distances for individual planets (which is more astronomically accurate). See II.10.
- **Unfortunate**. Normally, when a planet's condition is made more difficult through one of the **bearings** in IV.
- **Unlucky**. See **Benefic/malefic.**
- ***Via combusta***. See **Burnt path**.
- **Victor** (Ar. *mubtazz*). A planet identified as being the most authoritative either for a particular topic or **house** (I.18), or for a chart as a whole (VIII.1.4). See also *Search*.
- **Void in course**. Equivalent to **Emptiness of the course.**
- **Well.** A degree in which a planet is said to be more obscure in its operation. See VII.9.
- **Western**. See **Eastern/western.**
- **Whole signs.** The oldest system of assigning house topics and **aspects**. The entire sign on the horizon (the **Ascendant**) is the first house, the entire second sign is the second house, and so on. Likewise, aspects are considered first of all according to signs: planets in Aries aspect or regard Gemini as a whole, even if aspects by exact degree are more intense. See I.12, III.6, and the Introduction §6.
- **Wildness.** When a planet is not **aspected** by any other planet, for as long as it is in its current sign. See III.10.
- **Withdrawal.** Equivalent to **separation**.

BIBLIOGRAPHY

I. Sources for translated texts:

Al-Kindī: *The Choices of Days*

Wiedemann, Eilhard, "Über einen astrologischen Traktat von al Kindī," *Archiv für die Geschichte der Naturwissenschaften und der Technik*, v. 3/3, April 1911, pp. 224-26.

Bethen: *On the Hours of the Planets*

Bethen, *De horis planetarum* (Prague, APH, M. CVI 1466, 205f-06v)

Bethen, *De horis planetarum* (Basel: Iohannes Hervagius 1533, Part II, pp. 110-12)

Sahl bin Bishr: *On Elections*

Crofts, Carole Mary, "*Kitāb al-Iktiyārāt 'alā l-buyūt al-itnai 'asar*, by Sahl ibn Bišr al-Isra'ili, with its Latin Translation *De Electionibus* (Ph.D. diss., Glasgow University, 1985)

Al-'Imrānī: *The Book of Choices*

Paris, BNF lat. 16204, 13th Cent., 507-534

Madrid, BN 10,009, 13th Cent., 23v-38v

Paris, BNF, lat. 7413-I, 13th Cent., 45ra-57rb

Munich, BSB, Clm 11067, 15th Cent., 123ra-134vb

Vatican, BAV, Reg. lat. 1452, 14th Cent., 46ra-57vb

Al-Rijāl: *The Book of the Skilled*

De Iudiciis Astrorum (Venice: Erhard Ratdolt, 1485)

De Iudiciis Astrorum (Basel: Henrichus Petrus, 1551)

II. General Bibliography:

Abū Bakr, *On Nativities*, in Dykes, *PN 2* (2010)

Al-Bīrūnī, Muhammad ibn Ahmad, *The Book of Instruction in the Elements of the Art of Astrology*, trans. R. Ramsay Wright (London: Luzac & Co., 1934)

Al-Bīrūnī, Muhammad ibn Ahmad, *The Chronology of Ancient Nations* (Lahore: Hijra International Publishers, 1983)

Al-Bīrūnī, Muhammad ibn Ahmad, *Al-Bīrūnī's India*, trans. Edward C. Sachau (New Delhi: Rupa & Co., 2002)

Al-Qabīsī, *The Introduction to Astrology*, eds. Charles Burnett, Keiji Yamamoto, Michio Yano (London and Turin: The Warburg Institute, 2004)

Al-Tabarī, 'Umar, *Three Books on Nativities*, in Dykes, *PN 2* (2010)

Bonatti, Guido, *The Book of Astronomy*, trans. and ed. Benjamin N. Dykes (Golden Valley, MN: The Cazimi Press, 2007)

Bos, Gerrit and Charles Burnett, *Scientific Weather Forecasting in the Middle Ages: The Writings of al-Kindī* (London and New York: Kegan Paul International, 2000)

Burnett, Charles, "Al-Kindī on Judicial Astrology: 'The Forty Chapters'," in *Arabic Sciences and Philosophy*, v. 3 (1993), pp. 77-117.

De Fouw, Hart, and Robert Svoboda, *Light on Life: An Introduction to the Astrology of India* (Twin Lakes, WI: Lotus Press, 2003)

Dorotheus of Sidon, *Carmen Astrologicum*, trans. and ed. David Pingree (Leipzig: B.G. Teubner Verlagsgesellschaft, 1976)

Dorotheus of Sidon, *Carmen Astrologicum*, trans. David Pingree (Abingdon, MD: The Astrology Center of America, 2005)

Dykes, Benjamin trans. and ed., *Works of Sahl & Māshā'allāh* (Golden Valley, MN: The Cazimi Press, 2008)

Dykes, Benjamin trans. and ed., *Persian Nativities vols. I-III* (Minneapolis, MN: The Cazimi Press, 2009-10)

Dykes, Benjamin trans. and ed., *Introductions to Traditional Astrology: Abū Ma'shar & al-Qabīsī* (Minneapolis, MN: The Cazimi Press, 2010)

Dykes, Benjamin trans. and ed., *The Book of the Nine Judges* (Minneapolis, MN: The Cazimi Press, 2011)

Dykes, Benjamin trans. and ed., *The Forty Chapters of al-Kindī* (Minneapolis, MN: The Cazimi Press, 2011)

Evans, James, *The History and Practice of Ancient Astronomy* (New York and Oxford: Oxford University Press, 1998)

Hephaistio of Thebes, *Apotelesmaticorum Libri Tres*, ed. David Pingree, vols. I-II (Leipzig: Teubner Verlagsgesellschaft, 1973)

Hermann of Carinthia, Benjamin Dykes trans. and ed., *The Search of the Heart* (Minneapolis, MN: The Cazimi Press, 2011)

Holden, James H., "The Foundation Chart of Baghdad," *Today's Astrologer*, Vol. 65, No. 3 (March 2, 2003), pp. 9-10, 29.

Holden, James H., *A History of Horoscopic Astrology* (Tempe, AZ: American Federation of Astrologers, Inc., 2006)

Holden, James H., *Five Medieval Astrologers* (Tempe, AZ: American Federation of Astrologers, Inc., 2008)

Kunitzsch, Paul, Tim Smart, *A Dictionary of Modern Star Names* (Cambridge, MA: Sky Publishing, 2006)

Māshā'allāh bin Atharī, *The Book of Aristotle*, trans. and ed. Benjamin N. Dykes, in Dykes, *PN 1* (2009)

Niermeyer, J.F. ed., *Mediae Latinitatis Lexicon Minus* (Leiden: E.J. Brill, 1993)

Paulus Alexandrinus, *Late Classical Astrology: Paulus Alexandrinus and Olympiodorus*, trans. Dorian Gieseler Greenbaum, ed. Robert Hand (Reston, VA: ARHAT Publications, 2001)

Pingree, David, trans. and ed., *The Yavanajātaka of Sphujidhvaja* vols. I-II (Cambridge, MA and London: Harvard University Press, 1978)

Pingree, David, *From Astral Omens to Astrology: From Babylon to Bīkīner* (Rome: Istituto italiano per L'Africa e L'Oriente, 1997)

Pseudo-Ptolemy, *Centiloquium*, in *Liber Quadripartitus* (Venice: Bonetus Locatellus, 1493)

Pseudo-Ptolemy, *Centiloquium*, ed. Georgius Trapezuntius, in Bonatti (1550)

Ptolemy, Claudius, *Tetrabiblos*, trans. F.E. Robbins (Cambridge and London: Harvard University Press, 1940)

Ptolemy, Claudius, *Tetrabiblos* vols. 1, 2, 4, trans. Robert Schmidt, ed. Robert Hand (Berkeley Springs, WV: The Golden Hind Press, 1994-98)

Rhetorius of Egypt, *Astrological Compendium*, James H. Holden trans. and ed. (Tempe, AZ: American Federation of Astrologers, Inc., 2009)

Robson, Vivian, *The Fixed Stars & Constellations in Astrology* (Abingdon, MD: Astrology Classics, 2003)

Sachau, Edward C. trans. and ed., *Alberūnī's India* (New Delhi: Rupert & Co., 2002)

Sahl bin Bishr, *Introduction*, in Benjamin Dykes, *WSM* (The Cazimi Press, 2008)

Sahl bin Bishr, *On Questions*, in Benjamin Dykes, *WSM* (The Cazimi Press, 2008)

Sahl bin Bishr, *On Times*, in Benjamin Dykes, *WSM* (The Cazimi Press, 2008)

Sahl bin Bishr, *The Fifty Judgments*, in Benjamin Dykes, *WSM* (The Cazimi Press, 2008)

Sarton, George, "Notes & Correspondence," in *Isis* vol. 14 (1950), pp. 420-22.

Weinstock, Stefan, "Lunar Mansions and Early Calendars," *The Journal of Hellenic Studies*, v. 69 (1949), pp. 48-69.

Valens, Vettius, *The Anthology*, vols. I-VII, ed. Robert Hand, trans. Robert Schmidt (Berkeley Springs, WV: The Golden Hind Press, 1993-2001)

INDEX

This index is primarily confined to names of authors, rather than topics. For the most part, all topics in this book are organized according to the astrological house indicating them, and should not pose any problems for readers trying to locate them. Within the text itself, I have also cross-referenced topics through footnotes. Al-'Imrānī, al-Rijāl, and Sahl do not appear in this index, since references to them in the footnotes are so numerous that listing them here would be of little help.

Abraham bin Hiyya 32
Abū Bakr 5, 135, 216, 287, 406
Abū Ma'shar...4-5, 34, 36, 44, 49-50, 63, 86, 90, 141-42, 144-145, 150-52, 155, 167, 191, 194-95, 201, 207, 218, 229, 235, 240-42, 244, 267-68, 302, 326, 345, 398, 406-07
Alaçmin (unknown)..38, 157, 245-46
al-Bīrūnī...40-44, 46, 230, 269, 273, 398, 404
al-Fadl bin Sahl 37, 275, 313
Al-Hasan bin Sahl...37, 338, 387, 390
Al-Khasib (unknown)...35, 190, 192
al-Khayyāt, Abū 'Ali...5, 7, 14-15, 18-19, 24-35, 37-38, 50, 109, 133, 142, 159, 168, 172, 184, 190-92, 196, 200, 203, 207, 211, 213-14, 216, 221, 227, 229, 235-36, 247, 281, 283-84, 288, 297-98, 300, 326, 336, 340, 356, 373, 406
al-Kindī...1, 3, 25, 32, 34, 37, 39, 46, 56, 57, 59, 143-44, 148, 150-55, 156-58, 161, 167, 171, 174-75, 180, 185, 188, 190-91, 196, 201-02, 210-12, 218-20, 235, 238-45, 257, 281-82, 298-99, 301, 304, 316-18, 320-22, 375, 400, 404, 406
al-Mansūr, 'Abbasid Caliph 273
al-Nadim 32
al-Qabīsī...3, 32, 46, 167, 206, 263, 404-06
al-Shaibānī 37, 235
al-Tabarī, 'Umar...5, 7, 14-15, 23-27, 32, 35, 37, 47, 50, 126, 142, 144, 151-53, 156, 158-59, 171, 185-87, 191-94, 203, 205, 211, 215, 220-21, 228, 241, 244-46, 261, 273, 281, 285, 297, 300, 323, 334, 343, 365, 367, 373, 376, 386, 389-91, 393-94, 406
Anubio 27
Baghdad 273
Bericos (unknown) 38, 275
Bethen 1, 49, 50, 77
Bizidāj 36, 381
Bodyguarding 157, 237, 245
Bonatti, Guido...4, 22, 140, 165, 407, 429
Brennan, Chris 36
Burnett, Charles...3, 23-24, 40, 62, 64, 66, 68, 289
Bust 46, 404
Cadoros (unknown) 38, 266
Dawr ("turn") 168
Declination...104, 110, 184-85, 187, 199, 205-07, 210, 224,

262, 264, 266, 278, 294, 300, 371
Dignities and counter-dignities 396
Domain.... 119, 237, 276, 359, 404
Dorotheus of Sidon...1, 3, 5, 7, 14-15, 22, 24-32, 35, 43-45, 47, 50-51, 61-73, 86, 99, 102-03, 113, 116, 118, 126, 133, 182, 211, 222, 235, 253, 255, 281, 313, 334, 337, 346, 377, 405
Eclipse...100, 160, 170, 183, 228, 239, 253, 376, 385
Endemadeyg............36, 380, 384-85
Feytimus (unknown)..........38, 297
God...9, 21, 68, 106, 119, 121, 138, 140, 182, 189, 209, 219, 230-34, 236, 268, 270, 309, 311, 343, 345, 368, 376, 378, 388-389
Ḥalb..................................158, 278
Ḥayyiz........................*See Domain*
Hebeteth (unknown) 38, 310, 312
Hephaistio of Thebes...3, 5-7, 14, 27, 42
Hermann of Carinthia...24, 53-54, 180, 387, 389, 406
Houlding, Deborah.......................1
House-master (*kadukḫudhāh*) 362, 386
Hugo of Santalla...23-24, 151, 188, 196, 238, 239, 281-82, 301, 318, 321, 322, 325, 400, 402-03
Hurrazād al-Dārshād al-Khasib 27, 35, 37, 190, 192, 277-79
ibn Hibinta..........................38, 312
ibn Sayyid (unknown)....38, 49, 86
India, Indians...40, 42-44, 46, 61-73, 86, 153, 167, 320, 337, 404
John of Seville/Spain...1, 23, 53, 367, 387
Juste, David........................33, 230
Kant, Immanuel..........................11
Kardaja......................................101
Katarchē.............3-4, 6, 15, 16, 135
Lot of a kingdom and victory. 361
Lot of assets/money/substance 204, 212, 226, 260, 282, 400, 401
Lot of boldness........................359
Lot of captives and slaves.......218
Lot of children.........................401
Lot of dispute..........................312
Lot of Fortune...6, 102, 105-06, 120, 141-45, 149, 168-69, 172, 181, 185, 188, 204-05, 212, 226, 227, 237-38, 240, 255, 260-62, 266, 274-75, 279-80, 282, 311, 314, 355, 359, 361, 373-74, 380-82, 384-85, 392, 400-02
Lot of nobility/exaltation.......361
Lot of the matter...144, 180, 239, 401-02
Lot of victory (not Hermetic) 312
Māshā'allāh... 5, 7-8, 14, 19, 22-37, 47, 50, 92, 101, 113, 126, 133, 142, 151, 153, 157, 159, 167, 175, 180, 191, 196-97, 210-12, 214, 229, 235, 241, 245, 247, 254-55, 273, 281, 284, 295-96, 298, 316, 320, 326, 332, 334, 351, 365, 375, 377, 404, 406-07
Maximus.......................................42
Minegeth (unknown) 38, 298, 344
Nimagest (unknown) 38, 298, 344
Nufil (unknown)..38, 106, 262, 279
Olympiodorus..................100, 254
Paul of Alexandria... 100, 248, 254
Pingree, David.........7, 23- 25, 309
Plato of Tivoli.............................32
Ptolemy, Claudius...15-16, 35-37, 50-51, 53, 135, 151-53, 173, 232-33, 235, 241, 243, 297-98, 339, 343-44, 377-78, 385, 387

Pushing management 315
Pushing nature 235
Pushing power..................314, 315
Releaser...... 93, 180, 242, 362, 386
Robert of Ketton...151, 238, 400-03
Roots...2, 6-7, 9-10, 12, 15-18, 35, 84, 86, 91-93, 98, 122, 136-37, 163-64, 168-73, 181, 187, 216-17, 220, 222, 226, 229, 232-33, 236, 260, 268, 270, 289, 304, 311, 324, 336, 344-45, 353, 372, 375, 379, 382, 385
Scorched hours..........................318
Straight/crooked signs...55, 57, 81-82, 95, 97, 102, 105, 110, 119, 149, 167, 175, 185, 187, 193, 205, 216, 218, 250, 255, 261-62, 274, 278, 287, 294, 301, 311, 313-14, 323-24, 326, 403
Syzygies (New and Full Moons) 404
Thema Mundi 171
Theophilus of Edessa..37, 50, 235
Utuluxius (unknown)...29-30, 38, 236
Vettius Valens...36-38, 50, 58, 235, 266, 297-98, 378, 380-86, 391, 394
Victor (*mubtazz*)...164, 168, 171, 176, 180-81, 231
Yavanajātaka....................................6
Zaradusht.............................38, 338

CPSIA information can be obtained
at www.ICGtesting.com
Printed in the USA
BVHW072047050220
571511BV00004B/66

9 781934 586235